AMERICAN
FOREIGN POLICY

AMERICAN FOREIGN POLICY

Consensus at Home, Leadership Abroad

Karl von Vorys

 PRAEGER

Westport, Connecticut
London

Library of Congress Cataloging-in-Publication Data

Von Vorys, Karl.
    American foreign policy : consensus at home, leadership abroad /
Karl von Vorys.
        p.   cm.
    Includes bibliographical references and index.
    ISBN 0–275–95729–2 (alk. paper)
    1. United States—Foreign relations.   I. Title.
E183.7.V66   1997
327.73—dc21   97–1914

British Library Cataloguing in Publication Data is available.

Library of Congress Catalog Card Number: 97–1914
ISBN: 0–275–95729–2

First published in 1997

Praeger Publishers, 88 Post Road West, Westport, CT 06881
An imprint of Greenwood Publishing Group, Inc.

Printed in the United States of America

The paper used in this book complies with the
Permanent Paper Standard issued by the National
Information Standards Organization (Z39.48–1984).

10 9 8 7 6 5 4 3 2 1

Barbara

Since God created men,
there must be some use for them.

Contents

Acknowledgments

First of all I am very grateful to Professor Tom Davis of Cornell University. His immense knowledge and experience in Latin America helped guide my analysis in Chapter 9.

I also received well-informed advice and constructive suggestions from Professor Mauricio Baez of Universidad Simon Bolivar, Caracas; Mr. Javeed Burki, Vice President, The World Bank; Dr. William C. Nenno, U.S. Department of State; and Frau Ursula Lange, Europäische Schule, Berlin.

Mr. Chris Harth's contributions have been invaluable. He helped me check out the most elusive data to assure accuracy. I am grateful for his loyalty and integrity. Dr. Alan Lee, as always, gave me wise counsel.

Let me add this with personal pride. The preparation of the manuscript, including careful editing and quality control, was done by my wife Barbara and my daughter Beverly vonVorys-Norton. My granddaughter Brigid vonVorys-Norton in her own marvelous, intuitive way helped with the computer. For all the many hours of arduous work and above all for your inspiration, thank you, family.

Introduction

The decline and demise of the Soviet Union was sudden, swift, and spectacular. In an astonishingly brief time its power, which for more than a generation had dominated Eastern Europe, threatened Western Europe, and challenged the United States, broke apart. Its ideology, which insistently posited the historical inevitability of communist world revolution, is now smoldering in the ash heaps of history.

For Americans, decision-makers and citizens alike, it was a bewildering experience. After a collective sigh of relief we were swept into euphoria. We can save much money and the constant bother of worrying about becoming victims of aggression. Our national security is assured; it is time to concentrate on domestic matters and decide just how to spend the peace dividend at home. Lord knows we have enough problems at home. More than that. We may now seriously address without distraction and conquer the biggest challenge of our history: to build a stable and prosperous national community based on the full range of racial, ethnic, and cultural diversity. Few countries in history ever set so daunting a goal. None tried to accomplish it through mass-participatory democracy. And none ever succeeded. Our self-respect demands that we try; our pride assures us that we can master any task we set for ourselves.

It is a typical American reaction. Ever since the first European settlers landed on these shores, they, and those who followed from all the other parts of the world, preferred to concentrate their efforts on their own country. But there they set extraordinary goals and met unprecedented challenges. Having crossed an ocean, they mastered a continent. Pioneers, they cleared the land, moved mountains and rivers. American history marked a phenomenal expansion of power: from a narrow strip along the Atlantic coast to a continental colossus; from more or less prosperous rural communities with occasional trading centers to the world's foremost economic engine. Americans felt confident in their own system; they were inordinately proud of what they had accomplished—in America. They had no interest in conquering territories on other continents. Indeed much of the time they shied away from becoming involved in foreign affairs at all.

Occasionally Americans did become involved in world affairs. They did so reluctantly, usually after vigorous campaigns by their leaders who appealed to some grand moral cause. Then they rose in righteous indignation and set out to fix things for good, so they could return once again to their own business. By the end of the nineteenth century, Cuba was the last colony of Spain in the Western Hemisphere. A massive campaign of the New York press about its being a colony where slavery was still practiced and all kinds of other atrocities were being committed by the colonial power bore fruit when it was reported (accurately?) that the battleship USS *Maine* had been blown up in Havana harbor at the instigation of the Spanish government. We went to war and we promptly defeated Spanish forces in the Caribbean and the Pacific, signed a peace treaty, and returned to our ambitious economic and social agenda at home. Woodrow Wilson led us into World War I to fight a war to end all wars and to make the world safe for democracy. We decided the outcome of that war and our president attended the peace conference, but the country quickly returned to its pressing domestic business. The government (Senate) declined to join the League of Nations, and after a somewhat bruising political battle the country passed two constitutional amendments: (1) the right of women to vote and (2) the prohibition against the consumption of alcoholic beverages. Meanwhile the masses joyfully immersed themselves in all the innocent pleasures of jazz in the Roaring Twenties. Franklin Delano Roosevelt led us into World War II to prevent Nazi subjugation of Europe and its domination of the world. Our victory was spectacular as was the rapid dissolution of our massive military forces. Soon in the shadow of one hundred Soviet divisions there stood just one American division and three armored brigades.

The second half of the twentieth century saw a major, though reluctant, change in American attitudes. We may have learned two lessons from the world wars: that we can ignore the international environment only at a high risk and that there are no quick fixes in world affairs. More likely we recognized that for the first time in our history our national integrity itself was in peril from external forces. The source of peril was clearly identified, and its devastating magnitude was rather obvious. Some people may have been attracted to Marxist doctrine, some may have debated the extent to which our economic system is "fair," but clearly most Americans want to own property. They resent having to share it through taxation with their own government and would vehemently oppose being deprived of it by a foreign power peddling a foreign ideology. Some people may have seen Soviet military force as a liberator from fascist rule or class exploitation, but clearly most Americans saw its conquest of Eastern Europe and efforts to destabilize much of Western Europe, Asia, and Latin America as naked aggression driven by blatant imperialism. And clearly most Americans were very much concerned about Soviet intentions toward us. Most of us believed that given any opportunity the Russians would be ready to destroy us on a moment's notice. There was no ambiguity about the destructive power of Soviet nuclear weapons, and it requires no intellectual sophistication to want to live.

The Cold War is over, but the world is still a dangerous place. Indeed it is more dangerous because our perils are more complex and less obvious. It is all the more dangerous because they need to be explained, and with the pressure of fear removed not many people are inclined to listen.

To begin with there is still the matter of a strategic nuclear threat. Few believe there is any. In fact, during the 1992 campaign our president assured the American people time and time again that we had nothing to worry about. We could all go to bed at night and sleep in peace. Perchance to dream. We felt reassured by the statements of the current presidents of Russia, the Ukraine, Belorus, and Kazakhstan and by the fact that many of their missiles are deactivated or, at any rate, are no longer aimed at American civilian or military targets. Meanwhile we tend to ignore signs of reactionary resurgent nationalism,[1] and we pay little attention to the fact

---

[1] In the December 1995 elections to the State Duma (lower house of the legislature) the communists with 158 members (out of 450) emerged as the largest party. Shortly thereafter their leader Gennadi A. Zyuganov defined his goals, in an op-ed piece in *The New York Times*: "We would restore the might of the Russian state and its status in the world. . . . We would seek to restore our state's unique role as the pivot and fulcrum of the Eurasian continental block . . . we see the restoration of the union of the Soviet peoples—based on a voluntary association—as a historic necessity dictated by Russia's needs and those of world security." *The New York Times*, February 1, 1995, p. A21. The ultranationalist Liberal Democratic Party gained fifty-one seats. Its leader, Vladimir Zhirinovsky, was noted for extreme statements. For example, "Americans must leave the Balkans and the Middle East. . . . If you do not, you will find yourself on a court
(continued...)

that much of the vast nuclear arsenal assembled by the Soviet Union is still out there. Few are concerned that the command control of the current leaders may not be altogether sturdy, indeed, that on fairly short notice they themselves may be replaced. Fewer still worry that, although unlikely, in Russia new, reactionary leaders can come to power who quickly, easily, but secretly could reactivate and retarget the strategic capabilities at their disposal.[2] Simply put, the notion that the Soviet nuclear threat has disappeared was grasped quickly and easily; the reality that the danger from existing Russian (perhaps Kazakhstani) missiles is not zero, perhaps significantly above zero, needs explanation.

Then there is China. Many Americans are appalled by its human rights record, but few worry about its actual or potential power. It takes some effort to remind people that China is busy developing modern high-tech military capabilities. It is the country that most actively pursues the development of strategic nuclear capabilities. By 1993 China had four intercontinental missiles (DF-5A; U.S. designation, CSS-4) capable of delivering a three-megaton warhead over an 8,080 mile range. It is a country that in the face of worldwide condemnation has continued nuclear testing into 1996. It is a country that is busily manufacturing long-range missiles and constantly devising new models, missiles that it is ready to wholesale abroad. It is a country that is busily building a blue-water navy, including no fewer than three carriers. It is a country that since 1988 has

---

[1](...continued)
bench facing another Nuremberg. . . . there will be no joy when California will join Mexico, when a negro republic is founded in Miami, when the Russians take back Alaska." *USA Today*, December 15, 1993, p. A. Thus, together the two major extremist parties control some 46.4 percent of the lower house vote, quite enough to cause trouble. In turn, the two government parties (Our House Is Russia plus Oblique) could elect only a total of ninety-nine (22 percent) seats. Ibid., December 26, 1995, p. A. In the July 1996 presidential elections the communist candidate (Zyuganov) received over 40 percent of the popular vote. Boris Yeltsin won with 55 percent, but it is probable that his winning margin was contributed by his most recent ally, General Alexander Lebed. Earlier the latter vowed to rebuild and expand the armed forces. Just a few days before the election Yeltsin appointed him as his national security adviser. Had Lebed changed his mind? "Power," he proclaimed eight months earlier, "must be strong. Patriot will never be a dirty word, whereas 'democrat' has already become one." *Washington Post*, October 21, 1995, p. A.
    [2] Retargeting their strategic missiles on America, according to the Russian commander of Rocket Forces, would take all of twenty-two minutes.

increased its military budget by well over 75 percent after adjusting for inflation.[3] The budget of 1997 added another 13 percent increment. It is a country that is quite prepared for periodic saber rattling.[4]

It also takes some effort to explain the security problems we may face from newly emerging nuclear powers and the possibility of nuclear weapons in the possession of terrorists, worse still, terrorist states. What is most troublesome, however, is that a new, qualitatively different peril has been sneaking up on us. Especially troublesome is the fact that neither its nature nor its gravity is readily apparent.

A fundamental fact of our reality is that we now live in a transitional period at home and abroad. We have focused our efforts on our clearly defined domestic agenda—a determined expansion of integrated diversity within a steadily advancing democratic political system. To be sure, we do not quite know how to go about it, but we are actively engaged in a public debate on appropriate means. In contrast, we do not have an international agenda. The plain fact is that we have lost our bearings. We are just drifting along. Most American decision-makers and opinion leaders are still stunned by the collapse of the USSR and the passing of the simple, bipolar international model. We all believe in peace and freedom but do not have a clue as to what our world will look like in the twenty-first century. Neither do we have a clue as to just how to proceed toward a suitable global pattern of order. All the same, the most fundamental fact of international reality is that without active, constructive, even inspired American leadership we shall exist in a *perpetually and generally volatile international environment that is becoming progressively more explosive because of an increasingly dominant reactionary trend.* You may have to read the sentence twice, and perhaps a special explanation is required.

To begin with, we need to spell out certain basic assumptions. First, we propose it as a basic tenet that our foreign policy must be based on both power and virtue. We need power because it provides us the capability to act; without power we would be at the mercy of others. We need virtue as a guide for indicating what we ought and ought not do.

---

[3] Kent E. Calder, "Asia's Empty Tank," *Foreign Affairs* (March–April 1996), vol. 75, no. 2, p. 60.

[4] In September 1995 the Chinese government held large-scale military exercises in the Taiwan Straits. Some 40 naval vessels and more than 100 aircraft participated "in an orchestrated simulation of amphibious landing operations." In the spring of 1996 they planned another bigger set of exercises. *Washington Post*, February 5, 1996, p. 1.

This then leads us to the second tenet: the moral criterion of human development. If virtue is to serve as a guide, we need a system of morality. Admittedly morality has deep roots in religion, but in a pluralist secular society it is a very touchy subject. It needs a formulation that is all-inclusionary, a formulation with which all the diverse people on earth can identify. Actually this is not too difficult a task as soon as we recognize that history is not just an aggregate of events but much more than that. It is the record of the unfolding of human development.

All living beings change. They are born, grow, and die. When subjected to radical changes in their environment, species try to adapt. Some manage, others become extinct. Human beings are very special. They alone can take the initiative. They alone, through their own intellect and will, can change their environment, can even change themselves. Birds are still building the same kind of nests they did thousands of years ago; bees are still confined to the same "social and economic organization." Dogs may be trained, elephants may be domesticated—by man. But just see how human beings have modified nature itself and how they have changed themselves. Our homes where we are safe from the elements and where we can control the temperature by setting a thermostat are a long way from caves or even the houses of our parents where coal furnaces had to be banked each winter night. In our schools we can learn the intricacies of the universe and how to manage them for our benefit. We have come a long way since we believed that the earth was flat and the sun was circling it daily. In our hospitals physicians are performing organ transplants and experiments with genetic codes. We have come a long way since medicine meant reciting mysterious incantations and applying leeches. And in our societies we are learning human tolerance, even the value of diversity. We have come a long way since any stranger was seen as an enemy to be suspected, feared, and, if possible, harmed, better still killed.[5]

If human beings have the unique capability to develop, it stands to reason that they should have the opportunity to do so. No political system

---

[5] Human development provides the moral foundation of a modern state. On this all ideologies agree. The difference is this: communism and fascism look to the collective as the prime instrument of human development. The state through specially selected elites (e.g., the communist party or the SS) and all others assigned by them to their proper places would advance mankind. In direct contrast, democracies rely on the human individual as the prime instrument. Any person, any common man working by himself or through a political system whose officials he may help select and who are accountable to him, we believe, may move us ahead.

can be just unless it provides a favorable environment for human development. And if human development is a discernible historical process, we are part of it. We can try to retard, arrest, even reverse it, but we ought to help advance it. *Let us be very clear about this. We must understand it fully. For this is the moral foundation of our secular society.*

A few general characteristics of human progress need to be mentioned here. First, it is not a linear upward advance. It had its ups and downs: brilliant quantum leaps and perilous reverses. There were times when the human race in a reactionary binge barely escaped reverting into barbarism. We need to keep in mind that even now civilization is a very fragile condition and that unless constantly nurtured it can quickly be swept away by the fashions and passions of the moment.

Second, we need to keep in mind that civilization is not the property of any group: any religion, race, tribe, caste, class, or ethnic group. All cultures have contributed to human development. This means that all human beings have a vested interest and a right to participate in the benefits of the advancement of civilization. It does not mean, however, that the norms of all cultures past and present have the same value. Some have become obsolete during the human advance; some have become detrimental to it. Radical cultural relativism is absurd in the twentieth century. Cannibalism is not just a dietary preference.

Third, and most directly relevant here, we need to keep in mind that human development has many expressions, but politically it is recognizably marked by an expanding scale of integrated diversity—the family, the clan, the tribe. Starting from the smallest scale, we have been moving toward the unity of all mankind. Thus, some 200 years ago, after a long struggle, human interaction had reached the global scale. For a century and a half (European) Great Powers struggled with the problem of designing some minimally stable pattern that could manage so wide a range of diversity. They did have considerable success but ultimately could not quite cope with it, and the blood of two world wars washed away their achievements. It is now America's turn. We are a superpower, the foremost superpower. We may have rights, probably have advantages, and surely have obligations. Quite possibly, history will judge us on how we used this opportunity.

Essentially there are two main culprits of the current reactionary direction, intertwined like conjoined twins. First, if we look closely we can see the *reversion to political fragmentation.* Our international environment now includes nearly 200 members, each of them inordinately proud of its sovereignty and equality. In fact, many of them are economically underdeveloped and politically chronically unstable. Not a few are entities only by

United Nations illusory definitions. Nearly half hold territory less than that of the state of Pennsylvania—about 7 percent of U.S. territory—and 10 percent are not quite the size of Delaware with less than one-half of 1 percent of our country. In terms of population, two-thirds of the sovereign and equal states are below that of Pennsylvania and a little less than one-fifth (18 percent) are below that of Delaware. Forty years ago about fifty, twenty years ago about 120 were claiming national sovereignty, and the process goes on. Fragmentation is now in full swing. Just look at practically any part of the globe. The USSR broke up, and now the unity of Russia has become problematic. Yugoslavia was shattered, and now Bosnia is torn apart. The "fissiparous tendencies" in India are gaining the upper hand, as are separatist movements in Nigeria, Angola, Ethiopia, Somalia, Zaire, Sri Lanka, Burma, Lebanon, Cyprus, the Sudan. Even Britain, France, Spain, Italy, and Belgium are not immune. Indeed we need not look farther than our northern neighbor. We can no longer be sure that it will enter the twenty-first century as a united country.

Arguably the current trend of increasing fragmentation is detrimental to international order and peace. To begin with, small states are usually weak states. But weak states are not necessarily meek states. Some may seek to improve their position by gaining ascendance over other weak states whose weakness seems to invite aggression. It is theoretically possible that if small states in conflict are located in geopolitically insignificant areas, the tension may remain localized. With the growing global access, however, it is more likely that both will look for patrons among the major powers: the potential victim seeking protection from attack and the potential aggressor wishing cover for its attack. The major powers so involved may play a restraining role, but all too often they have their own aggressive designs that they seek to conceal. Even if not, they may become almost imperceptibly excessively entangled thus escalating the local conflict to a regional, even global crisis. Let us recall. At the beginning of this century conflict among the major powers was fueled by the antagonisms and local clashes among the smaller powers in peripheral areas (e.g., North Africa, the Balkans). Then suddenly: boom—World War I—with dazed leaders and puzzled scholars asking just how it had all come about. There is some danger that this can happen again. Not a pleasant prospect, but we need to think about it.

Small states, moreover, are also likely to be economically frail. They will be heavily dependent on a steady inflow of capital and technology. Unless they sit on natural resources in great international demand or benefit from a very special geopolitical location, they have much difficulty in acquiring and paying for such goods. All along, the domestic economy has considerable difficulty in generating a takeoff into self-sustained economic growth. The consequent persistence of mass poverty with pockets of highly visible wealth is a powerful source of political destabilization. It causes alienation from the domestic political system, which in any case is rarely sturdy. And it causes alienation from any existing pattern of international order. People acutely aware that they in their own country must endure a far lower standard of living than the average citizens of other countries enjoy easily become convinced that the "system" is exploitative and unjust. And let us face it, many people living in poverty throughout the world are aware of the much higher standard of living in the United States. In the past America has been an almost universal object of admiration. We now face the real danger that admiration will turn into envy. We will be blamed for their own condition and become a favorite target of hatred. Not a pleasant prospect, but we need to think about it.

All this is bad enough. But another reactionary culprit further exacerbates international volatility: the *resurgence of the ethnic focus of orientation*. Looking back into its earliest stages—once upon a time—the foundation of human communities was kinship. Gradually the scale expanded from extended family into clans and even tribes, but then it reached its limits. Any further expansion in scale, any further advance in human development, needed a quantum jump. Centuries passed, but this was accomplished only when and where kinship groups began to combine. Family ties still mattered—blood is thicker than water—but communities were being built with common culture (ethnicity) as the definitive mold. It was no longer once upon a time but recorded history: the ages of Moses in Israel, Solon in Greece, Chandragupta Maurya in India, and Ch' in Shih-huang-ti in China.

In terms of an expanding scale of integrated diversity, the ethnic focus of orientation was a genuine advance. It helped build empires that then served as engines of a new momentum of civilization. All the same, it retained one basic value of primitive orthodoxy: radical discontinuity within the human race. People were taught over and over again; they learned from experience over and over again: there is a fundamental difference between "us" in our community and all other human beings. The scale of the "we" expanded, but so did that of the "they." And as time went on, a record of grievances—real and imagined—sharpened the image of the "other." Military victories that glorified "us" were regularly recounted but so were defeats that demonstrated the perfidy of "others." Children were told terrible stereotypes about "them" and were instructed to keep away. Adults would treat "them" with heavy suspicion, would fear "them," and in adversity blame them for anything and everything. "They," by definition inferior, served as suitable scapegoats and proper subjects of discrimination. A double standard clearly and legitimately applied. "Others" could quite properly be cheated; many a story was told and retold to great popular acclaim and amusement of how "we" got the better of "them" or taught "them" a lesson. "Others" could be exploited, degraded, enslaved, and murdered.

It was an attitude that persisted and was reinforced over millennia in practically every part of the world. It was true of Attila the Hun and Tamerlane the Tatar. It was also true of "good" and civilized people. The Chinese were proud to be different from all others. In their scheme of things, living beings were divided into three categories: the Chinese, the barbarians, and the beasts; and the distance between the Chinese and the barbarians was very much greater than that between the barbarians and the beasts. The Chinese were the Middle Kingdom, the center of the universe, the only civilized people.

In the Bible we can read: "Thus said the Lord of hosts: I have reckoned up all that Amalec hath done to Israel. . . . Now therefore go, and smite Amalec, and utterly destroy all that he hath: spare him not, nor covet anything that is his: but slay both man and woman, child and suckling, ox and sheep, camel and ass. . . . And Saul smote Amalec. . . . And he took Agag the King of Amalec alive; but all the common people he slew with the edge of the sword." Because Saul spared Agag "the word of the Lord came to Samuel [the Prophet], saying: It repenteth me that I have made Saul king: for he hath forsaken me, and has not executed my commandments."[6] Jehovah punished Saul by preventing his son Jonathan from succeeding him and selecting David in his place.

Athens was the "cradle of democracy." All the same in 410 B.C. Athens sent thirty ships to Melos because the Melians "were unwilling to obey the Athenians like the rest of the islanders [in paying tribute]." Faced with the invasion, the Melians requested a conference. At the meeting they sought to reason with the Athenian general. They offered their friendship. "No," said the Athenian, "for your hostility cannot so much hurt us as your friendship will be an argument to our subjects of our weakness, and your enmity of our power." They appealed to justice. No again: "Since you know as well as we do that *right, as the world goes, is only in question between equals in power, while the strong do what they can and the weak suffer what they must.*" Being religious men, the Melians claimed divine protection. No, once again. "When you speak of the *favour of the gods, we*

---

[6] 1 Kings 15: 2, 3, 7, 8, 9, 11.

may fairly hope that as yourselves; of the gods we believe, and of men we know, that by a necessary law of their nature they rule wherever they can."

The conference broke up. The Melians fought valiantly, but after additional Athenian forces landed and some treachery among the Melians, they were forced to surrender. "The Athenians put to death all the grown men . . . , and sold the women and children for slaves, and subsequently sent out five hundred colonists and inhabited the place themselves."[7]

Some 400 years later Julius Caesar recounting his experiences in Gaul reports that a tribe of Helvetians escaped surrender by fleeing at night. He promptly ordered all who had given them sanctuary to turn them over or be treated as accomplices. "My orders were carried out," he observed casually "and the men were treated as enemies are treated." We may get a clue of just how enemies were treated from another section. When Vercingetorix surrendered, Caesar kept back some of the captives. "All the other prisoners were distributed as booty among the whole army, each man getting one Gaul." At another point Caesar records matter of factly: "I now set out on another expedition to devastate the country of the Eburones. . . Every village and every building they saw was set on fire; cattle from every part were driven in as booty; the grain. . . was consumed by the huge numbers of men and animals engaged in the operation, so that it seemed evident that even if some of the local inhabitants had managed to hide themselves for the time being, they would die of starvation after our troops had withdrawn."[8] These are only a few examples. There are many, many more, practically all through history.

The point is: like it or not, the existence of deep cleavages within the human race was a universally recognized norm even after the dawn of civilization. These cleavages legitimized claims of categorizations into superior and inferior persons and superior and inferior ethnic groups. They also legitimized, as a matter of course, slavery and genocide. *There is, however, another more important point: these norms of the past no longer hold true. In the vanguard of civilization, we no longer recognize radical discontinuities among human beings either as a scientific truth or as a moral imperative.*

The progress was slow, mostly tentative. Two great religions, Christianity and Islam, were solemnly committed to the unity of the human

---

[7] Thucydides, *The History of the Peloponnesian War*, translated by Richard Crawley (New York: Dutton, 1974), pp. 301, 302, 303, and 306. [Italics added.]

[8] Julius Caesar, *War Commentaries*, translated by Rex Warner (New York: New American Library, 1960), pp. 24, 181, 136.

race. St. Paul proclaimed that while Jesus Christ was a Jew, He died for all men and women. Muhammad the Prophet emphasized that the "Lord . . . created [mankind] from a single person, created of like nature. . ."[9] They spread the message (albeit with notable inconsistency) with word and sword. Vast was their reach but far from covering the globe.

The emergence of modern nation-states in Western Europe was another quantum jump. It shifted the focus of orientation from a social to a potentially much more flexible political community. Even so, it did not immediately affect ethnic solidarity. Usually these nations (e.g., Switzerland and Britain as well as Canada) were products of arrangements (at times facilitated by force) among ethnic communities with their autonomy respected. In some other cases (e.g., Germany and Italy) previously fragmented ethnic groups were reunited into one homogeneous political whole. There were, however, some growing inclusionary trends mostly fueled by democratic ideals. By the early nineteenth century Great Britain expanding its control over the global scale was investing much of its reputation and resources in an antislavery campaign. That kind of radical discontinuity among human beings was an affront to reason and morality. Admittedly there were some hierarchical differences among ethnic groups within the human race. But these were neither inherent nor immutable. Among its other initiatives, Spain carrying its crusade to the New World was very much concerned about the souls of the indigenous population. They too just like the Spaniards themselves should have the chance of salvation. For them too just like for the Spaniards Christ died on the cross. Great Britain, in turn carrying the White Man's Burden, assumed the responsibility of spreading civilization to the "natives," thus conceding they "could be civilized," and thereby implying they were at least potentially equal. British colonial administrators enforced laws against such primitive traditional practices as human sacrifice, suttee (burning a wife alive at the husband's funeral), maiming, and other forms of cruel and unusual punishments (e.g., death by a hundred cuts).   Christian missionaries taught and healed their fellow human beings in Asia and Africa.[10]

Meanwhile the United States kept the torch of its ideals burning—ideals that had their own momentum. In practice Americans treated Negroes as inferior and Indians as savages, but they proclaimed loudly and

[9] Sura IV:I, *The Holy Qur'an*, text, translation, and commentary by A. Yusef Ali (Brentwood, MD: Amana Corp., 1983), p. 178.

[10] There were, of course, other aspects of colonialism and missionary activities that were not so favorable to human development.

frequently the unity of the human race. *"All* men are created equal. . . . *All* men are endowed with certain inalienable rights." Not just we— *they* as well. Here was no radical discontinuity, no special premium for ethnic purity, no super race, no chosen people. It was not a cheap act of hypocrisy. Most Americans, unlike most other people in the world, actually believed in these ideals. Some may find pleasure in pointing a finger at all the imperfections of American society. There are many, and there is a strong element of self-righteousness in a democracy. Still looking at it with a historical perspective, surely the record will bear this out: It is quite proper to note the existence of slavery in the United States some 150 years ago, but it is a travesty to ignore the tens of thousands of Americans who died to eliminate it. More than anywhere else in the world, more than in Europe or Asia or Africa, almost from the beginning and at an accelerating rate, the thrust of American civilization has been toward the ideal, constantly pressing toward the reality of the unity of the human race.

Parenthetically we may note the contributions of Karl Marx. His economics proved to be wrong; his sociology was confused. But he added to the impetus of a quantum jump, transcending ascriptive (ethnic) solidarity as the basis of human communities. "Proletarians of the world unite." Actually it was only a half-jump. It did not take aim at the fundamental notion of radical discontinuity among human beings; Marx only tried to change its borders from ethnic to class lines. He retained and regularly proclaimed the legitimacy of the double standard, including the righteous hatred and violence against the "others" (class warfare).

The first half of the twentieth century, however, proved a serious setback. European nation-states were soon in mortal combat, and lines were drawn along ethnic lines. Marx was wrong. Germans fought the French in bitter and brutal battles. Ethnic solidarity prevailed. French workers were Frenchmen first and proletarians (even if they thought of it) second. German workers were Germans first, and until almost the end of the war they were proletarians second.

The salience of ethnicity was exacerbated by Allied war strategy. Germany was to be stripped of its allies: the Austro-Hungarian Empire and the Ottoman Empire. In a cold, calculating move they were to be divided and torn apart by ethnic mobilization. Ostensibly it was all done for a noble purpose. Democracy meant self-determination of people: the ethnic Czechs had this right as did all the ethnic minorities of the Austro-Hungarian Empire. The Arabs had this right as did all the other ethnic minorities of the Turkish Empire. Thus, democratic values that could have been used for inclusionary purposes overriding ethnic cleavages instead were tragically used to legitimize and reinforce them.

When the war was won, the Allies, seeking a long-term advantage over their defeated enemies, pressed the legitimacy of ethnically cohesive units. They received valuable and unwitting assistance from a man committed to an inclusionary vision of the human race: President Woodrow Wilson of the United States. Curiously more than any of his partners at the Versailles Peace Conference he proved himself to be intractable about the legitimacy of self-determination along ethnic lines. Thus, Central Europe and West Asia were fragmented. Ancient hostilities were rekindled and new grievances were piled on.

Although perhaps unintended, the reactionary movement gained momentum. The peoples of Asia and Africa who had been forced into a more inclusive colonial structure in search of their own political independence found the democratic concept enormously appealing. It reassured them about their own traditional ethnically focused way of life. It provided them with a powerful tool against their colonial masters. Meanwhile some of the larger European nation-states deified ethnic solidarity and promptly sacrificed on its altar democracy and most of the dearly won accomplishments of civilization. Fascism, Nazism, militarism were on the march. They reverted to primitive values and supported them with modern technology. They imposed all kinds of savage frightfulness upon people under their control and came perilously close to imposing their will on us all.

For about a decade Americans stood idly by. President Franklin Roosevelt's repeated warnings about the nature and gravity of the peril were ignored, even ridiculed. Finally, after Pearl Harbor, in the nick of time the United States emerged as a global force advancing the essential dignity of individuals and the unity of the human race. Then after World War II, with phenomenal generosity America helped rebuild war-torn lands whether their people had been our allies or enemies in the recent cataclysm. It pushed for the decolonization of Asia and Africa and the independence of countries regardless of the race, color, or creed of its people, helping them with tens of billions of dollars in economic aid.

Reactionary tendencies nevertheless persisted in much of our world. Most of the newly independent states of Africa and Asia continued an ethnic focus of orientation; indeed some were built on ethnic if not tribal solidarity. Thus, for example, the Indian subcontinent was partitioned into India and Pakistan, and later Pakistan itself was divided into Pakistan and Bangladesh. Meanwhile India organized itself with states mostly divided along "language" lines. Curiously the Cold War served as a restraint on such separatist tendencies. Hungarians and Rumanians were compelled to repress their mutual antagonisms; the French and the Germans recognized a common threat. The Greeks and the Turks felt American pressure to try to contain their centuries-old hatred. Indians and Indonesians were united in their anxiety about superpower hegemony.

Now with the end of the Cold War these brakes are off. We face an explosion of ethnicity. Democracy, which was the vehicle of the inclusionary value of the unity of the human race, once again has become the instrument of regression into human discrimination. In places where political and ethnic borders do not coincide, ethnic minorities are regularly outvoted in "democratic" processes. Often they are relegated to second-class citizens; at times they are abused and persecuted. All the grievances of the past are rekindled with new fervor. Hatred is once again becoming the dominant political attitude, ethnic hatred the legitimate expression of the "national" will. Even the pretense of democracy is in peril as ethnic majorities move with the full range of primitive brutality to "cleanse" themselves. Examples of atrocities are dramatic and widely reported in the territories of the former Soviet Union and Yugoslavia, but they abound in Africa and Asia from Nigeria to Iraq to Somalia to Rwanda to Sri Lanka.

There is a clear and present danger that these practices will continue in the future, indeed that ethnocentric separatism will gain momentum. There is also a clear and present danger that in the near future, many, not just a few, of these fledgling democracies will fail all over the world. Even lip service to the unity of the human race will be abandoned. *Fascism, no less an evil than communism, looms on the horizon.* Indeed we still live in a very dangerous world.

In all humility it can be said, the world, our civilization, needs American leadership. Then there is the question: can we successfully move toward our cherished goal of integrated diversity at home while ignoring the exclusionary (revolutionary) trend abroad? Can we ignore a world that is in upheaval, where violence abounds, and human rights are disdained? Can we be safe behind our fortress of missiles, bombers, and aircraft carriers in a world where all of the new barbarians make a fetish of hating us? Very vexing questions, but we need to think about them.

There is also this consideration. There is a reasonable possibility that in quite a number of countries efforts toward democratization could succeed—with a little help from us. Thus, it is not only a dangerous world, it is also one with opportunity. We may be at a historic turning point. Just a dozen years ago few countries were governed by democratic systems—a part of North America and Western Europe, Australia, New Zealand, Costa Rica, Venezuela, India, and Israel. Conceivably some along the Pacific Rim. Now their numbers have risen dramatically in Latin America, Central Europe, possibly in Asia (Pakistan) and Africa (South Africa). Meanwhile the political polarization of the world has receded. No radical ideological cleavages now reinforce political discontinuities. Once again the human race may be on the verge of a quantum jump in development. The United States, born of western civilization, in its youth instrumental in its protection, may have a historic chance to lead it into a new, even more advanced, global civilization. Admittedly it is an extraordinarily difficult task—but then again that has never deterred Americans. If we choose to assume a positive posture in foreign policy, we need to get a much better understanding about the real world around us and how we got where we are. We need a consensus on our goals, the kind of world we wish our children to live in, but first we need to address the means available to us. More specifically we need to recognize the problems that make the formulation of foreign policy an exasperating challenge.

1

The Conduct of Foreign Policy

The purpose of American foreign policy is easily defined: to advance the interests of the United States beyond its borders. Its conduct, however, poses an exasperating challenge. For it needs to meet two sets of criteria simultaneously: it must be effective abroad and popular at home: two sets of criteria that are likely to clash.

Foreign policy did not always pose an exasperating challenge. America meandered onto the stage of world politics in the twilight of imperialism. It was the system of major powers. They were responsible for international order; for all practical purposes they wrote international law. In case of conflict each power within its more or less discrete imperial sphere was expected to be competent to resolve all disputes by persuasion if possible or by force if necessary. Cross-cutting issues were settled by the major powers collectively, through negotiations at conferences (congresses) or by war. It was rather a simple system. There were few players; it was normatively cohesive; power was the universal currency. The United States had no ambitions of international leadership, nor was there any geopolitical need for it. Thus, during more than a century and a half U.S. foreign policy, often marked by expressions of idealism, had learned to relate to its external environment, but given the advantage of two wide oceans America could choose to ignore it.

The domestic environment of foreign policy making was not much more complicated. Americans believed in limited government; their principal concerns were economic and social. They worked very hard to make a living, a good living; they worshiped God and took pride in their honor. Politics was an occasional business with little impact on their daily lives. If it ain't broke, don't try to fix it, was their attitude, and most of the time most Americans thought their system was quite all right. To be sure, elections were held and issues were debated. Usually though, they focused on local, domestic concerns. Rarely, very rarely, did foreign policy become a campaign issue. Most Americans had no intention of getting involved in other peoples' affairs. For this there was a consensus—a passive consensus.

With foreign policy only an occasional preoccupation of the American polity, decision-making could afford to be simple. The Constitution granted the president the power to nominate ambassadors, negotiate treaties, and receive foreign emissaries. It also reserved some power to Congress. Ambassadors could not take office unless the Senate first confirmed them, and treaties should be negotiated with the "advice" and would become effective only after the "consent" of the Senate (a two-thirds vote was needed to ratify them). And the Constitution placed the power of declaring war entirely in the Congress.

In fact, however, the president was clearly in charge. To begin with, the Senate was quite willing to defer to the president on appointments. It had a constitutional reason. The president, the most powerful official in the country, must be held accountable. But accountability was impaired if Congress played too large a role in the selection of his closest advisers. Better to let him select his own team and be fully responsible for them and the policy advice he accepted. And, of course, there was a political motive. Senior political appointments, including ambassadors, were usually made on the recommendation of a senator, who, of course, benefitted from it politically (if not economically). His colleagues, who needless to say expected reciprocity, would be loath to defeat each other's recommendations.

Senators, moreover, were also broad-minded about their treaty powers. Early in his administration George Washington once sought their "advice" (in the case of a treaty with the Cree Indians). The Senate made a big stir about it. The president had to sit by in their chamber while they haggled over procedure and debated at length various ancillary trivia. Disgruntled Washington never again turned to them for advice, nor did his successors. And the Senate tacitly accepted this.

They were more insistent about the requirement of "ratification." Since for generations the United States was in its isolationist mode, the question rarely arose. Moreover, when toward the end of the nineteenth century American interests in international affairs rose somewhat, the president began to rely on "executive agreements." These were, in fact, personal commitments of the chief executive. He gave his word, and that was enough for foreign powers. Such commitments, of course, did not have the value of a treaty; they did not bind the United States, only its president—while he was in office. His successor was free to accept or decline such obligations. But executive agreements could be negotiated in secret and needed no Senate ratification. Often the senators did not even know about their existence.

Similarly Congress was quite broad-minded about its war powers. It exercised them sparingly: only three times in the nineteenth century (in 1812 against Britain, 1848 against Mexico, and 1898 against Spain). In the meantime it took a tolerant view when the president on his own dispatched the navy and the marines in harm's way. At the very beginning of the century Thomas Jefferson had hardly taken office when he was confronted by a challenge: the Pasha of Tripoli, with a record of capturing American sailors and holding them for ransom, declared war on the United States by cutting down the flagstaff of the American consulate. The president, as commander-in-chief, confident in his own constitutionally granted powers of the disposition of the armed forces, dispatched U.S. Marines "to the shores of Tripoli" with a demonstrably salutary effect. His successors followed his precedent. A century later by congressional courtesy it was an established practice.

If the president's position in making foreign policy for the government of the United States became predominant, his position on the subject within the executive branch was absolute. Simply put, he made his decisions any way he preferred. When Congress established the State Department it was noted in the debate that the secretary was as much an instrument of the president as the pen in his hand. Interestingly, George Washington chose to adopt a more collegial formula. He submitted all foreign policy decisions to a discussion in his cabinet. Indeed in the Genêt affair the president and his secretary of state were outvoted by the secretary of treasury, secretary of war, and attorney general, and George Washington accepted this kind of majority. In this he was not followed by his successors. The constitutional role of the "advice" of the Senate was gone, and the practice of the advice of the cabinet became entirely dependent on the personal pleasure of the president. He could prefer a "kitchen cabinet," a set of personal, informal advisors. But gradually there emerged a career Foreign Service and the secretary of state at its head as the principal advisor on international issues.

Actually it was a very gradual, at times very stressful, process. President Andrew Jackson upon his inauguration (1829) made it quite clear: "to the victor belong the spoils." Appointments of American representatives abroad were as a matter of course part of "the spoils." American representation abroad was beginning to spread. It was of two distinct kinds: (1) the political diplomatic interests of America throughout the world and (2) the personal interests of American citizens abroad. The latter clearly had the advantage. American consular representatives assigned to this duty rose from 141 in 1830 to 282 in 1860. Even after the Civil War when America once again turned inward, the number of offices delegated to handle the interests of Americans in places where no official American consulates were established jumped from 198 in 1860 to 427 in 1890.

Diplomatic representation, however, lagged far behind. In 1830 the United States had just fifteen such posts throughout the world. In 1860 this grew to thirty-three. But significantly (and all through nearly the rest of the century) although the Constitution specifically authorized "ambassadors," all American representatives were appointed at the level of "minister," which compelled them to a lower protocol status. This caused them some personal anguish but interested the average American, focused on the vast undertaking of a continental expansion, not at all.

Just before the end of the century a new salary, retirement scale, as well as representation (entertainment) allowances helped put the Service for the first time on a secure professional basis.[1] By tough standards and careful screening the Foreign Service began to form an elite: the best and brightest with exceptional talent, analytical skill, and good manners recruited from the upper echelons of American society and educated in its foremost private universities. They became the bulwark of the State Department and the mainstay of the secretary.

All along, since the nineteenth century, the secretary of state was established as the senior member of the cabinet in fact as well as in protocol. Interestingly this was due more to domestic than to foreign politics. Very early the secretary of state became the keeper of the Great Seal of the United States. He was designated as number two immediately after the vice president in presidential succession due to death or incapacitation—indeed for the first forty years of the Republic the secretary of state followed his president in office through the normal electoral process.[2] Later as the party system gained hold of American politics, heading the State Department became the highest-prized political plum.

---

[1] W. Wendell Blancké, *The Foreign Service of the United States* (New York: Praeger, 1969), p. 19.

[2] Jefferson was Washington's first secretary of state. Jefferson's secretary of state, James Madison, followed him in office. Madison's secretary of state, James Monroe, did the same. He in turn was followed by John Quincy Adams, his secretary of state.

With an elaborate and solid Foreign Service structure behind him the secretary of state could claim the role of the principal foreign policy adviser of the president. Often he was—when the president so decided. Otherwise it was someone else, a personal confidant (e.g., Colonel House for President Wilson, Harry Hopkins for President Roosevelt) or anyone the president chose.

World War II and its aftermath marked a high point of presidential foreign policy. The United States assumed leadership abroad. Moreover, the attack on Pearl Harbor united the nation. With the help of Senator Arthur H. Vandenberg Jr., the senior republican on the Senate Foreign Relations Committee, President Roosevelt forged a bipartisan foreign policy. He set the pattern of consulting with the leaders of Congress. They, in turn, through party discipline delivered to him the support of both houses. The American president, observed President Truman, had foreign policy powers that "would have made Caesar, Genghis Khan or Napoleon bite their nails in envy."[3] It could be said that politics stopped at the water's edge, for at home there was a *concurrent majority* in government and there was a broad *active consensus* among the people.

As we moved into the second half of the twentieth century, however, the external environment was no longer simple. Vast empires had disintegrated into many newly independent states of all sizes and capacities, each demanding regularly and vociferously the "dignity of equality." For American foreign policy to cope with this radical expansion of essentially inchoate diversity had become an exceptionally complex, multifaceted task. Worse still, the world had become a very dangerous place. Weapons systems capable of destroying our country and our people were now in the possession of an unfriendly power. We could ignore our international environment only at our extreme peril.

As we moved into the second half of the twentieth century, moreover, the domestic environment was no longer simple either. To be sure, as all the polls repeatedly testified, the American people were still only slightly interested in events abroad. "Meet the Press" programs featuring foreign leaders invariably suffered from a substantial drop in audience. Even toward the end of the century the NBC's exclusive, the headline-making presummit (December 1987) interview with Mikhail Gorbachev, attracted just half the usual Monday night audience accustomed to watching the fictional escapades of Alf, the extraterrestrial character. Worse still, somewhere along the way the popular consensus on national interest was

---

[3] Clinton Rossiter, *American Presidency* (New York: Time Inc., 1963), p. 30.

lost. People would listen to official statements on foreign policy, but they were also ready to hear other authorities as well. As before in the case of war, Americans could be mobilized by the government, but more than before—and especially so in times of peace—they were ready to ask questions, to be critical, and occasionally were ready to join together in opposing official actions and policies.

America was undergoing a rapid expansion in diversity. The diversity of ethnic origins now covered almost every nook and cranny of our globe. The range of diversity in values ran the gamut of all major religions, all the various sects, and atheism and agnosticism. The diversity in music included the Metropolitan Opera, Woodstock, and all the various discos. There were no limits on political diversity.

More voices, new voices were heard throughout the land. That they increased the range of alternatives helped build dissonance. That each started out from its own separate base of values and principles, applied its own particular perspectives toward its own special goal, invited cacophony. Foreign policy *special interest groups* have always been vocal; now they pressed their parochial causes single-mindedly with no inclination for compromise and scant courtesy to the national interest. Then a new set of lobbyists appeared, composed mostly of retired senior government officials and congressmen. They were paid handsomely by foreign governments or corporations to protect and advance their alien interests.

Television, a new and fascinating medium with its unprecedented access to the electorate, developed a capability to bring events from anywhere in the world into American living rooms practically at a moment's notice. Its approach to information also was very much its own. Reporters knew that news meant stories that got on the air, and that only stories supported by pictures that grabbed immediate attention got on the air. They had a vested interest in excitement; controversy was their meat. Criteria of national interest were rarely considered; when they were, they were generally subordinated to the American "people's right to know"—a right of which they claimed to be guardians. All the same, the media soon became part of the decision-making process. Government officials looked to them for information about what was happening abroad and what the people were thinking at home. Soon some of their members were serving in high-level (appointive) government positions.

Meanwhile the *academics* were also on the ascendance. With the phenomenal expansion of our educational system and especially with the dramatic rise in the number of college students, professors vastly improved their impact on future generations. But they too had their own perspectives. Their values imbued them with an idealistic view of mankind. They saw the practical hazard of the real world, man's inhumanity to man and its expressions, as unreasonable irritants to be explained away. Their training focused their attention on long-term regularities, and they had little patience with the exigencies of the moment. Their sensitivity regularly entangled them with their favorite causes. For instance, many an anthropologist who would be most reluctant to take a stand on cross-cousin marriages did not hesitate to assert with authority his feelings on Vietnam or disarmament. To say nothing about Nobel Prize laureates who would freely use their essentially specialized authority, for example in physics, to legitimize their political agitations on arms control. But they too were recruited by presidents to serve in the middle and upper echelons of government.

Most important, *Congress* was no longer content with periodic forays into foreign policy. The Senate had become more active and had begun to insist on a partnership, and the House of Representatives began to demand part of the action. When foreign policy became expensive, it had a case; when its peace-time costs ran up to a third and more of the federal budget, the House had a right. More than that, both houses were no longer willing to let the president use his constitutional powers to declare war. Just after the Vietnam involvement, an undeclared war, Congress passed the War Powers Resolution (1973). It provided that the president could commit the armed forces of the United States to areas of conflict or potential conflict only under three circumstances: (1) pursuant to a congressional declaration of war, (2) by specific statutory authorization, or (3) in a national emergency created by an attack on the United States or its armed forces. If the president acted under the third condition, he must (a) report immediately to Congress and (b) unless Congress confirmed his action he must within sixty days (maximum ninety days) withdraw the troops.[4] That was not all. With the decline of political parties and discipline in both houses, individual congressmen found their career prospects (popularity) increasingly dependent on the support of selected special interest groups and on their own media exposures. They were sorely tempted by the limelight shining on events abroad and often succumbed to it. They sought out occasions where they could advance their private, often parochial, views or

---

[4] The resolution was passed over President Nixon's veto. He and all subsequent presidents considered it unconstitutional. In fact, Congress chose not to test it in the courts. We may have a clue just how the Supreme Court would rule from *Chadha v. Immigration and Naturalization Service* (1983), which held legislative vetoes unconstitutional. *The New York Times*, June 24, 1983, pp. I, II, 5.

chose to ride the waves of popular emotions without any concern for long-term strategy or much understanding of the intricacies of complex multilateral relations.

Foreign policy decision-making, however, was slow in adjusting to the new realities in its domestic and international environment. Indeed the momentum carried it in the opposite direction. The country was moving toward the celebration of economic and social equality and was entering upon the historic experiment of setting diversity as one of its principal values. But all along the Foreign Service was reinforcing its special elitist élan and built a homogeneous group further homogenized by traditions of long service. Excellence remained the standard, but this rather intangible tie was reinforced by remarkably similar backgrounds. Most new Foreign Service officers came from the mid-Atlantic states. In college they majored in political science or history. They graduated from the Ivy League. As late as 1965–1968 at the time of the vigorous social initiatives of the Great Society 27.3 percent (141) of the newly appointed Foreign Service officers came from the mid-Atlantic states, nearly 65 percent (314) were majors in political science/government, and nearly 20 percent (98) were graduates of the Ivy League universities, i.e., 8 out of 255 schools whose graduates were appointed. When we add to this the graduates of Georgetown, California (Berkeley), and Stanford (another 55) the percentage rises to 30 percent.[5] In 1947 just 0.5 percent of the officers were women, and very much fewer were blacks.[6]

Once appointed, young FSOs entered a small, exclusive corps (in 1968: 3,363 of all ranks) within which they spent their lives until they retired. For most, the longer they served, the more they became part of it. They believed deeply that they played a vital role in shaping American foreign policy. To be sure, theoretically there was a lateral entry, Foreign Service Reserve (FSR). Recruited from a much broader base, talented persons in midcareer (e.g., university professors) were given a commission. It was a method used sparingly and with utmost caution. For FSRs,[7] their tenure,[8] and their career prospects were limited, as was their significance in policy input. There were exceptions, of course, but mostly they depended on the FSOs who

---

[5] Blancké, *The Foreign Service*, p. 50.

[6] The one usually cited example was Clifton R. Wharton, an FSO since 1925, who was appointed U.S. ambassador to Norway.

[7] In 1968 there were 1,729 such officers, mostly serving at the upper middle rank. Blancké, *The Foreign Service*, pp. 33–34.

[8] They were recruited as temporary specialists with needed skills.

used them, perhaps respected them, but all the same, saw them as not quite "quite."

Thus, the State Department remained in the hands of the best and the brightest. But remarkably, as time went on the qualifications for Foreign Services officers suffered. They were never really representative of the broad and diverse fabric of American society. This may not have mattered while Americans were fully absorbed in their domestic affairs, but by the second half of the twentieth century when the electorate was beginning to look beyond the water's edge, this was becoming a severe handicap. Moreover, Foreign Service officers with their long stretches of overseas assignments learned much about the rest of the world but were losing touch with their own country. They took it for granted that it remained the way they used to know it. That too could be manageable as long as change—cultural and social change—was slow. But when shortly after World War II change accelerated rapidly, Foreign Service officers became effectively disconnected from the people they were supposed to represent abroad. Indeed many simply did not understand the Civil Rights movement; looking at it from a distance they could only shake their heads at the turmoil of the 1960s.

Meanwhile the Foreign Service Corps was growing progressively out of sync with the rapidly changing international environment. One problem was that international relations was becoming multifaceted. The United States, entering global affairs at the time when technology was shrinking the scale of the planet, was becoming involved in a wide variety of contacts. They were not limited to diplomatic terms or commercial considerations. All kinds of other contacts were rapidly rising in salience: economic, social, cultural, and above all, those involving national security.

All the same, the State Department and the elite Foreign Service were quite determined to monopolize every aspect of our international relations. The legitimacy of all other contacts was more or less accepted, provided they were channeled through and coordinated by the State Department structure. Nondiplomatic interests handled by attachés (e.g., defense attachés, labor attachés, commercial attachés) would be given a place in the embassies but subordinated to the ambassadors. When absolutely necessary, new agencies for cultural relations or economic aid were established, attached to, and under the control of the State Department.

The monolithic approach dominated by an elite Foreign Service Officer Corps was beginning to reveal fundamental difficulties. Two were especially damaging. First, the dominance of diplomacy in foreign relations caused problems. It seemed to be such a plausible approach, really the American way. To be sure, there are disagreements among countries, just as among human individuals. But the proper, the democratic way is to discuss them, to negotiate, to bargain, and *then to compromise*. On the international level that is exactly what diplomats are supposed to do and for which they are especially qualified. Still there are issues that are essentially nonnegotiable. For us self-defense is an example, but not many other issues are as clear-cut. Almost everything else we would do is negotiable. Other states may look at issues in a fundamentally different way. Many of them do not have a democratic orientation; most of them do not have a democratic tradition. Negotiation and compromise are not their accustomed methods. We look on compromise as a means to *settle* disputes; much of the rest of the world looks on it as a *tactic to gain an advantage* for the next stage of the struggle. All issues to them are essentially moral issues, which sharply divide right from wrong, and between right or wrong there can be no negotiation, bargaining, or compromise. In this kind of confrontation reliance on diplomats is misplaced. They are determined to negotiate; alas they cannot do otherwise. Much of the twentieth century was marked by ideological struggle, but our Foreign Service tried and tried to negotiate. Confronted by evidence of fanaticism, it put a good face on it and then tried to compromise some more—which explains its difficulty to recognize fascist Italy and Nazi Germany for what they were, hoping to keep the door of negotiations open by placating and appeasing them. More recently their approach to Third World dictators suffered from the same handicap.

The other fundamental difficulty with the monolithic approach was that it mandated a single channel of communications. Basic information about foreign countries was assembled by State Department personnel in the field, often in the fields of far-away countries. Obviously decision-making on the highest level needs this database. But consider the road this information has to travel. It works itself up through channels from the lowest level, gradually step by step through the embassy to the country desk in the State Department, there through further layers possibly to the top. Along the way it may be amended or stopped altogether. It is, of course, a sensible procedure to review it at each level to assume the quality (i.e., probable validity) of the information. Moreover, it is useful through this process to integrate it with other information gathered from other sources. And, of course, it is advisable not to overwhelm the top levels with floods of information of various degrees of accuracy.

All the same, this makes for a slow and deliberate process, slower and presumably more deliberate than was the case with the news media even in its relatively primitive form. Crisis events may require rapid response. The longer it takes for information to travel, the shorter the time for ultimate decision. Thus, events may outrun decision-making. (This is probably what happened in Europe on the eve of World War I, and possibly in the United States on the eve of Pearl Harbor.)

In the case of longer-range policy decisions there is another aspect to consider. The single channel of the State Department runs in both directions. It is the same channel through which information moves upward and through which policy decisions move downward. In fact, this means that information on its upward advance is inevitably evaluated in terms of existent policy criteria moving downward. What happens with information that seems to contradict the current policy assumptions? Will it actually pass through all the various checkpoints—or will it probably get stuck at some level where career officers with their eyes on their future decide not to rock the boat and not to pass it along? The tightness of the cohesion of an elite may in fact support the integrity and independence of its members, at least in theory. In fact, all too often it reinforces the *status quo*. By the time of President Franklin D. Roosevelt there was a growing feeling that the latter was the more likely case. A few hours before his death at Warm Springs as he was signing the outgoing mail, the president stopped for a moment to remark: A typical State Department letter. It says nothing at all.

One significant step toward the modernization of foreign policy decision-making was the National Security Act of 1947. It established the Central Intelligence Agency as an independent arm of the government. This opened up a new channel of information. Moreover, it was authorized to coordinate all other intelligence agencies (military and civilian) thus evaluating the State Department's Bureau of Intelligence and Research. It also established the National Security Council, a top-level advisory group to the president. By statute the Council was composed of the president, the vice-president, the secretary of state, the secretary of defense, the director of defense mobilization, and *anyone else* whom the president chose to invite. It suggested a new appreciation of national security and with it the end of the Foreign Service monopoly and the secretary of state's preeminence, but it still depended on whom the president would invite for counsel and just how he would use the Council. In fact, President Truman and President Eisenhower relied principally on their secretaries of state, Dean Acheson and John Foster Dulles.

John F. Kennedy had every intention of being his own secretary of state, a reality that Dean Rusk, his actual secretary of state, recognized and respected.[9] Even before he took office, the president knew he had a

---

[9] Thomas J. Schoenbaum, *Waging Peace and War, Dean Rusk in the Truman, Kennedy and Johnson Years* (New York: Simon & Schuster, 1988), pp. 272–75.

problem. He preferred to retain the department's preeminent role but wanted to revitalize it by replacing "tired bureaucrats with young people." Shortly before inauguration he asked John Sharon for a list of men who should be retired or fired. During an excited discussion between the president-elect and his brother Bobby about plans for the Foreign Service, their father interrupted. The former U.S. ambassador to the Court of St. James had heard President Roosevelt discussing the State Department with the same heat. "He talked about razing the whole thing and starting from scratch. He didn't do a damn thing about it, and neither will you." Sharon submitted forty names. A month after the inauguration, the president had to admit that every one of the forty remained at their posts. It was perhaps for this reason that President Kennedy chose to bypass the State Department and establish a secret "confidential" foreign policy channel. Actually at first there were two such channels. One linked George Bolshakov, Washington Bureau Chief of Tass, the Soviet News Agency, with attorney general Robert Kennedy and press secretary Pierre Salinger. Bolshakov, who was also a senior officer of Soviet military intelligence, sent his coded messages to his boss in Moscow, who in turn reported directly to the minister of defense. The other linked Soviet Ambassador Dobrynin with Robert Kennedy.[10] After a year and a half the second "back channel" took over all the traffic and Bolshakov was recalled. Secretary of State Rusk knew nothing about this and kept assuring senior Foreign Service officers that there was not "a passive reliance but an active expectation. . .that this Department will in fact take charge of foreign policy."

The president later recognized that he could not in fact run American foreign policy single-handedly, and his confidence in Dean Rusk, his loyal, even self-effacing secretary, grew steadily. Rusk in turn was determined to act as the president's chief foreign policy advisor. Thus, for example, he was most reluctant to engage in a foreign policy debate in the cabinet or with other presidential advisers (including the national security adviser) as that would imply some sort of equality of status.[11] He also tried to

---

[10] Anatoly Dobrynin, *In Confidence, Moscow's Ambassador to America's Six Cold War Presidents (1962–1986)* (New York: Times Books, 1995) pp. 52–54. See also: Pierre Salinger, *P.S. A Memoir* (New York: St. Martin's Press, 1995), pp. 135–38. According to Salinger forty-four secret letters between Chairman Khrushchev and President Kennedy passed through this channel.

[11] Schoenbaum, *Waging Peace and War*, pp. 281–83. Incidentally, McGeorge Bundy, the national security adviser, respected Rusk's position and never tried to bypass him, p. 284.

streamline his department, but his administrative style favored decentralization, which puzzled his subordinates and did not suit John Kennedy.
Noticeably when it came to major decisions, the president looked to *ad hoc*
groups of advisers (Executive Committee). The secretary of state was
always included but was not the dominant voice.[12] Both during the missile
crisis (1962) and the debate over the instigation of a coup in Vietnam
(1963) he appeared to be busy with "other assignments." Moreover, the
president was often heard to vent his discontent. He called the State
Department "a bowl of jelly." It took them "four or five days to answer a
simple yes or no." Sending them instructions was like dropping it in a
dead-letter box. "They never have any ideas over there, . . . never come up
with anything new." Quite possibly by 1963 President Kennedy was ready
for fundamental structural changes.

---

[12] Robert F. Kennedy, *Thirteen Days* (New York: W.W. Norton & Company,
Inc., 1969).

2

An Exasperating Challenge

By the 1960s the new reality was taking shape. Abroad American leadership was challenged by the Soviet Union, its revolutionary ideology, its growing arsenal of nuclear bombs, and its intercontinental ballistic missiles. We could no longer neglect a dangerous international environment. At home, universities, their faculties and students, had become active; the coaxial cable made network news a powerful force, and political party discipline was breaking down in Congress. With a basic consensus gone, we could no longer neglect a fragmented domestic environment. Foreign policy therefore had become an exasperating challenge.

President Johnson did not recognize the new reality. He persisted in the traditional approach. He was confident that he could handle international issues by himself. "I always believed," he confided, "that as long as I could take someone into a room with me, I could make him my friend, and that included anybody, even Nikita Khrushchev." As far as Congress was concerned, he recalled that when he was majority leader in the Senate, he loyally, almost automatically, supported President Eisenhower on foreign policy and saw to it that the Senate did likewise. Sitting in the Oval Office, he expected no less from his former colleagues on the Hill. It was a big mistake. During the last years of his presidency when things seemed to go awry, he almost instinctively narrowed the decision structure and circled the wagons. He retired as a bitter man, certain that he had been badly treated because he was a southerner. He blamed the media, the Eastern Establishment, and the Ivy Leaguers.

President Nixon was quite aware of the radical changes in the decision environments. When in 1960 he left the vice-presidency, he saw the country at peace and in prosperity. Just eight years later he was shocked by the violence in the streets, the assassinations of national leaders, and the general loss of confidence in government. He was utterly appalled by the changes in the international environment. Conditions there had deteriorated far beyond his worst expectations. In a few short years the United States had become mired down on the other side of the globe, was suffering heavy casualties in a country about which most Americans knew little and for which they cared less, and in a war which they did not know how to win or how to quit. American leadership had become moribund; our alliances were in disarray; indeed for the first time since independence our national existence was genuinely in peril. Something had to be done right away to reverse this trend. The future of our country demanded it. He thought he knew just what to do. He decided first to restore American leadership abroad.

As the basis of his approach, the foreign policy decision structure would have to be reorganized into an effective modern instrument capable of dealing with the new global realities. It had become too broad, too public, too cluttered up with fuzzy thinkers. The base would have to be radically reduced. Elements outside the executive branch would be excluded altogether. Congress was petty and partisan; it might be placated by rhetoric and patronage. It would receive, of course, more or less useful and more or less truthful briefings but would not be consulted. The media was hostile; possibly it could be intimidated. Academics were irrelevant; they could be safely ignored. The electorate was ignorant and confused; it could be manipulated through media events. There would be time, just enough time, for historic breakthroughs. Once these were accomplished, the American people would acclaim the results and forget or care little about the method used to achieve them.

Inside the executive branch the State Department had proven itself to be empty of new ideas but full of policy leaks. It could still be entrusted with routine diplomatic matters but otherwise would be systematically kept in the dark and, if necessary, intentionally misled. Foreign policy would be conducted by the president from the White House, supported by a National Security Council built into a lean and tough command center, managed by its brilliant and articulate director, and manned by the best talent available.

Dr. Henry Kissinger maneuvered deftly in the bureaucratic maze of Washington. He vigorously, and at times temperamentally, controlled the flow of foreign policy advice to the president. All communication from the White House senior staff had to be passed through him, as did all communication from cabinet officers. Sometimes he let it go through, sometimes he adjusted it to his liking, sometimes he blocked it altogether. He was deeply annoyed when Nixon pretended to discuss foreign policy options with the cabinet after he believed that he, Henry Kissinger, and the president had already made a decision. In the meantime Kissinger was busy rebuilding and reinforcing "back-channels" to foreign governments and leaders which bypassed the entire Foreign Service. Working indefatigably he set out to bypass and force out the secretary of state from decision-making. He quickly developed a special relationship with Anatoly Dobrynin, the Soviet ambassador in Washington, DC. With the expressed approval of President Nixon, he had an understanding with the Russian that the latter would not reveal to the Secretary Rogers the content of some discussions he had with the national security adviser. The most dramatic example of the operation of the back-channel was the "opening to China." Here the confidential intermediary was President Zia ul-Huq of Pakistan. Even Secretary Rogers was kept ignorant of the Nixon initiative and especially its culmination: Kissinger's secret visit to Beijing. Alternatively cajoling and whining, he would oppose practically anything the secretary of state proposed. He was constantly complaining about the sinister manipulations of the State Department and Secretary Rogers, even going so far as to accuse them of planting "adverse stories" about his dating Jill St. John and thus trying to destroy him.[1] Regularly he threatened resignation.[2] All along, he moved systematically to gain monopoly of official briefings on and off the record. He sought to endear himself to the press, constantly offering to serve as a news source and "confiding" in them artfully, and more or less truthfully. Gradually he managed to improve his own reputation for brilliance and influence. It took about three years, but then it was there for all to see. The national security adviser emerged as the preeminent adviser and executor of foreign policy. President Nixon generally tolerated the obvious ambitions of his stellar aide but was not always amused.

---

[1] H. R. Haldeman, *The Haldeman Diaries* (New York: G.P. Putnam's Sons, 1994), p. 176.

[2] "Monumental flap with K[issinger], who called accusing P[resident] and me of playing games with him yesterday about boat ride, etc. to cover up plan to have Rogers up to Camp David. Incredible . . . Guess they sat there all day stewing . . . Guess K is uptight about Middle East and is imagining things. He made reference to several early morning phone calls from P yesterday, with quick hangups . . . P realizes K basically jealous of any ideas not his own, and he just can't swallow the apparent early success of the Middle East plan because it is Rogers'. In fact, he's probably actually trying to make it fail for just that reason. Of all people, he has to keep his mind clean and clear, and instead he's obsessed with these weird persecution delusions." Ibid., p. 189.

The radically reduced role of the secretary was resented by William Rogers, but he was loyal to the president, an old friend.[3] Within the established Foreign Service elite, however, the resistance was fierce, as it was with other bureaucratic elites, including the military. Presidential policies announced through the National Security Council were restated, reinterpreted, even contradicted by State Department spokesmen, at times by the secretary himself. Worse still, secret deliberations and decisions were regularly leaked to the press.

Considering the problem realistically it soon becomes clear that it is a hopeless quest to keep secrets for very long in the American government. To begin with, we are too open a society for that, and we are too diverse. Then there are the practical exigencies of policy making. Facing major decisions, presidents "task" them out. In other words, they consult their advisers. That is, after all, why they have been appointed. Advisers turn for help to their assistants, and they in turn look to their staffs. Unavoidably quite a number of people get involved. Each works very hard for many hours to prepare what he considers the best advice. In time, the process is reversed. After extended discussion staffs put together their analysis of what they see as available options and their preferred choices. Assistants meet to evaluate these, make their own adjustments and selections, and pass them up to presidential advisers, who in turn bring them to the highest level for decision. But as this process unfolds, people develop loyalties to positions they have advanced. After all, they have invested much work in these solutions, which they consider the very best of their judgment. They want to know from their superiors just what the final outcome was. Coming back from a cabinet meeting, for example, the top advisers will inevitably face questions and/or curious looks. They can say, "I cannot tell you about our secret deliberations, what the Man decided, and why," but if they do so, the morale of their closest associates will suffer. Therefore, most of the time they give some explanations in confidence; sometimes (often) the explanations disappoint someone who was really committed to his own position, and he may seek relief through the media. The strain is acute where civil service officials intersect with political appointments. Even in the best of times there is tension here, and when the president puts on the pressure the temptation for vindication through the "fourth estate" (media)

---

[3] Bryce Harlow, one of the key men in the transition team, confided that Nixon was surprised (disappointed?) that Rogers turned out to be so lazy and did not assert himself more. Presumably he had hoped for a balance between his secretary of state and the national security adviser.

may become irresistible. There are just too many possible sources of leaks for even the most drastic security measures to locate. Still it is not entirely unusual for presidents to try .

As early as September 12, 1969, H. R. Haldeman, the president's chief of staff, confronted by a leak, saw "something new to worry about. Were the Camp David phones tapped for the Defense Department?" he wondered.[4] Soon leaking of classified information to the press reached epidemic proportions. Henry Kissinger blew his stack regularly. The president, to the chagrin of his national security adviser, was reluctant to discipline the State Department, but then the National Security Council itself became affected. During the Indo-Pakistan war secret deliberations by the president's closest advisers were published by columnist Jack Anderson in December 1971. Suspicion soon focused on Navy yeoman Charles Edward Radford, an aide to Adm. Robert P. Welander, USN, who headed the Joint Chiefs' liaison with the National Security Council. He was suspected partially because he was a Mormon like Jack Anderson and because just a few days before the leaks he had been invited by the columnist to a Chinese restaurant.

When Radford was interrogated under a lie detector, he denied being the source of the leak and the lie detector supported him on this.[5] Then almost by accident a remarkable story began to unravel. When Radford was asked the routine question: "Have you ever furnished classified documents to uncleared persons?" he became tense and embarrassed then answered, "yes." Pressing the point the interrogators discovered that the liaison office was engaged in systematic spying. They were spying for the Joint Chiefs of Staff, our highest military leaders, on the president of the United States, their commander-in-chief. Indeed during the supersecret Kissinger trip to China Radford rifled the national security adviser's briefcase, photographed its contents, and sent it on to the chairman of the Joint Chiefs! What extraordinary goings on! Since rigorous security measures had proved ineffective, extreme measures were instituted. Lie detector tests were required; the office and home telephones of senior assistants were bugged. A special White House security force ("the plumbers") was organized. More than that, it seemed necessary to engage in active deception for the good of the American people. Even so, once the great foreign policy achievements were accomplished, President Nixon still

---

[4] H. R. Haldeman, *The Haldeman Diaries*, p. 86.

[5] Len Colodny and Robert Gettlin, *Silent Coup, the Removal of a President* (New York: St. Martin's Press, 1991), p. 16.

fervently hoped the American people would cheer the successful ends and ignore or at least forgive the distasteful means.

In January 1975 Ray Price, discussing the approach the former president should adopt in his memoirs, urged that instead of being embarrassed by the "darker side" of his personality Nixon should acknowledge it.

If the country were ever to be restored to its senses, the public would have to recognize that a measure of scheming and duplicity is necessary in the real world of power politics. . . .
I could see some of the tension drain away, and at one point, he looked out of the window, then turned back and grinned, and commented: "Of course, it's true. We never could have brought off the opening to China if we hadn't lied a little, could we?"[6]

Actually the Nixon administration did rather more than just lie a little. The president no doubt was disappointed when the extraordinary security measures did not work. That the office and home phones of the senior national security staff were being tapped was soon discovered. So were White House efforts (under the guise of a "security check for a senior appointment") to intimidate an unfriendly CBS reporter. So was the burglary of a psychiatrist's office in search of derogatory information on the man accused of improperly releasing the secret Pentagon papers. And so were efforts to involve the CIA in a cover-up of Watergate. Most disappointingly, Nixon's major and dramatic foreign policy accomplishments did not yield *ex post facto* validation of his emergency procedures. People applauded President Nixon's foreign policy coups, but they did not forget or forgive the manner in which he went about achieving them. The congressional, media, and academic excoriation was devastating.

The prohibitively high cost in public confidence of the Nixon approach was dramatically demonstrated in October 1973 less than a year after his reelection by a landslide. When during the Arab-Israeli War in perilous confrontation with the Soviet Union the president ordered a *global nuclear alert* and very much needed broad public support, he received mostly scorn and skepticism. At the State Department press conference reporters questioned whether the confrontation in general and the alert in particular were actually ploys designed to distract from the president's domestic difficulties (Watergate). Henry Kissinger was close to tears. "We are

---

[6] Raymond Price, *With Nixon* (New York: Viking Press, 1977), p. 34.

attempting to conduct the foreign policy of the United States with regard for what we owe not just to the electorate but to future generations. And it is a symptom of what is happening to our country that it could even be suggested that the United States would alert its forces for domestic reasons."[7] His complaint went directly to the heart of the matter. All too soon after the splendid achievements of the China trip, the Moscow Summit, and the Vietnam settlement, the paralysis of American foreign policy was there for all to see.

President Ford felt compelled to try a different approach. The international environment, he thought, was manageable. What was needed was to bring the foreign policy decision-making process into harmony with its domestic environment. Henry Kissinger had in the meantime become secretary of state and the department was regaining its central role. His relations with Congress were good: he would build on them and try to restore confidence. The preoccupation with secrecy was abandoned. Congressional demands to become privy to all government secrets were honored to the point of severely impairing CIA overseas operations. President Ford had no intention whatsoever of deceiving the American people for their own good.

President Carter moved even farther along this path. He focused on restoring the domestic consensus of national interest. Just before the election in 1976 Cyrus Vance, the future secretary of state, in a memorandum to the Democratic presidential candidate put it plainly:

The new Administration will accept the necessity *to make Congress and the American people joint partners* in foreign policy matters. To do so, the president will assume major public leadership on foreign policy matters, and make a major investment in educating the public to perceive the difference between its long-term interest and short-term interests and the difference between the interest of the nation as a whole and the interests of particular subconstituencies and interest groups within the United States.[8]

It was a move in the right direction, but in its implementation it was a failure. As far as the "joint partnership" with Congress, the media, and academia was concerned, President Carter was cautious, his staff inept. In his partnership with the people he went to the populist extreme. He would at least ostensibly dissolve the boundary between decision-making structure

---

[7] Henry Kissinger, *Years of Upheaval* (Boston: Little, Brown, 1982), p. 596.

[8] Cyrus Vance, *Hard Choices: Critical Years in America's Foreign Policy* (New York: Simon & Schuster, 1983), pp. 441–42. [Italics added.]

and domestic decision environment. All American citizens would be able to participate in foreign policy making. They could do so vicariously. They were invited by gestures and style to recognize and appreciate that their president was just like them. During the campaign he let it be known that he was "Jimmy," not "Governor," not "Mr. Carter," not "Sir," not even "James."[9] He was opposed to luxury and ostentation; he wanted to live just like an average Joe. He complained about too many television sets in the White House and too many large cars available in the motor pool. He demanded that their numbers be reduced and that his own big black limousine be changed.[10] He sold the presidential yacht as a luxury. Sitting before the fireplace wearing a sweater, he discussed foreign policy (the energy crisis) with the folks.

More than that, President Carter at least during the first two years of his administration also invited the American people to participate directly in foreign policy making. They were encouraged to offer their comments and suggestions directly to the president by mail and at one point by telephone. The president himself would travel across the country, stay in private homes, and hold "town meetings" to seek the advice of the good people. During his famous retreat to Camp David to ponder the causes of the "national malaise," he consulted a wide range of experts, then went into the streets of nearby Thurmont, Maryland, to tap the wisdom of the good people. No one was to be excluded. In 1980 during his debate with the Republican presidential candidate, he revealed in all sincerity that he sought advice on nuclear policy from his twelve-year-old daughter, Amy.

President Jimmy Carter also started the destruction of the State Department cadres. His populist approach was hostile to the significance and utility of their special expertise. His egalitarian proclivities reinforced by a devout religious rebirth (we are all God's children) were inimical to the elite cohesion of the Foreign Service. The special position of the FSO

---

[9] Shortly after he moved into the White House, his staff sent in a memo asking him how he wanted to be addressed. It had little boxes with a wide range of alternatives from "Jimmy" to "Mr. President" to be checked to mark his decision. When the memo came back, none of the boxes had been checked.

[10] One reason for multiple television sets in White House offices was the desire to cover all the networks. It would have been a very delicate matter to reduce the number of TV sets to one and thus exclude two of the networks. Which ones? Moreover, as the Secret Service explained, presidential limousines for essential reasons of security needed heavy bulletproof reinforcement, something that simply could not be put on a Volkswagen. In the end President Carter compromised. He had a large, heavy limousine, but it was painted tan.

was degraded, then practically abolished. In recruitment the pretense of searching for the best and the brightest became a thin, transparent veneer. Representativeness and political sensitivity became the dominant criteria. A massive effort of affirmative action to recruit women and minorities moved into high gear and gained irreversible momentum.

Accompanying the progressive decline of the State Department during the Carter administration was a sharpening conflict between the secretary of state and the national security adviser. When Secretary Cyrus Vance resigned, Zbigniew Brzezinski, Assistant to the President for National Security Affairs, was a clear winner.

Possibly President Carter never had a chance. The challenges in the domestic environment, which he had inherited from the truncated Nixon and the short Ford administrations, were quite probably no less intractable than those in the international environment left to President Nixon by a disoriented Johnson presidency. It takes little time to lose the confidence of the people, much more time to regain it. Determined and hard-working, meticulous in detail, President Carter did not have the skills to teach the complexities of foreign policy or the time for "a major investment in educating the public." Even so, the Carter presidency did significantly alleviate domestic tension. By the time it was over, gone was the paranoiac suspicion of government and its elected leaders. The American people once again were willing to trust their government. That was no mean achievement for them and for President Carter.

In the international environment, however, his posture was mostly reactive. We suffered serious setbacks. The Camp David agreement, which many hail as an accomplishment, was gained at a cost of direct U.S. involvement in Middle East affairs on a wholly unprecedented and possibly excessive scale.[11] Soviet indirect intervention through surrogates (e.g., Cuba) in Angola, Ethiopia, and Yemen was exacerbated by direct intervention in Afghanistan. Personal relations with foreign leaders were not good; the country's reputation abroad was no better. Meanwhile international lawlessness was reaching new heights. American ambassadors were assassinated; some fifty diplomats were held hostage for over a year,

---

[11] Successful negotiations require a basket of issues of various degrees of difficulty. Starting with the easier ones, negotiations may build a momentum making the difficult ones more manageable. Camp David removed all the easier, compromisable issues without building a momentum for general settlement and leaving only the intractable ones. Incidentally it was conducted in strict secrecy. It is doubtful that the American people have yet learned its dollar cost to us.

and we could do nothing to stop it! It was not an attractive state of affairs. With all the benefits gained at home through an all-inclusionary decision style, the costs abroad were prohibitive.

President Reagan developed the assets accumulated by his predecessors: Nixon's *détente* abroad and Carter's confidence building at home. The president's values and style touched the emotional strings of the American people and built the rich resonance into a massive popular support which lasted through much of his second term. His approach to decision-making was conventional. He believed in presidential leadership but also in delegation of authority. In the White House he depended on his three-member senior staff, two of whom (Ed Meese and Mike Deaver) were long-time California friends and the third (James Baker III) whose management skills he greatly admired.

In fact, President Reagan had very little expertise in foreign policy. He did have a "vision" but no detailed large-scale design. America militarily strong and ideologically unambiguous was quite enough for him. He made his general convictions clear to everyone. His advisers could read them easily enough and were expected to act accordingly. He wished to be informed of the more important international events and trends, and when decisions were required he made them, but he left implementation and resolution of details to others. His three closest advisers in foreign policy were also personally known to him since way back in California. He trusted: Caspar Weinberger, the secretary of defense; William Casey, director of the CIA; and after a short initial period, George Schultz, the secretary of state.

It was Reagan's original intention to avoid any clash between cabinet officers and his national security adviser. There would be no back-channel during his administration. All communications with foreign governments were to be channeled through the State Department.[12] For most of the first term the arrangement worked well. The national security adviser, Richard Allen, a former deputy of Henry Kissinger, had to accept a visibly lesser role. His office was moved down into the White House basement; his direct access to the president was curtailed. He, it was revealed, would have to report through Counsel to the President Ed Meese.

The National Security Council itself was staffed mostly by military and naval officers and former CIA agents. They were essentially "yes sir, can-do" people, nary an intellectual with a global perspective among them. Complicating matters was a remarkably high turnover in national security

---

[12] Dobrynin, *In Confidence*, p. 52.

advisers. Richard Allen stayed for less than a year. He was succeeded by Judge Clark, a close confidant of the president, but otherwise with practically no qualifications for the job. The first term ended with yet another, the third national security adviser. Previously unknown to Reagan, he was a Marine Corps Lieutenant Colonel, Bud McFarlane.[13] The weakened position and the instability at the top of the NSC left staffers chafing at the bit.

While President Reagan was concentrating on domestic, economic problems—interest rates and inflation were well in the two-digit figures—his administration had significant foreign policy accomplishments. First, American rearmament progressed steadily. With remarkable ease the United States more than doubled its defense budget. It built new planes, new ships, new tanks, *and* it dramatically improved the quality and morale of its servicemen. This worried the Soviet leadership no end.

Second, the Reagan administration demonstrated that the United States had recovered from the paralysis of its post-Vietnam syndrome. When the president thought it necessary, on his own initiative he projected American military force. Twice in 1982 he sent U.S. Marines to Lebanon. When the press with the War Powers Resolution in mind asked him just how long he expected the marines to stay, Reagan replied, "as long as necessary."

In turn, when the mission became ambiguous and 241 Americans were killed in their barracks by a suicide bomber, the president withdrew the forces from Lebanon. This action demonstrated clearly that America had indeed learned the lessons of Vietnam. It would not by gradual escalation become bogged down in foreign civil wars. To underscore the new position, on the very day when the decision was made to withdraw the marines from Lebanon, the president ordered U.S. forces to land on the island of Grenada where a communist terrorist coup had overthrown the ruling communist leader (Maurice Bishop) and then murdered him and his six cabinet colleagues.

Third, the Reagan administration moved to tackle the pestilential problem of international terrorism, especially state-supported terrorism. Persistently, high administration officials spoke out, indeed lectured regularly, on this subject they called "ambiguous warfare" or "low-intensity warfare." The American people would have to be educated on the subject: there could be no compromise with terrorists.

---

[13] One of his first ideas was to send American divisions to Egypt and invade Libya. Casper W. Weinberger, *Fighting for Peace, Seven Critical Years in the Pentagon* (New York: Warner Books, 1990), p. 361.

Behind the words there was muscle. The United States would abandon a passive position of waiting for a terrorist atrocity and then responding. Within the CIA a special Counterterrorist Center (CTC) was organized. Its purpose included the development of human assets through which terrorist groups could be infiltrated. It was not altogether successful, but it did have some notable achievements, e.g., the infiltration of the Abu Nidal terrorist organization (ANO).[14] Meanwhile Congress passed the Omnibus Crime Act (1986), which established the United States' legal right to capture abroad terrorists who had committed acts against American citizens and to return them to the United States for prosecution.

On October 7, 1985, a radio station in Göteborg, Sweden, picked up an emergency message from the Italian cruise liner, the *Achille Lauro*. A group of armed men who identified themselves as members of the Palestinian Liberation Front had seized the ship, which had Jewish passengers, many of them American. The terrorists demanded the release of fifty Palestinians held in prison by the Israelis, or they would execute their hostages (presumably Jewish passengers). They did not do that, but before they negotiated their own free passage, they brutalized the passengers and in an extraordinary display of savage criminality they abused Leon Klinghoffer, an American who was physically handicapped. Then they killed him and threw him in his wheelchair overboard. In cooperation U.S. and Israeli intelligence learned that the terrorists were to leave Egypt on an Egyptian airline. Lt. Col. Oliver North, an able, ambitious, and vain war hero serving as a middle-level officer on the National Security Council, worked out a plan to intercept the plane, seize the terrorists, and fly them to the United States for trial. The president approved and later explained, "Here was a clear case in which we could lay our hands on the Terrorists. . . . I didn't think there was any way that I could not approve a mission of that kind with what was at stake."[15]

The operation was carried out flawlessly—up to a point. The Egyptian plane was intercepted and forced to land at the NATO base of Sigonella, Italy. It was quickly surrounded by fifty Delta Force (U.S. Army special unit) troops, but they in turn were surrounded by Italian forces. An unpleasant shouting match between commanders highlighted the standoff. In the end, on the assurance of Italian Prime Minister Craxi that Italy would

---

[14] Duane R. Clarridge, *A Spy for All Seasons, My Life in the CIA* (New York: Scribner, 1997), pp. 323–29, 332, 336–37.

[15] Quoted in: Gregory F. Travertine, *Making American Foreign Policy* (Englewood Cliffs, NY: Prentice-Hall, 1994), p. 266.

arrest and try the terrorists, President Reagan agreed to withdraw the American troops. In fact, the leader of the gang was secretly spirited out of the country. The terrorist convicted of the murder of Mr. Klinghoffer was given prison leave in February 1996. To the "surprise" of the Italian authorities he did not return.

Six months later there was another incident. Muammar al-Qaddafi, Libya's ruler, had been preening his feathers. He threatened U.S. Mediterranean forces, declared 200 miles off his coast Libyan territorial waters, and even fired on American ships. His pinpricks ended in a disaster for him. American forces ignored his provocative declaration and when challenged responded forcefully. Libya lost planes and ships. Frustrated, on March 28, 1986, al-Qaddafi called on "all Arab people" to attack anything American, "be it an interest, goods, ship, plane, or person." A week later (April 5) a Libyan bomb, placed there by Libyan-employed terrorists, exploded in La Belle Discothéque in Berlin, killing an American serviceman and a Turkish woman and injuring 230 people, including about fifty American soldiers.[16] This time no one could interfere with a firm U.S. reaction. The president was determined to teach the terrorists a lesson, to preempt, disrupt, and discourage further Libyan operations abroad. At 2:00 A.M., Libyan time, April 15, U.S. carrier planes and Air Force F-111s from Britain delivered a massive blow on mostly military targets of the two largest Libyan cities, Tripoli and Benghazi. Thereafter the secretary of state noted dryly, "the man crawled back in his box."

The most difficult component of the antiterrorist strategy was a determination not to deal with kidnappers. The Palestinians, abetted by Iranian, Syrian, and Iraqi governments, had developed quite a habit of seizing American civilians and holding them for ransom in Lebanon. They would demand all kinds of things: the release of their fellow terrorists captured mostly by Israel, U.S. pressure on Israel, an Arab Palestine, and, of course, money, always money. The hearts of Americans and most civilized people went out to the innocent hostages who were brutally abused by some fanatics and to the relatives of the hostages. They wished to do something, anything at all, to bring the hostages' suffering to an end. But, in fact, dealing with kidnappers, even if it would relieve the misery of some hostages, would only *place at risk more and more innocent Americans.* Hard logic but also tempered compassion mandated no trafficking with and no concessions at all to terrorists seeking to parlay their brutality toward innocent American citizens into profit. We must have nothing to do

---

[16] Weinberger, *Fighting for Peace*, pp. 187–201.

with kidnappers and under no circumstances would we pay ransom was the repeatedly declared American position.

It was a tough position. The American people had to be persuaded; our allies had to be, to put it diplomatically, constantly reminded. The Reagan administration did all that with uncompromising firmness. The people around the president, however, were acutely aware of his compassion for the hostages and his desperate wish to find some way to relieve their plight. And so this third thrust of Reagan's foreign policy through the flaws of the decision-making structure left open the chance for fraud, a scandal, and the near-destruction of the Reagan presidency. Late in the first term the NSC, anxious to serve the Boss, reasserted itself, assumed the initiative, and the Reagan-style decision-making broke down.

Curiously the action-oriented officers in the National Security Council may have been misled by a theory of statecraft, a European, not an American, theory at that. Nineteenth-century imperialist leaders had a special fondness for a balance of power. International order is safe when the major powers are balanced in capabilities. In turn, regional balance of power would assure peace in the area and the opportunity for a major power (or the major powers) to guide the direction of development at relatively small cost. The national security advisers of both president Nixon and Carter were profoundly devoted to this notion. Thus, Henry Kissinger, who was especially concerned about the Middle East, felt reassured by an emerging powerful and pro-American Iran under the shah. Zbigniew Brzezinski fervently hoped that the shah would survive. But then in January 1979 the shah had to flee his country, and Iran fell under the rule of the Ayatollah Khomeini, who saw in America the Great Satan. The situation further deteriorated when American diplomats were held hostage by the Iranian government for 444 days. Since another U.S. friend in the area, Pakistan, in spite of a Nixon "tilt" in its favor had been dismembered by India just a few years earlier (1971), in the vast area between Israel and Thailand we had no powerful friend we could rely upon in our strategic need.

As we moved into the 1980s, senior NSC officials, frustrated by distressing reality, looked for hopeful signs. They watched with glee the Iraqi invasion of Iran (1981) and the war that proceeded toward a pro-longed, bloody stalemate. They noted that the Ayatollah Khomeini was old and was getting visibly feeble. He could not last long, and then an "inevitable" power struggle would follow. The outcome of the power struggle could not be predicted, but it would be helpful if beforehand we could establish contact with a probable winner and in the process woo him over to our side. On August 31, 1984, Robert McFarlane, the president's national security adviser, formally requested "an interagency analysis of American relations with Iran after Khomeini" (NSSD 5-84). When it was completed in October, its findings were negative. There was little the United States could do, it concluded, with the existing constellation of Iranian groups in power.[17] Robert McFarlane and William J. Casey, the director of the CIA, disagreed[18] as did Gen. George B. Crist, USMC, Commander-in-Chief, U.S. Central Command. The negative report notwithstanding, they went ahead with their plans.

The problem was just how to make contact. It was a big problem. We had no diplomatic relations; indeed the State Department had designated Iran as a sponsor of international terrorism. In turn, any Iranian who would be found to deal with the Great Satan would incur the deadly wrath of the Ayatollah. His only approved approach to America was terrorism.[19] Thus, we entered the murky world of covert operations.

There are always people who offer themselves for a price as go-betweens. Most of them are frauds, individuals falsely advertising inside knowledge and special contacts for psychological or economic motives. But occasionally there are a few genuine articles. How can we tell which is which? Unlike among official representatives, there can be no formal designations. There are only innuendos, rumors, and vague "I know someone who knows someone." Hence the first task for each side is to test the *bona fides* of their contact. Is this person just a big-mouth with an illusion of self-importance? Is he or she an enemy *agent provocateur* seeking to entrap us? Or possibly can he be useful?

McFarlane was encouraged by his knowledge that the Israelis already had contacts in Iran and wanted to expand these further. Needless to say, the Israelis had their own rationale. They were concerned about Iraq and its president's military ambitions. They thought that Iran could well be a useful balancer. Moreover, they were worried about the fate of 30,000 Jews living in Iran under a militant, fundamentalist Muslim regime.[20] To advance their objectives the Israelis were quite willing to transfer arms to Iran but

---

[17] Ibid., p. 362.

[18] United States Court of Appeals for the District of Columbia Circuit, *Final Report of the Independent Counsel for Iran/Contra Matters*, Washington, DC, August 4, 1993, vol. I, p. 88.

[19] In 1985 six Americans were being held hostage by pro-Iranian Shi'ite Muslims in Lebanon. A TWA jet was hijacked and one of its passengers, U.S. Navy diver Robert Stetham, was murdered.

[20] Oliver North, *Under Fire* (New York: HarperCollins, 1991), p. 25.

did not want to lose by it. They needed U.S. consent for such a transaction and wanted an assurance that the Americans would replace the weapons transferred.

In the spring of 1985 the National Security Council took the initiative. Michael Ledeen, an "NSC consultant," indicated that an Iranian, Manucher Ghorbanifar, might be helpful. Robert McFarlane suggested that Ledeen travel to Israel and explore with his Israeli friends the possibility of a useful Iranian contact. It was, however, understood that neither of them "would keep anything in writing regarding this initiative." Indeed two months later when Secretary of State Schultz confronted McFarlane about the Ledeen visit to Israel, the national security adviser assured him that "Ledeen was there on his own, not on NSC assignment."[21]

In Israel, Ledeen met with his various contacts and even had a session with Prime Minister Shimon Peres. On his return he reported that indeed covert contact could be established with Iranian officials, who were very much interested in getting American spare parts for their military equipment. In fact, Israeli arms dealer Yakov Nimrodi and Iranian entrepreneur Ghorbanifar were already in contact. The Iranian offered as proof of his *bona fide* that he could cause the release of an American hostage held in Lebanon but requested as a sign of Nimrodi's *bona fide* the delivery of 100 U.S.-made TOW antitank missiles. Ledeen later testified before a grand jury that McFarlane gave his okay for the one exchange. McFarlane insisted that he did not remember the conversation.

On June 17, 1985, McFarlane circulated a draft National Security Decision Directive (NSDD). It recommended a policy that would "encourage Western allies and friends to help Iran meet its import requirements so as to reduce the attractiveness of Soviet assistance and trade offers, while demonstrating the value of correct relations with the West. This includes provision of selected military equipment as determined on a case-by-case basis."[22] Two weeks later (July 3, 1985) during his visit to Washington David Kimche, the director-general of the Israeli foreign ministry, met with McFarlane. "In the conversation, there was no request for arms, in any respect, not linkage between arms and the release of the hostages although Mr. Kimche did advert [*sic*] to the possibility that arms might be raised in the future." Soon the pace accelerated. On July 7 Kimche, Nimrodi, Adolf Schwimmer (an adviser to Prime Minister Peres), Ghorbanifar, and "international financier" Adnan Khashoggi met in

---

[21] Ibid.

[22] Weinberger, *Fighting for Peace*, p. 363.

Geneva, Switzerland. The next day the same group met in Hamburg, Germany, with Ghorbanifar's Iranian contact. On July 11, 1985, at Kimche's direction Schwimmer called on Ledeen in Washington. Each was circumspect, but by implication the Iranian contacts would prove their *bona fides* through the release of an American hostage, while the Americans could do the same by making available 100 TOW missiles.[23] Indeed Israel was quite willing to transfer them from its arsenal provided the Americans would not object and would replace them. As it turned out, just one American hostage, Reverend Benjamin Weir, was released and the Israelis transferred an additional 408 TOW missiles.[24] What started out as a strategic effort to improve U.S.-Iranian relations after Khomeini—an acceptable goal—was becoming through the murky world of covert operation perilously close to an arms-for-hostages deal. After four years of public disavowal of negotiating with terrorists and paying ransom to kidnappers that was a big NO-NO.

On July 14 McFarlane informed Schultz of the Israeli proposal to ship 100 TOW missiles to Iran. The secretary of state thoroughly disapproved. Two days later the secretary of defense formally opposed the draft NSDD of June 17th. "Under no circumstances should we now ease our restrictions on arms sales to Iran. [Such a] policy reversal would be seen as inexplicably inconsistent by those nations whom we have urged to refrain from such sales and would likely lead to increased arms sales by them and a possible alteration of the strategic balance in favor of Iran while Khomeini is still the controlling influence. *It would adversely affect our newly emerging relationship with Iraq.*"[25]

Meanwhile McFarlane was developing doubts about his Iranian go-between. Ghorbanifar, he later testified, "seemed to have a rather agile and creative mind for intrigue and in retrospect, a rather accurate view of the politics within Iran, [but] he was a person of intrigue and conspiracy and not a diplomat. Kind of a north end of a south bound horse. And I did not think we should do business with the man."[26]

But we did. The secretary of state and the secretary of defense were generally excluded from such deliberations. They, in turn, while suspecting much, chose to ask little or nothing. American weapons began moving to

---

[23] Ibid.

[24] Robert C. McFarlane, *Special Trust* (New York: Cadell E. Davies, 1994), pp. 38–40.

[25] Weinberger, *Fighting for Peace*, pp. 363–64. [Italics added.]

[26] *Independent Counsel's Report*, pp. 93–94.

Iran first through Israel and by 1986 directly from the United States. Soon things got completely out of hand. McFarlane resigned, and his successor turned the initiative over to Lt. Col. Oliver North of *Achille Lauro* fame, who had recently completed successfully several difficult assignments close to the heart of the president.

The Israelis kept up the pressure for further arms shipments. We were getting in deeper and deeper. Through the murky channels of covert operations a high-level meeting was set up for May 25, 1986, in Tehran. The American delegation would be headed by McFarlane and included not only Lieutenant Colonel North, but also Amiram Nir, the Israeli prime minister's special adviser on terrorism. Each, of course, had false passports[27] and flew on an Israeli Air Force plane repainted with the markings of the Irish Airlines: Aer Lingus. They expected to meet high-level Iranian officials, including the prime minister and the speaker of their parliament. They were ready to negotiate for big things: massive U.S. military supplies and the release of all American hostages. They carried on their plane some arms and a chocolate cake purchased in Tel Aviv for "the aging and widowed mother" of Ghorbanifar. Incredibly their plane landed at the main commercial airport in Tehran.

If negotiations were to move along successfully, two plane loads of arms waiting in Israel would be delivered to Iran. But negotiations did not proceed successfully. They were a farce. McFarlane never met a high-level Iranian official. The Iranians kept demanding the other two plane loads of arms. They were highly deceptive and vague in the extreme about the release of hostages. In the end, just about the only thing that could be said for the Tehran caper was that all our officials returned safely.[28]

Shipments of arms to Iran continued. Still no American captives were released. If trading arms for hostages was very bad policy, and so it was seen by the secretaries of state and defense, by Congress, and by most American people, the story now turned into a sordid scandal and a crime. Lieutenant Colonel North, always sensitive to President Reagan's desires, now thought he had a solution for aiding the anticommunist forces in Nicaragua. Congress through the Boland amendment prohibited such support by any U.S. government agency it could think of. It did not think of the National Security Council. Oliver North with his "can do" attitude saw a solution: a "neat idea" to let the Ayatollah pay the freedom fighters in Nicaragua. Through secret arrangements by the National Security

---

[27] McFarlane's bore the name Sean Devlin; North's was John Clancy.

[28] McFarlane, *Special Trust*, pp. 53–66 and North, *Under Fire*, pp. 36–63.

Council we would sell arms to Iran at inflated prices and then divert the profits to the Contras. The problem was that constitutionally appropriations—the spending of U.S. public funds—are the prerogative of Congress, not Oliver North personally, not even as an official of the National Security Council.

The secret, of course, did not remain a secret long. Within a year (November 8, 1986) information about the whole operation began to leak dooming the Reagan administration to having to defend itself against investigations: internal investigations (Attorney General Meese), congressional investigation, and finally the investigation of the independent counsel, Judge Lawrence E. Walsh. It also doomed any opening in U.S. relations to Iran for some time to come.

Thus, the strategic problem remained the same but became much more pressing. Devoted to the concept that U.S. security and international stability rested on a friendly regional power balancing other unfriendly ones, we desperately needed a new candidate for the vast region between Israel and Thailand. We had to find one. All we could think of was Iraq.

3

Anatomy of a Decision: The Persian Gulf Crisis

Just before 8:30 P.M. Washington time on August 1, 1990, Robert Kimmitt, the undersecretary of state for political affairs, was informed by the State Department's operation center that the U.S. ambassador to Kuwait reported gunfire in the emirate's capital. Kimmitt's conclusion: the Iraqi invasion of Kuwait had begun.

THE BACKGROUND

Just how it came to this, as to so many others in the Middle East, is a long, complicated, and wildly controversial story. Indeed it is difficult to say when it started. Did it start after World War I in March 1921 when the Kingdom of Iraq was carved out of the former Ottoman Empire mostly by British will and power? But Kuwait, which was part of the same Ottoman province, was separated from it. Or did it start in July of 1958 when a coup by Brigadir Abdal-Karim Quasim overthrew the Iraqi monarchy; executed the king, his closest relatives, and his prime minister; and embarked on an anti-British, anti-Western, then anti-American campaign? Did it begin when in 1961 Brigadir Quasim declared his determination to "liberate" Kuwait and backed down only when Britain sent warships to the area? Did it start when Karim Quasim himself was overthrown and executed in February 1963 and a new dictator, Saddam Hussein, began his ascent and then in 1979 grabbed total power for himself? Or did it start with the Iran-Contra scandal and its subsequent single-minded U.S. determination to enlist Iraq's friendship and entice its support?

If opening relations to Iran presented a complex and a difficult task, wooing Iraq was something of a psychedelic experience. It was only in

1984 that we resumed diplomatic relations, and even then the American Embassy was a modest operation in a rather unimposing building. Few Americans knew and fewer still cared about Iraq. Most Iraqis were unfriendly to Americans and outright hostile to American foreign policy. The biggest problem was Saddam Hussein. The Iraqi president (dictator) had little international experience, practically none with the West. Nevertheless he held strong views. He did not like the British, and toward the United States he had nothing but grievances. Regularly he recited his litany about America's provocative presence in the Persian Gulf, its conspiracies to suppress the Arab nations and to overthrow his own government, and its single-minded support of Israel. He held grandiose ideas about his own international destiny. Since 1973 Iraqi oil revenues had skyrocketed—one estimate was to $100 million a day. Much of it he invested in his armed forces. He increased the size of his army, trained it thoroughly, and equipped it with modern weapons. He built armored divisions with formidable concentrations of advanced Soviet T-72s. More than that he sought to build a nuclear arsenal and developed chemical weapons. In short, he wanted to build Iraq into an Arab superpower.

Saddam Hussein did have some setbacks: the Iraqi attack on Iran (September 21, 1980) was checked by the latter, and the following year Israeli jets in a surprise attack destroyed his nuclear weapons facility in Osirak. Still by 1987 the Iran war was turning in his favor; he successfully developed chemical weapons and was busily rebuilding his nuclear weapons program. To be free to move toward his international goals he proceeded with ruthless efficiency to eliminate all domestic opposition. Persons, relatives and close associates included, anyone who would challenge him, even those who might be suspected of challenging him, were executed without trial or ceremony. The Kurdish minority, which resisted his and Iraq's control, was gassed in September 1988.

All these things, of course, did not escape the attention of the U.S. government. But it was working hard on the concept that stability in the region depended on a balance of power in the area, and Iraq seemed to be the only suitable balancer of a hostile and vituperative Iran. Indeed senior American decision-makers were very much worried about the "nightmare . . . that the Ayatollah Khomeini would lead Iranians across the desert to Lebanon. The export of revolution appeared very possible."[1] Whether

---

[1] United States House of Representatives, Subcommittee on Europe and the Middle East of the Committee on Foreign Affairs, *Hearing on United States–Iraqi*
(continued...)

through conquest or cooperation such a future prospect threatened the oil supply of the industrial world, not to mention the security of Israel. Thus, throughout much of the 1980s the United States felt compelled to tilt in favor of Iraq. It provided some satellite intelligence about Irani troop dispositions and movements. The State Department listed Syria as a country that exported terrorism and thus was subjected to sanctions, but Iraq was kept off the list. When on May 17, 1987, the USS *Stark* was attacked by an Iraqi Air Force plane killing thirty-seven U.S. sailors, in spite of evidence to the contrary the United States accepted the Iraqi explanation of an "error" and the promise of $27 million compensation to the sailors' families (which then took three years to collect). When the Iraqi government refused to let U.S. officials interrogate the errant pilot, we did not press the issue. When we learned that indeed the pilot had been promoted and given charge of the air force college,[2] we kept quiet about it. When the following year the Kurdish minority was gassed, the United States protested and protested. The Iraqi government first denied the atrocity, then on television it explained that it was a preemptive strike against an uprising, and finally emboldened, the "Defense Minister, in an effort to diffuse western criticisms, made the following statement, this in an effort to diffuse criticism. He said for every insect, there is insecticide."[3] Undeterred, in the summer of 1989 the U.S. embassy in Baghdad sent a message to Washington arguing that Iraq "had demonstrated 'a modicum of political maturity,'" and urged conducting military exchanges."Supporting the proposal, Gen. H. Norman Schwarzkopf's Central Command . . . proposed ten possible initiatives, including training the Iraqi military in disabling mines and aerial reconnaissance and outfitting Saddam Hussein's personal aircraft with flares and others [*sic*] devices to protect it against missile attacks by coup plotters or insurgents."[4] As late as May 21, 1989, a CENTCOM study, *Security Environment 2000*, delivered this judgment: "Iraq is not expected to use

---

[1](...continued)
Relations, March 21, 1991 (Washington, DC: Government Printing Office, 1991), p. 20. Hereafter referred to as HR SCEME.

[2] Hussein Sumaida, *Circle of Fear, My Life as an Israeli and Iraqi Spy* (Washington, DC: Brassey's, 1994), p. 182.

[3] Testimony by April C. Glaspie, U.S. Ambassador to Iraq, before the House Subcommittee on Europe and the Middle East. HR SCEME, p. 46.

[4] Michael R. Gordon and Bernard E. Trainor, *The Generals' War, the Inside Story of the Conflict in the Gulf* (Boston: Little, Brown & Co., 1995), p. 12.

military force to attack Kuwait or Saudi Arabia to seize disputed territory or resolve a dispute over oil policy."[5]

The Iran-Contra scandal, which killed any opening to Iran for some time to come, further focused American government attention on our need for Iraq. On October 2, 1989, National Security Directive (NSD) 26 ordered the exploration of the possibility of moderating Iraq's position in the Middle East and steering it toward a more friendly position toward the United States. Four days later the secretary of state met with Tariq Aziz, the Iraqi foreign minister.[6] For openers James Baker stated that "the United States valued the relationship with Iraq and wanted to see it strengthened and broadened. There was every reason to believe the potential existed to move the relationship in a positive direction." The foreign minister responded in kind but then launched into a long litany of grievances. It was a pattern regularly repeated by Iraqi leaders. The secretary of state tried to remain positive, which in turn was a pattern the Americans repeated. Three weeks later Baker urged the secretary of agriculture to grant $1 billion in credits to Iraq. All along, NSD-26 was implemented with caution but pressed single-mindedly. The new U.S. Ambassador April C. Glaspie, arriving in Baghdad, set two goals. First, "that we should constantly think of ways in which we expose to him [Saddam Hussein] and to other senior decision-makers all those things about us, our values, our policies, and the intricacies of our constitutional structures, relationship between the Congress and the media and government and the Supreme Court, all of which are totally misunderstood by Iraqi decision-makers . . . [and second that we] see if we could find any way to get in to see him."[7]

Simply put, if he could only get to know us, he would learn to love us. Some members of Congress, for example, subcommittee chairman Lee Hamilton (D, Indiana), Tom Lantos (D, California), and Steven Solarz (D, New York), were aghast at such naïveté, but Glaspie persisted. Since 1981 when Saddam Hussein met a British journalist as part of a BBC program, he had had no contact with the Western media. When in 1990 Diane Sawyer sought an interview with him, the American embassy pulled out all stops. In the end it was successful; the interview was granted. By the time the Iraqi Ministry of Information got through with it, the interview was something else. Again in late February 1990 the State Department felt it

---

[5] Ibid., p. 14.

[6] James A. Baker III, *The Politics of Diplomacy, Revolution, War and Peace* (New York: G. P. Putnam's Sons, 1995), pp. 265–66.

[7] Ibid., p. 57.

necessary to be soft on Iraq following a Voice of America broadcast beamed on Eastern Europe. The editorial had "deplored the existence of secret police and regimes which depend on brutality to remain in power." It went on to warn that "as Eastern Europeans demonstrated in 1989, the tide of history is against such rulers," and then closed with the line: "the 1990s should belong not to the dictators and secret police but to the people." On instructions from the State Department the American ambassador felt it necessary to explain to the Iraqi Foreign Ministry that the editorial "could have given rise to misinterpretation."[8] All along, Glaspie resisted any initiative in Congress to impose sanctions on Iraq because of its international conduct and/or its domestic atrocities.

Saddam Hussein remained confident to go his own way. In February Ambassador Glaspie saw him "viciously attacking the United States, and providing a new logic by which the Iraqi government would announce and analyze foreign policy." The basic principle, he said, was "that the Soviet Union had withdrawn from the Middle East, leaving the United States as the sole superpower . . . in the area, and this was very dangerous for the area."[9] America protested. On April 1, 1990, Saddam Hussein "boasting that he had acquired advanced chemical weapons threatened . . . to annihilate half of Israel if it moved against his country."[10] America protested again. The Iraqi president in a gambit then asked King Fahd of Saudi Arabia to send a special envoy to Baghdad. When Saudi Ambassador to Washington Sultan Bandar appeared, Saddam complained that he had been misquoted. He had not threatened aggression against anyone, only a fearsome retaliation if Iraq became a victim of aggression. Bandar carried the assurance to President Bush. Bush was skeptical.[11]

Developments were building toward a crescendo. On July 16 Tariq Aziz, the Iraqi foreign minister, sent a provocative letter to the Arab League. "He charged that Kuwait's refusal to resolve the border disputes with Iraq, its rejection of Iraqi demands that its multibillion dollar debts be canceled, and its insistence on pumping oil in excess of OPEC quotas were tantamount to military aggression."[12] The next day Saddam Hussein made another speech. It named no targets, but his grievance was clear. Some

---

[8] Ibid., pp. 38–39, 60.

[9] Ibid., p. 2.

[10] *The New York Times*, April 3, 1990, p. A1.

[11] U.S. News & World Report, *Triumph without Victory* (New York: Random House, 1992), p. 17.

[12] Gordon and Trainor, *The Generals' War*, p. 14.

Arab states did not curb their excess oil production and thus weakened oil prices. "They are inspired by America to undermine Arab interests and security." And the threat was vehement: "O God almighty, be witness that we have warned them. . . . If words fail to protect Iraqis, something effective must be done to return things to their natural cause and to return things to their owners."[13]

Several factors made the move especially ominous. First, there was the evidence that Iran seemed to have joined Iraq. "Concerning oil policies, our views conform with those of Iraq," its oil minister declared. Second, Saudi Arabia, the "economic godfather" of the smaller Persian Gulf states, appeared to be sympathetic to Iraq's complaint. "A senior Arab oil official who participated in the talks," reported *The New York Times*, "said any further infraction of the production quota by Kuwait would 'not be tolerated' by Saudi Arabia. That, said the Arab official, who asked not to be identified, suggested that Saudi protection would not be extended to Kuwait in the face of Iraqi anger at the breaking of quotas."[14] Third, Defense Intelligence was reporting the movement of Iraqi Republican Guard divisions with their heavy, modern armor toward the Kuwait border.[15] On July 23 the British military attaché counted some 3,000 vehicles moving rapidly. Washington's reaction was almost instantaneous. The Iraqi ambassador was called to the State Department where in writing he was informed that if Iraq "thought that we have changed our policy, they were wrong. We would continue to defend the right of navigation in the Gulf through the Straits of Hormuz and above all . . . . we continued to be strongly committed to the individual and collective self defense of our friends in the Gulf."[16] At the request of the United Arab Emirates, joint military exercises were started in the Gulf.

During a hastily arranged visit to Baghdad in a private meeting, Egyptian President Mubarak asked Saddam Hussein a clear, direct, definitive question: "Do you have any intention for a combat action against Kuwait?" Saddam Hussein told him not to worry. The Iraqi movements were designed to throw a scare into the Sabahs [the Kuwaiti ruling family]. They were terrified, frightened, and that was enough. On his return Mubarak stopped off in Kuwait City where the royal family met him at the

---

[13] *The New York Times*, July 18, 1990, p. D1.

[14] Ibid., p. D4.

[15] Colin L. Powell, *My American Journey* (New York: Random House, 1995), p. 460.

[16] HR SCEME, p. 3.

airport. He advised them not to worry. When asked what the Iraqi leader wanted, Mubarak laughed. "It seems he needs some money."[17] As soon as he got back to Cairo, Mubarak called President Bush to give him the good news.

The next day (July 25) Ambassador Glaspie suddenly found her fervent wish fulfilled. She was called to see the Iraqi president and had an extended meeting with him. It was an uncomfortable session. She had to sit around for a half hour while at one point Saddam Hussein went off to take a phone call from President Mubarak. And she had to sit idly by while for an hour and a half the president "railed" at her. But Glaspie was eager to please. "I admire your extraordinary effort to rebuild your country," she beamed. "I know you need funds. We understand that. We are of the opinion that you should have the opportunity to rebuild your country, but what we hold no opinion about are the inter-Arab disputes, such as your border disagreement with Kuwait. I was in the American Embassy in Kuwait during the late 1960s. The instruction we had at the time was that we should not have anything to do with this issue, and this issue was not connected with US concerns."[18] At another point Ambassador Glaspie sought to explain an ABC news profile of the president and his interview with Diane Sawyer. "That program was cheap and unjust," she said. "And this is the picture of what happens in the American media—even to American politicians themselves. These are methods the Western media employs. I am pleased that you add your voice to the diplomats who stand up to the media. Because your appearance in the media even for five minutes, would help us to make the American people understand Iraq. This would increase mutual understanding. If the American President had control of the media, his job would be much easier."[19] Back and forth. Saddam Hussein railing and the American ambassador placating. Toward the end of the interview the Iraqi president informed her that in response to a request of President Mubarak, he had agreed to negotiate with the Kuwaitis. Glaspie was ecstatic. "This is good news . . . Congratulations." Returning to the embassy she reported to the State Department and conveyed her optimism:

---

[17] Ibid., pp. 22–23.

[18] Quoted by Congressman Harry Johnston (D, Florida) from the Iraqi transcript, during the testimony of the ambassador and not contradicted by her. Ibid., p. 19.

[19] Quoted in Bob Woodward, *The Commanders* (New York: Simon & Schuster, 1991), p. 211–12.

Speaking of his conviction that our Governments do not sufficiently understand each other, especially since "some circles" of USG continue to work to undermine his Government and his policies, Saddam stressed that he put his hope in President Bush and Secretary Baker, who are fine and honorable men, as is NEA Assistant Secretary Kelly. He asked me to return to the U.S. to explain Iraq's concerns to the President, who he supposed might have questions. Comment: Saddam, who in the memory of the current diplomatic corps has never summoned an ambassador, is worried. He does not want to further antagonize us. With the UAE maneuvers, we have fully caught his attention, and that is good. I believe we would now be well advised to ease off on public criticism of Iraq until we see how the negotiations develop.[20]

In Washington a major debate about the right response raged among the top advisers of the president. The State Department preferred a very mild answer. The Defense Department objected. It wanted a stern warning, but meanwhile the cable was sent on July 28 to Baghdad. On that day the Iraqi foreign minister assured the American ambassador that there would be no invasion of Kuwait, that she could safely leave Baghdad for Washington. Then the following day Saddam Hussein's son-in-law, the Minister of Military Industrialization, gave her the same assurance.[21] About the same time Sultan Bandar, the Saudi Ambassador, reported to General Powell that King Fahd was being assured by everyone in Iraq and the Middle East that Saddam was not going to invade Kuwait.

The Chairman of the Joint Chiefs did not share in the optimism. He had seen Defense Intelligence reports that continued Iraqi military buildup along the Kuwait border reached 100,000 of its best troops, far beyond any force necessary for a bluff or political intimidation. Even the command tanks had taken a forward position. The attack was coming soon, in a day, perhaps two. All the same in the intelligence community there was disagreement. "On July 30, many of the [CIA's] top experts met to discuss the tense situation in the Gulf and a pending report by the National Intelligence Council . . . on Iraq's intentions. It was clear that [Defense Intelligence Agency] assessment was a minority view. When [they] argued that Iraq was preparing a major attack, their views were shunted aside."[22] The next day General Schwarzkopf briefed the top military leadership at the supersecure Tank of the Pentagon. Secretary Cheney wanted to know

---

[20] "Saddam's Message of Friendship to President Bush," cable from Baghdad 04237, July 25, 1990. Quoted in Gordon and Trainor, *The Generals' War*, p. 22.

[21] HR SCEME, p. 4.

[22] Gordon and Trainor, *The Generals' War*, pp. 24–25.

what the Iraqis had in mind. "'I think that they are going to attack,' Norm said. He thought it would be a limited attack to seize the Kuwaiti part of the Rumaila oil field and Bubiyan Island. He did not think that Saddam intended to swallow all of Kuwait and topple the ruling family."[23]

Clearly the signals from Washington were ambiguous. Speaking for the State Department, Richard Boucher refused to say whether the United States would provide military help in case of attack. On July 27 Ms. Tutweiler [the principal State Department spokesperson] said, "We do not have any defense treaties with Kuwait and there are no special defense or security commitments."[24] The OPEC meeting was held in Geneva with harsh words from Iraq against Kuwait. Then followed the meeting in Jiddah where Iraq further detailed its demands. Kuwait must follow Iraqi lead in OPEC. It must forgive some $32 billion in loans Kuwait extended to Iraq in support of the latter's war with Iran. It must further finance a program to help rebuild Iraq. And it must make territorial concessions to solidify Iraqi oil production.[25] The Kuwaitis resisted the demands; the conference was adjourned presumably for a few days. When Kuwait was informed by the United States of its imminent peril, it showed no anxiety. It did not need outside help. On the evening of August 1 the Iraqi deputy prime minister responsible for Kuwaiti relations announced that the Jiddah talks were about to resume in Baghdad.

The mixed signals raises the question: were they mistakes, products of bureaucratic bungling, or policy confusion, or were they part of intentional sophisticated strategy? Michael Gordon and General Trainor, called it a "war by miscalculation." Others offered a different slant. "It must be said that the U.S. never explicitly warned Saddam against the use of force in his dispute with Kuwait," wrote General Khaled bin Sultan, the Saudi Joint Forces Commander of Desert Storm. "Curiously enough, it was an error which the U.S. repeated a number of times and which led some people to speculate that it had set a trap for Saddam."[26]

In any case, Iraq was engaged in strategic deception. A surprise attack would conquer Kuwait; a *fait accompli* would intimidate his Arab

---

[23] Powell, *My American Journey*, p. 461.

[24] Ibid., p. 7.

[25] Iraq claimed that by slanted drilling into its Rumaila oil field Kuwait was robbing it of its material resources.

[26] HRH General Khalid bin Sultan, *Desert Warrior, a Personal View of the Gulf War by the Joint Forces Commander* (New York: HarperCollins, 1995), p. 162.

neighbors, the small states along the Persian Gulf, even Saudi Arabia. They would be fearful lest they arouse Saddam Hussein's ire. They would hem and haw but do nothing. And a *fait accompli* would discourage U.S. response. The Americans would bluster, threaten dire consequences, but in the end they too would do nothing, or more accurately, all they would do is to explain why they would not do anything. Soon they would find new reasons for appeasing Saddam.

Within twelve hours of his aggression it seemed to Saddam that he had indeed succeeded. He was ready to celebrate. Just for good measure he announced to the world that (1) negotiations with Kuwait would indeed be resumed in Saudi Arabia, (2) Iraqi forces had entered as liberators at the request of democratic forces in Kuwait, and (3) within a few days all Iraqi forces would be withdrawn. Actually he had miscalculated. He did not know about Americans; indeed he had never really tried to learn much about them. And as far as global strategy was concerned, he was so far below the class of George Bush that it was pathetic.

Just what President Bush thought about Saddam Hussein's strategic deception so successful with the Arab leaders was not known. He did not share the optimism flowing from the Middle East; he saw the evidence of an impending Iraqi invasion. He did not for a moment believe that the Arabs could handle the matter satisfactorily. When General Scowcroft rushed over to the residence to inform him that the invasion had started, Bush took the news calmly. He decided to act promptly. He ordered a diplomatic initiative in the United Nations to condemn the aggression, the seizure of all Iraqi and Kuwaiti assets in the United States, and an NSC meeting for the next morning. Beyond this he did not show his hand.

THE DECISION

A full National Security Council meeting convened 8:00 A.M. next morning. Just before it started some reporters were ushered in by the press secretary. An exchange was highly significant. "We are not discussing intervention," the president said. Question: "You are not contemplating any intervention or sending troops?" Answer: "I am not contemplating such action."[27] It was an unequivocal statement. I do not think it was accurate. I think already at this early stage the president's approach was taking shape: vigorous personal diplomacy, military action, and his own strategic deception. Visibly, however, it was a step-by-step evolution.

---

[27] Woodward, *The Commanders*, p. 225.

At this meeting the president expressed his pleasure with the performance of the State Department. Within hours of the aggression the U.N. Security Council with a 14:0 vote (Yemen did not participate) condemned it. He was also pleased with the Treasury, which in so short a time had ferreted out all Iraqi and Kuwaiti funds within its reach and frozen them. All in all, however, "the meeting seemed routine . . . there wasn't an overpowering atmosphere of crisis." That was the vice president's impression,[28] and others shared his view. The CIA reported that Kuwait was overrun by more than 100,000 troops, much more than would have been necessary, troops that were currently being resupplied. Gen. Colin Powell, Chairman of the Joint Chiefs of Staff, spoke little. With some admiration in his voice he reported that the Iraqi invasion was a very professional one. He also listed U.S. forces ready for immediate response. A squadron of F-15 was on alert, and some KC-10s, large tanker planes, had been moved to Saudi Arabia. Then Powell introduced Gen. Norman Schwarzkopf. The Commander in Chief, U.S. Central Command—the cop on the beat—offered two options and then quickly knocked each of them down. One possibility, he said, was to use retaliatory air strikes. But they would be no more than pinpricks and could possibly provoke Saddam to attack Saudi Arabia. Another possibility was contingency plan 1002-90 (or 90-1002). It was designed to defend Saudi Arabia and would require a massive U.S. military buildup. It would also require time, months to deploy some 200,000 U.S. military personnel. And it would take a Saudi invitation, which he thought was unlikely. All along, there was much discussion about international economic sanctions and oil, its importance, and the means to punish Iraq. Bombing pipelines, for example. White House Chief of Staff John Sununu pressed for some method to cut off the flow of Iraqi (now also Kuwaiti) oil. Noticeably in all the oil discussion one person present did not participate, the one who knew most about it, George Bush. Sure enough, there was also some finger-pointing. Richard Darman, Director of OMB, "thought the situation was pathetic. Given the vital U.S. interests in the region and Saddam's past aggressions, it was just short of dereliction that U.S. intelligence hadn't had a clue this was going to happen and that the military didn't have an adequate and updated contingency plan."[29] The discussion meandered along, and then the president had to leave for a speaking engagement in Aspen, Colorado.

---

[28] Dan Quayle, *Standing Firm, a Vice-Presidential Memoir* (New York: HarperCollins, 1994), p. 205.

[29] Woodward, *The Commanders*, p. 229.

His advisers were left without guidance. General Powell was impressed about the wide range and the detail of the president's questions. He could not guess his intentions. Secretary of Defense Cheney thought that the president was very much interested in the military options. Gen. Brent Scowcroft, the national security adviser, suspected that Bush wanted a firm response. C. Boyden Grey, counselor to the president, who had known the president for many years, saw him at his firmest. Whatever others among the advisers, the American public, or foreign officials might think, Bush was determined to take very strong steps, and people were foolish to miss the signs.

On his flight to Aspen the president was accompanied by General Scowcroft, and presumably they had some discussions about Iraq. Just what these concerned no one knows until George Bush will reveal them in his forthcoming book. But Scowcroft did say this: "The President was way out in front of most of his advisers."[30] At Aspen the president met with British Prime Minister Margaret Thatcher. It was like two soulmates finding each other, thought the national security adviser. She told him in the clearest and most straightforward terms: First, aggressors must never be appeased. We learned that to our cost in the 1930s. Second, if Saddam Hussein were to cross the border into Saudi Arabia, he could go right down the Gulf in a matter of days. He would then control 65 percent of the world's oil reserves and could blackmail us all. Therefore, not only did we have to move firmly to stop the aggression, we had to do so right away.[31] The president then recounted the advice he had received from King Hussein of Jordan and President Mubarak of Egypt. They urged that the United States keep calm and let the Arabs work it out among themselves. Margaret Thatcher was profoundly skeptical about that approach and so was George Bush. By the afternoon of August 2 the president's formula for response to media questions about U.S. intervention had changed markedly to "no options have been ruled out."[32] Public emphasis, however, was on sanctions.

Next morning back in Washington, another National Security Council meeting was held. There was general agreement that we would have to defend Saudi Arabia. But then what? Schwarzkopf asked, "Are we prepared, should we be prepared to go forward and fight for Kuwait?" His

---

[30] WGBH Educational Foundation, *Videotape cited.*

[31] Margaret Thatcher, *The Downing Street Years* (New York: HarperCollins, 1993), p. 817.

[32] *The New York Times*, August 3, 1990, pp. A1, 6.

commander in chief did not answer.[33] General Scowcroft led the discussion: "We have got to examine what the long term interests are for this country and the Middle East if the invasion and taking of Kuwait become an accomplished fact. We have to begin our deliberations with the fact that this is unacceptable."[34] The discussion covered some of the previous points, e.g., oil and the need for economic sanctions, but a new idea emerged: Saddam Hussein was determined to become an Arab superpower, and we just could not permit that. Quite probably sanctions would not be enough. We shall have to use force to stop it. Using force in the area, however, depended on having bases in Saudi Arabia. But the Saudis showed no eagerness to grant them. Indeed they had not responded even to our offer of sending a squadron of F-15s. Somehow we would have to persuade King Fahd that he needed us and that we would not abuse his hospitality.

Meanwhile Prince Bandar, the Saudi ambassador in Washington, was very much concerned. He was concerned about the Iraqi aggression in the face of Saddam Hussein's solemn promises to his Arab brothers, and he was concerned about the Americans. Can they be depended on? Will they act?

That same Friday afternoon he was visiting General Scowcroft. They were engaged in some diplomatic maneuvering when President Bush walked in. He reminded the ambassador of all the Arab assurances that Saddam Hussein would not invade Kuwait. Obviously they had been victims of deception. Turning to matters at hand, he said he was disturbed because the Kuwaitis refused to ask for U.S. help until a few minutes before they were invaded. Will Saudi Arabia follow the pattern and hold out until it was too late?

Prince Bandar, in turn, recounted one of his favorite gripes. Just a decade earlier when the shah of Iran was forced out of power, President Carter urged the kingdom to accept a couple of squadrons of F-15s as a warning to the new revolutionary Iranian government. His Majesty reluctantly agreed. While the planes were still in the air, President Carter felt it necessary to announce that they were unarmed. Such empty gestures were dangerous to Saudi Arabia. They provided no help, only incensed possible aggressors.

In one of the dramatic moments of history President Bush spoke calmly and deliberately: "I give my word of honor. I will see this through

---

[33] WGBH Educational Foundation, *Videotape cited.*

[34] Woodward, *The Commanders*, p. 237.

with you."[35] The president of the United States had given his pledge, a president who was not a newcomer, some upstart politician, but a man of proven integrity, a member of the traditional American elite. His word was sacred. Ambassador Bandar was overawed. He was ready to move into action. That afternoon he stopped over at the Pentagon where he, on the orders of the president, was shown U.S. satellite photos about heavy concentration of Iraqi armor in positions that could be interpreted as preparatory to an invasion of Saudi Arabia. Impressed, the ambassador ordered his private plane and flew back to see his king.

Next day (Saturday, August 4) the National Security Council met at Camp David. This time the issue of military intervention was discussed; indeed that was pretty much all that was discussed. The military leaders were cautious. They were reluctant to use force, and they could not read the president's mind. General Schwarzkopf in his briefing emphasized the weakness of the Saudi armed forces and in contrast the size of the Iraqi army (the fourth largest in the world). Its modern equipment (5,743 tanks, including 1,072 advanced Soviet-made T-72s) was also cited. Added to this was the vast distance of American supply lines. We would need about three months of military buildup to assure the defense of Saudi Arabia, but "if we ever wanted to kick the Iraqis out of Kuwait, we'd have to go on the offense—and that would take a whole lot more troops and a whole lot more time." At least six more divisions and eight to ten months of preparations.[36] General Schwarzkopf also favored deterrence, i.e., a defensive position. "I don't recall anybody saying we were going to take back Kuwait," he testified later.[37]

After the briefing a vigorous discussion ensued. Two special concerns underlay most of the deliberations. First, the appropriate level of response. Colin Powell, Chairman of the Joint Chiefs of Staff, emphasized that any military intervention, including the defense of Saudi Arabia, could not be carried by the air force alone. To be useful it needed heavy involvement of the army. The danger in this was that by acting vigorously we would provoke Saddam Hussein to move not only into Saudi Arabia but also into the smaller Persian Gulf states before we could bring any effective resistance to the area. General Powell, whose detractors have called a

---

[35] Ibid., p. 241. cf: U.S. News & World Report, *Triumph without Victory*, p. 73.

[36] H. Norman Schwarzkopf, *It Doesn't Take a Hero* (New York: Bantam Books, 1992), p. 301.

[37] WGBH Educational Foundation, *Videotape cited.*

political general, may also have had the domestic environment in mind. Less than a year before, after the U.S. intervention in Panama, the popular approval rating of the president soared. Perhaps with this memory the chairman rather vigorously insisted that this would not be another Panama.[38] Third, there was a pervasive concern that the Saudis would not agree to a massive U.S. deployment on their soil. They still had not agreed even to accept a few squadrons of fighter planes, and the king seemed to have been resisting the suggestion of a formal visit by a high-level U.S. delegation to discuss American military involvement. Indeed when the president called King Fahd from Colorado, the latter was at best ambiguous.[39] Most members of the National Security Council were pessimistic about Arabs in general and doubted that King Fahd would act firmly. The Saudis might choose to compromise and as in the past try to buy themselves out of the predicament by paying blackmail. President Bush was much more optimistic; he did not believe the Saudis would pay blackmail.

In fact, Ambassador Bandar was already at work in the Saudi capital. He moved with skill, but he faced a difficult task. Quite apart from the traditional reluctance of the kingdom to permit foreign troops on its soil, especially Western troops that lacked familiarity with, if not respect for, Muslim ways, the imminent danger from Iraq was not altogether so obvious to them. The American satellite photos were not unambiguous. Moreover, when Saudi scouts on a special royal order entered Kuwait, they did not find any Iraqi forces approaching. As late as Sunday noon when General Scowcroft spoke to Ambassador Bandar on the telephone, King Fahd was still unwilling to accept a cabinet-level mission. In a few hours, however, permission was granted, and the American delegation, headed by the secretary of defense and including the Commander in Chief, Central Command, was in the air.[40]

The next day the delegation was received by King Fahd. General Schwarzkopf outlined the plan to defend Saudi Arabia. The troops the United States was ready to commit were massive. He wanted "to make sure the king understood that we were talking about flooding his airfields,

---

[38] U.S. News & World Report, *Triumph without Victory* (New York: Random House, 1992), p. 71.

[39] Ibid., p. 74.

[40] Sunday morning when Chairman Powell briefed General Schwarzkopf on the mission, the latter was informed that the United States was prepared to commit forces. "I was stunned," recorded the general. Schwarzkopf, *It Doesn't Take a Hero*, p. 302.

harbors and military bases with tens of thousands more Americans than Saudi Arabia has ever seen."[41] Secretary Cheney added a reassurance. "Here is the message that President Bush has instructed me to convey. We are prepared to deploy these forces to defend the kingdom of Saudi Arabia. If you ask us, we will come. We will seek no permanent bases. And when you ask us to go home, we will leave." After a remarkably short discussion between the king and his advisers, King Fahd turned to Cheney and said in English: "Okay." The American delegation left. They had what they came for. Within hours U.S. forces started moving to Saudi Arabia.

On Monday, August 6, Mrs. Thatcher was visiting the White House on her way home. She was impressed by the president. "He was firm, cool, showing the decisive qualities which the Commander-in-Chief of the greatest world power must possess." George Bush had made his decision; he was not going to go wobbly. "I always liked George Bush," she wrote. "Now my respect for him soared."[42] Just four days after deployment of forces had begun, the president declared at a press conference: "This aggression will not stand."[43] When General Powell heard it, he thought it was the first direct guidance. "I said: 'wow'."[44]

THE IMPLEMENTATION: DIPLOMATIC OFFENSIVE

There were three major elements in the president's decision. First, the protection of Saudi Arabia and the Gulf states. Second, the liberation of Kuwait. Last, but not least, *the destruction of Iraq's capacity to become an Arab superpower*. If we were successful, we could put an effective end to the unhappy Vietnam episode. It could then be relegated once and for all to a minor footnote of American history, roughly equivalent to the debacle at Little Big Horn a century earlier. We could not be successful, however, unless our huge military buildup in the Gulf was accompanied by two essential components: one, a massive diplomatic initiative, and two, *a daring game of strategic deception*.

First, a diplomatic offensive was necessary to legitimize the use of American arms. We needed international approval as a minimum requirement for mobilizing domestic opinion. And we needed international approval because we never felt comfortable with the use of force strictly

---

[41] Ibid., p. 305.

[42] Thatcher, *The Downing Street Years*, p. 820.

[43] *The New York Times*, August 6, 1990, p. 1.

[44] WGBH Educational Foundation, *Videotape cited.*

as a means to advance American interests. We wanted to do the right thing, and we wanted others to believe that we did. Accordingly, the diplomatic initiative had to have two simultaneous thrusts. One was an effort on the global scale, the other in the specific region, the Middle East. Regarding the first, the United States insisted that aggression was a universally condemned offense against international peace and order. Hence, the whole world community needed to be convinced that Iraq was the guilty party and had to be mobilized against it. In this, all sovereign states were important. All the same, the members of the United Nations Security Council were a little more so, and the five permanent members were rather more so.

We could expect that Britain, an old friend, would vote with us, and perhaps reluctantly France would too. But the Soviet Union had been in the habit of vetoing American initiatives. Lately though its position was more congenial. Its president, Mikhail Gorbachev, was very much interested in cooperation with the United States. In fact, he hoped for an international order based on a Soviet-American partnership. His Foreign Minister, Eduard Shevardnadze, was an enthusiastic advocate of the idea. To be sure, Iraq was a traditional Soviet ally, but that was a regional matter. Relations with the United States were global in scope, and global rationale should override regional considerations. Indeed through official meetings and private visits Shevardnadze had developed a genuine respect for James Baker III, the secretary of state.

As it happened, at the time of the Iraqi invasion Baker was in Irkutsk, a guest of Foreign Minister Shevardnadze. The visit started out in a very congenial atmosphere, and the discussions were proceeding well when the secretary of state received the message from Washington about the invasion. He passed it on to the foreign minister, who at first would not believe it. When his own sources confirmed it, he hurried back to Moscow for consultation. Baker proceeded as scheduled to Ulan Bator, Mongolia. There he was informed that Shevardnadze requested that on Baker's way home he stop off at Moscow. When an exhausted secretary of state got off at Moscow's Vnukovo airfield, his colleague was waiting for him. Before the assembled reporters, in firm tones Shevardnadze made a public announcement. Although the Soviet Union had enjoyed long and friendly relations with Iraq and some 7,830 of its citizens were still working there, Moscow was urging a worldwide halt of arms deliveries to Baghdad.[45] It was a very positive signal for all to see. We could feel confident of his

---

[45] U.S. News & World Report, *Triumph without Victory*, pp. 35, 55.

support in the United Nations Security Council. The Soviet Union was enlisted for the duration.[46]

Gorbachev himself saw the Iraqi foreign minister on September 5. It turned out to be a weird conversation. The president tried very hard to impress Tariq Aziz of Iraq's perilous position and urged rapid movement toward a political solution. He made no impression. The foreign minister "unleashed a tirade about the Iraqi leadership's 'confidence' that 'the present confrontation between Iraq and the United States will eventually bring Iraqi success.'" Exasperated Gorbachev concluded the conversation:

You may be receiving instructions direct from the Almighty, but I would still like to give you some advice. You should not reject the search for a political solution on a realistic and constructive basis. We get the feeling that you still don't see it that way. You should bear in mind, though, that in the future the situation is only going to deteriorate.[47]

On November 29 the Security Council was debating Resolution No. 678. It was a particularly difficult position for Shevardnadze. James Baker wanted explicit authority to use military force against Iraq; he had spent ten weeks traveling 100,000 miles to meet personally with all the world leaders to enlist this support. The Soviet president, however, was most reluctant to go along. Gorbachev did not want the Americans to use force, and he certainly did not want to add his troops to the coalition managed (commanded) by the Americans. What he wanted was a grandstand—a massive international conference on the Middle East linking Iraq's aggression with the Palestinian problems.[48] But when the chips were down the Soviets went along. They did get some time, all of December and half of January, to come up with a peaceful solution; and they got slightly ambiguous wording, "all necessary means" instead of use of force, but

---

[46] Security Council Resolution No. 600: Condemned Iraqi invasion of Kuwait; No. 661: imposed trade and financial sanctions; No. 662: declared Iraqi annexation of Kuwait null and void; No. 664 demanded Iraq free all detained foreign nationals; No. 665: gave U.S. and other naval powers the right to enforce an economic embargo; No. 667: condemned Iraqi aggressive acts against diplomatic missions in Kuwait; No. 670: expanded embargo to include all air cargo traffic; No. 674: held Iraq liable for war damages and economic losses.

[47] Mikhail Gorbachev, *Memoirs* (New York: Doubleday, 1993), p. 553.

[48] According to Baker, President Bush at the Helsinki Summit on September 9 thought he might have to give Gorbachev a joint statement, including a reference to such a conference. Baker, *The Politics of Diplomacy*, p. 293.

everyone understood what Resolution 678 sanctioned. In case they did not, after the vote the secretary of state made it explicit: the resolutions, he said, granted "unambiguous authority" to use force. He was not contradicted by his Soviet counterpart.

It came at a very high cost to Shevardnadze. Time was running out not only for Saddam Hussein; the opposition to the Soviet foreign minister was rising to a fierce crescendo. Early in November Gorbachev had already dispatched Yevgeny Primakov, the Foreign Ministry's senior Arabist, to Baghdad as his own special envoy. Whatever this move was designed to do, one of its principal results was the undermining of Shevardnadze's position. Conflict was raging in the Kremlin and becoming increasingly personal. At one point one senior adviser to Gorbachev shouted at the foreign minister: "There will be blood on your hands."[49] The latter had to endure all the rudeness, the recriminations, and the imprecations. But what hurt most: he saw very little support from Gorbachev. After the Security Council vote it only got worse. Soon he had enough. On December 20 he rose in the Congress of People's Deputies. He spoke of the vicious infighting, the devious manipulations at the center of power. He warned that the Soviet Union was sliding back into a dictatorship. Then to the surprise of all, he resigned and walked out.

The world and specifically the Americans were surprised and shocked. All the same, by the end of December matters had gone too far for the Soviet Union to turn back. No new votes in the U.N. were needed. The American buildup in the Persian Gulf was nearly complete. Nothing but world war could stop the American coalition. The last thing Mikhail Gorbachev needed was a confrontation with President Bush. Soviet internal problems were getting worse daily. Primakov was sent back to Baghdad in a last-minute face-saving move, but the overt Soviet support remained steady.

The fifth major power needed in the Security Council was China. Relations between our two countries had been improving when in 1989 they took a turn for the worse. In June that year the Chinese government decided to disperse by force the tens of thousands of demonstrators who had occupied for some six weeks Beijing's main Tiananmen Square.[50] A wave of political arrests followed. Congressional reaction in the United

---

[49] U.S. News & World Report, *Triumph without Victory*, p. 180.

[50] Chen Xitong, the mayor of Beijing, claimed that 200 civilians died and more than 3,000 were wounded. Amnesty International estimated the number of dead to be closer to 1,000. *Time*, June 4, 1990 p. 59.

States was blistering. Demands for political and economic sanctions were heard throughout Congress and the media.[51]

President Bush with considerable experience in China sought to resist the pressure. He decided to renew China's most-favored-nation status in trade with the United States. He could not resist imposing some sanctions, however. Shipment of military equipment and related aid was halted. High-level official contacts were suspended. Most significant of all, he decided that through American voting power and influence in the World Bank, pending loan agreements would be held up. In vain did Barber Conable, the president of the bank, plead with Bush (June 13, 1989) to exclude from the ban seven development (e.g., transport and power) projects already negotiated that primarily benefitted the common people. The president felt that he could not go along. The United States would vote against them at the Board meeting and would persuade its industrialized friends to follow suit. Given the weighted voting in the World Bank Board, that was all that was needed to hold up the projects, if not kill them altogether. The Chinese were annoyed.

The American ambassador to China, Winston Lord, did not help much. He had strong views about the bloody confrontation at Tiananmen Square. His wife, Chinese born, kept expressing them while in Beijing. What did help was the Chinese ambassador in Washington, Zhu Quizhen. He had come to Washington with the assignment of improving China–U.S. relations, which he personally believed to be the right course for his country. It helped enormously that he was a scholar, a man of style, and a man of wit. He urged patience on his government and cooperation. He urged understanding in Washington. To help on both counts he suggested the resumption of high-level contacts. They were held, but in secret. On two weekends (July 4 and December 8, 1989), General Scowcroft and Deputy Secretary of State Lawrence Eagleburger met with high Chinese officials in Beijing. The Chinese mood visibly improved when at the Houston G-7 Summit (July 9–11, 1990) the president decided not to press his colleagues on the World Bank projects. The United States would still vote against them, but the others could break rank, which meant that in fact World Bank aid could proceed.

Shortly after the invasion (August 4–5, 1990) Richard Solomon, assistant secretary of state, visited the Chinese capital. Then by special arrangement Secretary Baker met with the Chinese foreign minister Qian

---

[51] 101st Congress, 1st session, 135 Congressional Record H2312 and S618, June 6, 1989.

Qichen in the VIP lounge of Cairo airport.[52] The secretary was very anxious to enlist Chinese support in the Security Council. That, he suggested, would be the "best thing." The Chinese were noncommittal. They wanted some kind of *quid pro quo*. All that Baker was willing to give was a promise that toward the end of the year he would send his deputy to Beijing to discuss a possible visit in 1991. He made it clear: "We don't hold it against our friends that they are not joining us, but we *do* ask that they do not stand in the way."[53] When the vote in the Security Council came on November 29, China abstained, and that meant that the military operations in the Persian Gulf could proceed with UN approval.[54]

The other thrust of the U.S. diplomatic initiative was toward building support in the region. We had gained Saudi permission to deploy our military forces. Now we needed their help to finance the operations. After a visit by the secretary of state they agreed to it, and they were as good and generous as their word. At the end of October (as a first payment) they turned over to General Schwarzkopf the biggest check he (or probably anyone else) had ever seen. Drawn on an account at the Morgan Guaranty Trust it was made out to the Government of the United States. The amount: $760 million.[55]

Egypt, another moderate Muslim country, was also ready to help. It was "shocking, shocking," President Mubarak felt, that Saddam Hussein after all his personal assurances did invade Kuwait. Besides Mubarak possibly hoped that a grateful United States would forgive billions of dollars of Egyptian debt. So Egypt too came aboard almost immediately. The small Gulf states followed suit. Turkey, another Muslim country, was a member of NATO. Its president, Turgut Ozal, was one of the first President Bush called after the Iraqi aggression. Ozal quickly agreed to cutting the flow of Iraqi oil in the pipelines across Turkey and, when asked, gave permission to use NATO air bases against Iraq. All of which was to the good, but not quite sufficient. Somehow we would have to ward off a very troubling prospect.

Saddam Hussein was essentially a secular leader with uncertain loyalty to his "Arab brothers." When in trouble though, he could be expected to appeal to religious and ethnic solidarity. He would picture himself as a

---

[52] U.S. News & World Report, *Triumph without Victory*, p. 175.

[53] Baker, *The Politics of Diplomacy*, pp. 308–9.

[54] Some American observers were surprised. "The Chinese turned out not to be much of a problem." Woodward, *The Commanders*, p. 333.

[55] Schwarzkopf, *It Doesn't Take a Hero*, p. 37.

hero engaged in a fight against Western (American) imperialism and a victim of an anti-Muslim, Zionist conspiracy. And that was exactly what he did. Hardly had the first U.S. planes arrived in Saudi Arabia, when he unleashed a propaganda barrage. If he could not persuade the heads of governments, he might intimidate them by enticing their people against them.

The imperialists, deviators, merchants, political agents, the servants of the foreigner and Zionism all stood up against Iraq only because it represents the conscience of the (Arab) nation and its ability to safeguard its honor and rights against any harm. . . .
O Arabs, O Moslems and believers everywhere. This is your day to rise and defend Mecca which is captured by the spears of the Americans and the Zionists. Revolt against oppression, corruption, treachery and backstabbing. . . . Keep the foreigner away from your holy shrines and raise your voices and evoke the honor of your rulers so that we all stand as one to expel darkness and expose those rulers who know no sense of honor.
Revolt against the oil emirs who accept to push the Arab women into whoredom.[56]

Many heard him. His appeal was undeniable. About 7,000 Muslim militants demonstrated in Jordan declaring a *jihad* (holy war) on the United States.[57] And the barrage continued. Three days later very much the same theme was expressed:

Arabs, Muslims, believers in God, wherever you are. This is the day for you to stand up to defend Mecca, which is the captive of the spears of the Americans and Zionists. This is the day for you to rise to defend the Prophet Muhammad Bin Abdullah, who spread his sublime message from this noble land so that it would stay sacred. Revolt against injustice, corruption, treason and treachery! Keep the foreigners clear of our sacred places! Speak up and rally to the worthy among the rulers so that all may take a united stand of pride, dispel the darkness, expose the rulers who do not know pride and revolt against whoever deems it acceptable for oil emirs to allow Arab women to be exposed to harm and driven to obscenity.[58]

And so on and on. Response by Arab moderates would help little. Vulnerable to the charge of America's friends they could be easily

---

[56] Text of Saddam Hussein's address to Arabs, Reuters, BC Cycle, August 10, 1990.

[57] Ibid., Byline Samia Nakhoul, August 10, 1990.

[58] Saddam Hussein's call to the Arab masses and all Muslims, BBC Summary of World Broadcasts, August 13, 1990.

castigated as America's vassals. Indeed they themselves were under Iraqi propaganda attack. What was needed was an Arab country (leader) in the region with credentials of anti-Americanism to line up against Iraq and thus delegitimize its claims. Theoretically the choice was Syria or the PLO. In fact, there was no choice at all. Our only possibility was Syria. Surely not an easy course.

The problem was that Syria had been designated by the State Department as a country supporting terrorism and, as such, was under congressional mandate subject to severe sanctions. On the other hand, Hafeez al-Assad, the president of the country, had for some time fought Saddam for the preeminence of the Ba'thist Party and had become his mortal enemy. Then there was also the practical consideration. Since the late 1970s Saudi Arabia had been subsidizing Syria at an annual rate of about $2 billion. With Jordan and the PLO joining the wrong side in the conflict, there was the opportunity that Syria could pick up their share of Saudi subsidy as well, another $2 billion a year.

So it was worth trying. As early as August 13, 1990, Assistant Secretary of State for Near Eastern and South Asian Affairs John Kelly visited Damascus and met with President Assad. "Assad said enough to satisfy Kelly."[59] On September 14 Secretary Baker called on Assad. The latter wanted to know about U.S. military intentions. "We think it's important that we do not have public discussions of that possibility," Baker responded, "except to say that we have not ruled out any options."[60] Things looked promising. Then in November shortly before the U.N. Security Council vote President Bush himself met with Assad in Geneva.[61] They were photographed together, causing much unease among Americans in and out of government. Their unease, however, was probably nothing compared to that experienced in Baghdad. Saddam Hussein and Iraq were for all practical purposes diplomatically isolated.

The anti-Iraqi coalition, a masterpiece of President Bush, General Scowcroft, James Baker, and the State Department, however, was not a very robust structure. All kinds of strains could easily and almost on the spur of the moment develop. And one of them was the issue of Israel. Only Egypt had signed a peace treaty; other Arab states were more or less formally at war with her. Any prominent, active role for Israel in the crisis could easily break up the coalition.

---

[59] U.S. News & World Report, *Triumph without Victory*, p. 104.

[60] Baker, *The Politics of Diplomacy*, p. 297.

[61] *The New York Times*, November 24, 1990, A1, 6.

Specifically the problems were (1) Israel was a well-armed, powerful country, (2) it had no sense of humor about being attacked, and (3) in any U.S. move against Iraq it was expected to be attacked without provocation. All the same, there were many good reasons for Israel to follow U.S. requests for staying out of the conflict. For one thing there were quite a number of areas where U.S. and Israeli interests coincided. The elimination of Iraq as an Arab superpower with weapons of mass destruction was one of them. Moreover, Israel needed America. It was almost entirely dependent on U.S. weapons. It had become accustomed to massive annual economic aid (minimum $3 billion). In addition, it now sought help with financing the influx of Soviet Jews by requesting the U.S. government to guarantee Israeli loans up to $10 billion.

Israel would certainly try to be helpful. On August 27 while the regional coalition was being built by the secretary of state, Prime Minister Shamir sought to be reassuring. Israel, he declared, "has no interest in attacking any Arab state—not even the most extreme among them."[62] So far so good, but what about the prospect of an Iraqi attack on Israel? Would Israel retaliate? David Ivri, the director general of the Israeli defense ministry, thought that the possibility had to be considered. In that eventuality it would be invaluable for the Israeli air force to know the secret IFF codes, which identified friend and foe in the skies. Only thus could accidents of Israeli planes shooting at Americans or vice versa be avoided. Late in August he formally raised the issue. The Americans thought it would be better altogether if in this instance the Israelis would keep out of the fighting.

The issue, however, could not be settled. It was complicated in October when the United States supported two resolutions in the United Nations Security Council critical of Israel: one condemned "the excessive Israeli response" in the Temple Mount incident when peaceful Muslim worshipers were killed by Israeli military forces; the second called for a special United Nations fact-finding mission to be dispatched to Jerusalem. In November Secretary of State Baker raised the issue of possible Israeli retaliation with King Fahd. The Saudi monarch was understanding. "He could not expect Israel to stand by idly if attacked. If Israel were to defend herself," he said, "the Saudi armed forces would still fight by our side."[63]

As the date of the commencement of operations approached, the question was still not settled. On January 12, 1990, Deputy Secretary of

---

[62] U.S. News & World Report, *Triumph without Victory*, p. 130.

[63] Schwarzkopf, *It Doesn't Take a Hero*, p. 373.

State Lawrence Eagleburger visited the Israeli prime minister. He transmitted a formal presidential commitment that (a) any Iraqi attack on Israel could be considered a *casus belli* and (b) the United States had assigned high priority to targets that might threaten Israel. But the Americans would go no further. When Israel proposed their own air attack on Iraq and in the process overfly Jordan and Saudi Arabia, we said "no," and we would not share the IFF codes. In turn, the Israeli prime minister reaffirmed his commitment that Israel would not launch a preemptive strike but made no promises that Israel would not retaliate if attacked.

It remained touch and go. When later in January Israel was actually a victim of Iraqi missiles, Eagleburger had to return to Jerusalem to calm Israeli indignation. U.S. Patriot missiles (interceptors) were quickly deployed in Israel. An extravagant amount of time was spent by the U.S. Air Force on hunting down Iraqi missile (often mobile) sites. All the same, the Israeli government showed admirable restraint and earned American gratitude.[64]

THE IMPLEMENTATION: STRATEGIC DECEPTION

The massive U.S. military buildup and the spectacular diplomatic initiatives, impressive and even brilliant as they were, however, would not be sufficient for a successful outcome. There was a second requirement for success of the president's agenda: strategic deception.[65] For all along, almost on a moment's notice Saddam Hussein could ruin the American effort.

Consider the harsh reality of the situation: during all of August and part of September 1990 Iraq could, if it chose, successfully invade Saudi Arabia and the Gulf States. Against 100,000 well-trained Iraqi troops in Kuwait (with their numbers rising), stood less than 70,000 Saudi troops with only one small unit in the way of the Saudi oil fields. By August 15 one brigade of the 82nd Airborne Division, 4,000 lightly armed U.S. soldiers, was being deployed. In another week a brigade of marines, some

---

[64] Ibid., pp. 416–19, 499; U.S. News & World Report, *Triumph without Victory*, pp. 208–11, 258–59.

[65] It will be interesting to see just how history (and George Bush's memoirs) will treat this subject. At the Conference of the Washington Society of Association Executives on the "Meaning of Leadership" (John F. Kennedy Center for the Performing Arts, January 22, 1996) the president listed only two overt goals. He referred to three only obliquely.

special forces, and more airborne troops were arriving, tripling the U.S. ground forces in the area, but still no match for the Iraqis. Only after a month of the buildup could heavier divisions, so essential against Iraqi armor, begin to arrive.[66] Consider the calculus: had Saddam Hussein decided to invade Saudi Arabia and the Gulf States, Iraq would suffer heavy casualties and ultimately be defeated—no worse a fate than it had in the end. But in the process the United States would also suffer heavy casualties, very much more than it did in the end. Under those conditions would President Bush persist in his purpose? Indeed would American public opinion remain supportive and permit him to do so? Even if the answer was in the affirmative, as an act of vengeance, Iraq could devastate practically all the oil wells in the Gulf at extraordinary costs to the leading industrialized countries of the world. Quite possibly though, the answer would be in the negative, and then there would be negotiations—all of them benefitting Iraq. Thus, during this initial period we would have to deter (or at least not tempt) Iraqi attack by hiding our military goals and letting Saddam Hussein believe that America was all bluster and that ultimately he could make major gains if not, in fact, get away with a *fait accompli* of annexing Kuwait.

As the buildup proceeded first to a level that would assure Saudi defense (with moderate U.S. casualties) and continued far beyond it, the problem became progressively more difficult. If anyone thought about it for a minute, the essence of the situation would have become apparent quickly enough. First, there was no way the United States could have deployed hundreds of thousands of troops in Saudi Arabia for an indefinite period, all waiting there to repel a possible attack by Saddam Hussein at a time of his choosing. The Saudis would not accept it; the American electorate would not tolerate it. And as far as the troops were concerned, to stay in the desert indefinitely without wine, women, and song was just plain absurd.[67] Second, if they were to go on the offensive and simply push Iraq out of Kuwait (goal number two) that would not make much sense either. After suffering some casualties in a direct attack the United States could declare Kuwait liberated, but that would be all. We would then

---

[66] Schwarzkopf, *It Doesn't Take a Hero*, p. 301.

[67] American forces were trained, exercised, exercised, and trained some more. Apart from their military value, such exhausting schedules made them (at least theoretically) too tired for hanky-panky. "American troops in the region had less than usual rates of misconduct. I was proud of their discipline." Powell, *My American Journey*, p. 474.

withdraw leaving the best Iraqi troops still intact within an hour's march and leaving Iraqi capacity of mass destruction undiminished.[68]

If anyone thought about it, it would soon become apparent that the key to our strategy was a determination to cripple for some time to come any Iraqi aspiration to become an Arab superpower or, in other words, to destroy the core of its military power and its development of weapons of mass destruction. Anywhere, including in Iraq itself.

The invasion of Iraq, which had to be a central element of the American plan, however, had to remain a secret. Its logic and the determination with which President Bush pursued it could not be explained to the American people. Had it been, it would no longer remain a secret. It would seriously impair whatever solidarity the American diplomatic offensive had built within the coalition, and especially with the Arab leaders who were still loath to admit publicly that they had cooperated in an attack on another Arab country.[69] Worse still, it would convince Saddam Hussein that his best course would be simply to withdraw all his troops from Kuwait, leaving General Schwarzkopf and his massive forces all dressed up and no place to go.

For an American president to keep secrets from the American people, however, was not only fraught with political risks, it was also a task difficult to carry out in practice. The lessons of the Nixon administration just two decades earlier could not have been forgotten. All the same, these were different times. It was not a hostility-laden, high-decibel domestic environment. Confidence in the national government was largely restored;

---

[68] After the war the United Nations discovered that Iraq was within three to six months of developing a nuclear warhead. It was very close to installing a long-range (300 miles) gigantic artillery piece. It also had nearly 1,000 SCUD missiles and thousands of bacteriological and chemical warheads.

[69] Five years after the war General Khaled bin Sultan has a chapter in his book devoted to "The War Aims of the Arab Alliance." In it he parallels the American logic. "Saudi Arabia, Egypt, and Syria were united in a determination to defeat Iraq's bid for regional hegemony—a hegemony which would have undermined Saudi security and exposed it to extortion, marginalized Egypt in Arab affairs, and exposed the Syrian regime to extreme danger. Had Saddam not posed a deadly threat to the interests of these Arab states the coalition would not have been formed and the war would not have been fought—or would have been fought very differently without Arab participation." Khaled bin Sultan, *Desert Warrior*, p. 172. If indeed the Arab leaders did understand the hidden, third goal of the American strategy and therefore, as is a fact, they did not challenge or leak it, they and President Bush deserve special credit.

there were no persistent public assaults on the integrity of the Chief Executive. President Bush's decision style also helped. He asked his advisers a lot of questions but generally kept his own views to himself. They knew that the president would make the final decision but were rarely sure just what that would be. Their uncertainty could be *honestly* passed on to the American people.

All through the crisis the persistent theme emanated from the administration: No decision has been made. All options were open, none were ruled out. It was, no doubt, confusing for Saddam Hussein. The American leaders seemed unsure of themselves; the American people seemed undecided. Quite possibly he might still win the confrontation.

It was also confusing to very high-level American officials. In mid-October General Powell had a private talk with the secretary of state. They both agreed that existing policy was "drifting."[70] Powell was convinced that the sanctions should be given more time to work, perhaps much more time. Baker was more cautious. He saw merit in a massive offensive. Both went to see the president, spoke of alternatives, but neither pressed them. Looking at the situation from a distance, General Schwarzkopf found it was especially confusing. He was pleased with all the troops that were arriving to serve under his command. He was unclear what their mission was to be. By early October he had enough forces to draw a very firm and secure line in the desert. Still the troops kept coming. They were more than enough to meet their publicly stated purpose, the defense of Saudi Arabia. Was there another purpose as well? The offensive option?

On October 5 General Schwarzkopf spoke to the Chairman of the Joint Chiefs on the phone. Colin Powell assured him that no decisions had been made, but that the offensive option would have to be looked at. He ordered Schwarzkopf to send a team to Washington to brief the Joint Chiefs "and possibly the President." General Schwarzkopf was rather less than enthusiastic about the demand, and when Gen. Carl Vuono, Army Chief-of-Staff, visited him the next day, he was a CINC (commander-in-chief) with a grievance. Dramatically as is his wont, he complained that "some son-of-a-bitch was going to wake up some morning and say, let's get the offense rolling." He had two more months' work to do on defense, and he had told the president in August it would take eight to twelve months to be ready for the offense.[71] The general did not understand what it was all about.

---

[70] Woodward, *The Commanders*, p. 303.

[71] Ibid., p. 303.

Schwarzkopf's team arrived in Washington and met with the Joint Chiefs on October 10. They presented a plan for the offensive option. After massive air strikes it was essentially a direct, frontal, land and sea attack on Iraqi forces in Kuwait. This would have met the second item of the agenda. Quite probably it would have pushed the Iraqis out of Kuwait. But it had two problems. First, the projected casualties of such a direct attack were high: an estimated 10,000 with 1,500 killed in action.[72] Second, it did nothing about the hidden number three item of the agenda. The team returned to Saudi Arabia somewhat chastened, and General Schwarzkopf remained agitated and puzzled.

On October 21 General Powell flew to Saudi Arabia to discuss matters with Schwarzkopf. He started with the now-standard formula. The president had not yet made a decision. "The mood in Washington shifts every week," he said. "Ten days ago it was hawkish; in the past four or five days people have been talking about giving the economic sanctions time to work."[73] All the same, Powell wanted to discuss the offensive option. Schwarzkopf was reluctant; first he wanted to get a commitment for additional forces. He would ask for the moon: the Seventh Corps, the best U.S. forces stationed in Germany, in fact, the troops that were supposed to protect Western Europe. That would surely discourage those crazy guys in Washington. To his surprise the chairman did not turn him down. More than that. He offered an additional armored division from the United States. "Plus, we would also send another Marine Division," the chairman recalled. "I beefed up his request for additional fighter squadron. Aircraft carriers? Let's send six. We had paid for this stuff. Why not use it? . . . 'Norm,' I said, 'you've got to understand that the President and Cheney will give you anything you need to get the job done.'"[74] Powell then visited some troops. "I know you want to know the answer to two questions: What are we going to be doing here? And when are we going to go home? Because I can't give you answers to two questions, we are giving our political leaders time to work this out."[75]

Schwarzkopf in a long interview to the *Atlanta Journal* was sounding his own theme. "Now we are starting to see evidence that the sanctions are pinching. So why should we say, 'okay, gave them two months, didn't work. Let's get on with it and kill a whole bunch of people?' That's

---

[72] Gordon and Trainor, *The Generals' War*, pp. 132–33.

[73] Schwarzkopf, *It Doesn't Take a Hero*, p. 366.

[74] Powell, *My American Journey*, p. 487.

[75] Woodward, *The Commanders*, p. 311.

crazy."[76] All the same, by the end of the month he was fully absorbed in planning an offensive option that, in fact, met both item #2 and item #3 of the president's agenda. The offensive option was now on the fast track.

Watching it from the outside, Saddam Hussein could reasonably conclude that the Americans were confused, and their leaders would argue each other into paralysis. He did not know of the discussion on October 31 when the military requirements for the offensive option were presented to the president. "He never hesitated," Cheney recalled. "When it was time, when we said, 'Look, Mr. President, we're going to want to send a total of six aircraft-carrier battle groups. We've got one Marine division over there now; we're going to want to send another one. We want to send another division [the Big Red One] from Kansas. Et cetera, et cetera'. . . . He never blinked. He signed off on it, and he said, 'Do it.'"[77]

Early in November Secretary Baker set out on a whirlwind tour of twelve countries, some of which he visited twice. His message was that no decision had been made, but that the United States needed the offensive option and sought the approval of foreign powers for it. In Dharan he explained the position thus: "While we are still seeking a peaceful, political and diplomatic solution, we have to, I think, put ourselves in a position where we would be able to exercise any option that might be available. I don't think we can—nor should we—rule out the use of force."[78]

Congress had adjourned on October 28 but the majority of Democrats, seeing only what appeared to be confusion in the White House, thought they had a constructive alternative to offer or perhaps a partisan opportunity to exploit.

The day before U.N. Resolution 678 authorizing the use of any necessary means was passed, Senator Sam Nunn, the widely respected Chairman of the Senate Armed Services Committee, opened public hearings on the administration's policy in the Persian Gulf. His staff arranged for a list of distinguished witnesses: two chairmen of the Joint Chiefs, Gen. David Jones, USAF, and Adm. William J. Crowe, USN; the assistant secretary of state for Near Eastern and South Asian Affairs, Richard Murphy; plus two *éminences grises*, George Ball, undersecretary of state in the Kennedy and Johnson administrations, and Paul Nitze, an adviser at the highest levels regardless of party at least since Eisenhower.

---

[76] Ibid., p. 313.

[77] U.S. News & World Report, *Triumph without Victory*, p. 171.

[78] Ibid., p. 175.

All counseled against military action. "We can outlast him" was Nitze's considered view. It was democracy at its best; everyone had a right to his opinion. All of it must have appeared as cacophony to Saddam Hussein.

President Bush contributed to it. Suddenly just a day after the United Nations authorized military action against Iraq, the president announced a "peace-initiative." He knew in his heart that Saddam would not blink but was convinced that for world opinion a last initiative was necessary. So he announced that he was ready to send the secretary of state to Baghdad at a mutually convenient time between December 15 and January 15 of next year. "The President's announcement brought the contradictions between the needs of the international coalition and a domestic consensus to the fore,"[79] the secretary of state observed. The decision didn't sit well with some of our friends. Bush saw the risk that the Baker mission would shake up the coalition to the core. But he knew that the time fuse was very short and that he would instruct Baker not to give an inch. Prince Bandar, the Saudi ambassador, missed the point. "Why did you not consult with us," he asked Scowcroft. "The timing could not have been worse. The offer to meet right up to the deadline of January 15 would be an invitation for Saddam to stall. . . . To you sending Baker is good will, to Saddam it suggests you are chicken."[80] Which was just fine with Bush.

All through December there was much public discussion about the best course to be pursued. There was, for example, a lengthy network (CBS) interview with the vice president. Should we wait for economic sanctions to work? What if Saddam says that he will get out and is willing to take only a bit of Kuwaiti territory in the north? "Dan Rather threw all his political acumen into this conversation," recalled Dan Quayle, "raising possibility after possibility and I left glad that Saddam Hussein hadn't been able to overhear it, because if he had followed Rather's line of thinking he might have come closer to outfoxing us."[81]

Abroad, other powers chimed in. The French wanted to help negotiate a peaceful solution. The Yugoslav secretary of foreign affairs, on behalf of the "Non-aligned Movement" approached Secretary Baker, the secretary-general of the United Nations, and the foreign ministers of the European community.[82] President Bush watched all the goings on with equanimity. His only comments were that all initiatives toward peace

---

[79] Baker, *The Politics of Diplomacy*, p. 351.

[80] Woodward, *The Commanders*, p. 336.

[81] Quayle, *Standing Firm*, p. 216.

[82] U.S. News & World Report, *Triumph without Victory*, pp. 192–93.

would be appreciated, provided they achieved the unconditional withdrawal from Kuwait. Almost unnoticed went a subcondition of U.N. Resolution No. 674 that raised the ante by demanding Iraqi payment of reparations for war damages and economic losses.

Early in January when Congress reassembled, "Senator Harkin surprised Majority Leader Mitchell in demanding immediate debate on Persian Gulf. I continued to call on Harkin," Vice President Quayle noted in his diary, "as he is good fodder for us."[83] The debate, which most members wished to avoid, was on. Back and forth it went in the Senate. Should Congress authorize U.S. military action in the Gulf? In the end just before the January 15 deadline, by a narrow almost party-line majority (53:47) the Senate voted in the affirmative. In the House over the most vigorous objections of the Speaker a more bipartisan margin was much wider, 250:183.

There were still last-minute movements in what had become a diplomatic charade. A meeting between Secretary Baker and Iraqi Vice President Tariq Aziz in Geneva; a visit by U.N. Secretary General Pérez de Cuéllar to Baghdad; French President Mitterand's "eleventh hour appeal"; and President Gorbachev's plea for more time. At home Congressmen Gonzalez and Gedjenson filed impeachment papers against the president. Ramsey Clark suggested that the president should be tried as a war criminal. It really made no difference but may have given hope to Saddam Hussein. Senator Edward Kennedy, who evidently did not understand what was going on, exclaimed: "We have not seen this kind of arrogance in a president since Watergate."[84]

The deadline passed. It was early in the evening of the next day in Washington that the war started by a heavy bombing of Baghdad and other strategic targets. For a month it was an air war. Coalition air forces (principally American and British) systematically destroyed Iraqi command centers, radar stations, ground-to-air missile bases, communication networks, highways, and railroads. They shot down Iraqi war planes and annihilated them on the ground. They vigorously sought out SCUD missile sites. The biggest problem was that many of those were mobile. Some were actually launched at Israel, causing some anxiety that Israel would not keep out. Once again Deputy Secretary of State Eagleburger had to fly to Jerusalem. The Israeli government made no commitments but continued to act with restraint.

---

[83] Quayle, *Standing Firm*, p. 224.
[84] Quoted in *U.S. News & World Report*, op. cit., p. 206.

Meanwhile our efforts of strategic deception continued. Even after the air offensive was underway, Saddam was still confident that the land war, "the mother of all battles," favored him. He would cause so many U.S. casualties that the president would be compelled to negotiate, in the end leaving him, Saddam, with significant net profits. Specifically he counted on a move so reckless that the Americans would never expect it. He would ignite the Kuwaiti oil fields. The marines trying to land would get a surprise: an impenetrable wall of fire along the coastline. Actually by now the original Schwarzkopf plan was long abandoned. The "Hail Mary" strategy of a wide western sweep into Iraq itself was already in motion. Still the Iraqis did not know this; their radar and all other intelligence means had been blinded by the steady month-long air attacks. It was not in our interests to enlighten them. Better still, it was useful to reinforce Saddam's confidence in his false premise. Let him believe that we were planning as the main attack an amphibious offensive from the Gulf. We had six attack carriers assembled there. We had regularly conducted amphibious exercises in the Gulf (Oman). We kept bombing the shoreline.

Listening with all they could (mostly their ears), they kept hearing sounds of heavy armor moving along the coastline opposite the troops in eastern Kuwait. They did not know that the sounds came from loudspeakers, which amplified audiotapes. They kept watching everything they could, mostly American television. Each night the network news included analysis by experts. Notably the CBS consultant was Gen. George B. Crist, USMC (ret.), Schwarzkopf's immediate predecessor as commander-in-chief, Central Command. There were always colorful maps on display on which the general carefully and persuasively described the "logical" American strategy: a direct, amphibious attack against the shores of Kuwait. And then suddenly the general's analyses stopped. It was said the commandant himself ordered his silence as they revealed too much of America's strategy. Saddam was reassured—and thoroughly deceived.

After a month of massive aerial attacks the ground offensive took off. The marines, with Saudi and Kuwaiti forces on the right, drove up along the coastline. They made rapid progress. The Iraqi troops, dazed from all the bombing, were no match for them. In two days they liberated Kuwait. Meanwhile the main force struck with a knockout left punch. They encircled all the Iraqi forces in Kuwait and even some of the elite Revolutionary Guard divisions

After a hundred hours of the ground war (390 deaths, 146 battle deaths and 244 nonbattle deaths, and 467 wounded for a total of 857 American casualties) the president ordered a cease-fire. Saddam Hussein, who just a day earlier had been reduced to despair, felt saved. We have won, we have won, he kept repeating to his closest associates.[85] In terms of American goals it was something of a puzzle, for the job was not quite finished.

A number of explanations have been offered. First, President Bush had no intention of getting involved in the conquest of Iraq, a doubtful objective with consequent obligations that neither he nor the American people were willing even to contemplate. Moreover, his Arab coalition partners were growing restless. Some could not get rid of their lingering suspicions that America was much like the Europeans in the nineteenth century. In the guise of liberating Kuwait, she really wanted to make oil-rich Iraq a colony or a satellite. There was no reason to fuel this prejudice. Second, George Bush, with his global view and experience and touched by the conventional wisdom of the balance of power theory, did not wish to create a power vacuum along the western borders of Iran. Third, George Bush, actually a gentle, sensitive person, was distressed to see television pictures of the devastating bombing of the withdrawing Iraqi forces. Gen. Colin Powell kept warning him that we were entering a stage that was "un-American," "unchivalrous," events that would be unpleasant to see. The American people probably would not like it, and others would get the wrong impression of Americans as monstrous, merciless brutes.

All of these explanations may have played a role, but in the final analysis they are not satisfactory. For they do not answer the question: why did we not continue operations *for twelve more hours*, say a day maximum, when they could have completed the military defeat of Saddam Hussein? Nor do they answer the question: why did we let Iraqi troops who were guilty of all kinds of outrages in Kuwait but were practically surrounded escape capture and leave with their weapons, including their modern heavy tanks? Perhaps a more accurate explanation may be found in mistakes in communications. In the morning (EST) of February 27 General Schwarz-kopf held his controversial press conference. With great flair he described his own brilliant planning of the military operations and its extraordinary successes. The elite Republican Guard units were surrounded. "The gate was shut." Does that mean that coalition troops have cut the Guard's line of retreat to Basra? a reporter asked. "No." Can they withdraw to Basra? "No, that is why the gate is shut."[86] In fact, the gate was not shut. Later that afternoon General Powell told the president: "We have destroyed the

---

[85] WGBH Educational Foundation, (Videotape) *Frontline*, January 10, 1996. Testimony by Gen. Wafic al Sammarai, Iraq Intelligence.

[86] Ibid. Press conference of General Schwarzkopf.

Republican Guard."[87] which was not accurate either. More than a third of them got away, many with their heavy armor.

Epitomizing the situation is this vignette. General Schwarzkopf decided to hold the armistice meeting with the Iraqis at Savran, an airbase in Iraq a short distance beyond Kuwait. His maps based on field commanders' reports indicated that it was well within U.S. military control. While preparing for the event two days after the official cease-fire announcement he learned that actually we did not have any troops in the area. There followed a typical Schwarzkopf outburst and an order to promptly occupy the airfield. The next morning he learned that the Iraqis held the airfield with fifteen Republican Guard tanks. So three days after the cease-fire he ordered: Go take the place. Later still he learned that the Iraqi commander refused to move. "Fine," Schwarzkopf burst out. "Here is what you'll do. You have got the entire 1st Infantry Division there. Dispatch overwhelming force and surround the guy completely, and make sure he sees. Tell him 'we cannot tolerate Iraqi units this close to our forces. You must leave the area or we will take you prisoner. We are doing this for the protection of our troops. If you fight, we will destroy you.'"[88] At first the Iraqi commander refused to move, but then after a short discussion, he thought better of it.

In any case, by the end of February 1990 the war was over. Saddam Hussein still ruled in Baghdad, but Iraq was forced out of Kuwait, and it was forced to destroy under international supervision all of its weapons of mass destruction and forgo the development of a nuclear arsenal. The Iraqi army suffered heavy casualties; the country would remain under international economic sanctions for some time. When George Bush went to Congress, in the very best traditions of American democracy he received universal accolades led by his most vigorous opponent: the Speaker of the House of Representatives.

---

[87] Ibid.

[88] Schwarzkopf, *It Doesn't Take a Hero*, pp. 475-77.

4

Rebuilding the Consensus at Home

The Persian Gulf crisis (1990–1991) was exceptionally well managed. President Bush's decision-making approach was effective abroad and popular at home. He accomplished his external goals, and according to the polls in March 1991, his domestic approval rating soared to a phenomenal 80-plus percent. All the same, in terms of instruction for the future the Gulf crisis is only of limited value.

It was an exceptional achievement under exceptionally favorable circumstances. Our relations with the Soviet Union in its twilight were particularly fortuitous. The United Nations Security Council for the moment was veto-free. No Soviet "no" votes blocked action; indeed the Soviet Union staunchly supported the United States. *And at home* the strong Israeli interests in the success of the enterprise undoubtedly mitigated the expressions of articulate and vehement opposition to the use of force in the influential liberal intellectual circles of American society.

President Clinton in his first term did not advance us toward a solution of the decision-making conundrum. More than any recent president, he acted as though foreign policy was an extension of domestic politics. He himself had few qualifications in foreign relations, and he suffered seriously in his staffing decisions by the handicap of not being wired into the American establishment. He just did not know who were the key people and the most qualified in the professions, in business, in bureaucracy (civilian and military), or even in the media. His team included only one member whom he had personally known for many years, the deputy secretary of state, a former newspaper reporter. In fact, several other senior appointments had long careers in the media. His national security council was not noted for academics or military officers. Its senior members were partners in a prominent Washington law firm; some had been active in special interest lobbies. Outwardly they did not engage in intramural struggles with the State Department. The secretary of state had considerably more experience than the national security council people or his own senior assistants, but he was not widely seen as a forceful personality. He is a gentleman with becoming modesty, a hard-working, (at times exhausted) professional who presented an easy target in the capital's cynical bloodsports. "None of this would be happening if Warren Christopher were alive."[1] A supposedly funny remark making the rounds.

The secretary of state regularly warned—sometimes dramatically— "that our diplomatic readiness was deteriorating. . . . In Tajikistan, our staff operated out of a hotel for four years, through a civil war and its aftermath. In Sarajevo, our officers were sleeping beside their desks until just last month. . . . Until very recently, the post's communications system was a Rube Goldberg model. When I visited in February, I was amazed to see a barbecue grill used to rig a satellite dish to the roof of the embassy."[2] All the same Warren Christopher supported and implemented the reduction of his department's budget: for fiscal year 1995, for example, $110 million less than the State Department received for FY 1993.[3] Fiscal year 1996 would see a further drop of nearly 4 percent ($178 million). Three years of steep cost cutting reduced staffing by 2,482 (9 percent), including 452 Foreign Service officers (-5.7 percent).[4] International discretionary programs dropped from $21.1 billion (1993 actual) to $18.5 billion (1996 estimate), about 12 percent.[5] Simply put, it was a venture into "diplomacy on the cheap," two former ambassadors concluded.[6]

All along, the secretary stood by while the destruction of the foreign service professional cadres was completed. Begun during the Carter

---

[1] *Economist*, June 8–14, 1996, p. 28.

[2] "The International Affairs Budget: Large Returns from a Small Investment," statement by Secretary Christopher before the Subcommittee on Commerce, Justice, State, the Judiciary and Related Agencies of the House Appropriations Committee, Washington, DC, May 15, 1996, *U.S. Department of State Dispatch*, May 20, 1996, vol. 7, no. 21.

[3] U.S. Department of State, *Magazine*, March 1994, p. 2.

[4] Presentation Document, Secretary Christopher's statement before the House Subcommittee, May 15, 1996.

[5] U.S. Office of the Management and Budget, Budget Supplement, Fiscal Year 1997 (Washington, DC: Government Printing Office, 1996), vol. 5, p. 40.

[6] *Washington Post*, June 18, 1996, p. A13.

presidency and somewhat slowed during Reagan and Bush, the pursuit of affirmative action had become single-minded under President Clinton. In 1993 18 percent of the eligible males and 27 percent of the eligible females were promoted. Similarly 19 percent of the eligible "nonminority" and 23 percent of minority officers were promoted.[7] In 1993 Foreign Service Recruitment Examinations show an increase of 46 percent over 1992 of minority and 4 percent of "white" passers; and an increase of 18 percent of women and 2 percent of men passers.[8]

On January 11, 1994, a Town Meeting on Foreign Service Personnel Reform was held in, of all places, the Dean Acheson Auditorium. "We must get rid of the notion that merit has been such a success that we don't have a problem," declared Conrad K. Harper, the department's legal adviser. He then added what he considered to be a reasonable justification. "What our own sense of shame is telling us to do [is] to change." Ms. Genta Hawkins Holmes, director general of the Foreign Service and director of personnel, explained the new practice of bringing in new employees through detours around the examination system. While some "assume that we want to give a free pass to people who couldn't pass the exam," it is rather the opposite, she said, explaining there are persons who are so highly sought after that the department could never hope to recruit them if it had to wait for the lengthy exam process. Richard M. Moore, undersecretary of state for management, conceded that the assignment process was convoluted and that people suspect it is "susceptible to manipulation." The legal adviser was not much concerned. "As we try to level the playing field," he asserted, "those are some incidental costs that all of us are going to have to bear."[9] And so it went. Under President Carter the process of the deprofessionalization of the Foreign Service had taken off. By the mid-1990s it has produced a set of officials, no longer a corps, where each new recruit's qualifications were increasingly political and specific to the moment of recruitment. They were well below the best and the brightest of America in knowledge, expertise, and style.

Regrettably, *a successful decision-making process that meets the criteria of both the international and the domestic environment still eludes us.* We may have to confront the reality that the pressures of the two environments are in fundamental conflict.

---

[7] U.S. Department of State, "From the Director General," March 1994, pp. 21–22.

[8] Ibid., April 1994, p. 16.

[9] U.S. Department of State, "News Highlights," February 1994, p. 2.

THE REALITIES OF THE INTERNATIONAL ENVIRONMENT

If we look closely enough, we find that our world is most accurately described not as a community but as an arena. Its actors are states that jealously guard their sovereignty. As a closed legal order, each reserves the right to define the value of its own actions and the right to resort to force when it so chooses. Though physically constrained by a relatively small planet, billions of human beings still do not think in terms of the unity of the human race. They feel no solidarity with other persons just because they are fellow human beings. They are accustomed to think in terms of ascriptive (often ethnic) divisions, centuries-old grievances and hostilities. Instinctively most people still think in terms of a double standard. Indeed they cannot imagine shared values that would bind us all, and they have little concern for the good of us all.

The unhappy fact remains that in the real world truth and virtue rarely prevail and justice is seldom triumphant. The common currency in the international arena is by tradition and default: power. Every kind of power matters, but at the basis is military power and the political will to use it. Without military power and the reputation for using it as a last resort, negotiations and compromise do not have much of a chance. A diplomat might as well be crying in the wilderness.

Thus, for American foreign policy to be *most effective abroad requires that we keep our military capabilities in good repair*. We need to retain our lead in military technology; we need to continue to attract some of the best of our youth to the armed forces of the country and train them well. If we were to *maximize* our effectiveness we would need much more. We would need military capabilities to handle all the possible challenges of the present and all imaginable challenges of the next decade. (The lead time of developing many new weapons systems is about seven years.) And we would need the full range of military capabilities to provide for the flexibility of multiple options. As a minimum we need credible deterrence of any strategic attack upon us. Add to this conventional forces that we could project into all various trouble spots on the globe. And we must not neglect our capacity for covert operations, since actions of the "hidden hand" on the small scale are enormously useful. Because they are not clearly attributable, indeed are often officially denied, they do not push the other side to respond. It could pretend to ignore them and thus avoid the perils of escalation. All this, of course, would require fabulous expenses.

Second, for American foreign policy to *maximize its effectiveness abroad our government also needs to protect its reputation for steadfastness*. To be sure, there are times when calculated vagueness could serve diplomatic purposes, and there are times when conditions have changed radically so that previous official commitments may have to be adjusted. There is no need to bully and no profit in swagger, but if we choose to rattle our sabers, we ought to use them when we are taunted. A reputation for bluffing, worse still for indecision and waffling, does not serve us well. A case in point may have been the Korean War. The Truman Administration sent out conflicting signals regarding our interest in South Korea. In January 1950 the secretary of state speaking before the Washington Press Club drew a line of our defensive perimeter in the Pacific which by intention or inadvertence ran east of South Korea.[10] Six months later the North Koreans attacked, and we were reduced to a choice between appeasement and war. Unfortunately since there is often doubt abroad about our political will to use force, *maximum* foreign policy effectiveness requires that we regularly rattle our sabers, and unless that has a salutary effect we predictably proceed to use them.

Third, a foreign policy that *best serves our international interests still needs the narrowest possible decision base*. It has to be carefully crafted to balance its various (political, economic, strategic, etc.) consequences. Its costs and benefits have to be accurately calculated not just in terms of our bilateral relations with any specific country, but also in its impact on relations with many others. It requires special skills and experience. It is not likely to be the product of extended discussions and elaborate compromises in every segment of our democratic system.

Fourth, *maximum effectiveness of our foreign policy abroad requires our government's ability to maintain secrets*. To begin with, secrecy is very useful in negotiations. History-making diplomatic breakthroughs require clandestine preparations. New ideas, new initiatives have no organized domestic constituencies; in fact, they are quite often perceived as threatening by established special interest groups. Had secret arrangements between China and the United States become prematurely known, President Nixon and Chairman Mao probably would have been prevented from proceeding by their respective domestic opponents (and supporters). Similarly secrecy was very useful in the Kennedy administration during the Cuban missile crisis when the president agreed to dismantle (obsolete) U.S. missile sites in Turkey.[11] Had it become known, the domestic reaction could have proved highly negative. Furthermore, the reaction in Turkey and other

---

[10] Speech of Secretary of State Dean Acheson, the Washington Press Club, January 12, 1950, *The New York Times*, January 13, 1950, pp. 1, 3.

[11] Dobrynin, *In Confidence*, pp. 81–90.

NATO countries, which might have seen this as evidence of U.S. unreliability, would have been disastrous.

Less dramatic, incremental progress is also facilitated by secrecy. Statesmen all over the world, in democratic as well as authoritarian countries, are more comfortable when they talk in confidence. They are worried by any prospect that their remarks might become public. Negotiations necessarily involve a give and take. To identify concessions (strategic or tactical) publicly is difficult in a democracy, as it exposes the government to partisan attacks by the opposition. In an authoritarian system where concessions may be seen as ideological compromises, nothing short of heresies, negotiations are more difficult still. Communist, fascist, religious fundamentalist negotiators do at times compromise, not easily, but they do, and only in secret.

Most important though are national security considerations. It is essential that much information about our weapons technologies, our orders of battle, our strategic plans, just to mention a few, are kept secret. Foreign countries, sometimes our friends, are prepared to go to great lengths to spy on us, even to turn our citizens traitors. After World War II some were turned by ideological appeals. America was a fraud; communism and the Soviet Union were the true beacons of morality, which was absurd and over time could be exposed. Nowadays the bait is likely to be money, and money, especially big money, is not likely to go out of fashion.

John A Walker, Jr., warrant officer in the Navy, after 1968 turned over secrets, including naval codes, to the KGB, even recruited his family into spying against his country. He put it succinctly and clearly: "Political belief had nothing to do with it. Spying was business."[12] Jonathan J. Pollard, who worked for naval intelligence, was a somewhat more complicated case. The initiative actually came from the American. "I'm Jewish. I want to help you," he told a startled Israeli officer.[13] Mossad,[14] however, had "no interest in meeting him." It was the Defense Ministry, Office of Scientific Liaison (LAKAM) that established the contact. Pollard met his Israeli controller first on May 29, 1984. He soon passed on reams of classified documents. Some contained information about American weapons systems, but most contained information on the Middle East gathered by American intelligence agencies. Pollard was especially pleased by the Israeli air attack on the PLO headquarters in Tunisia on October 1, 1985. He knew he had

---

[12] *Los Angeles Times*, May 12, 1986, p. 3.

[13] Wolf Blitzer, *Territory of Lies* (New York: Harper & Row, 1989), p. 9.

[14] Israel's intelligence agency.

played a major role in it. It was he who passed along classified American intelligence about the location of Yassir Arafat's headquarters and his secret residence, both of which were demolished. (Arafat was not hurt.) It was Pollard who also provided Israel with information about Libyan and Tunisian air defenses and about the disposition of the U.S., Soviet, and French naval vessels in the area.[15] Afterwards he frequently justified his treason by "moral" explanations, that Israel was not treated fairly "by the American [one would have thought his own] government." All the same, according to Israeli testimony, by July 25, just two months later, he accepted an envelope with $2,000 in cash and three days later a second envelope of $2,000 in cash. Pollard consistently denied this. However, he admitted he was promised "a flat $1500 monthly salary for espionage" and, in fact, was paid $10,000 for services and expenses. In August 1985 Pollard was given an Israeli passport and the number of a Swiss bank account opened for him in the name of Danny Cohen. He was told that "$30,000 would be deposited in the account each year for the next five years. . . . This amount was in addition to the direct cash payments that Pollard received for a total of nearly $50,000, a big chunk of which covered his travel expenses."[16] That, of course, was just the beginning.

If Pollard was a somewhat ambiguous case, Aldrich Ames was not. If the Walkers and Pollard betrayed very important U.S. secrets, Ames, a senior CIA officer, did much more for much more money. He wanted "to level the playing field" by identifying Soviet citizens who were giving us information. To be sure, he had a grievance to tell.

Beginning with TRIGON and later with Arkady Shevchenko, we were getting really good—and I mean first class—political information about the Soviets. We were getting really top-notch military information from Tolkachev and Polyakov, too. I mean we were getting it all. Don't forget we also had our spy satellites sending us back intelligence. And do you know what all this data . . . kept telling us over again and again and again? It told us that we were disproportionately stronger than the Soviet Union and the Warsaw Pact. It told us that Soviet forces couldn't compete with us. The bottom line was that with only the most minor exceptions we were consistently superior militarily to the Soviets . . . everything you could think of—we were light years ahead of them. . . .
I read TRIGON's reports, and those diplomatic cables showed a feeling of helplessness among Soviet policymakers. They believed that they were under terrific pressure. Their cables were filled with statements about how the Soviets felt

---

[15] Blitzer, *Territory of Lies*, pp. 91, 95, 113.
[16] Ibid., p. 102.

that they were losing in every way. . . . And yet Henry Kissinger and Gerald Ford and later the Democrats all blustered about the resurgence in Soviet aggressiveness and military power. . . .

I knew it, and I began to realize that much of what we were doing really was just part of a silly game.[17]

All the same: "Why did I do it? I did it for the money. Period. I am not lying. I wanted the cash."[18] He was in love with a woman, and he was going through a costly divorce. He considered robbing a bank but rejected the idea because that would not gain him enough. So on April 16, 1985, after being fortified by several double vodkas, he walked into the Soviet embassy in Washington, D.C. and gave the guard an envelope addressed to KGB General Stanislav Androsov. In it was a note: "I am Aldrich Ames and my job is branch chief of Soviet counterintelligence at the CIA. I served in New York when I used the alias Andy Robinson. I need $50,000 and in exchange of the money, here is information about three agents we are developing in the Soviet Union right now." In a month (May 17) he had his answer. At the embassy he was handed a note: "We accept your offer. . . . Mr. Chuvakhin is NOT a KGB officer, but . . . he will be able to give you the money and be available to have lunch with you if you care to exchange more messages." Ames was concerned that the room was bugged so he did not speak, but on the back of the note he wrote: "Okay. Thank you very much." That was all there was to it.[19] Several exchanges followed during which Ames betrayed twenty Soviet citizens. Fifteen were executed; five are alive in Russia.

Two days after his first deposit of Soviet money in the bank, Ames read about the arrest of John A. Walker, Jr. It brought him a new justification for his continued treason: fear. "I immediately thought, 'Oh, God, they are going to find out about me too! What I did.'" To minimize that chance, he decided to give the Soviets every CIA "human asset" that he knew about with the exception, he insisted, of two names. Ames's life-style soon changed for the better. On his CIA salary, which did not exceed $68,000 a year, he ran up credit card bills of $50,000. His monthly American Express

---

[17] Pete Earley, *Confessions of a Spy, the Real Story of Aldrich Ames* (New York: G. P. Putnam's Sons, 1997). pp. 84–85.

[18] Ibid., p. 147.

[19] Ibid., p. 139–41. There is something wrong with this part of Ames's story, particularly with the April 16 note. For one thing, neither the FBI nor the CIA believe it. For another thing, during several polygraph tests, the machine indicated that he was "deceptive." Ibid., p. 177.

charges ranged from $18,000 to $30,000. He and his wife also charged thousands of dollars on other credit cards. He paid $540,000 in cash for a home in Arlington, Virginia, and in 1992 he bought a new Jaguar. The FBI estimates that the Soviets and later the Russians paid $2.5 million for Ames's treason.[20]

Walker, Pollard, and Ames, of course, were the big fish caught. There may be others who were not, and quite probably there are many more of lesser significance, perhaps some under surveillance. In August 1993 "FBI agents across the country were investigating allegations by a former KGB employee that many hundreds of Americans and possibly more than 1,000 provided the former Soviet intelligence agency with information in recent years."[21] Ames thought that could be correct, and it fits in fairly well with MI-5 estimates "that there were upward of 200 spies currently active in Britain."[22] Those who had hoped that a more friendly Russia would end its intelligence operations in the United States were rudely awakened on November 21, 1996, when Harold J. Nicholson was indicted for selling national defense information. The traitor, a senior CIA officer, regularly passed to Russian agents information on CIA recruits and training procedures. His take since 1994 was over $180,000. And still another, this time senior FBI agent Earl Edwin Pitts, who was arrested on December 18, 1996. He told persons he thought were Russian intelligence officers, "I have provided you with everything that I was aware of." His haul was $224,000.

Like it or not, we have enemies who want to know about us, all about us, in order to be able to take better advantage of us and to do us harm. It makes no sense to help them. In order to *maximize* the security of our secrets, they should be deprived of all information about us. Since we cannot keep the American people informed without others also listening in, this maximalist position would mean keeping almost all foreign and national security policy information from the American people as well. At the same time, our officials who deal with sensitive information should be required to submit to extraordinary security measures, such as regular lie detector tests. Surely Americans would not put up with such practices.

Finally, a *maximally* effective foreign policy in the international environment requires that we engage vigorously in broad-range efforts to

---

[20] *Los Angeles Times,* April 20, 1994, p. A1.

[21] Ibid., August 18, 1993, p. A13.

[22] Peter Wright, *Spy Catcher, the Candid Autobiography of a Senior Intelligence Officer* (New York: Viking, 1987), p. 345.

get all the intelligence information possible about practically all countries in the world. When we do not, the consequences can be serious. In the 1970s our government decided to rely on the Iranian SAVAK for intelligence about the stability of the shah's regime. Our policy was a failure. In 1983 American students had to be rescued from Grenada, but our military operations were seriously handicapped by the absence of reliable maps of the island. During the Watergate era congressional investigators weakened the CIA and some CIA members went public. Worse still the CIA director, Stansfield Turner, thought it wise to concentrate on technical means (for example, satellites) and neglected to place agents under deep cover. The consequences were disastrous. We had insufficient assets for learning in time the predatory plans of terrorists.

When we do get sufficient intelligence, it can make quite a difference. In October 1962 with multifaceted intelligence (ground assets and U-2 spy plane reconnaissance) President Kennedy became convinced in the nick of time that the Soviets were deploying offensive missiles in Cuba. He could thus thwart their adventure toward hegemony. In general, through a well-developed Central Intelligence Agency we can more accurately gauge the dimensions of a crisis and improve the rationality of our response. We do not want to overreact, but we cannot afford to underestimate the dangers.

On August 18, 1991, a coup was in progress in the Soviet Union. We had warnings. When Richard Nixon visited Moscow in March 1991, he was surprised that many of Gorbachev's closest associates were freely discussing the probability of the Soviet president's overthrow. Indeed, according to Nixon's notes, he was even told the name of the chief plotter: Vladimir A. Kryuchkov, head of the KGB. Needless to say, he passed this information on to the White House. Then on June 20, 1994, John Matlock, American ambassador in Moscow, sent a top-secret message reporting the imminence of a coup. His source was Kryuchkov himself. Presumably the conspirators were testing the international waters. (Secretary of State Baker personally passed along the warning to the Soviet foreign minister without any visible effect.) Less than two months later suspicions intensified when spy satellites orbiting over Gorbachev's Crimean retreat reflected evidence that his Volga limousine was still in place after he was supposed to have departed and that an unusually high number of armed guards had surrounded the building. About the same time, I believe, a deep cover agent in Kazakhstan—Aldrich Ames had burned all the CIA assets in Moscow—flashed a message to Langley, Virginia, that the coup had actually begun. Thus, while the people in Moscow were still going about their business ignorant of unfolding events, the president of the United States was quite well informed.

On short notice most European leaders, including prominently President Mitterand of France and Foreign Minister Genscher of Germany, were scrambling to find out who the "new leaders" were and hoping to establish a working relationship with them. Most American scholars, newspaper editors, and members of Congress were inclined to take the same line. President Bush did not. He publicly condemned the action. Although Soviet power shifts had a habit of succeeding, he made an emphatic point that coups do fail. In the ensuing hectic days he had intelligence that pointed to the vulnerability of the coup leaders, for example, the doubtful support from the security forces.[23] He also knew the strong and effective resistance of the Russian government's leadership with Boris Yeltsin, Ruslan Khasbulatov, head of the Russian Supreme Soviet, and Anatoly Sobchak, mayor of Leningrad. He had a variety of sources; curiously they included the fax system of the U.S. Information Agency. The bottom line is this: Had President Bush lacked the intelligence resources that helped him gain a fairly accurate assessment of the realities in Moscow, he might not have been able to resist the general trend. And had he gone along with the assumption of a *fait accompli*, quite possibly the assumption would have become the reality. And then, where would we be now?

One caveat: our intelligence organization has to be especially well developed so that it can effectively sort out the quality of information. Acting on unreliable reports is no better than acting on ignorance; indeed it may be worse. A story told by a long-time Soviet ambassador to Washington illustrates the point.[24] The day President Kennedy alerted the nation to secret Soviet efforts to install intermediate-range ballistic missiles in Cuba and the world teetered on the brink of nuclear war, it was vital that policy mistakes be avoided. On that day, October 22, 1962, as it happened, the Soviets arrested Oleg Penkovsky, a colonel in Military Intelligence who had provided secret information to the United States. His American handlers had allotted him two coded telephone signals, one indicating the danger of his immediate arrest and the other warning of an imminent Soviet attack on the United States. Before his arrest Penkovsky had several minutes to send a signal. He chose to send the second signal. His CIA handlers, however, did not pass this information along to the president. Just imagine what would have happened if during the perilous confrontation, the

---

[23] Anatoly Sobchak, *For a New Russia* (New York: Free Press, 1992), pp. 175–82.

[24] Dobrynin, *In Confidence*, p. 81n.

national decision-makers, engaged in a desperate effort to avoid war, had been told that the Soviet Union was about to launch an attack on us.

THE EXIGENCIES OF THE DOMESTIC ENVIRONMENT

In sharp contrast, the demands of our own polity keep pushing in the opposite direction. Part of the problem is our tradition of complacency marked by a wait-and-see attitude. The inward orientation of Americans is exacerbated by the confidence that if any major international crisis of direct relevance to us were to arise, we would have ample time to develop successful responses. We did, in fact, have time in World War I, in World War II, and just recently in the Gulf War. We had time to prepare and solve even such gigantic troubles. There is no need for America to keep looking for future difficulties, no need at all to become an international busybody.

Another part of the problem is our habitual self-centeredness. When most Americans look beyond our borders, out of pride or ignorance, they simply extend with confidence and idealism their perceptions of our domestic reference base. We have a community at home, or so we like to think. Therefore, we see a community on the outside. We speak as a matter of course of an international community. Our citizens (most of them anyway) relate to each other within the framework of the rule of law. We hopefully assume that beyond our borders sovereign states do so as well. We speak of international law, international morality, international public opinion as rules of restraint and standards of conduct, and most of us believe this. Projecting our own conditions, we consider negotiation, bargaining, and compromise, not violence and coercion, the proper means of settling disputes. We are most reluctant to consider our world an arena.

A foreign policy that is *most sensitive* to public opinion needs to recognize *that military considerations are no longer fashionable* in America. The number of senators and congressmen who have served in the armed forces is steadily declining. The number of professors or media stars who did so, and did so without rancor, is rapidly approaching zero. Few people can now remember an experience with a good and victorious war. Even the recent Persian Gulf conflict arouses few positive emotions. Fewer still consider military service as a patriotic duty. Recruits apparently have to be bribed by rewards of special educational opportunities and *money*. Americans share a profound wish that reason should prevail and that all human conflict *can and must* be settled by negotiation and compromise. Suspicion prevails that our armed forces ought to be kept at the minimum necessary for defense and that they bear watching. Otherwise we would spend most of our treasure on unnecessary armaments and be all too prone to project force overseas into undeserving conflicts in irrelevant parts of the globe.

For foreign policy to *gain and retain maximum public support*, moreover, it *must be conducted openly*. Most Americans recognize that our government must have secrets and that it cannot deny information to others without keeping it from the American people as well. All the same, the American people do not like to be systematically kept in the dark; opinion leaders thoroughly resent secrets, and they can no longer be ignored. Pressure groups with vested interests in special foreign policy decisions are too well connected and too deeply embedded. If anything, they can be expected to multiply and become more vocal. News reporters with all their biases, brashness, errors, and excesses are highly competent in gathering news and too highly valued to be brought under government control. Academics with all their abstruse theories, floods of verbiage, and even peculiar personal styles have developed sophisticated analytical methods and improved their societal influence. And Congress is not likely to resume its former docility. Any member of the National Security Council staff who thinks he can keep secrets from the Senate or the House and exclude them from participating in foreign policy decisions will soon find himself on television. In other words, the toothpaste is out of the tube; we cannot put it back.

Incidentally, most Americans feel quite uncomfortable about our massive foreign intelligence operations. The country has come a long way since 1929 when Secretary of State Henry L. Stimson closed down the department's code breaking agency with the words: "Gentlemen do not read each other's mail."[25] Nevertheless since they consider others' spying on us or trying to subvert our citizens as bad, by a kind of visceral logic they cannot easily consider our spying on others and subverting their citizens as good.

So the question arises: are the demands of the external environment and those of the domestic environment altogether irreconcilable? If they are, we face an impossible situation. Since, however much we wish it, we cannot ignore the outside world, the clash will, as it did in the recent past, chew up presidents and produce a wildly fluctuating foreign policy, leaving most people abroad and at home in uncertainty about our intentions. There ought to be alternatives. We ought to try to develop an approach that may be less than maximally effective abroad and less than maximally popular

---

[25] Henry L. Stimson, *On Active Service in Peace and War* (New York: Harper & Brothers, 1947), p. 188.

at home but possibly achieve an optimal balance of being effective enough abroad and popular enough at home.

TOWARD A CONSENSUS ON NATIONAL INTEREST

In our search for a successful reconciliation between our international challenges and our cherished values, we shall have to give much thought to new policy-making arrangements. Within the Executive a reassessment of the proper role of the State Department is in order. Experimentation with interdepartmental committees could prove helpful. Limits on the National Security Council's role in directing covert operations are obviously necessary. Even so, it seems wise to increase this Council's capacity to generate fresh approaches and innovative ideas and above all to help design an overall strategy. Regarding relations between the branches we may have seen some progress recently. Still more work is needed to accomplish a satisfactory arrangement that would assure (1) that Congress is consulted early in the process, and (2) that Congress refrains from using its constitutional power over the purse to manage, even micromanage, the president's constitutional prerogatives in the conduct of foreign policy. That its members should give up their opportunity to grandstand is probably too much to expect.

New ideas and more work are also needed to overcome the recent predisposition of opinion leaders to take an adversary position to presidential decisions. It might involve informal but persistent cultivation of interpersonal relations or, as President Nixon suggested, a more formal council composed of a broad selection of influential members in the private sector. A group that would meet regularly (e.g., twice a month) to consider in confidence foreign policy issues of the president's choosing could build valuable bridges, in addition to providing him with a further dimension of advice. All these are very important questions and need to be addressed.

The point, however, is this. None of these revisions and innovations in the decision-making process will help much unless we can find a common set of basic assumptions upon which the deliberations among the branches of government and the public dialogue rest. If any member of Congress, any newspaper pundit or television commentator, any professor, any special interest lobbyist, any citizen who decides to make a pronouncement may properly choose his or her own private criteria based on his or her own particular values, the discussion is apt to produce more heat than light. We need to restore and build an active *consensus*, at a minimum a concurrent majority, among the executive branch, the Congress, and private opinion-leading groups on the basic principles of *our national interest*.

It will not be easy. One problem is that the American people have only a vague notion that national interest is a good thing and a proper standard for foreign policy. A much bigger problem is that the government much prefers it that way. The concept of national interest is too valuable to government as an instrument of *postpolicy mobilization*. By leaving it vague, it could be fitted to suit any course decided upon. From the very beginning of the Republic, policy came first, and then it was (or was not) sold to the people by proclaiming it to be our national interest. By leaving it vague, moreover, it could be fitted to reflect lofty, inspiring absolutes: our manifest destiny, the tenets of Christian faith, or the will of God. Whenever publicly proclaimed by the government, American national interest by a remarkable and felicitous coincidence was always identical with the dictates of moral law. The American people expected it and would have accepted nothing less.[26]

The traditional approach may have served its purpose in the past, and it did mobilize popular support behind policy. In our time, however, there are at least two things wrong with it. First, it is prone to mistreat the American people. Once a decision is made by the government, citizens are called upon to close ranks promptly and blindly support it with no time at all for a general discussion of the pros and cons. For an American it is disturbing enough to be presented with an accomplished fact, a decision made by an exclusive government group. But when it is cloaked in national interest reinforced by moral imperative to make it unassailable, when the polity is confronted with a choice reduced to acquiescence or feeling unpatriotic and immoral, it provokes a vague, and soon not so vague, feeling of discomfort in many citizens of our Republic.

Second, national interest, an instrument of postpolicy mobilization, is not without pitfalls for the government. To be sure, in case of severe national peril no debate is necessary. Pearl Harbor effectively ended it all. Mass support will naturally follow. Few Americans would doubt that the existence of the United States is worth defending. There are, however, only very few international problems that genuinely threaten our national existence. Most of them present less drastic dangers where public opinion has no instinctive response. Public debate is necessary and useful, but it runs the risk that it may not reach the same conclusion as government. Concerned with this contingency, decision-makers are apt to resort to a shortcut: sound a patriotic note and redefine the issue as a threat to our

---

[26] For historical examples of the uses of national interest as an instrument of postpolicy mobilization see: von Vorys, *American National Interest*, pp. 12–14.

national survival (e.g., the domino theory). When told by our government that our vital interests are at stake, the nation will respond. It will unite behind policy. But here is the problem.

Once public support is given, even if enthusiastically given, a timer will start ticking. Their attention attracted, the American people will look closer at the issues and official justifications. The media will cover them; the academics will examine them, each from his own perspective, each with his own standards and interest. The process will take time and periodically could be distracted by good news, but sooner or later this democratic scrutiny will expose the excesses of the official position. The claim: it was a good cause, the danger was real, but it had to be exaggerated to get public attention and support, cannot prove convincing. The timer keeps ticking and winding down; popular support declines. Public confidence not only in the policy, but far worse in the integrity of the government itself, is steadily impaired. To illustrate the point. The Nazi menace was a peril to our civilization and a mortal challenge to our friends in Europe, but there was no chance at all that the German forces, which could not cross the Channel, would invade America. Even so, the government insisted that the danger was acute. Volunteers watched our coasts. We "blacked-out" our cities at night and collected "pots and pans for victory." World War II was clearly a "good war"; the enemy was evil, no question about that. We fought for the right, we won glorious victories, and we had relatively few casualties. Still the reaction had set in. In the very first congressional elections the president's party lost both houses to the Republicans. Soon a congressional committee began investigating the causes of the war, then found considerable fault with our president, even raising the specter of official deception. It was no coincidence that Congress passed and the states hastily ratified the Twenty-second Amendment limiting the president to two elected terms.

Similarly communist aggression in Vietnam may have been a serious challenge to international order, but there was no chance that it could improve the Soviet strategic threat. Even so, public officials spoke of dominoes, which, once falling there, would soon knock us down here. As the military buildup intensified in Southeast Asia, American people at home lined up behind the president. The Gallop Poll reported the ratio of favorable to unfavorable public reaction to be: 50:28 in January 1965, 52:26 in April 1965, and 64:21 in October 1965.

Vietnam was never a good war. It was an example of good intentions going awry. For a while it was perceived as a necessary military action. Within two years, however, public support was rapidly eroding. By July 1967, according to the Gallop Poll, 41 percent of Americans considered our military involvement there a mistake with 48 percent still supporting it. By October of the same year those who thought it was a mistake were in the majority (46:44), and President Johnson had lost his credibility. By January 1969 when his successor took office, the opponents were in a heavy majority (52:39). In April 1971 when people were asked whether they thought that President Nixon was telling all they should know about Vietnam, 24 percent answered yes, 67 percent said no. Confidence in the presidency as an institution was badly shaken as well.

In short, given the past record it is not surprising that there is skepticism about the contributions of the concept of national interest to public policy. All the same, our foreign policy conundrum may be resolved by trying a fresh approach to national interest. First, instead of its being defined in the highest councils of government, national interest will need to be developed by the polity at large. Second, instead of its being used by government postpolicy as an instrument of public mobilization, it will need to become a *publicly set prepolicy standard.*

We must not have any illusions. It is most unlikely that we can through public dialogue and compromise develop a consensus on every aspect of our foreign policy. Our society is too diverse for that; our people are too busy to pay attention to all the goings on in all the various countries in the world. All we might be able to achieve with much effort is a consensus on a common general framework. Surely this would be valuable. For it would make possible effective foreign policy decisions by the president that would be backed by public support, and it would provide a reliable and predictable standard by which government actions could be evaluated. It could provide the parameters within which the president could be free to determine just which of his proper options would best serve our national interest. He could have flexibility in negotiations, even keep secrets—*within this framework and within the appropriate range of options.* In this contract on honor, the administration could count on the support of our democratic system as long as its foreign policy is successful *and* as long as it does not transgress the parameters of the understanding. If new circumstances would require new options, the administration would be bound to seek a new understanding.

The Carter administration intended to move along this road by making "a major investment in educating the public . . . [on] the difference between the interest of the nation as a whole and the interests of particular subconstituencies and interest groups."[27] In turn, President Reagan regularly explained his own views of the world and our interest in it. His administra-

---

[27] Quoted: Ibid., p. 7.

tion made an especially significant attempt to build consensus on the relatively new and vexing problem of international terrorism.

Enormous progress was made along these lines, but then the Reagan administration crossed the boundaries of consensus in the secret mining of Nicaraguan harbors, the arms-for-hostages deal, and the illegal diversion of government funds to the Contras. The chorus of censure ran the full gamut of the American political spectrum. Indeed in the Iran-Contra hearings, Congress made a major contribution: an increased popular awareness of the central problem of conducting effective foreign policy only with means acceptable to our democratic society. And popular awareness leading to vigorous public discussion in a democracy usually helps in the search for a solution.

It is not, and should not be, the task of the government alone to build a consensus on American national interest. In such an effort all opinion-leading groups, all Americans, have a role to play. The time has come for a great debate on foreign policy. Not like the one we had on Vietnam, in which we argued about specific decisions regarding a particular country, in which we pointed a finger in righteous indignation about past mistakes upsetting and dividing the nation. What would serve us well is a broad-based and thorough discussion now in relatively tranquil times about the realities of our international environment and our proper and popularly preferred posture to them. In the process we may develop a *prepolicy standard* of national interest, one which is not vague and ambiguous, but offers an identifiable structure. It should define for some time to come: first, challenges to our vital interests, our national existence; second, challenges to our special interest, our friends and allies; and third, challenges to our general interests, international order. In turn, it should identify and classify the *range* of appropriate policy options. We have some interests for which we should be ready to fight; we have some interests for which we should be willing to pay; we have some interests for which we should be prepared to work; and we have some interests that should warn us to leave some international problems alone. Before proceeding constructively along these lines, however, it would serve us well to take stock of where we are and review how we got here.

5

National Security

Building a domestic consensus for a framework of our foreign policy may best begin by reaffirming a self-evident truth: for all Americans regardless of their diverse backgrounds and diverse orientations the secure existence of the United States is an altogether nonnegotiable commitment. It is never in our national interest to be subjugated by a foreign power. It is never in our national interest to voluntarily delegate or transfer to any foreign country or international organization our right to control our internal affairs and our right to conduct our foreign policy according to our own purposes.

This does not mean that a national focus of orientation shuts out the universalist perspective. A foreign policy conducted according to our own purposes definitely does not mean that we may callously disregard the interests of mankind. Sensitivity and concern for the needs of our fellow human beings throughout the world are in the best tradition of the American people. In order to help, we have been prepared to bear many burdens and make many sacrifices. We have been driven by altruism or motivated by enlightened self-interest. Still, in our national interest these sacrifices must stop short of sacrificing the United States for any purpose however exalted. We had better be clear on this to others and to ourselves.

Nor does the preeminence of our national community delegitimize the personal and group perspective. The individual is a very cherished value in democracy. Indeed he or she is the *raison d'être*, the essence of the logic of popular sovereignty. That a person should pursue his own personal happiness is an inalienable right. That he could do it through free associations is constitutionally guaranteed. The standard of national interest does not contradict or threaten these values—unless they are projected into the extreme. For this right, like all rights, is not absolute. Special interest groups may lobby vigorously but the line must be drawn when they seek to dominate and try to impose their special concerns on all others. Individual rights are limited by the rights of other individuals, and they cannot be constitutionally pushed to deny the national community its right, when its very existence is in peril, to properly demand the sacrifice of individual happiness, even individual life. The contention "better red than dead" may have merit in some private logic but is repugnant to the standard of national interest. On this too, we had better be clear to others and to ourselves.

In the past the imperative of national security has generally been of little concern to us. We were busy with many other things; besides we simply took it for granted that we were safe. It was a reasonable assumption. Two vast oceans protected much of our borders; two more or less friendly, but in any case far weaker, countries were our neighbors. God was in His Heaven; the major powers were far away and otherwise preoccupied.

The threat of aggression has changed fundamentally. Our vulnerability to attack from a major power is no longer a rare, occasional problem. It is not one that will just go away, not one we can solve by a stroke of genius or remove by bold action. The problem will remain for a long time. The best we can do is to learn to live with it—by successfully coping with it.

Worse still, the potential consequences of being attacked have also changed fundamentally. The airburst of a one-megaton bomb "burns out" sixty square miles and destroys or radically deforms human life over a much larger area. For example, such a bomb detonated 8,500 feet above the Empire State Building "would glut or flatten almost every building between Battery Park and 125th Street, . . . and would heavily damage buildings between the northern tip of Staten Island and the George Washington Bridge." The heat would be great enough to melt metal and glass from Greenwich Village to Central Park and to ignite all readily inflammable materials in all five boroughs and west to the Passaic River in New Jersey. A lethal radioactive fallout would almost immediately cover an area 15 miles wide and 150 miles long, depending on the wind, from New York City to Wilmington, Delaware. Sublethal fallout, which could still cause serious illness and birth defects, would extend another 150 miles downwind, perhaps to Washington, DC. A single one-megaton bomb.[1]

The Soviet Union had an estimated 32,000 nuclear warheads. Russia still has at least 20,000, some smaller but others larger than one megaton. Several other countries are busily building deliverable nuclear warheads;

---

[1] Jonathan Schell, *The Fate of the Earth* (New York: Alfred A. Knopf, 1982), pp. 47–51.

still other nations are in the process of trying secretly to develop them. Simple arithmetic quickly reveals the stark reality. For the first time in our history we are now vulnerable to attack that could effectively destroy our national existence: most of our people, much of our country, and our entire way of life. As a result, the traditional policy of maintaining just sufficient capacity to *defeat* aggression while not irrelevant is no longer acceptable. *To deter aggression* has become the prime requirement of national interest. *Surely we can all agree on that.*

How can we avoid becoming targets of aggression? This is a vital question that raises complicated issues with considerable areas of controversy. Some of the technical details, of course, are best left to the experts to debate, but if we take a closer look at the problem we find three identifiable preconditions to aggression. First, aggression requires *hostility*. It stands to reason that people or states would not attack unless they wanted to do so and that takes a powerful urge. Second, aggression requires *capability*. An enemy must be able to do serious harm to its victim. This depends fundamentally on direct access to the latter's national territory and may explain why in international relations neighbors rarely have developed lasting friendship. Indeed it has become part of conventional wisdom that my neighbor is my enemy, my neighbor's neighbor is my friend. It also may be the reason why most countries historically sought to protect themselves with natural barriers, such as swift rivers or high mountain ranges, or by weak, preferably neutral or neutralized neighbors. Capability also depends on an exportable surplus of coercive capacity, the military forces an aggressor can bring to bear upon its target. Napoleon's armies were a formidable might, but their capability to attack England was nil. He no doubt wanted to attack but could not. England was safe after Trafalgar. Napoleon knew it too. Thus, capability for aggression begins when the level and composition of the aggressor's forces are sufficient to overcome any physical barriers to access. It becomes significant when they can challenge the defensive forces and decisive when they can overwhelm them. Finally, aggression requires *utility*. Wanting to attack and being able to do so may together produce a powerful temptation, but as a practical matter it will rarely if ever prove irresistible unless the aggressor expects to gain by aggression. The gain may be sheer aggrandizement in the form of material benefits (better access to raw materials, markets, or cheap labor force, perhaps rich plunder) or in the form of power and prestige. No less significantly the gain may be defensive, the successful elimination of the constant anxiety of a perceived threat. But gain there must be. Few people and fewer governments would embark on aggression that they know would end in defeat or produce costs that would prove to be ruinous. Each of these preconditions may provide a policy focus. If any one of them could be prevented, aggression would be deterred. They are worth considering.

HOSTILITY

As a country and as a people America and Americans have a relatively favorable image abroad. In most places people are curious and pleased to meet visitors from the United States. A few may find Americans puzzling, difficult, and even offensive at times but are usually impressed by our open friendliness. American acquaintances are often discussed and regularly quoted. Even in countries where government actively discourages it, people are attracted to the cultural and consumption patterns in the United States. American forms of entertainment, even social styles, are emulated; American consumer products are at a premium. Many people from all walks of life want to visit and would love to emigrate to the United States. Thus, there is a receptiveness to positive actions by the U.S. government. It seems simple enough. If we could just keep people from becoming hostile to us, we could live in peace.

Actually it is not quite as simple as that. Unfortunately, and we must admit this candidly, America's image also has negative aspects. To begin with, the global appeal of our culture runs roughshod over the ethnocentric values and ascriptive hierarchies of billions of people in Africa and Asia. They get comfort from routinely following their own long-established rules of right and wrong, norms that they apply asymmetrically to those in and outside the community. They are bound by age-old classifications of their traditional hierarchies. It is not at all our intention, but we confuse them. Worse still we tempt them, tempt them most awfully with our standard of living and alien methods of democracy. When they succumb, and very often they do succumb, they feel guilty perhaps but certainly insecure. Their leaders feel resentful and hostile. Some deride the United States as a rotten, decadent, and exploitive system or castigate it as the "Great Satan." Their righteousness moves many to a fanatical defense of their own causes and not just a few to a passionate hatred of America.

Second, our quality of life, which people admire all over the world, also has a negative by-product. About a billion and a half of our fellow men in Asia, Africa, and Latin America live under conditions of relative poverty, and another billion exist in abject, absolute poverty where the human animal can subsist but rational man has no chance to function. Being aware of our phenomenal standard of living, they want to share in it. They resent that as yet they have not shared in it and that there is little chance that they in their lifetimes, probably their children in *their* lifetimes, will share in it.

They have little patience with explanations, all the more so as they observe that Americans, while they zestfully enjoy their marvelous material benefits and comforts, also loudly proclaim to all the world their devotion to human equality. Billions believe that they have a grievance, that they have a right to a new economic order. Their own political leaders often are pleased to promote this view. The last thing they want are popular grievances directed at themselves. Much better to point the finger at an external culprit. Foreign exploitation, "American imperialism."

Curiously the end of the Cold War made it all worse. The demise of the Soviet Union left the United States as the only superpower. Shortly thereafter our awesome power even in conventional forces was dramatically demonstrated by the Gulf War. The American people really have no intention of attacking anyone, and our government regularly proclaims our purest motives and our friendliest intentions. Even so, most people know that if at any time we would choose to project our military might, we could do so with catastrophic consequences for them. Instinctively they are disturbed by their own helplessness. During the Cold War many people felt reassured when the Americans were challenged by an aggressive Soviet Union. That there might actually be a balance was a comforting thought. It liberated them from the necessity of constantly playing up to the Americans. It was fascinating to observe the average "intellectual" in India enthusiastically applauding *Sputnik*. Here at last was evidence that the almighty Americans could be beaten after all. Thus, it is well to keep in mind that we are admired abroad but also envied; we are respected abroad but also resented.

CAPABILITY

If we cannot be sure of preventing people from wanting to hurt us, we must try to prevent them from being able to do so. The United States has been extraordinarily fortunate in its geopolitical location. Our northern and southern neighbors were weaker states that did not have a significant capability of aggression. To the east and west we were protected by vast oceans. In the past only the greatest powers had any capability of harming us, and they presented only a peripheral threat. Great Britain could reach our shores, but she was a friend; indeed throughout the nineteenth century she was our protector. Japan could bomb Pearl Harbor but could not land even on Midway. The Germans could do even less: they could sink some of our ships at sea, that was all.

Scientific breakthroughs developing nuclear weapons and long-range strategic delivery systems made the problem acute for us. The question arose: just what could be done to moderate, if not eliminate, the *existing* capability of a superpower to do us mortal harm? In the 1970s and 1980s the answer was partially arms control, even arms reduction negotiations. The theory ran along these lines. Since we cannot compel the Soviet Union through military force to give up its capability of doing us serious, even mortal harm, it is imperative that we make every diplomatic effort to persuade her to do so voluntarily. This means hard bargaining and predictably substantial sacrifices in our own military capabilities. If we could succeed, even if we would have to give up most of our own strategic capabilities in exchange, we would still have made a marvelous bargain: we would trade our capacity to destroy them, something we never had any intention of doing, for their capacity to destroy us, which we feared they had every intention of doing. We could once again enjoy the conditions of an America fully secure in its national existence. Unfortunately our reality was not quite as simple as that. Had we entirely disregarded other salient components of our national interest, such as the security of our allies, and concentrated single-mindedly on our national existence, the rationale of disarmament would still have had serious flaws.

The heart of the problem is what we may call the uncertainty: risk factor. Given the enormous stakes of national survival no country can afford to take any risks. Each *at a minimum* must be certain (1) of the other's position, (2) of the sincerity of the other's intentions, and (3) of its own capability to discover all the other's relevant, even covert actions.

This kind of certainty is difficult among major powers. It becomes elusive when at least one of them is an authoritarian and/or totalitarian system. For authoritarian governments are inclined to regard their own special interest as a *non plus ultra*, an end that would justify all means. Treaties could be summarily dismissed as "ein fetzen Papier," a slip of paper.[2] They could be unilaterally reinterpreted or canceled at will. Worse still, where a totalitarian government exercises anything approaching effective control over the polity, the economy, and the society, the possibility of secret decisions to break out of treaty commitments covertly carried out is a demonstrated practical possibility. The risks of relying on their oral and/or written commitments would increase enormously.

Without the minimal requirements of certainty each would need a positive margin of weapons over the other commensurate to its risks, just to make sure. Authoritarian/totalitarian governments dealing with

---

[2] A phrase used by the German chancellor describing the treaty neutralizing Belgium when in August 1914 Germany decided to violate it.

democratic systems would seek a significant margin; democratic governments dealing with authoritarian/totalitarian systems, a very much wider
margin. With each needing a positive edge and determining that any
arrangement should perpetuate such an edge, the equation is mathemati-
cally and diplomatically insoluble.

Our ventures to negotiate arms control agreements with the Soviet
Union kept constantly butting up against this barrier. It was not so much
that most Americans did not trust the Soviets, and we did not,[3] but rather
that we, our people *and* our government, did not know much about them.
We really did not know how their leaders made decisions, just how, for
example, Gorbachev gained his ascendancy. We did not know whether the
course he announced was no more than a tactical maneuver (as was Lenin's
New Economic Policy) or a genuine long-term commitment. We may wish
to trust, explained President Reagan, but we must verify. Indeed in 1996 we
had no accurate knowledge about President Yeltsin's health, and we still
could not be sure to what extent the Russians could be relied upon to fulfill
their treaty obligations.

Worse still, what we did know in the 1960s, '70s, and '80s did not
ameliorate, but actually exacerbated, uncertainty. We knew that the Soviet
Union possessed an advanced system of science and technology. Although
in the past it had rarely originated a new weapons system, we could not
assume that it was unable to do so. We had to keep constantly in mind that
they might accomplish a breakthrough in arms technology and if they so
chose, they could break out of any arms control treaty.

We also knew that normative and structural asymmetries between us
gave them enormous advantages for a *clandestine* breakout and rapid
buildup. The Soviet Union was a closed society. It went to unprecedented
extremes to keep the rest of the world from learning anything but the
official version of itself. Its values were ideologically determined; its
causes justified any means. Its government was authoritarian; decisions
were made in strictest secrecy, but once they were announced, all people
were compelled to obey promptly and unquestioningly. Its economy was

---

[3] Since the 1950s the Gallup Poll found consistently that a large majority of
Americans had an unfavorable attitude, often very unfavorable attitude, to the
Soviet Union. For example, to the question: "Do you think the USSR is doing all
it can to keep the peace of the world?" 84 percent in November 1981 and 81
percent in November 1984 answered "no." George H. Gallup, *The Gallup Poll:
Public Opinion, 1983* (Wilmington, DE: Scholarly Resources, Inc., 1984), pp.
78–79, 227.

centrally planned, capable of shifting priorities and resources from civilian consumption to military purposes without public notice and within a short time.

We tried to negotiate all kinds of safeguards, aerial or radar surveillance, verification by on-site inspections. After a long and tiresome process there still was no way that we could eliminate altogether the uncertainty that the Soviets might break out and violate an arms control or arms reduction agreement. All this was very depressing.

Curiously about two decades ago in the midst of all the hostility and frustration, conditions were beginning to change for the better. Conventional wisdom at the time held and popular opinion firmly believed that the higher the level of arms, the higher the insecurity produced by uncertainty. This is true enough up to a point. In the late 1960s, however, this point was crossed by the United States, and what is more relevant here, by the Soviet Union.

The strategic capabilities of the two superpowers had moved beyond the level where each could destroy the other and had crossed the threshold into the qualitatively different realm of overkill. Very large stockpiles of long-range missiles and nuclear warheads, so the theory goes, need not exacerbate uncertainty; paradoxically they may actually mitigate the risks. In the realm of mutual and multiple overkill decisive breakthroughs that would fundamentally change the balance of capabilities have become much less likely. There is not much point in building more missiles and more nuclear warheads if all we would gain is a capability to destroy the Soviet Union, not three times but four or five times over. In turn, there was not much risk in trading capabilities if the worst that could happen in case they broke out of the treaty was that instead of killing us twice over they could do so four, five, even ten times over. After the first time we would not feel a thing. Here then is the paradox: treaties providing for massive arms reductions, which would take us back below the overkill boundary would entail extravagant risks for us. At the same time treaties that contain arms levels still above overkill would jeopardize neither side and save public expenditures for both.

UTILITY

This leads to the third requirement for aggression: cost:benefit calculation. No leader, no country would embark on a predatory adventure if they were not confident that they could win, indeed if they knew that in the end they would be much worse off. Thus, it follows that aggression may be prevented by a prudent military preparedness.

Actually once again it is not quite as simple as that. Cost:benefit calculations in case of national policy (ours, as well as those of a potential aggressor) are not based on some rational, universal standard, but on more particular societal values. We in our democratic system, for example, place a great value on the individual, his or her life and well-being. But this is a very unusual position. Throughout much of history most people have believed, indeed even today most people still believe, that the individual is an instrument of the state and that personal interest must always be subordinated to the collective good. "You cannot make an omelet without breaking some eggs," we hear regularly from apologists of revolutionary bloodbaths. According to Soviet sources, not necessarily the most reliable on the subject, Chairman Mao was quite prepared to sacrifice millions of human lives, including millions of Chinese lives, in a nuclear war. The next war, he explained to Chairman Khrushchev, will kill 300 million Chinese, 200 million Russians, and 200 million Americans. It will leave a few Russians, a few Americans, and 300 million Chinese! Krushchev was appalled and told this story to President Kennedy at their summit in Vienna.

Even among democratic countries human life is not always cherished to the same extent. In 1983 when over 241 U.S. Marines were killed in their billets in Beirut, Lebanon, a similar attack on a French paratroop barracks cost fifty-nine casualties. The loss for both countries was roughly proportional. Americans were shocked; Congress and the media were inflamed. The French accepted it more philosophically. *C'est la guerre*. The point is that in our efforts to identify just what is an unacceptable price in human lives for a potential aggressor, we cannot simply project to them what we would consider an unacceptable price for us. Others' tolerance of human casualties may well be very much higher. What is unacceptable for us may even seem a bargain to some.

This problem is exacerbated by the fact that decision-making is never a wholly rational process, and in times of crisis the forces driving irrationality are especially rampant. The stakes—war, the survival of the country, that of the human race—are usually incomprehensible. The pressures, often formulated in "no choice" terms, are unbelievable. The time within which a decision must be taken—if it is not, that itself becomes a decision—is pitifully short. Deliberation is quickly reduced to a few tense men, then to still fewer, still more tense and tired men, creating an environment ripe for miscalculation. Only wholly unambiguous evidence recognizable even to an unstable, fanatical mind that no attack upon the United States under any circumstances can possibly yield any profit, and if attempted there surely will be hell to pay, can assure us successful deterrence.

This may be the place to consider the piquant possibility of *self-deterrence*, the possibility that major nuclear powers may be restrained not just by the others, but by their own nuclear capabilities. According to calculations by a group of prominent scientists widely publicized by Dr. Carl Sagan, the detonation of 500 to 2000 nuclear warheads would predictably induce a climatic catastrophe: a long, stark, dark, freezing nuclear winter. To quote the conclusion of the distinguished biologists who met to assess these calculations:

Species extinction could be expected for most tropical plants and animals, and for most terrestrial vertebrates of more temperate regions, a large number of plants, and numerous freshwater and some marine organisms. . . . Whether any people would be able to persist for long in the face of highly modified biological communities; novel climates; high levels of radiation; shattered agricultural, social and economic systems; extraordinary psychological stresses; and a host of other difficulties is open to question. . . . Coupled with the direct casualties of perhaps two billion people, the combined intermediate and long-term effects of nuclear war suggest that eventually there might be no human survivors in the Northern Hemisphere.[4]

Dr. Sagan's purpose, of course, was to emphasize the need to reduce strategic nuclear arms well below the "threshold" of 500 warheads, but there is another implication of these calculations as well. In the late 1980s the United States and the Soviet Union each had well over 2000 strategic targets, such as missile launchers, bomber bases, and command and communications centers. Assuming that for a successful first strike an aggressor must assign at least one warhead but for many strategic targets it probably must use two or more warheads, we quickly reach a total of 3000 warheads, far above the number predicted to induce a "climatic catastrophe." This does not include any warheads to be detonated over cities and economic targets. And this does not include any warheads fired by the victim in retaliation. In other words, a Soviet surprise attack on us, even so fantastically successful that the United States could not or would not retaliate with a single nuclear warhead, would nevertheless have created such changes in the ecosystem of the Northern Hemisphere that the people of the Soviet Union would have surely been destroyed as well—not in a quick, blinding flash, but after a slower, painful agony.

---

[4] P. R. Erlich, M. A. Harnwell, Peter H. Raven, Carl Sagan, G. W. Woodwell, et al., "The Long-Term Biological Consequences of Nuclear War," *Science*, vol. 222 (December 23, 1983), p. 1299.

Theoretical calculations by respected scientists, it goes without saying, deserve deference. Speculations about their practical implications in turn are quite appropriate and can be fascinating, but scientists' calculations at times are conjectural and have their own uncertainties. It is even conceivable that at times, perish the thought, they are affected by partisan convictions. Thus, they can be made the basis of policy only with caution—in case of national security policy only with extreme caution. It would be marvelous if we could rely on the assumption that aggression has become synonymous with suicide. Perhaps in the future, in the twenty-first century, we may have reason to do so.

6

The Soviet Menace

The mushroom cloud rising over Hiroshima on August 6, 1945, carried with it many things. One was our traditional geopolitical context. Suddenly our relatively small planet became very much smaller still, so small that human beings using our ingenuity could destroy it all. A horrible thought; we all know that. There is, however, an alternative. The human race, recognizing its common peril and its shared destiny, may on reflection find a vital push to bring us together. Conceivably we may direct our unique ingenuity in that direction, and this is a much more hopeful prospect.

At the time, however, most Americans were noticeably unconcerned about it all. They were busily celebrating the end of the war. It took longer than originally expected, but the "happy days [were] here again." We could once again enjoy the economic advantages of America, and we could resume our advance in democracy through a "fair deal." Some scientists were worried about the new nuclear reality. Much of their devotion to the nuclear project had been motivated by a fear that the Nazis would get the weapon first, but that threat was now gone, hopefully forever.

Meanwhile the U.S. government was actively shaping its own position. "Ever since Hiroshima I had never stopped thinking about the frightful implications of the atomic bomb,"[1] recalled Harry Truman in his autobiography. There was general consensus that atomic energy in the United States

---

[1] For a detailed description of U.S. government efforts see: Harry S. Truman, *Memoirs* (Garden City, NY: Doubleday & Co., 1955), vol. I, pp. 419, 523–28, 533 and vol. II, p. 11.

must be controlled by a civilian authority. Even before the weapon was tested, in fact just a day after the German surrender (May 9, 1945), a top-secret Interim Committee composed entirely of civilians met to consider whether the bomb should be used at all. After much discussion this committee decided unanimously that it should be.

On June 14, 1946, an American (Baruch) plan on gradual international-ization of atomic energy was presented to the United Nations Commission. It eventually adopted, over objections from Poland and the Soviet Union, what was substantially the American plan. The commission's report was sent to the Security Council. There, backed by the use of the veto, the Soviet Union was able to block all further action.

Indeed the Soviet Union had its own agenda. In an astonishingly short time, by September 1949, they were ready to test their own atomic device. Then while Americans were debating whether to go one step farther and develop a thermonuclear superbomb with almost all scientists opposed, indeed publicly campaigning against it, the Soviets had no hesitation. The first American H-bomb test took place on November 1, 1952, followed shortly by the Soviet test on August 12, 1953.

The determined and rapid Soviet weapons development was not reassuring. Nor was the steady propaganda barrage from Moscow. American good will toward its former ally, so carefully nurtured during the war, was fading fast. "In Europe," Churchill warned, "an iron curtain had descended across the continent. Behind that line lie all the capitals of the ancient states of Central and Eastern Europe. Warsaw, Berlin, Prague, Vienna, Budapest, Belgrade, Bucharest, and Sophia, all these famous cities and the populations around them lie in what I must call the Soviet sphere, and in many cases, increasing measure of control from Moscow."[2] Many Americans whose ancestors came from Eastern Europe tended to believe him. Newly arriving displaced persons who had fled from communism were sure he was right. When communists gained control over China (1949) and soon thereafter aided North Korean aggression (1950) causing heavy U.S. casualties, the American reaction was fierce. How can they behave like this after we have done so much for them? They are conquering countries and people for whose liberation from Nazi and Japanese tyranny we fought together. They are screaming falsehoods at us and about us when they should know better.

Curiously, we were not much concerned about what their military might could do to us. Instead popular anger was directed at our own

---

[2] *The New York Times*, August 6, 1947, p. 1.

people—those traitors who gave atomic secrets to our enemy and those subversives who echoed communist propaganda about us. Suspicion spread against intellectuals, "eggheads," especially those sophists in academia who equated U.S. and Soviet behavior. The targets spread farther. Soon they included practically everyone. Fueled by demagogues who were abetted by timid academics and sensation-oriented journalists, people were gripped with fear. Americans were afraid that other Americans, perhaps their friends and neighbors, were disloyal; they were afraid that they themselves would be suspected of disloyalty by their friends and neighbors. Great universities demanded that their faculty members sign loyalty oaths, sometimes even requiring that they be fingerprinted. It took years into the mid-1950s before sanity returned and the lessons were learned, at least for the moment.

But then as fear of communist subversion subsided, awareness of the threat posed by Soviet military power suddenly crashed in on us. On August 26, 1957, Moscow radio announced the successful testing of a "super-long-distance intercontinental multi-stage ballistic missile." Six weeks later they launched *Sputnik*, the first man-made earth satellite. In quick riposte the United States announced that it too would launch a satellite. Since we are a democratic system, moreover, we would do so not in secret as the Soviets had done, but in public, on radio and television. In due time our missile, U.S. Navy-built Vanguard I, was rolled out to the launching pad. Walter Cronkite was reporting; the nation was listening and watching. The countdown proceeded: 3-2-1. Ignition. The missile rose slightly—then blew up.[3] Two months later the same spectacle was repeated.[4] Humorists in Washington reflected the general popular disgust. Why don't we just blow up the missiles at the factory; we could save the transportation costs.

But, in fact, it was not funny. Suddenly we faced a challenge to our national security. In quick succession the Soviet Union presented us with a major threat and then with a mortal peril. We had never had such an experience before. The last thing we wanted was to get involved with a military competition. The last thing young Americans wanted was to think of new weapons systems in a nuclear age. But WE HAD NO CHOICE. Surely we had to defend ourselves. Young Americans had to realize this. Actually they were inclined toward different priorities, but most of them were willing to listen and learn—and make sacrifices. Faced with the

---

[3] Ibid., December 7, 1957, p. A6.
[4] Ibid., February 6, 1958, p. D8.

unprecedented challenge American society had to become preoccupied with national security matters.

Just what exactly were our special problems with Soviet missiles? First, it was their range. They could bring the war to us. Since the 1950s the possibility that the United States could become vulnerable to a devastating direct nuclear attack, while worth considering, seemed a contingency with only a modest probability for some time to come. Now it became a predictable certainty in the near future. Suddenly a well thought out and highly, if not absolutely reliable, deterrence strategy became a vital imperative.

The second problem was their speed. They could surprise us. Soviet missiles could be expected to cover the entire range more than twenty times faster than a bomber. As long as the Soviet strategic threat was based on their bombers, even if they could very much improve them, we would have time, not much, but some. During the hours it would take for their planes to reach their targets, we would have time to respond; we would have time to move our decision-makers and our retaliatory capacity to safety; we would have time to warn the people, many of whom would have time to evacuate to safety; and we would have time to unleash a devastating counterattack. During the less than thirty-minutes' flight of the missile we would have time for a few, possibly none, of these. Now with a surprise attack becoming a realistic possibility, the whole calculation of deterrence had to be revised. Retaliatory forces-in-being became at best only of academic significance. What counted for deterrence was strategic retaliatory capability, which could be expected to *survive* and could be rapidly made operational *after the absorption of a nuclear attack*.

DETERRENCE CONDITION ONE: SOVIET SOFT-TARGET CAPABILITY

Chairman Khrushchev's boasts and President Kennedy's campaign rhetoric notwithstanding, it was not until well into the 1960s that the Soviet Union developed the capacity of a severe, direct strategic nuclear attack on the United States.[5] By the end of the decade, however, the Soviet Union did

---

[5] John M. Collins, *U.S.-Soviet Military Balance: Concepts and Capabilities, 1960–1980* (New York: McGraw-Hill, 1980), p. 32; Stewart Menaul, *The Illustrated Encyclopedia of the Strategy, Tactics, and Weapons of Russian Military Power* (New York: St. Martin's Press, 1980), pp. 87, 91, 206. In January 1989 at

(continued...)

achieve strategic soft-target capability. Their missiles could reach practically any place throughout our country. They would not be accurate enough for direct hits; in fact, we could expect that some of them would be detonated well above their targets. But they could come close enough for their nuclear warheads to destroy our cities, our factories, our transportation networks, even some of our military establishments. We could have peace as long as our deterrence was credible, but our deterrence remained credible only as long as our retaliatory forces remained survivable.

It was an enormous challenge. First we had to assure credible deterrence for the present (short-term). Admittedly some protection for our strategic retaliatory forces could be gained by concealing their location, as an enemy cannot hit unknown targets; some protection could be gained by their mobility as an enemy might find it difficult to hit moving targets; and some protection could be gained by a defensive shield—heavy armor, sophisticated electronic countermeasures (ECM), or reinforced shelters—as an enemy might find it difficult to penetrate them. All the same, it seemed most unlikely that we could make any weapons system invulnerable. Prudence demanded that we expect losses, probably heavy losses. In order to assure that they would not become crippling, so the argument ran, we needed *redundancy*. Only if we would maintain strategic forces *several times* the size needed to devastate the Soviet Union could we be sure and, what is more important for deterrence, would *they* be sure that even after absorbing an attack the United States could still deliver a devastating blow.

Second, we had to assure a credible deterrence for the future (long-run). We could not count on the Soviet Union's accepting the *status quo*. It was wise to assume that our enemies were constantly engaged in research designed to overcome our protective measures to gain the critical advantage. It was wise to assume that in order for these breakthroughs not to become decisive, this argument ran, we needed *diversity*. Only if we relied on several different autonomous weapons systems could we and they be sure that any technological breakthrough would at most neutralize a part of our strategic forces. Neither the enormity nor the certainty of our retaliation would be decisively affected.

---

[5](...continued)
a meeting in Moscow of U.S., Soviet, and Cuban officials reviewing the missile crisis, the Soviet delegation reported that in October 1962 they had installed or were about to install forty-two medium-range missiles in Cuba. They had only twenty ICBMs in the Soviet Union that could reach the United States. *The New York Times*, January 29, 1989, pp. 1, 10.

Specifically the United States adopted a system of deterrence marked by redundance and diversity. It was generally referred to as the Triad, a system supported by three legs. Its "airleg" was provided by manned strategic bombers. Some 538 long-range B-52s each capable of carrying up to four multimegaton bombs were already operational shortly after President Kennedy took office. The "groundleg" was to be made up of fixed-site intercontinental ballistic missiles (ICBMs) placed in heavily reinforced shelters or silos. In addition to 54 heavy Titan IIs we planned to deploy 1,200 lighter Minuteman solid fuel missiles. The former carried nine-megaton, the latter one- to two-megaton warheads. Finally, the "sealeg" was to be composed of 45 nuclear-powered Polaris/Poseidon submarines with a total of 720 submarine-launched ballistic missiles (SLBMs). A formidable and credible system of deterrence. "In planning our second strike force," explained Secretary of Defense McNamara to Congress in 1963, "we have provided . . . a capability to destroy virtually all of the 'soft' and 'semi-hard' military targets in the Soviet Union and a large number of their fully hardened missile sites, with an additional capability in the form of a protected force to be employed or held in reserve for use against urban and industrial areas."

It was clearly a second-strike design. The United States was not trying to destroy "any very large portion of the fully hard ICBM sites" even if the Soviets were to build them in large quantities. "Fully hard ICBM sites," the secretary explained further, "can be destroyed but only at a great cost in terms of the numbers of offensive weapons required to dig them out. Furthermore, in a second-strike situation we would be attacking, for the most part, empty sites from which the missiles had already been fired."[6]

The Soviet Union for its part made every effort to build up its strategic forces. However, it followed its own strategy. Unlike the United States it chose not to rely heavily on diversity. Soviet heavy bombers (turbo-prop Bears and jet-powered Bisons) were inferior in performance to the B-52s and remained much smaller in number.[7] "Antiquated submarines, each armed with three short-range SLBMs accounted for much of Moscow's sea-launched missile strength as late as 1970. Half were diesel powered." In missiles, however, the Soviet effort was spectacular. From about 100 ICBMs, that is less than a quarter of the U.S. number in 1963, they

---

[6] Quoted in Harland B. Moulton, *From Superiority to Parity: The United States and the Strategic Arms Race, 1961–1971* (Westport, CT: Greenwood Press, 1973), p. 114.

[7] A total of 210 in 1966, which then steadily declined throughout the decade.

increased their arsenal to 1,300, or 25 percent above the American level. The improvement was not only quantitative. Three new missiles (the SS-9, SS-11, and SS-13), some heavier, all more accurate, were deployed. There could no longer be any question of U.S. strategic superiority, only equivalence. We had reached the stage of mutual-assured destruction. Each superpower would have sufficient survivable second-strike capability to impose unacceptable damage on the people and territory of the other.

It was something of a psychedelic experience. Quite a few people actually found the condition comforting. We could feel safe because our retaliatory forces could survive an attack and still assure the destruction of one-fifth to one-fourth of the Soviet population and one-half of Soviet industry.[8] The Soviet Union could feel safe because they too had a survivable retaliatory force and could be confident that we would not resort to strategic nuclear attack against her for any reason at such exorbitant costs. So everyone could feel safe, and we could have peace. Mutual-assured destruction would mean mutual-assured deterrence. What could be better for international stability? "The doctrine," recalled Henry Kissinger later, "led to the extraordinary conclusion that the vulnerability of our civilian population was an *asset* reassuring the Soviet Union and guaranteeing its restraint in a crisis. 'Assured destruction' was one of those theories that sound impressive in an academic seminar but are horribly unworkable for a decision-maker in the real world and lead to catastrophe if they are ever implemented."[9]

Indeed there was a corollary to the theory. Mutual-assured destruction *could* mean mutual-assured strategic deterrence *provided* both sides were content with their own survivable second-strike capability. But only then. If either side were to move beyond that and seek to develop new weapons systems that would threaten to impair the other's retaliatory forces, it would destabilize the balance. If, to be more specific, as the result of improved Soviet weapons our capability to deliver a devastating retaliation would be imperiled, our deterrence would be seriously degraded. We could no longer safely assume that they would not be tempted to attack. Still late in the 1960s American decision-makers could not simply take it for granted that the Soviet Union would necessarily reject the balance of mutual-assured destruction and clandestinely seek to subvert it. It was worth a try, a cautious experiment.

---

[8] Pentagon definition of "assured destruction" in 1968.

[9] Henry Kissinger, *White House Years* (Boston: Little, Brown & Co., 1979), p. 216.

The United States responded to the massive Soviet buildup of the 1960s with remarkable restraint. It did not develop any new types of missiles. It did not seek to increase the number of its launchers. On the contrary, the Minuteman program was compressed from 1,200 to 1,000. Plans for 45 Polaris submarines with 720 missiles were cut to 41 boats with 656 missiles. All along, the B-52 losses were not replaced. By 1970 their total had dropped to 465.[10] Above all, we did not try to improve the accuracy of the warheads. We could have done so; we knew how—but we did not. All the United States did was to develop the technology for the Multiple Independently Targetable Re-entry Vehicle (MIRV). We would arm our missiles with more than one warhead: our Minuteman III ICBMs with three, our Poseidon SLBMs with ten. In short, throughout the 1970s our strategic offensive forces significantly increased the redundance in our second-strike soft-target capability, but we intentionally did not improve on our limited capability to destroy Soviet missiles in their heavily reinforced shelters. We made a point of not threatening the survivability of their second-strike capability.

DETERRENCE CONDITION TWO: SOVIET HARD-TARGET CAPABILITY

It was devoutly hoped that the Soviet Union would reciprocate. Instead their leaders chose to embark on a desperate gamble: to break out of strategic parity. By developing a first-strike capability they set out to gain global hegemony through force or blackmail. Perhaps a clarification may be useful here. First-strike capability means the ability to carry out a *successful* surprise attack. It is not enough that the victim of aggression be surprised; it is necessary that the attack be successful, and a strategic attack can only be considered successful if it would paralyze the victim's retaliatory (second-strike) capability. Both the United States and the Soviet Union if they so chose could plan a surprise attack on each other. After the 1960s the United States could not make it successful. Until the 1970s it was clear that neither could the Soviet Union. The question arose: what about the 1980s?

Actually there were early warning signs. In 1961, and this requires not only thinking the unthinkable but also imagining the unimaginable, the Soviet Union detonated a 58-megaton weapon—almost 3,000 times the yield of the Hiroshima bomb! Then in 1967, on the fiftieth anniversary of

---

[10] Collins, *U.S.-Soviet Military Balance*, pp. 128, 454.

the Bolshevik Revolution, it unveiled the SS-9 (Scarp). It was an awesome sight. The missile was over 100 feet long, about 10 feet in diameter, and had a throw weight (payload) of at least 12,000 pounds, twice the size and more than six times the payload of the Minuteman. It could carry a single warhead of twenty-five megatons, more than twelve times what the Minuteman could do.

In terms of the doctrine of mutual-assured deterrence the weapon was incomprehensible; it added neither to the survivability nor to the meaningful destructive force of the Soviet second-strike capability. It was perplexing to see them being actually deployed at a rate of about four a month (their total reaching 308 by 1972). It was worrisome to see them being tested as satellite weapons. Moreover, it became especially worrisome to observe them being tested with three warheads, since these dummy giant warheads were independently targeted in a peculiarly close cluster. It made no sense to target them so close if they were intended to destroy three cities, and it surely made no sense to use three warheads against one city. Were they planning to target our ICBMs? In a tight cluster one may come close enough to destroy them.

All the same, Americans remained patient. Many, including some prominent public officials, just could not believe what they saw. They eagerly embraced arguments that the SS-9's "mammoth size could be seen as a function of Soviet technological inferiority, rather than a harbinger of Soviet strategic superiority. . . . the USSR was impelled toward a reliance on heavy missiles by the backwardness of its propulsion and guidance systems. The less accurate the warheads or cluster of the warheads the bigger it has to be to destroy its target."[11]

Throughout the late 1960s popular pressure was building to augment our military posture with vigorous diplomatic initiatives toward a strategic arms limitation treaty. During the Nixon administration we seemed to make progress. At the Moscow summit in 1972 the SALT I treaty[12] was signed. It was done in a televised atmosphere of bonhomie among equals. It froze for an interim period of five years the total number of strategic missiles but permitted "modernization" of ICBMs and the deployment of a limited number of additional SLBMs, provided an equivalent number of older ICBMs or SLBMs were taken out of service. It froze the number of heavy missiles and prohibited the conversion of light missiles into heavies, but it

---

[11] Strobe Talbott, *End Game, the Inside Story of SALT II* (New York: Harper & Row, 1979), p. 28.

[12] Kissinger, *White House Years*, p. 811.

did not define clearly the weight boundary between the two. SALT I did have some positive features in that it helped reduce the decibels of Cold War rhetoric. It also had some negative elements: the Soviet advantage in ICBMs remained close to 17 percent; their advantage in the very large, heavy missiles remained at 308:54. Worse still, by the time the treaty was signed the critical issue was shifting from missiles to warheads. The number of missiles was frozen, but not the number of warheads, and the Soviets took full advantage of this initial flaw.

Those who hoped to find hopeful signs of Soviet intentions in SALT I were all soon to be disappointed. As a matter of fact, Soviet missile development did not slow down. Quite the contrary. While the United States did not deploy a single new missile system, the Soviet Union deployed three: the SS-17, SS-18, and SS-19, each at least three times heavier than our Minuteman III, and one (SS-18) about nine times heavier. By 1977 there was a rough numerical equivalence in launchers.

The problem was by this time the terms of relevant comparison had changed. The United States had proceeded with MIRVing its strategic missiles, placing three warheads on the Minuteman III. The Soviet union soon began MIRVing as well with four warheads on the SS-17 (Mod 1), six warheads on the SS-19 (Mod 2), eight warheads on the SS-18 (Mod 2), and ten warheads on the SS-18 (Mod 4)! Since targets are destroyed by warheads, not missiles, the equivalence in missiles became irrelevant, and the disparity in warheads (by 1979 this meant a ratio of 4,306:2,154 in favor of the USSR) became alarming. Unfortunately that was not the worst of it.

It was soon noted that the new, modernized Soviet missiles were powered by liquid fuel. Why? Some found comfort in seeing this as further evidence of the backwardness of Soviet technology; we had long since shifted to solid fuel. Others wondered. Liquid fuel cannot be stored in missiles, and it takes many hours before launch to fill up the tanks. Liquid fuel missiles could not be launched in the short time available after warning of an impending attack. Were the Soviets leaders confident that their ICBMs were quite secure, that the United States not only lacked strategic hard-target capability but could not develop one in the foreseeable future? Or could the explanation be found in a more sinister motive? Did they use liquid fuel because they expected to launch their missiles at the time of their choice? A defender does not have a choice; only an aggressor planning a first strike does!

Most ominous, however, was the remarkable improvement of their guidance system. Its consequences were no less than the fundamental change in the conditions of deterrence. Since the mid-1960s Soviet missiles had soft-target capabilities. They could reach our country, destroy our cities, destroy our industries, even destroy some military installations. They could not, however, hope to impair our devastating retaliatory capability. More specifically, our ICBMs (the ground-leg of our Triad) were secure in their concrete-reinforced silos. The accuracy:yield ratio of Soviet missiles was not sufficient to threaten them. Their smaller warheads could come close, but their explosive yield was insufficient to hurt our silos. Their larger warheads could destroy them but could not come close enough. By the late 1970s, however, it had become clear that the Soviet missiles were steadily approaching the accuracy:yield ratio necessary to qualify as silo-buster.[13] It had become clear to all but the most determined wishful thinkers that neither a 2:1 ratio in warheads in favor of the Soviet Union nor an American soft-target strategic capability matched by a Soviet soft-target capability *plus* a Soviet hard-target capability do parity make.

The combined effect of these disparities was especially serious because they added to the approaching Soviet first-strike capability a first-strike temptation. The time was rapidly approaching when the Soviet Union in a surprise attack could make the very favorable trade of warheads for missiles. For example, one single SS-18 could destroy ten Minuteman IIIs (together with their three warheads each); or to put it in its crassest, most disturbing form: the 240 SS-18s that make up less than 20 percent of the Soviet ICBM force in 1979 could conceivably in a sudden strike destroy the entire American ICBM force.

Threatening an important component of our retaliatory capability, the very thing that protected the American people from nuclear attack, made Soviet intentions unmistakable. They would not be content with their own security (through assured deterrence), they also wanted to be free of the high cost of aggression.

These potential realities of the mid-1970s produced the projected scenario of the "window of vulnerability" of the mid-1980s. Without warning, Soviet nuclear submarines just off the U.S. coastline could fire in a shallow depressed trajectory their SLBMs at our soft strategic airbases. At the same time, they could launch a portion of their ICBMs with sufficient warheads to destroy all our Minuteman missiles in their hardened silos. As a result, practically all our ICBMs and about 70 percent of our B-52s (i.e., all those not on strip-alert) would be eliminated. The decimated B-52 force would then have little chance to penetrate the fully prepared and

---

[13] The SS-19 (Mod 2) could carry a ten-megaton warhead with a circular error probable of only 0.14 nautical miles.

wholly intact powerful Soviet air defenses. We would still have available our SLBMs, which could kill a lot of Soviet citizens and devastate much of Soviet territory but could not damage Soviet strategic missile forces. Would we use them—would it be rational for us to use them? The Soviet Union could combine its nuclear first-strike with a massive propaganda campaign. Look, they would say to the American government and the American people, we have gained the decisive military advantage. We admit that you could kill many of our citizens, but we have not yet used most of our missiles, indeed some of our missile silos can be repeatedly reloaded and you have no defense against them. Admittedly you have suffered some human casualties, but we have not yet begun to aim at your population centers. If you use your second-strike capability, we will turn our full, irresistible force against them. You Americans may start a senseless carnage but you simply cannot gain the military advantage. Be sensible, save the lives of tens of millions of Americans, and surrender. Surely you must see that being red is better than being dead.[14]

Even the possibility, however remote, of being confronted with the only choice of surrender or death was utterly unacceptable for the United States. Indeed American patience was wearing thin. Still our preference for diplomatic solutions remained foremost. We were determined to try to negotiate a meaningful arms control treaty. Late in 1974 President Ford at Vladivostok sought to move forward. He agreed to an equal total of 2,400 offensive strategic nuclear launch vehicles, including an equal subtotal of 1,320 launchers with multiple warheads. But overall progress was slow. The United States was willing to appease the Soviet Union on legitimacy. In July 1975 President Ford traveled to Helsinki to sign the European Security Conference Charter, which spoke of human rights and the free flow of information but which dramatically demonstrated American acceptance of Soviet hegemony over Eastern Europe. The United States was also prepared to offer concessions on weapons, concessions that would increase Soviet deterrence of a U.S. nuclear strike. What it was not prepared to offer were concessions that would weaken American deterrence of a Soviet nuclear strike.

By the time Jimmy Carter became president, it was evident that the United States had not prevented a Soviet advance toward a first-strike capability: not through the SALT I negotiations and not through a decade-

---

[14] To be sure, the scenario was not without its flaws. See: Karl von Vorys, *American National Interest: Virtue and Power in Foreign Policy* (New York: Praeger, 1990), pp. 42–43.

long unilateral self-restraint. To assure that the Soviet Union could not under any circumstances see a profit in a surprise attack on our retaliatory second-strike forces had become an imperative of national security. The question was: Could the USSR be persuaded to limit the number of its "time-urgent hard-target capable" missiles?

President Carter decided to try. He presented a comprehensive proposal in our first high-level contact with the Soviet Union. It would cut deeply into the Vladivostok ceilings, reducing the total strategic launchers of each side from 2,400 to 1,800 or at most to 2,000, limiting all the MIRVed strategic launchers to 1,100 or not more than 1,200, all the MIRVed ICBMs to 550, and all the heavy ICBMs to 150. All these would have represented major Soviet sacrifices. Their arsenals would drop below the minimum level necessary to cripple our land-based strategic missiles. In turn, President Carter offered to sacrifice the development of American "hard-target killers." The development, testing, and deployment of *any* new ICBM would be banned and flight testing of existing missiles severely curtailed. In short, President Carter offered to return to the conditions of the 1960s. Mutual-assured destruction could once again become mutual-assured deterrence: neither side would have a chance to launch a successful first strike; both would possess a survivable second-strike capability.

The Soviet leadership turned him down flat. At the meeting President Brezhnev called the American proposal "unconstructive and one-sided" and "harmful to Soviet security." Afterwards in a press conference Foreign Minister Gromyko denounced it as a "cheap and shady maneuver" aimed at achieving "unilateral advantages."[15] The secretary of state was shocked. President Carter was surprised. Henry Kissinger himself, it was explained, thought that the Soviet Union might welcome our proposal. Now it was rejected, and rejected brutally. There seemed to be no alternative but to rely once again on our strategic offensive weapons for deterrence of a nuclear attack. To be sure, the president canceled the B-1 strategic bomber program, but his decision was made on cost-effectiveness grounds. The B-52 modernized, loaded with new sophisticated electronic equipment and armed with Cruise missiles, would perform just as well at very much less cost. Either approach, moreover, would have been only a stopgap measure until the ultramodern "Stealth bomber" could be developed and deployed in the 1990s.[16] In any case the deployment of the new Trident submarine was now within sight. The modernization of the Minuteman with a much

---

[15] Vance, *Hard Choices*, pp. 53–54 and Talbott, *End Game*, pp. 70, 74.

[16] Vance, *Hard Choices*, p. 57–58.

improved guidance system and a more powerful warhead was now moving ahead, as was the testing of Cruise missiles and the deployment of the MX.

Negotiations toward a SALT II treaty continued but with a fundamental difference. Any expectations that the Soviet Union might be prepared to trade away its emerging first-strike capability fell victim to realism. When SALT II was signed in 1979, it did project (into 1981) a reduction in the aggregate number of missiles and bombers from 2,400 to 2,250 and a limit of MIRVed ICBMs of 820, but it did not significantly affect the rapidly expanding Soviet arsenal of warheads. At the time they possessed some 5,500 warheads, but under the treaty these could quite legitimately expand to more than double this number. Indeed by 1985 the total of Soviet ICBM and SLBM reentry vehicles passed the 8,800 mark.[17] This would allow a combination of SS-18s and SS-19s capable of raining some 5,500 highly accurate 550-kiloton warheads (the Minuteman's most advanced 12A warhead had a yield of 335 kilotons) on a thousand missile silos and perhaps a few hundred command and communications centers. Even so they would still have had 600 warheads left, many of them in the megaton range, to devastate American cities and the countryside. Under the treaty the United States in turn also could build enough warheads to destroy most of the Soviet Union several times over and build the MX, which could destroy Soviet missile sites. In fact, SALT II did impose a constraint on the factor of overkill. Possibly with its limits Americans could not be destroyed ten times over, only three or four times. Quite evidently SALT II was not an instrument of the "real arms control" President Carter and most Americans fervently sought. It contributed little to our strategic deterrence. In any case, for that and a variety other reasons SALT II was never ratified. After all the effort we had reached an impasse.

DETERRENCE CONDITION THREE: THE END OF CONFRONTATION

By the time President Reagan took office, American patience was thoroughly exhausted. The president himself orchestrated a massive U.S. response. The defense budget at $89.6 billion in 1976 and at $134 billion in 1980 jumped to $237.5 billion in 1984. Much of it went to the very accelerated modernization of strategic offensive weapons, which now included the reinstated B-1 bomber as well. The new Triad was no longer

---

[17] *Soviet Military Power, 1985*, Washington, DC: Government Printing Office, 1985, pp. 30, 33.

restricted to soft-target capability. It could destroy hard targets as well. Indeed some of our warheads were targeted with confidence on Soviet strategic weapons.

Negotiations with the Soviet Union continued, but they made little progress. Critics blamed the president's ignorance and inattention as well as conflict and anarchy among his advisers.[18] Actually it may have been due mostly to the fact that the president ordered substantive changes in the American negotiating position.

The United States remained interested in diplomatic benefits, and the president himself was quite aware of the popular appeal of "nuclear disarmament," but clearly the transcendental criterion for the negotiations had become the elimination of Soviet first-strike capability. To make sure that no one missed the point, the title of the negotiations was changed to Strategic Arms Reduction Talks (START). The "consensus option" approved by the president in a National Security Council meeting on May 3, 1982, set the goal of much more drastic cuts in the Soviet arsenal than had President Carter's "comprehensive proposal" five years earlier. While protecting the MX, the Cruise missiles, and the rapid advance of American strategic forces modernization, it required the Soviet Union to sacrifice most of its recent gains: to reduce ICBM warheads from 6,000 to 2,500, its total launchers from more than 2,300 to 850, its SS-18 "heavies" from 308 to 110, and its SS-19 "mediums" from 300 to 100 and to eliminate its SS-17 "mediums" (some 150 missiles) altogether. Had the Soviet Union agreed to these terms, and there is some question whether anyone thought they might, it would have meant real arms reduction, a sacrifice of their cherished first-strike capability, and the restoration of the "stability" of mutual-assured destruction.

President Reagan also ordered changes in the negotiating posture. The American delegations in the past tended to be activist, at times almost compulsively so. They were always anxious to advance negotiable positions; thus, throughout their preparations much time and thought went into finding some incentives for the other side. The Soviets could then peremptorily turn down our proposals and remain comfortably certain that the Americans, either through their formal delegations or through a "back-channel," would come back with new ideas, at times offering further concessions. President Reagan was not in any great hurry. He was quite prepared to let the Soviet Union take the negotiating initiative, and then *he* would think about it. His chief negotiator, Gen. Edward Rowny, USA,

---

[18] See, for example: Talbott, *Deadly Gambits*, pp. 224, 250, 263, 273–74.

knew how to say "no" as firmly and as frequently as the Soviets knew how to say "nyet". Rowny could outstonewall the master stonewallers.

The absence of progress was punctuated when on December 8, 1983, their chief delegate, Viktor Karpov, ended the fifth round of START and declined to set a date for the resumption of talks. Strobe Talbott, the diplomatic correspondent of *Time*, epitomized the grossly erroneous "authoritative" judgment of the media pundits. "If talks did resume," he wrote, "the agenda would be more complicated, and the Americans' expectations would have to be far more modest."[19]

The keystone of President Reagan's approach, however, turned out to be the Strategic Defense Initiative, which he formally announced on March 23, 1983. Few remembered that it was actually the second such initiative following by about two decades President Kennedy's program. He and President Johnson (who was rather less interested) were not successful.[20] The psychological costs for an effective passive defense (civil defense) proved to be exorbitant while the political costs for an ABM (active defense) system proved to be too much for Presidents Johnson and Nixon while they were deeply engaged in Vietnam. The ABM, it may be recalled, also had several technical problems, the most fundamental being that under the best of circumstances a successful interception would require the detonation of its nuclear warhead over Canadian or U.S. territory.

The situation, however, was changing. Longer-range radar (perimeter acquisition radar) and longer-range interceptors (Spartan) have now become available. The point of interception could be pushed farther out into space and farther away from North American targets. These advances, however, were largely counteracted by the development of MIRVed missiles and a catalogue of penetration aids, all kinds of decoys, balloons, and chaff, which are relatively cheap to produce and easy to release during the flight but which enormously complicate the identification and tracking of hostile missiles. Other technological advances included a whole family of Airborne Warning and Control Systems (AWACS) featuring radar, fast-reaction computers, and reliable communications, all very useful in defense against planes and cruise missiles, but less so against ICBMs. The most far-reaching technological advance, however, was in the development of satellites. By the mid-1970s they could be used for warning of an impending missile attack. The question invariably arose: Could space be used for strategic defense? Could a combination of developments in space technol-

---

[19] Ibid., p. 314.

[20] See: von Vorys, *American National Interest*, pp. 52–57.

ogy and directed energy (laser or particle beam) technology wholly overcome the most serious ABM flaws and achieve interception with nonnuclear means *and* over territory of the aggressor rather than its victim? Could we, in fact, intercept a slowly rising enemy while all of its warheads were still aboard?

The logic of interception in the booster stage was always theoretically sound but appeared practically beyond reach. Still if American ingenuity combined with American technology could actually accomplish this, it would in a single stroke eliminate the Soviet advantage of MIRVed missiles. In fact, it would cripple Soviet first-strike capability and very much improve the survivability and credibility of the U.S. second-strike capability. It would be a decisive contribution to our strategic deterrence and our national security. President Reagan was convinced that it should be tried and committed the country to making the effort.

To be sure, the technological problems were formidable.[21] But we have overcome difficult technological problems before, which not even our leading scientists considered insoluble (e.g., the hydrogen bomb). There were also some legal difficulties. Given the criterion of national security, they could be managed as well with the help of a couple of Philadelphia lawyers.[22]

But the most fundamental problem with the Strategic Defense Intiative was this: If we could develop an effective booster stage intercept, the Soviet Union would become strategically helpless. Our defense, which

---

[21] See: Ashton B. Carter, *Directed Energy Missile Defense in Space* (Background Paper) (Washington DC: Office of Technology Assessment, April 1984); Hans Bethe, Richard L. Garwin, Kurt Gottfried, and Henry W. Kendall, "Space-based Ballistic Missile Defense, *Scientific American* (October 1984), vol. 251, no. 4, pp. 39–49; and U.S. Congress, Office of Technology Assessment, *Strategic Defenses, Ballistic Missile Defense Technologies, Anti-Satellite Weapons, Countermeasures and Arms Control* (Princeton: Princeton University Press, 1986).

[22] Article V of the ABM Treaty in 1972 states: "Each Party undertakes not to develop, test or deploy ABM systems or components which are sea-based, space-based or mobile land-based." But during the final days of negotiations the U.S. chief negotiator made a unilateral statement that included the passage: "If an agreement providing for more complete strategic offensive arms limitations were not achieved within five years, U.S. supreme interests could be jeopardized. Should that occur, it would constitute a basis for withdrawal from the ABM Treaty." United States, *Treaties and Other International Agreements*, Washington, DC: Government Printing Office, 1973, vol. 23, Part 4, p. 3460. In any case, the treaty provided for regular reviews every five years.

could thwart their first strike, could also thwart their retaliatory second strike. In fact, the Soviet Union after forty years of massive exertion would be where she was in 1946—or perhaps not even that. Its desperate gamble for gaining ascendance over the United States was all for naught. Indeed America, want it or not, like it or not, would have global hegemony.

Ronald Reagan, by all accounts, was not about to shed any tears over the Soviet predicament, but some Americans were outright hostile to SDI. Foremost among them were much of the scientific and academic establishment, the media executives, and public personalities. Quickly they mounted a campaign to discredit the program. Their first salvo: dubbing it "Star Wars." It was just a Hollywood fantasy, deserving just as much respect in public policy deliberations.

The Soviet leadership, however, was not prepared to dismiss it as a fantasy. They thought they knew the stubborn determination of Ronald Reagan and his implacable hostility toward the "evil empire." They have always been impressed by American ingenuity and especially our scientific and technological propensities. Whenever Americans made up their minds to do something, somehow they always succeeded. "Just imagine," Gorbachev noted in his *Memoirs*, "there could have been nuclear and laser weapons in space in 1997!"[23]

Worse still, the Soviet leaders knew, none better, that their system had reached the brink of ruin. They still had considerable resources of coercion, but terror, which was the linchpin of state security under Lenin and especially under Stalin, could no longer be relied on. Noticeably during his final days Stalin could not carry out his purge of the "doctor's plot." Shortly after his death, his henchman, Beria, was tried and executed.

As a matter of fact, the whole notion that a state's security could be built on terror was fundamentally flawed. To be sure, human beings may be intimidated to act almost like sheep—but not quite. While they may appear to obey blindly the commands of tyrants, they resent having to do so. Invariably some may resist. To discover just who these are and then break them and their resistance, the state needs an ever-expanding secret police. Even if the numbers of this force grow rapidly, they are not likely to find all the dissenters. Realizing this, in all their eagerness they will predictably overreach and brutalize innocent people as well. In the process all the people whose families, relatives, or acquaintances were affronted by the injustice will join the resisters and further swell their ranks. It is a mathematical race that the tyrant, especially a secular tyrant without

---

[23] Mikhail Gorbachev, *Memoirs*, p. 445.

extramundane legitimacy, has no chance of winning. The number of new dissenters mobilized by terror will multiply faster than the secret police-men can be recruited. Moreover, as secret police numbers multiply, the quality of recruits will inevitably drop. It is never particularly high because those who seek the profession of terrorizing their fellow human beings are usually at the fringes of society (not to mention human sanity). But soon the state will have to reach down to the bottom of that stinking barrel. The question then arises: can the secret policemen and their commanders be trusted? Even sane rulers would doubt it, and an anxious tyrant would always worry about it. How then do they keep their secret police under control? By bribes? But is that not similar to, and as hopeless as, paying a blackmailer? By terror? But would the guards in their own fear not turn on their masters? The self-contradictions of a system resting on terror were revealed by Nikita Khrushchev, the communist boss who succeeded Stalin, in his secret address to the 20th Party Congress. Some excerpts will prove revealing.

Instead of proving his political correctness [*sic*] and mobilizing the masses, [Stalin] often chose the path of repression and physical annihilation, not only against his actual enemies but also against individuals who had not committed any crimes against the Party and the Soviet government. . . .

It was determined that of the 139 members and candidates of the Party's Central Committee who were elected at the XVIIth Congress 98 persons, i.e., 70 percent were arrested and shot . . . of the 1,966 delegates with either voting or advisory roles, 1,108 persons were arrested on charges of anti-revolutionary crimes, i.e., decidedly more than a majority.

Then conditions became progressively worse.

We must state that after the war the situation became even more complicated. Stalin became even more capricious, irritable, and brutal; in particular his suspicions grew. His persecution mania reached unbelievable dimensions. . . .

[Stalin] personally issued advice on the conduct of the investigation and the method of interrogation of the arrested persons. He said that the academician Vinogradov should be beaten. . . . Stalin told [former Minister of State Security Ignatiev] curtly: "If you do not obtain confessions from the doctors, we will shorten you by a head."[24]

---

[24] Strobe Talbott (translated and edited), *Khrushchev Remembers* (Boston: Little, Brown & Co., 1970), pp. 559–618. Specifically pp. 569, 572–73, 577, 597, 601.

After Stalin, voices of dissent were heard throughout the empire, often led by their best and brightest: Pasternak, Solzhenitsyn, Sakharov. At the same time, the economy, still capable of producing advanced weapons of war, was also in visible trouble. It too was based on a fundamentally flawed notion: the viability of centrally managed command economy. Simply put, such a system lacks the self-corrective mechanisms of a market system especially when the latter is combined with a democratic political system. In private enterprise an erroneous economic decision will quickly translate into an easily recognizable loss; a big mistake will probably mean bankruptcy. Those prospects are likely to focus the mind marvelously and generally will help prevent error, waste, and structural disruption. Not so in a socialist government-controlled economy. When the Soviet economic czars were making mistakes, these were rarely discovered and practically never remedied, causing dislocations at increasingly exorbitant costs. Worse still, looking toward the future, if and when the Soviet system hoped to advance into the postindustrial stage, its prospects were just plain dismal. The information revolution has brought us into an age of decentralization with effective personal centers of telephones, computers, faxes, e-mail, Internet, and who knows what else tomorrow will bring. One thing is predictable: they will not be easily controlled or commanded by an authoritarian central authority. Clearly the future was antithetical to the Soviet system. Khrushchev desperately sought a way out. He had no clue about the "third wave," the information revolution, but he tried very hard to find self-corrective mechanisms in a command economy and then to implement them. He never found them and in any case had no time to implement them. After him Brezhnev apparently gave up. Presumably on the principle "make hay while the sun shines," he and his cohorts fully enjoyed all the material perquisites they could attach to their offices.

The failure of the system, moreover, was exacerbated by psychological factors. First, the public became increasingly aware of the fraud of the "classless society." A Soviet citizen did not have to be brilliant or very observant to recognize that a new class of government officials was assured special privileges in every aspect of their daily lives. They enjoyed special housing plus vacation homes. Their children were treated preferentially in schools. Their wives could go shopping in special stores with no need to stand in line hours on end or to suffer shortages. They were driven around in official cars that could ignore traffic patterns. A lane with no speed limit was specially reserved for them; no need to worry about intersections or red lights.

About the same time the Soviet people became increasingly aware of the fraud of the "communist paradise." The Iron Curtain, then the Berlin

Wall, was designed not to protect the Soviet Union from military aggression. It was designed to protect against a far more real and perilous threat: public information about the far superior quality of life of the average citizen in the capitalist West.

Relevant sequels followed. As part of the thaw in Soviet-American relations each country agreed to host an exhibition for the other. When the time came, the Americans proved to be the more imaginative. In Moscow instead of a picture gallery about the beauties of our country, its phenomenal technological achievements, or the heights of our standard of living, we built a sample of a typical American home. It had a modern, well-equipped kitchen; a den with a TV; and a garage with a Chevrolet—actually the quality of life of an American. The Russian people stood in line for hours to get in to see the American exhibit. Surely a bad omen for Soviet propaganda. Vice President Nixon was the official host when Khrushchev arrived. Seeing long Moscovite lines, the chairman's mood was dark and soon turned thunderous. He accused Nixon of a deception, a false pretense about how American workers lived. In the famous kitchen debate Nixon could not resist trumping the chairman's outburst by remarking wryly that the exhibit was actually an understatement. Soon average American homes would be even more modern. Color television was about to become available to all.

Indeed by the time of Chairman Khrushchev the Iron Curtain was becoming porous and even the Berlin Wall could not patch it up. The Soviet people, very much like any other people, wanted to be respected abroad. They were less and less satisfied with the propaganda pictures painted by their government. They wanted to see for themselves. Cultural contacts with the West were expanding. Soviet citizens won Nobel Prizes; at the Olympics their athletes won championships. The winners and their country were proud of the international recognition. Peeking through strict security arrangements they caught glimpses of the actual standard of living in the West—very different from what they had been told officially. The disparity stimulated curiosity, then raised doubts. The slide had begun. What made it a very slippery slope were the previously unimaginable quantum leaps in communications technology: from radio to television, to audio tapes, to VCRs and video tapes, and to minicams.

These advances tore the Iron Curtain apart and thus removed the foundation of the phony political stability of the Soviet Union. It was one thing to jam Radio Free Europe or the Voice of America. Trying to intercept the smuggling of small audio and video cassettes was quite another. It was one thing to lay down a phalanx of words to combat oral messages from foreign official sources and another to argue with private motion pictures in color. Evidently life in the "proletarian paradise" was not only not far better than under "capitalist exploitation." It was, in fact, far worse. When in the mid-1980s the Soviet government felt compelled to follow the West by installing a direct-dial telephone system, Soviet people could talk on the phone without some official operator listening in. And they talked to each other within and across borders. They talked and talked. About what? They gossiped a lot, discussed their own problems, but they also talked about the pictures they saw of the West and, more specifically, about life in the United States.

It was not merely a matter of material comparisons. Russians, communist Russians no less, wanted to be *kulturny*, roughly translatable as "civilized." They were inordinately proud of their cultural achievements of the past. They loved their museums; they were enchanted by their poets, their novelists, and their composers. Now they needed reassurance from the West. In official cultural exchanges the Russians sent us their very best artistic accomplishments, sources of pride of their elites: gala performances by the Kirov Ballet of Tchaikovsky's Swan Lake. The top layer of Washington society, headed by Secretary of State Schulz, attended, listening to and watching the very special, graceful beauty of harmony. But, of course, they were already familiar with it. We, in turn, reciprocated by sending the Russians the most popular expressions of our mass culture bubbling up from below. Few of them had ever heard anything like it. Alexander Solzhenitsyn condemned it bitterly as "liquid manure seeping underneath the Iron Curtain," but most Russians were fascinated by the sensuous, rousing call of rhythm.

It was an incredibly wrenching experience for a people who were taught, and generally believed, that they were on the right track. They had made enormous sacrifices in blood to protect their homeland from foreign aggression and to serve as the vanguard of social justice in the advance of the human race. Suddenly it all seemed to be a fraud. Indeed it was Americans, more than their own government and society, that represented the very things they wished for and their communist masters had promised. Time was running out for the Soviet system. All that remained was the desperate gamble of a strategic military breakthrough. If the Soviet Union could gain a credible first-strike capability while America slept or was distracted by its curious domestic upheavals, the Soviet state might still survive.

Actually the evidence was increasing that America was no longer sleeping, nor was it paralyzed by domestic partisan squabbles. With growing anxiety the Soviet government watched when under President Carter the U.S. reaction took off and under President Reagan it accelerated to full force. When in 1983 the United States moved to trump all Soviet aspirations with SDI and the prospect, admittedly nebulous but frightening, of U.S. first-strike capability, it was time to launch lifeboats.

While President Reagan was considering strategic defense, a top-level meeting was taking place at the Kremlin. General Secretary Andropov was briefed by a senior intelligence analyst about the U.S. armament program and specifically the new basing modes of American strategic missiles. All of the information was based on reports from "Bill," a Soviet agent with access to Pentagon secrets. At the end of the meeting, according to a Soviet source, the General Secretary, visibly depressed, drew his conclusions.

It's over then. We can't do anything at this level of technical sophistication. Further military competition with the Americans is pointless unless we are willing to destroy our economy completely. We have to come to terms with the U.S.—even at the price of major concessions. And the sooner we do it, the less we'll have to concede. We must prevent them from embarking on these projects before it's too late. Also, we'll have to revise our military doctrine. In light of what we've just heard, a first strike against America would be suicidal. We'll be lucky if we manage to retain some deterrence potential.[25]

It was an astonishing turn in Soviet policy. Andropov did not live long after that nor did his successor, Chernenko. When Mikhail Gorbachev came to power, indications that the Soviet government was anxious to resume strategic arms reduction negotiations were increasing and persistent. Still the Soviets continued to pretend that they were bargaining from strength, that if necessary they could match U.S. technological innovations. "We have our own space defense program and our research is making progress in different ways than yours is," insisted Gorbachev to Nixon.[26] Their anxiety, however, was evident when not even the death of their party leader

---

[25] Yuri B. Shvets, *Washington Station, My Life as a KGB Spy in America* (New York: Simon & Schuster, 1994), p. 129. Personally I suspect that there is something bogus about this book, so I am not at all certain about the accuracy of this quote. But Shvets has been vetted by U.S. security agencies, his book has been published by a highly reputable U.S. firm, and CBS's "60 Minutes" has based a program on his testimony, so I cannot ignore it. In any case, whether that meeting in the Kremlin actually took place, whether Andropov actually said what he was quoted as saying, subsequent Soviet government actions indicate that their thoughts went along those lines.

[26] Memorandum to President Reagan from former President Nixon on a conversation with General Secretary Gorbachev at the Kremlin, July 18, 1986.

(Chernenko) would keep them from the resumption of arms reduction talks scheduled in Geneva for March 12, 1985. They were met there by the new head of the American delegation. Max Kampelman could say no as often as General Rowny, but his main skill was bargaining.

Soviet leaders now missed no chance to let the world know that they quite understood that a nuclear war could not be won. The implication was clear: they wanted to assure the United States that they planned no first strike. Indeed they sincerely wished to get an agreement for a massive cut in strategic offensive forces. Suddenly it rained Soviet arms reduction proposals. The Americans could hardly catch their breath, let alone say no before a new one was coming. At the hastily arranged Reykjavik Summit (October 1986) Gorbachev caught the president unprepared.[27] The former was determined to prevent the development of the Strategic Defense Initiative at almost any cost.[28] Going well beyond President Carter's "comprehensive proposal" and Reagan's "consensus option" and going far, far beyond Brezhnev's position, Gorbachev offered a mutual reduction by 50 percent of all strategic missiles and aircraft. All he wanted was an American commitment not to develop, test, or deploy SDI for ten years. It was a stunning suggestion. The Defense Department had no inkling that it was coming; they had been more or less kept out of the preparations. Our allies were not consulted On the spur of the moment the president made a counter proposal: a ten-year delay in the deployment of SDI in exchange for the complete elimination of *all* ballistic missiles from the arsenals of both nations. In effect the president suggested a nuclear disarmament of the superpowers without any restraint on other nuclear states. The conversation was assuming fabulous proportions.

The summit meeting broke down. As they were parting Reagan reproached the Soviet president: "You planned from the start to come here and put me in this situation." Gorbachev: "No. I am ready to go right back into the house and sign a comprehensive document on all issues agreed if

---

[27] Gorbachev reportedly was prepared for the meeting by a KGB agent in Washington, a former high-ranking official in the Carter Administration (OBM), code name Socrates. According to the KGB agent, Socrates learned about the U.S.-Iranian contact *and* the diversion of funds to the Nicaraguan Contras. He urged Gorbachev to blackmail Reagan by threatening to leak the information to the press unless Reagan was willing to make concessions demanded by the Soviets. If this is true, it is noteworthy that Gorbachev did not take his advice. He did pass on the information about "Iran-Contra" to Reagan but strictly in private and as a gesture of good will. Shvets, *Washington Station*, pp. 148–50, 161.

[28] Dobrynin, *In Confidence* (New York: Random House, 1995), p. 621.

you drop your plans to militarize space." Reagan: "I am really sorry."[29]
"The President's performance was magnificent. And I have never been so
proud of my President as I have been in these sessions, and particularly this
afternoon,"[30] the exhausted and probably relieved Secretary of State Shultz
proclaimed just an hour later. Back home the president himself assured the
American people: "The door is open and the opportunity to begin eliminating the nuclear threat is within reach."[31]

Significantly Reykjavik marked the final turning point. The last Soviet
gambit did not work. Underlying the at-times-surreal negotiations was the
message: President Reagan, reelected by a landslide, would not bargain
away American technological advantages and would never permit the
Soviets to gain Soviet first-strike capability against us. It was a tough
message to swallow, but Gorbachev had no choice. As a practical matter
the Soviet menace was over.

To be sure, the Soviets continued to build missiles. They were
developing two new strategic models, but noticeably these did not
aggravate the menace. The SS-24 was comparable in size to the MX and
could carry ten warheads. It was expected to be fully deployed in the early
1990s. Like conventional ICBMs, it could have been placed in a heavily
reinforced silo, but possibly it could have been made mobile by mounting
it, just as we were trying to do with the MX, on a railroad car. The SS-25,
which had been deployed since 1985,[32] was a fully mobile missile and
carried one warhead. That these missiles were or could have been mobile
clearly increased the survivability of land-based missiles, but their
deployment did not enhance Soviet first-strike capability. Possibly it may
have been construed as a retreat from such intentions. Both were solid-fuel
missiles. Their mobility somewhat decreased their accuracy:yield ratio and
with it their utility as silo busters. Finally the SS-25 with its single warhead
reduced the "MIRV temptation," that is, that advantage in a surprise attack
of trading warheads for missiles. With double-targeting conceivably it
would have taken just 240 SS-18s to destroy our entire ICBM force, but it
would have taken more than 2,000 SS-25s! Could it have been that we were
moving back to Deterrence Condition I, that is, to the relatively stable
position where mutually assured destruction produced mutually assured
deterrence?

---

[29] Gorbachev, *Memoirs*, p. 419.

[30] *The New York Times*, October 13, 1986, p. A10.

[31] *The New York Times*, October 14, 1986, p. A1.

[32] By 1990, 300 had been deployed.

Meanwhile negotiations were resumed and gained momentum. The succession of George Bush, not even the collapse of the Soviet Union and the emergence of Russia under Yeltsin, could slow it down. In July 1991 Strategic Arms Reduction Treaty I was signed by Bush and Gorbachev. It pledged to reduce strategic warheads by about 50 percent.[33] It was followed by a Bush-Yeltsin agreement in June 1992 with a further massive reduction. There remained some problems about ratification and the warheads located in the former Soviet Union but outside Russia. Even so, at least for the moment they do not seem insoluble. As of July 1, 1996, Russia had 5,169 ICBM warheads, 2,496 SLBM warheads, and 921 bomber-carried warheads for a total of 8,586.[34] In turn, we had retained 2,382 ICBM warheads, 3,904 SLBM warheads, and 1,820 bomber-carried warheads for a total of 8,106.[35] For the first time we had a rough equivalence in warheads. Indeed mutual confidence was growing that the targets set for 2003 would actually be met—no more than 3,500 nuclear warheads on each side. Most significantly the United States and Russia pledged to dismantle all MIRVd missiles by 2003. To be sure, circumstances may change, but as of now there is a genuine prospect that MIRV temptation and a first-strike capability for Russia are altogether obsolete—and, in fact, that Russia has no interest in them.

Thankfully we have returned to more secure times. Our national security will still require military power that would deprive any attack upon the United States of any *utility*: it could not succeed and would have a predictably exorbitant price. Now we could address with some confidence the element of *capability*. There still may be risks in arms limitation agreements, but they are tolerable. They can save us money and enhance our security. We can now also rely with some confidence on addressing the dangers of *hostility*. Massive state-sponsored hate campaigns against the United States are not yet features of the past, but at least for the moment they emanate from lesser powers that lack the capability of doing mortal damage and can under no circumstances find utility in attacking us. Our security once again rests on a Triad, this time a Grand Strategic Triad where military power is accompanied by a posture of negotiation and an

---

[33] For the USSR: from 11,012 to 6,163; for the United States: from 12,646 to 8,556. *The New York Times*, October 2, 1992, p. A6.

[34] By summer 1995 there remained only 4,000 Soviet strategic nuclear warheads. Interview with head of Soviet rocket forces, CBS, "60 Minutes," June 18, 1995.

[35] *Washington Post*, October 16, 1996, p. A17.

attitude of tolerance and good will—a position much more congenial to the American people.

The position is comfortable but not entirely without perils. They include foremost an infectious complacency and a reactionary neglect of other components of our national interest, in other words: a return to our tradition, for generations quite congenial isolationism.

7

Friends and Allies

A consensus on the survival of the American community is just the beginning, the easy part. When it comes to exertions beyond our borders, consensus comes hard. It always takes some persuasion and much public discussion. When all is said, however, given a realistic evaluation of our current condition, it makes sense to have friends. To begin with, although the mortal peril to our existence has abated, there are still military reasons for allies. We are fortunate that the rimlands of Eurasia are in the hands of friendly states. It is in our interest that they remain friendly and secure. We do not want hostile forces gaining control over areas that could serve as staging areas and jumping-off points against us.

In turn, in a contingency of our own global force projection we need special access to geopolitically key areas. To enable our rapid response we may have to pre-position military equipment on foreign soil; we may need arrangements that would make available forward staging areas; and we may need permission to use foreign air space. We should keep in mind though that because the military challenges may be changing, the rationale for the selection of our special relations may also be changing. We may need new allies, and we might be able to dispense with some whose salience in the altered circumstances has been reduced. Not a pleasant task, but unless endowed with unlimited resources, reality is often unpleasant. Mostly though, the reasons for our special interests are not security concerns; they are those of economics and culture. Americans want to live in peace. More than that they want to live in peace in their own way.

We do enjoy a very high standard of living. We want to continue to enjoy a high standard of living, and what is more, we want to improve upon it. The United States is rich in resources; the American people are highly skilled and talented. Their propensity for innovation is legendary. We have done and can do much with our own resources. Much, but not quite all. We need to import some raw materials for strategic (national security) purposes; we are dependent on imports to satisfy our consumer demands. And in order to pay for our imports, we need access to foreign markets where we can sell our goods.[1]

To be sure, Americans are willing to make sacrifices in their standard of living for the sake of national security or, as was the case in the 1973 oil embargo, to resist foreign countries blackmailing our foreign policy, but they'd rather not. They prefer giving special attention to countries where their economic interests lie.

The American way of life, however, is not only notable for the pleasures of material affluence but also for the satisfaction of our intangible values. One of these is a commitment to a democratic polity. Americans cannot imagine living without basic constitutional rights, which would be upheld if necessary by the courts even against the government itself. They have become very much accustomed to electing their public officials and to holding them accountable for their actions. Indeed they take it for granted that those are the terms of the only proper relationship between citizens and their government. Looking beyond their borders they feel a measure of solidarity with people and governments that share these values. They dislike authoritarian and especially totalitarian governments,[2] feel sure that these are up to no good internationally, consider their rule immoral, and have sympathy for the people who must serve under them.

The other basic American value is a preference for a pluralist society, a devotion to diversity: diversity in values, opinions, tastes, and, most to the point here, diversity of national origins. This was not always so. At the time of independence we were primarily a homogeneous nation. We treated

---

[1] U.S. imports in billions of current dollars amounted to 15.0 in 1960, 40.0 in 1970, 244.9 in 1980, and 325.7 in 1984 or, respectively, 3.0 percent, 4.0 percent, 9.3 percent, and 8.9 percent of gross national product. In the same years U.S. exports amounted to 19.6, 42.7, 220.6, and 217.9 billions of (current) dollars or 3.9, 4.3, 8.4, and 5.9 percent of gross national product, respectively. United States, Department of Commerce, *Statistical Abstract of the United States, 1986*, 106th Edition (Washington, DC: Government Printing Office, 1986), pp. 431, 807.

[2] Authoritarian governments are selected by means other than free elections and are not accountable to the electorate; totalitarian governments do not concede any rights to the individual (any civil liberties); they insist that *they* have the right to control and regulate *all* aspects of human behavior, even human thought.

Indians as foreigners. We negotiated with the tribes and regularly fought wars with them. We treated blacks even worse, as inferior creatures worth three-fifths of a human being. Yet from the very beginning this was a country of immigrants. Five delegates to the Constitutional Convention were born abroad.

At first people came from Western Europe, soon from Southern and Eastern Europe, and then from practically every part of the globe. By the end of the nineteenth century the Statue of Liberty proudly proclaimed: Give me your tired, your poor, your huddled masses yearning to breathe free. *Our* ancestors came. They were attracted by political freedom and economic opportunities. Some alas we compelled by force. They came and all helped develop the land, helped build the railroads, helped build vast industrial plants, helped build great universities. They helped to build America.

Gradually the attitude toward racial and ethnic diversity changed. It was still cautious. Laws were passed to limit the number of immigrants and favored them according to their countries of origin. Still diversity was beginning to be accepted—as a temporary, transitional condition. Newcomers with different racial and cultural backgrounds were welcome to live with us, to share in the wealth, to learn our language, to *assimilate* into our way of life, and then in a generation or so to become accepted as Americans. The "melting pot" was our favorite symbol for the country—the melting pot in which the additives to native iron would produce the steely alloy of our nation.

More recently, however, public attitude has been changing further. Diversity, many now argue—and at times the Supreme Court appears to agree with them—is not just a useful temporary inconvenience. On the contrary, it is a subject of national pride. Surely one can see that immigrants should not be stripped of their heritage. Without it people would lose their balance, like a fiddler on the roof. Surely one can see that America in turn is enriched by the variety of cultures. They keep us from becoming smug and stagnant. Never mind the melting pot. Never mind the assimilation of diversity. Integration is a better course. Perhaps the tossed salad is a better metaphor. Bring the tomatoes, the cucumbers, the radishes, the lettuce together. Do not homogenize them. If you process them through a blender, all you get is a dull, insipid mess. Let this be a nation of minorities working together, each bringing its own unique contributions and all being held together by just one common belief that America is the greatest nation.

Diversity in cultural heritage, however, is not without political consequences. Ethnically based special preferences are minority expressions that are difficult to convert into a general consensus. Indeed they are likely to facilitate special-interest-dominated politics at home. In our international relations they are likely to produce partiality in favor of or prejudice against a specific foreign country or people. In a pluralistic democracy these are not necessarily indications of separatism or disloyalty. Indeed they are part of the dynamic of integration *provided* (1) these cultural solidarities are not held fanatically and abet radical discontinuities among American citizens and thus tear apart our national community, and (2) these special interest groups do not pursue single-mindedly their parochial goals by rudely overriding the interests of all other Americans, worse still by ignoring the interests of the nation as a whole. The tossed salad needs a salad bowl, or all its various ingredients roll around or roll off the table altogether.

SPECIAL OBLIGATIONS

It follows from our special needs that good relations with some governments, the friendship of some people, are especially desirable for us and that we should try to build special relationships with them. These may be ceremoniously proclaimed in treaties of alliance or may be the products of less formal diplomatic "understandings," but they are far from easy.

Two conditions make our special relations particularly strenuous. One problem is that they are *inherently asymmetric.* Foreign countries may be moved by a variety of motives toward a special relationship with us. They may feel a solidarity to a common cultural heritage, they may remember a past history of mutual good will, or they may admire our democratic form of government. In these situations there can be a measure of reciprocity, even symmetry. The position is more complicated with economic motives. Contrary to contemporary wisdom, the argument that free trade means "a level playing field" and hence is mutually and equally advantageous is flawed. In fact, access to our vast consumer markets offers special, differential benefits to practically all but the Western European countries. When we export goods to others, even without trade restrictions imposed on us, we benefit from the expansion of our total market by a relatively small *fraction*. When they export to us, they benefit from an increase by a large *multiple* of their own market.[3]

---

[3] The Japanese, for example, sell about five times as many VCRs in the United States as at home. Without the efficiencies of scale gained by such a quintuple expansion, the unit price of their product would be far above any international competition, quite possibly even above their domestic demand.

The asymmetry is even more clear in mutual security arrangements. Foreign countries seek special relations with us because they need our protection. They may feel vulnerable because they are weak in the proximity of a larger, aggressive power. They may worry about ancient grievances feeding strikes of revenge. They may feel vulnerable because they are placed in key geopolitical locations or have natural resources that others covet. And we should not forget that some may be vulnerable exactly because they are our friends. But the bottom line is: when push comes to shove they *need us for their survival*. We in turn may seek and appreciate the support of others in time of need; indeed we may benefit from it, but in all candor our national *survival* will not be critically affected by their support.

Perhaps most troublesome is the *asymmetry of perspectives*. In spite of the advance of technology they may count on a relatively small radius of effectiveness. Even large, former imperial powers, for example, Britain, France, or Japan, have (or should have) not much more than regional horizons. To be sure, this is often traumatic, but that is the contemporary reality. Neither by sea nor by air do they have a longer reach. But the United States does. It is a superpower, arguably now the only superpower. Our foreign policy perspective can be and ought to be global. We have looked with friendship on countries of Western Europe and Latin America for quite a long time. We have developed special relations with others throughout the world: Turkey, Israel, Saudi Arabia, Egypt, Pakistan, Thailand, the Philippines, Kenya, Australia, and many others. We have special interests in the areas around the choke points of global maritime routes: the Suez and the Panama Canals and all the various straits (e.g., Gibraltar, Bosphorus, Hormiz, or Malacca). The disparity of perspectives causes unease even among our friends. Some may be envious and keep recalling with nostalgia the not-so-distant past when they played a global role. Some are certainly anxious that with a global perspective America may subordinate their important, perhaps vital, interests. Our fellow OAS member Argentina found out that in its war over the Falkland Islands (Malvinas) the United States gave decisive support to Britain. Also the Republic of China and Japan, diplomatically faithful and true, were shocked to learn that we were secretly opening relations with the People's Republic of China, Red China. This aggravates another problem. "Special interest" is by mutual consent left ambiguous: it means something between total commitment and no interest at all.

There is a good reason for this. Most of our friends do not want to be saved by American military intervention. They much prefer to be protected by American deterrence of attack against them. The problem is that when we seek to extend our deterrence from the protection of our own existence to that of others, we have to meet the requirements of a different dimension of credibility. Deterrence of aggression against our *vital* interests rests almost wholly on visible evidence of our military capabilities. But deterrence of aggression in the areas of our *special* interests depends heavily on more elusive indicators of political *will to project force.* Few would doubt that we would defend ourselves with everything we had, but many might wonder whether we would resort to nuclear retaliation in case of a subnuclear attack on one of our friends. In case the aggressor is a nonnuclear power, Americans would be repelled by the prospect of raining mass devastation on a defenseless people even though their government was guilty of aggression. In case of a nuclear power, Americans would be most unenthusiastic about the prospect of its in turn raining mass devastation upon us. There is, of course, the possibility that the United States would come to the aid of its allies with conventional forces. The question is: how much of a possibility?

Ambiguity, of course, has its uses in foreign policy. When predators are unsure of our response, they may be restrained because they do not want to take a chance that we would do nothing. They have after all miscalculated before, in Korea for instance.[4] All the same, ambiguity has a serious negative consequence: it invites others to test us. This is exactly why it is to the interest of both our friends and ourselves that our commitment should *appear* to be iron-clad. President Nixon in his last book identified our "interest in the survival and security of Israel" to be critical but apparently of a lower order than the "vital interest the West had" in maintaining access to Persian Gulf oil.[5] While technically of course he was right, by speaking of our commitment to Israel in less than unequivocal, total terms he made a lot of people nervous and conceivably encouraged some others. As a matter of fact, there have always been doubts about the steadfastness of democracies. The Europeans, and not just the Europeans, remember Munich well. Europe, and not just Europe, knows the awesome

---

[4] On January 12, 1950, "in a general review of the position as of 1956" before the National Press Club in Washington, the secretary of state declared that our defensive perimeter "was one which runs along the Aleutians to Japan and then goes to the Ryukyus." (U.S. Department of State, *American Foreign Policy 1950–1955, Basic Documents*, Washington, DC: U.S. Government Printing Office, 1954, p. 2317.) Although in his speech he mentioned Korea several times, that country (North or South) was outside of this perimeter.

[5] Richard Nixon, *Beyond Peace* (New York: Random House, 1994), pp. 142, 143.

military power of the United States, but the question lingers on: does America (Congress, for example) have the will to use it? Indeed even when our threat to use force was only thinly veiled, we were tested.

At his press conference on September 13, 1962, President Kennedy made it "clear once again": "If Cuba should ever . . . become an offensive military base of significant capacity for the Soviet Union, then this country will do whatever must be done to protect its own security and that of its allies."[6] All the same, in six weeks he had to use the navy to impose a "quarantine." In June 1973 during a late-night session at his home in San Clemente President Nixon made it perfectly clear to President Brezhnev that the United States would not abandon Israel. Four months later after the Syrian and Egyptian invasion of Israel the president had to order a gigantic airlift to counter the Soviet resupply of Syria and then in a few days a global nuclear alert of U.S. forces in response to Soviet threats to intervene unilaterally in the war.[7] Actions speak louder than words.

The actions of President Kennedy and President Nixon were salutary because they were successful. But actions speak louder than words in failure as well, and words followed by a failure to honor them are disastrous. They undermine deterrence and invite hostile forces to gamble on aggression. They raise doubts in our friends about the value of special relations with us (is America after all just a paper tiger?) and tempt them to appease our adversaries.

It is a conundrum. The success of special relationships depends on (1) that our friends and allies understand that our commitment is limited and (2) that potential aggressors believe that it is absolute. Whenever an aggressor is prepared to test our commitment, our friends and allies may face disappointment, perhaps a mortal outcome.

As a practical matter, a special relationship is a high-wire act. It requires enormous skills of statesmanship on both sides and a very generous measure of luck. A strong power—and its people know this—constantly risks becoming excessively involved in the fate of a friend and then paying exorbitant costs for it. Most of us recall our misfortunes with the shah's Iran and with South Vietnam.[8] In turn, a weaker power—and its people do not want to think of this—risks becoming abandoned in its hour of need. Most of us have a vague idea about the

---

[6] *The New York Times*, September 14, 1962 p. 12.

[7] Nixon, *Beyond Peace*, pp. 142, 143.

[8] See von Vorys, *American National Interest*, pp. 82–92; and chapter 11 this volume.

Munich Pact, but Europeans keep it in mind and hope that the world has learned a lesson.

THE CASE OF THE MUNICH PACT

The story started at Versailles in 1919. The victorious allies of World War I decided to break up the Austro-Hungarian Empire. They had military reasons: they were determined to prevent a powerful German-dominated state from ever again reinforcing Germany in the heart of Europe. They, especially the Americans, also had ideological reasons: they deeply believed in the self-determination of people, and Austria-Hungary ruled over millions of Czechs and Slovaks, not to mention Rumanians, Croats, Slovenes, Serbs, etc. (many who incidentally had helped the allied war effort).

A Risky Experiment

So the new state of Czechoslovakia would be established by the fiat of the victors, period. The question was what should constitute its boundaries. It was a tough question. The boundaries could run along ethnic lines, but if so Czechoslovakia would have to remain primarily an agricultural state with few mineral resources and little industrial capacity. It would also be an extremely vulnerable state, without any natural borders in the midst of hostile, revenge-seeking, and, in the case of Germany, potentially powerful, states. Or Czechoslovakia could have a significant industrial capacity and natural borders, but at the cost of violating the cherished principle of self-determination: an empire where millions of ethnically diverse and unfriendly people were dominated by Czechs (and Slovaks). In fact, a somewhat hypocritical ideological position.

When the head of the Czech delegation, Dr. Edouard Beneš, addressed the Peace Conference, as the British prime minister recorded, "he larded his speech throughout with phrases that reeked with professions of sympathy for the exalted ideals proclaimed by the Allies and Americans in their crusade for international right." "Czechoslovakia," Dr. Beneš intoned, "had not fought for territory, but for the same principles as the Allied nations. It had risen against a medieval dynasty backed by bureaucracy, militarism, the Roman Catholic Church, and, to some extent, by high finance."[9]   He

---

[9] David Lloyd George, *The Truth about the Peace Treaties* (London: Victor Gollancz Ltd., 1938), vol. II., p. 931.

addressed the problem of minorities only to dismiss them. The Austrian census notoriously overstated the size of the German population. Their actual number would be less, probably more than a million less. In any case, the territory where they lived was historically joined to the areas populated by Czechs and for economic reasons must not be severed. As far as the Hungarian minority was concerned, their number was an even worse exaggeration. Moreover, these were people who had invaded (presumably 1,000 years earlier) Slovak land, and in any case Czechoslovakia needed the Danube as a natural border. The Poles of Teschen were cavalierly dismissed as "cheap labor" brought there for purposes of industrial exploitation. And so it went. Dr. Beneš even demanded a corridor sliced out of Austria or Hungary that would link Czechoslovakia to Yugoslavia. It would, of course, have no Czech population, but no matter, it would improve the country's security and give it access to a Mediterranean port. In any case, there was no need to worry, as the new state, he pledged, would be a fair one with the minorities enjoying full rights. Czechoslovakia would be something like Switzerland. "Of the many misfortunes that befell Austria in the day of her great calamity," the British prime minister concluded, "one of the worst was that Czechoslovakia was represented at the Peace Conference not by her wise leader, President Masaryk, but by an impulsive, clever but much less sagacious and more short-sighted politician, who did not foresee that the more he grasped, the less he could retain."[10]

The French did not give it a thought, the British agonized, and the Americans chose to close their eyes. Except for the grossest of his demands, that is, the corridor to Yugoslavia over entirely alien lands, Dr. Beneš received everything he wanted. Czechoslovakia's borders were drawn along the river Danube and the Sudeten mountains rich in minerals and offering good physical barriers. Within it some six million Czechs (and to a much lesser extent two million Slovaks) ruled three and a half million Germans, one million Hungarians, and about three hundred thousand Poles. The Czechoslovakian government soon forgot all about any Swiss model and saw no pressing reasons to be concerned about the minorities. *It chose to depend on its special relationship with France.*

The borders were secure enough against a defeated, disrupted, and militarily disarmed Germany. But just for good measure the Czech government signed a treaty of mutual assistance with France in December 1925. In it Paris pledged to support Prague in the event of unprovoked

---

[10] Ibid., vol., II, p. 942.

aggression by Germany. It seemed to be an altogether satisfactory cover. Germany, of course, was not at all pleased with the developments. The Weimar Republic wished it could do something about it; when in January 1933 Adolf Hitler came to power, his Third Reich soon moved to change things.

The Czechoslovak government, which ruled its minorities with no more empathy (probably much less) than had the Austro-Hungarian empire, was getting nervous. It had no intention of making any concessions on its treatment of minorities. Internal stresses would continue to be managed through external relations. In May 1935 Czechoslovakia signed a treaty with the Soviet Union. Moscow pledged its military support provided that (1) Czechoslovakia became a victim of unprovoked aggressions *and* (2) France had extended prior aid.[11]

For a decade and a half France and Czechoslovakia enjoyed a special relationship. They supported each other diplomatically. In terms of security it was a typically unsymmetric relationship. In case of a German threat Czechoslovakia was important to France; in case of a German threat France was *vital* to Czechoslovakia. And then came the German threat.

French support for Czechoslovakia was formally enshrined in a treaty, but as a practical matter it depended on France's ability to bring tactical aid to Czechoslovakia before it would be overwhelmed by a German invasion. As long as Germany was nearly disarmed and her western borders (the Rhineland) were demilitarized, French forces could quickly cross the narrow stretch of southern Germany and effectively intervene on the Czech side. But soon after Hitler came to power, Germany began to rearm (1935), to remilitarize the Rhineland (1936), and to build a string of fortifications (the Siegfried line) along its western borders. Then in March 1938 it incorporated Austria into the Reich. Suddenly Czechoslovakia found itself in a deadly German pincer with little chance of timely tactical support. To reach her, Soviet troops would have to cross unsympathetic Poland or fearful Rumania; French troops would have to overcome fortified positions manned by a revitalized German army.

The realities of the situation were being faced in London. The prime minister of Great Britain, Sir Neville Chamberlain, and the foreign secretary, Lord Halifax, were conferring with the prime minister of France, Edouard Daladier, and his foreign minister, Georges Bonnet. Their agenda

---

[11] The last thing Stalin wanted was for communist Soviet Union to become involved in a war with Nazi Germany while the capitalist West was sitting on the sidelines smirking.

was long and varied, ranging from relations with Italy to problems in the Far East. Item four was Czechoslovakia. The French were clearly worried that Hitler had decided to eliminate Czechoslovakia. "Mr. Daladier had explained that France would scrupulously respect her obligations, . . . France must respect her signature and Great Britain, whose school-children were taught the importance of honoring their promises, would readily understand the attitude of France." What France needed was British help in bringing diplomatic pressure on Berlin and in case of war, British military support.

The British position was noticeably cautious. Lord Halifax reported that:

in the judgment of His Majesty's Government if he might be allowed to state the problem quite crudely, . . . if the German Government decided to take hostile steps against the Czechoslovak State, it would be impossible, in our present military situation, to prevent those steps from achieving immediate success.

Regarded purely as a military proposition, any reestablishment of the Czechoslovak State would have to wait the issue of a war in which we had been victorious. It might be necessary to wait a long time before such a conclusion had been reached, and it was perhaps impossible to exclude from our minds the question whether, even at the end of a victorious war, it would in fact be possible to reestablish the Czechoslovak State on its present basis.

The prime minister himself was concerned that Dr. Beneš (who in the meantime had become president of Czechoslovakia) would "count on greater support from us, in the event of certain circumstances arising, than would, in fact, be the case." On this, as on other subjects, in spite of French appeals the British did not waver.[12]

Time of Troubles

On May 20 a draft of "Operation Green" was presented to Hitler for his signature. Its first paragraph read: "It is not my intention to smash Czechoslovakia by military action in the immediate future without provocation, unless an unavoidable development of the political conditions *within* Czechoslovakia forces the issue, or political events in Europe create a favorable opportunity which may perhaps never recur."[13] But May 20 was

---

[12] Documents on British Foreign Policy 1919–1939 (London: His Majesty's Stationary Office, 1949), Third Series, vol. 1, pp. 198–235.

[13] Documents on German Foreign Policy, vol. II, p. 300.

an otherwise eventful day. In the afternoon Czechoslovakia announced partial mobilization. Its justification was "reliable reports" of heavy German troop concentrations on its borders.[14] The British ambassador in Berlin, Sir Neville Henderson, called on the German State Secretary for Foreign Affairs, Dr. Ernst von Weizsäcker, to inquire about troop movements. Dr. Weizsäcker categorically denied any such military activity and in the presence of the ambassador called General Keitel of the High Command, who also denied the charges. Next morning the British military attaché and his assistant toured the entire area in question where they could find no sign of unusual or significant troop activity.[15] Nevertheless on instructions from the Foreign Secretary the ambassador delivered a warning to Germany: "If a resort is had to forcible measures, it is quite impossible for me or for him to foretell the results that may follow, and I would beg him not to count on this country's being able to stand aside if from any precipitate action there should start European conflagration. Only those will benefit from such catastrophe who wish to see the destruction of European civilization."[16] Other Western countries publicly expressed similar views. The press, moreover, treated the false reports of German troop movements as though they were true. Hitler blew his stack. What annoyed him was not so much that the Western powers had acted in unison against him but that the world might think that he was intimidated into halting a planned attack. And what he really could not stand was the crowing of the Czech press that their firm military action stopped (defeated) the German juggernaut. On May 30, 1938, Hitler signed the Directive for Operation Green. Its first paragraph now read: "It is my unalterable decision to smash Czechoslovakia by military action in the near future. It is the business of the political leadership to await or bring about the suitable moment from a political and military point of view."[17] In fact, the German political leadership had no intention of awaiting the suitable moment; they set out to bring it about.

Examining their task, the German or, more accurately, the Nazi political leaders saw a determined, even defiant Czechoslovakia relying on her allies. They were not particularly worried about the Soviet Union. The Soviet armed forces were large but their high command was demoralized by Stalin's purges. Just recently the Commander-in-Chief, Marshal

---

[14] John W. Wheeler-Bennett, *Munich, Prologue to Tragedy* (New York: Duell, Sloan and Pearce, 1962), p. 55.

[15] *Documents on British Foreign Policy*, vol. I, p. 335.

[16] *Documents on German Foreign Policy*, vol. II, p. 320.

[17] Ibid., p. 300.

Tukhachevsky, and a dozen top generals had been arrested for treason and executed.[18] Moreover, the Soviet Union did not have a common border with Czechoslovakia, and neither Poland nor Rumania was likely to grant it transit.[19]

Czechoslovakia's ally, France, was strong in force, but weak in will. French governments were highly unstable. The people did not want war; they did not even want to hear of war. The enormous human losses of World War I were still fresh in memory. If necessary they would defend France from behind the heavily fortified Maginot Line, but to send troops into another country was to most unthinkable. And that is exactly what they would have to do if they were to come to the aid of Czechoslovakia. Even then it might be too late.

There was one power that worried the German leaders, however: Great Britain. Great Britain did not have a treaty with Czechoslovakia and did not have a chance to make a tactical impact.[20] But they were allied to France, and they did have a formidable strategic weapon: the Royal Navy. Germans who remembered the economic chaos and personal misery caused by the British blockade in World War I, and few did not, feared British intervention. Thus, the German planners knew if they were to succeed they somehow would have to manage His Majesty's government.

In this, Germany was not without assets. The British were never at ease with French power or with Frenchmen. They had serious doubts about the Treaty of Versailles and were genuinely uncomfortable with the German litany of its hypocrisies. The electorate was against war, any war, even armaments, practically all armaments.[21] Most important perhaps, the British

---

[18] It now seems highly probable that the evidence against these officers was fabricated by the Gestapo in collusion with the NKVD and fed back into the Soviet Union through Czechoslovakia by Soviet agents in Paris. Leonard Schapiro, "The Great Purge," in B. H. Liddell Hart (ed.), *The Red Army* (New York: Harcourt, Brace & Co., 1956), pp. 70–71.

[19] When during the May 20 crisis France inquired about their position, it was told by both that they would not voluntarily permit the Soviet army to cross their territories or the Soviet air force to fly over. Georges Bonnet, *De Munich a là Guerre, Defense de la Paix* (Paris: Plon, 1967), pp. 74–83.

[20] In March at Downing Street the British made it clear: "with the best will in the world . . . the greatest measure of help . . . would be two divisions." *Documents on British Foreign Policy*, Third series, vol. 1, p. 201.

[21] During the mid-1930s mass-demonstrations for disarmament, even unilateral disarmament, were frequent in England. One distinguished participant was Albert Einstein.

government needed peace in Europe. They had troubles to attend to in the Empire. Their major political concessions to the Indian nationalists on "home rule" in 1935 did not seem to placate them. They wanted more; they wanted independence. The "most precious jewel" of the imperial crown was in danger of being plucked out.

Hence in June 1938 German strategy followed three distinct lines. First, it sought to demonstrate the depravity of Czechoslovakia and its government. Its birth was illegitimate; it had behaved like a bastard. It had betrayed its promise of minority rights, its pledge of building a system on the Swiss model. Instead it had persecuted and brutalized helpless people—Germans, Hungarians, Poles, Ruthenians, even Slovaks. It would therefore logically follow that if Germany could come to the aid of its subjugated brethren it would have to attack, but the attack would not be unprovoked. Under these circumstances France would not be bound to honor its treaty obligation; indeed if it did give military aid to Czechoslovakia, it, France, would be guilty of aggression!

The British, the Germans thought, were a dispassionate people. Their government was not swayed by emotion and calculated national interest very carefully. Thus, the second component of German strategy was designed to address British strategic supremacy. Obviously Germany could not build a navy matching Britain's. Not in many years, certainly not in the short time available. But Germany was busy building its own strategic force, the *Luftwaffe*. The British people had some unpleasant memories of German air raids. They did not exactly fear them but they would rather not have them recurring. Germany could therefore emphasize the condition of strategic balance. Admittedly the Royal Navy could impose enormous suffering upon the German people, but the *Luftwaffe* could match it by bringing destruction to British cities. In fact, a strategic stalemate would result. Once the British would recognize this reality, they would see German reason.

All the time in the background, mostly by soft innuendo but at times breaking out into gross patronizing, was the third component of German strategy: Germany could do much for the British Empire. By being a power in Europe Germany would contribute to the continental balance. By becoming a "satisfied" power it could assure continental peace. And by being a great power it could, if worse came to worst, generously offer its military might to help assure that the sun would never set on the British Empire.

Germany's war of nerves moved into full swing. Dr. Josef Göbbels, minister of propaganda and national enlightenment, in a speech at Dessau on May 29, opened the campaign. He spent most of his time attacking

Czechoslovakia. After that the *Völkischer Beobachter*, the Nazi daily, devoted much of its front pages, almost daily, to "Czech Imperialism" (July 6), "Jewish Wirepullers in Czechoslovakia" (July 12), "Deceit of the Sudetens" (July 13), "Inciters against Peace" (July 15), "Czech Troop Movements" (July 18), "Feverish Military Activity" (July 19), "Czech Pretense of Concessions" (July 20), "Instruction in Hatred in School and Army" (July 23), etc. All along, the foreign minister and his state secretary officially played similar themes for the benefit of the British, French, and American ambassadors. "Prague was treating the Sudeten German area as a war zone" (June 23), "In schools and among soldiers, insulting songs about the Führer were being sung" (July 3), "There was absolutely no sign of the Czech catastrophe-politicians [*Katastrophenpolitiker*] being discouraged" (July 9); "The Czech regular army, as is generally known, has been almost in a state of full mobilization since May" (July 20); and so on.[22] The month of August saw further escalation. The *Völkischer Beobachter* reported provocative air space violations (August 4), assaults on Sudeten German civilians by Czech police (August 6), the Czech sabotage of the Sudeten youth movement (August 7), and then on August 13 the three column headline: "Blood, Death and Agony of the Sudetens," listing a page of incidents and Sudeten victims. The people of Germany were systematically aroused: more important, the international democratic news media was being fed a steady diet of atrocity stories. Some resisted it; some did not. There is after all no smoke without fire!

By August, however, the other line of the strategy was also in operation. German military power, especially air power, was emphasized.[23] Foreign air experts were invited to observe the capabilities of the *Luftwaffe*. They included the Commander in Chief of the French Air Force. Driving back to Berlin General Vuillimin confided in the French ambassador, André François-Ponçet: "Should war break out as you expect late in September, there won't be a single French plane left within a fortnight."[24]

All this time there were "negotiations" in Czechoslovakia. The Sudeten German leader, Konrad Henlein, set forth his demands: reorganize the system along Swiss lines. When Berlin discovered that he actually expected to negotiate, he was promptly superseded. Karl Hermann Frank, who called

---

[22] *Documents on German Foreign Policy*, vol. II. pp. 428, 453, 481, and 502.

[23] Instructions by "The Foreign Minister to German Missions Abroad," August 3, 1938. *Documents on German Foreign Policy*, vol. II, pp. 529–31.

[24] André François-Ponçet, *The Fateful Years*, translated by Jacques LeClerq (New York: Howard Fertig, 1972), p. 265.

the shots, was quite candid with his colleagues. "The negotiations make no difference. . . . There could be no question of a settlement of the Sudeten question except by force."[25]   By the end of August the demands had reached full autonomy and were about to be raised further still.

In any case, Prime Minister Chamberlain was anxious to give negotiations a chance. He sent a close associate Lord Runciman to mediate. Still in Berlin the strategy was running its course. Alfred-Ingemar Berndt, a young counselor in the Propaganda Ministry, had a large office that served as a factory of atrocity stories. Several tables were loaded down with maps, telephone, and city directories. Drawing information from them he made up "reliable reports," which were then released by the official news agency and beamed to the rest of the world—an awful lot of smoke. The foreign minister, of course, was doing his share. He explained to the British ambassador:

(1) The alliance of the French with the Czechs was a thoroughly immoral one, as it was based on the mentality of Versailles and aimed at establishing completely unjustified claims to hegemony.

(2) This alliance was immoral because it meant the oppression of 3 1/2 million Sudeten Germans.

(3) Not only was France under no obligation to intervene in any conflict provoked by the Czechs, but she was not even justified in doing so.[26]

There is no evidence that the German tales of horror were credited by the British government or that they appreciated German Foreign Minister von Ribbentrop's logic. But the British public and "influential circles" were affected. By the end of August the German ambassador in London reported a "growing British comprehension of the Czech problem," and an "increasing British readiness to take our demands into consideration."[27] On September 7 the lead article in the *London Times* suggested that it might be "worth while for the Czechoslovak government to consider whether they should exclude altogether the project which has found favor in some quarters of making Czechoslovakia a more homogeneous state by the secession of that fringe of alien populations who are contiguous to the nation to which they are united by race."[28] And the British government was getting very worried that French stonewalling might get them too entan-

---

[25] *Documents on German Foreign Policy*, vol. II p. 556.

[26] Ibid., p. 688.

[27] Ibid., p. 620.

[28] *London Times*, September 7, 1938, p. 13.

gled. Lord Halifax especially wanted Paris to have no illusions. "Whatever we might feel about any action that Germany might take in Czechoslovakia," he warned the French ambassador, "I did not think that British opinion would be prepared, any more than I thought His Majesty's Government would be prepared, to enter upon hostilities with Germany on account of aggression by Germany on Czechoslovakia."[29] So there it was as plain as could be. The linchpin of Czechoslovakia's security treaties was gone.

By then Czechoslovakia had made enormous concessions. It accepted the Swiss model. "My God, they have given us everything!" exclaimed Karl Frank.[30] He would have to find some pretext to torpedo the negotiations altogether. His masters in Berlin did not want autonomy. They wanted annexation. Two days later during a mass demonstration a German deputy was allegedly struck by the riding whip of a Czech policeman. "An unprecedented atrocity," cried the Sudetens and broke off negotiations! In any case, by then it was too late. France was about to crack.

When the Chips Were Down

The French foreign minister was searching for support. He had none from Poland, very little from Rumania, and a lot of awkward words from the Soviet Union. He turned to the United States. He received sympathy but no military promises whatsoever.[31] He broke down. On September 13 the British ambassador reported:

M. Bonnet was very upset and said that peace must be preserved at any price as neither France nor Great Britain were [sic] ready for war. Colonel Lindbergh had returned from his tour horrified at the overwhelming strength of Germany in the air. . . . He declares Germany has 8,000 military aeroplanes and can turn out 1,500 a month. M. Bonnet said that French and British towns would be wiped out and little or no retaliation would be possible.

M. Bonnet's collapse seems to me so sudden and so extraordinary that I am asking for an interview with M. Daladier.[32]

---

[29] *Documents on British Foreign Policy*, Third Series, vol. II, p. 276 (*Documents on German Foreign Policy*, vol. II, p. 732). Incidentally this secret conversation, which took place on the evening of September 9, was known to the German embassy and reported "Urgent, Top Secret" to Berlin at 3:30 P.M. September 10.

[30] Wheeler-Bennett, *Munich, Prologue to Tragedy*, p. 927.

[31] Bonnet, *De Munich a là Guerre*, pp. 123–26.

[32] *Documents on British Foreign Policy*, Third Series, vol. II, pp. 310–11.

Prime Minister Daladier was calm but essentially supported Bonnet. To a "point blank" question "he replied, but with evident lack of enthusiasm, that if Germans used force, France would be obligated also." But, he added quickly, and this was a crucial point, "of course he would have to be sure . . . [about the] rights and wrongs of recent bloodshed in Czechoslovakia." The British ambassador concluded: "I fear French have been bluffing, although I have continually pointed out to them that one cannot bluff Hitler."[33] In just three and a half months the German strategy had accomplished its purpose. As a practical matter Czechoslovakia stood alone. Next day Prime Minister Chamberlain offered to go to Hitler for direct negotiations, and Hitler was delighted.

On September 15 Chamberlain was cordially received at the German Führer's home in Berchtesgaden. He appreciated, Hitler said, the British prime minister's devotion to peace and his willingness to travel, which at his age was quite a distance. Had he known that Mr. Chamberlain had never flown before, he would have suggested a place much closer to Britain. And then the negotiations started. Hitler wanted the Sudetenland; he threatened war and offered peace. He cited atrocities and appealed to the principle of self-determination. He proclaimed his commitment to peace. There remained only one problem, Czechoslovakia, and Europe would have peace. But Czechoslovakia must give up the Sudeten territories. All Chamberlain wanted was a fig leaf. If there was to be cession of Czechoslovak territory, it would have to be the result of democratic processes: the people would have to have a chance to express their choice through a plebiscite. Such a plan could gain his support after discussions with his colleagues. He could then return to Germany for further negotiations. Hitler made a show of being generous.

The Führer declared that he would gladly save the British prime minister a second journey to Germany, for he was much younger and could undertake a journey of that kind; but he was afraid that were he to come to England anti-German demonstrations would complicate rather than simplify the situation. But in order somewhat to shorten the prime minister's journey he proposed for their next meeting the Lower Rhine area, Cologne, or Godesberg.[34]

Upon his return, the British prime minister had to face his French counterpart. The full day's session of the Anglo-French delegations, nearly

---

[33] Ibid., p. 312.
[34] Ibid., p. 350.

8 1/2 hours of work, included some very instructive exchanges.[35] Confronted by the demands and military threats of the German dictator the heads of the two most powerful democracies in Europe were, in fact, debating appeasement. Hitler had taunted Chamberlain at Berchtesgaden. He asked how democratic countries could refuse the application of a principle which they, and not he, had invented, "specifically 'the right of self-determination.'" Hitler, of course, did not give two hoots for the principle; he was chiefly interested in "racial unity," which, he said, had been his dominating preoccupation since birth. But the devil quotes the Bible, so a tyrant could use and abuse democratic principles by turning them against democracies. Chamberlain had endured the exposition of Hitler's views in Berchtesgaden. Now in London he was prepared to start from there. "The issue was, in the first instance," he argued, "a very simple one. It was a question whether or not to accept the principle of self-determination." Daladier cared a great deal for democracy, but he did not think it was intended to be a suicide pact. Self-determination was a sound principle, but it should not be pursued single-mindedly. He explained that such a solution would be very difficult for the French government to accept because clearly the German object in accepting a plebiscite would not be to solve the Sudeten problem but to disintegrate Czechoslovakia. At the same time, it would create a precedent capable of subsequent application elsewhere and liable to cause infinite complications throughout Europe.

The British put on the pressure. Lord Halifax, the foreign secretary, pointed to "the practical realities of the situation." From that perspective the conclusion was unavoidable: "whatever action were taken by ourselves, by the French government, by the Soviet government, at any given moment, it would be impossible to give effective protection to the Czechoslovak State. We might fight a war against German aggression, but at the Peace Conference which followed such a war he did not think that the statesmen concerned would redraft the present boundaries of Czechoslovakia. The British Government, like the French Government, had to face hard facts." The French resisted; they kept repeating the long-term perils of giving in to an aggressor. Its appetite is insatiable, and with each advance it will gain in power. "Germany's real aim was the disintegration of Czechoslovakia and the realisation of pan-German ideals through a march to the East. . . . The result would be that in a very short time Germany would be the master of Europe. . . . Within one year we might expect her to turn back against France and Great Britain who would then have to meet her in much more

---

[35] Ibid., pp. 373–99.

difficult circumstances than those existing today." Daladier used practically any argument. At one point he even let loose the heavy artillery of bombast. "In his view the problem was . . . to discover what could be done as a practical measure to avoid conflict and preserve what could be preserved of a State which might have made mistakes—and what great State had not made mistakes?—but to which France was bound as an ally and whom she could not desert without committing a crime." He tried everything to persuade Great Britain to do more for Czechoslovakia than she intended. The British, in turn, were determined to persuade France to do less than it said. In the end the strategic superiority of Britain prevailed. The French agreed. It was certainly very distressing in view of France's very close relations with a friendly country to whom she was bound by treaty. "They had to consider, Daladier said, the interests of European peace and, . . . they had to consider the interests of Czechoslovakia at this decisive moment in the history of Europe." There would be a joint Anglo-French message to Prague making it clear that "both Governments have been compelled to the conclusion that the maintenance of peace and the safety of Czechoslovakia's vital interests cannot effectively be assured unless these areas are now transferred to the Reich."[36] The appeasement had been only a fig leaf: the Czech territories to be relinquished would be determined by popular will: a plebescite.

The British-French note was delivered to Prague on September 19. Around the clock the government deliberated, then in the evening (7:45 P.M.) of the 20th rejected it. They offered a number of reasons, including that "the question of peace would not be resolved because (a) minority problems would again arise, (b) the balance of power would be destroyed," and begged Britain and France to reconsider.[37] Within hours (1:21 A.M., September 21) the British and French ambassadors in Prague were instructed to point out "to Czech Government that their reply in no way meets the critical situation which Anglo-French proposals were designed to avert" and to warn: "If on reconsideration Czech government feel bound to reject our advice, they must of course be free to take any action that they think appropriate to meet the situation that may thereafter develop."[38] Czechoslovakia was left no choice. By 6:30 A.M. it accepted.

On September 22 the British prime minister was back in Germany—halfway between London and Berchtesgaden. As he landed at

---

[36] Ibid., p. 405.

[37] Ibid., p. 424.

[38] Ibid., pp. 437–38.

Cologne airport, the band played "God Save the King," and an honor guard of a battalion of SS stood at motionless attention. The drive in an open car to Godesberg led through city streets decorated with flags—swastikas and the Union Jack flying side by side—and with friendly crowds waving from the sidewalks. They drove through the peaceful countryside and along green hills. Down below white boats could be seen cruising down the Rhine. The weather was fine; all in all it was a very pleasant drive. Finally they reached the Hotel Petersberg.[39] The rooms were comfortable; everything was arranged to serve even the slightest desires of the guests. Late in the afternoon Chamberlain and his party drove to Hitler's hotel. The greetings were friendly; they moved on to the conference room.

Chamberlain was in a good mood.[40] He was rather pleased with himself. He summarized the situation that existed at the close of their last meeting. He described all the dangers and all the problems he had faced, but in the end he had, in fact, succeeded. Czechoslovakia had accepted the principle of territorial cession; only the details would have to be agreed upon. Surely that could be accomplished peacefully. He went on to describe some proposals which would, he believed, satisfy the Führer's requirements. Then almost as though waiting for applause, he looked around.

All along, Hitler had been interrupting with queries, usually rather petty. Now he asked whether the proposals presented had actually been submitted to the Czechoslovak government. Yes, replied Chamberlain. In that case, said Hitler, he was sorry, since the proposals were no longer enough. Then followed a harangue about past injustices and the present wave of atrocities, about demands by Poland and Hungary, about the servitude of the Slovaks, about the Czech government being perfidious and unable to control its military and police personnel. And so on and on. There remained only one course: immediate German military occupation of the Sudetenland. Britain would not be allowed a fig leaf. Chamberlain was devastated. He was, he said plaintively,

both disappointed and puzzled at the Führer's statement. The Führer had said during their previous conversation that if he, the Prime Minister, could arrange for a settlement on the basis of self-determination he would be prepared then to discuss procedure. . . . [In the meantime] he [the prime minister] had induced his colleagues, the French and the Czechs to agree . . . , in fact he had got exactly what the Führer wanted and without the expenditure of a drop of German blood. In

---

[39] Ten years later it served as the seat of the Allied High Commission.

[40] *Documents on British Foreign Policy*, vol. II, pp. 463–73 and *Documents on German Foreign Policy*, vol. II, pp. 870–86.

doing so, he had been obliged to take his political life in his hands. As an illustration of the difficulties which he had to face, he mentioned that when he undertook his first flight to Germany he was applauded by public opinion. Today he was accused of selling the Czechs, yielding to dictates, capitulating, and so on. He had actually been booed on his departure today.

Hitler was unmoved. A report was brought to him: Twelve Sudeten Germans were shot in Eger as hostages![41] A diatribe against the Czechs ensued. Chamberlain tried to negotiate. Nothing doing. Hitler had no use for commissions, committees, etc. Only an immediate military occupation would do. No agreement was possible. The meeting broke up. At the door Hitler shook hands and said: "I am so sorry, I really wanted to show you the splendid view of the Rhine, but now it has become dusky and foggy."[42]

The next day there was an exchange of letters. Hitler repeated his position, and Chamberlain suggested a memorandum of the German position. Just before midnight the two met again.[43] Hitler was ready with his memorandum. It demanded Czech evacuation of the Sudetenland by September 26. At this point a message was passed to him. His foreign minister announced: Czechoslovakia was mobilizing. "In that event," exclaimed Hitler, "things were settled." The prime minister was not so sure. He tried to negotiate, but Hitler was not interested in negotiation. He preferred to harangue. "An end, even with terror, is better than terror without end!" He added that his memorandum did, in fact, represent his last word.

The prime minister had become subdued. In that event, there was no purpose in negotiating any further. I shall go home with a heavy heart, he said, "since I saw the final wreck of all my hopes for peace in Europe. But my conscience is clear;   I had done everything possible for peace. Unfortunately, I had not found an echo in Herr Hitler." The German foreign minister was worried: But what about the memorandum? It was not a memorandum, retorted Chamberlain, but an ultimatum. Embarrassed, very much like a schoolboy caught in a petty infraction, Hitler pointed to the paper. But, look here, at the top it says clearly "Memorandum." Chamberlain retorted that he was more impressed by contents than title. Almost pointlessly, the discussion went on. Hitler agreed to extend the deadline to

---

[41] This too proved later to be a lie.

[42] Erwin Wickert, *Dramatische Tage in Hitlers Reich* (Stuttgart: Steingrüben Verlag, 1952), p. 162.

[43] *Documents on British Foreign Policy*, vol. II, pp. 499–508 and *Documents on German Foreign Policy*, vol. II, pp. 898–908.

October 1; Chamberlain agreed to pass on the Memorandum to the Czech government.[44]

Within a day the answer came back from Prague. Hitler's demands were rejected as "absolutely and unconditionally unacceptable. . . . The nation of St. Wenceslas, John Hus and Thomas Masaryk will not be a nation of slaves." The note closed poignantly with: "We rely upon the two great Western democracies, whose wishes we have followed much against our own judgment, to stand by us in our hour of trial."[45]

The problem was, Jan Masaryk, the Czech minister in London, was not that confident in the British government. In a dispatch ten days earlier he had described Chamberlain as seeking peace at all cost and his advisers Horace Wilson and Sir Neville Henderson, as outright enemies. Now he reported: It is a misfortune that this ignorant, poorly informed, little man is the prime minister, and I am convinced, that he shall not remain so for long.[46] And the problem was that when after Godesberg the British and French statesmen met at Downing Street, they had no hope of saving Czechoslovakia. All they could discuss was what each would do in case of an attack. What would, for example, France do. Daladier always emphatic of French support for Czechoslovakia was curiously evasive. He cited Goethe and referred to Cassandra, he spoke of many things, and was carried along by eloquence. "There was one concession, however, he could never make, . . . which had for its object the destruction of a country and Herr Hitler's domination of the world and of all that we valued most. France would never accept that, come what might."[47] And what about Britain. What would she do? It was Chamberlain's turn to be evasive. Everything would depend on circumstances.

It was past noon of September 26 when the meeting adjourned. Chamberlain had sent a special envoy to urge Hitler to hold his hand. Later he met with the High Commissioners of the British Dominions who

---

[44] Ernst von Weizsäcker, *Memoirs of Ernst von Weizsäcker*, translated by John Andrews (Chicago: Henry Regnery Co., 1951), p. 152; Wickert, *Dramatische Tage in Hitlers Reich*, pp. 158–67; and *Documents on British Foreign Policy*, Third Series, vol. II, pp. 499–508.

[45] *Documents on British Foreign Policy*, Third Series, vol. II, p. 519.

[46] Vaclav Kral, *Das Abkommen von München 1938* (Praha: Nakladatelstri Ceskoslovenske Akademie Ved, 1968), pp. 223–24 and Wickert, *Dramatische Tage in Hitlers Reich*, p. 172. Presumably the British Secret Service knew about these and other indiscretions of Jan Masaryk and informed the prime minister.

[47] *Documents on British Foreign Policy*, Third Series, vol. II p. 529.

uniformly expressed doubts that Czechoslovakia was worth fighting over. In turn, Hitler addressed a mass meeting in Berlin. His personal attack on President Beneš was venomous, but he praised Chamberlain and offered to guarantee the borders of Czechoslovakia after territorial cession, ("We want no Czechs"). He promised "to have no further territorial claims in Europe."

By September 27 the war of nerves had reached intolerable levels. German propaganda was blaring in crescendo, but Counsellor Berndt, head of the atrocity reports factory, had reached his limit. "Something must now really happen," he exclaimed, "otherwise my imagination can no longer invent further atrocity stories."[48] Chamberlain had already written to President Beneš: "I feel bound to tell you and the Czechoslovak government that the information His Majesty's Government now have from Berlin makes it clear that German forces will have orders to cross Czechoslovakia frontier almost immediately, unless by 2.00 P.M. tomorrow Czechoslovak Government have accepted German terms." He had replied to Hitler: "After reading your letter, I feel certain that you can get essentials without war, and without delay. I am ready to come to Berlin myself at once to discuss arrangements for transfer."[49] In the evening he addressed the nation on the BBC. "How horrible, fantastic, incredible it is that we should be digging trenches and trying on gas-masks here," he complained, "because of a quarrel in a far-away country between people of whom we know nothing. . . . *However much we may sympathize with a small nation confronted by a big and powerful neighbour, we cannot in all circumstances undertake the whole British Empire in war simply on her account.*"[50] Later he met with the Cabinet. His emissary to Hitler reported no progress. But from Rome, Lord Perth, the British ambassador, cabled a suggestion. Perhaps if he were to ask the Italian dictator, Mussolini, to help out. The Foreign Office approved with alacrity. Something had to be done. The democracies were defensive and confused. Hitler knew what he wanted and the democracies believed that Germany stood united behind him.

This was the biggest deception of all. Resistance to Hitler had been growing steadily. The State Secretary of Foreign Affairs had warned on

---

[48] Theo Kordt, *Nicht aus den Akten* (Stuttgart: Union Deutsche Verlagsgesellschaft, 1950), p. 266.

[49] Feiling, *The Life of Neville Chamberlain* (Hamden, CT: Archon Books, 1970), p. 372.

[50] Keith Robbins, *Munich 1938* (London: Cassell, 1968), p. 306. [Italics added.]

August 30: "In this situation the leaders of German policy, must, in my opinion, revise their plans. If they do not do so, the war—shortly after the German action—would develop into a European one. This war would sooner or later end in a German capitulation."[51] Senior military officers had been hostile for years. On July 16, 1938, the Chief of the General Staff urged all military leaders to joint resistance to war. On August 4 the Commander-in-Chief of the Army after a conference of all army group commanders and commanding generals declared: "I hereby conclude that the higher leaders of the Army are united in their views opposing a war."[52] On August 18–19 Ewald von Kleist, a secret emissary from the German General Staff, visited London. He saw Winston Churchill, but in the government only the Undersecretary of Foreign Affairs. His message: hold fast, do not be intimidated by Hitler. Chamberlain saw the report of the visit, then wrote to Lord Halifax: "I think we must discount a good deal of what he says. Nevertheless I confess to some feeling of uneasiness and I don't feel sure that we ought not do something."[53]

By mid-September a conspiracy was in full progress. It included among others senior generals (Beck and Halder), the commanders of the military districts of Berlin and Potsdam (von Witzleben and von Brockdorff), the head of military intelligence and his deputy (Canaris and Oster), the Controller of Armaments (Thomas), and the Chief of Police of Berlin and his deputy (Count Helldorf and von der Schulenburg). Even the Commander-in-Chief of the Army (von Brauchitsch) was in sympathy. The moment Hitler gave the order to invade Czechoslovakia they would act and remove Hitler from power.

In the evening of September 27 a motorized division was passing through Berlin. Hitler had ordered it in the hope that it would stimulate a patriotic outburst. In August 1914 German troops marching through the capital were wildly cheered. But this time the Berliners thought the troops were on their way to war. There was no applause, no cheering, only quiet anxiety. As the motorized units approached the Reich Chancellery, Hitler ordered the lights turned off in his office and watched from behind the drapes. He saw the troops and he saw the people. He turned suddenly and exploded in anger: One cannot make war with this nation.[54]

---

[51] *Documents on German Foreign Policy*, vol. II, p. 663. (His son is now the president of West Germany.)

[52] Wickert, *Dramatische Tage in Hitlers Reich*, p. 185.

[53] *Documents on British Foreign Policy*, Third Series, vol. II p. 686.

[54] Kordt, *Nicht aus den Akten*, p. 268.

It was a fine morning in Rome on September 28. Lord Perth was calmly and systematically working through his breakfast. A highest-priority message from Lord Halifax had arrived. The ambassador finished what he was doing and then read the message. It instructed him to deliver immediately a personal message of the prime minister to Mussolini asking his support with Hitler. The ambassador called Foreign Minister Count Ciano to arrange an interview with the Italian dictator. The appointment was quickly set. Italy had been on the sidelines of the great European drama. Mussolini did not like that at all. Here was his chance to act. He demanded immediate telephone connection with the Italian ambassador in Berlin. To his surprise the telephone operator succeeded. (After the crisis she received a decoration for her work.) Mussolini ordered his ambassador (Attolico) to see Hitler immediately to request a 24-hour delay in German military action and then to propose a four-power summit. Attolico called the German Foreign Office. He shouted into the phone (in English): "I have a personal message from il Duce. I must see the Führer at once, very urgent, quick, quick."[55] Please come ahead. To facilitate his passage through Hitler's SS guards he gave his car's license number and then ran out to his car. Alas his driver was taking a midmorning break, and the ambassador had to find a taxi.

At the Reich Chancellery the tension was nerve-wracking. Ambassadors, generals, SS men were rushing around. Outside Hitler's office in a large room the tables were being set for a luncheon Hitler would give for the commanders of the invasion. It was scheduled to begin at 1:00 P.M. Shortly after 11:00 A.M. François-Ponçet, the French ambassador, arrived. Hitler received him, and they debated Czechoslovakia. Hitler was nervous and tense; his arguments were lame and relatively tame. Back and forth, back and forth. The door opened. An SS adjutant spoke to Hitler: Attolico had an urgent message. Hitler left the office, listened to the Italian ambassador, and accepted Mussolini's request. It was just before 12:00 noon. He returned to François-Ponçet but hardly listened any more. When a little later Henderson came with a message from Chamberlain, Hitler told him of Mussolini's initiative and issued the invitations for the summit. The leaders of the coup soon got the news. Their cause had become hopeless. Depressed they disbanded.

In London Parliament was in session.[56] The galleries were full. People sat in the aisles waiting for the prime minister to speak. Queen Mary, the

---

[55] Ibid., p. 271.
[56] *London Times*, September 29, 1938, pp. 6–7.

Duchess of Kent, the Archbishops of Canterbury and York, the ambassadors of the major powers, everyone was there. The prime minister entered and was greeted by applause. He took his place as the House proceeded with its regular business. They were debating a bill on worker's compensation. The speeches droned on. Finally the prime minister rose. Slowly and carefully he reviewed the history of the Czechoslovak conflict and described its issues. Everyone listened in silence. For more than an hour the prime minister droned on. Lord Douglass, one of Chamberlain's private secretaries, entered, tiptoed to the front bench, and passed a paper to Sir John Simon, the Chancellor of the Exchequer. He glanced at it and tried to attract the prime minister's attention. But Chamberlain was not to be distracted. The tension became unbearable. Finally at 4:15 Sir John succeeded in getting the message through. They whispered but the microphone picked up the question: Should I tell them? Sir John urged yes. Chamberlain turned to the House, smiled, and declared: "This is not all. I have something further to say to the House yet. I have now been informed by Herr Hitler that he invites me to meet him at Munich tomorrow morning. He also invited Signor Mussolini and M. Daladier. Signor Mussolini has accepted and I have no doubt M. Daladier will accept. I need not say what my answer will be." The applause was deafening and prolonged. As the prime minister prepared to leave, Members, government and opposition, crowded around him to shake his hand. Only Harold Nicolson sat quietly and Anthony Eden walked out. "There was a loud cheer," reported the *Times*, "when Mr. Churchill went up to the Prime Minister and cordially shook his hand."

About this time Mussolini's special train was leaving Rome. Il Duce was in excellent spirits. In the politics of great powers he was once again center stage. With great vivacity he pronounced on many subjects. Obviously he had no respect for the British. "In a country where animals are adored to the point of making cemeteries and hospitals and houses for them, and legacies are bequeathed to parrots, you can be sure that decadence had set in," he declared. "Besides, other reasons apart, it is also a consequence of the composition of the English people. Four million surplus women. Four million sexually unsatisfied women, artificially creating a host of problems in order to excite or appease their senses. Not being able to embrace one man, they embrace humanity."[57] At the border Hitler joined them on the train. He was not particularly interested in

---

[57] Count Galeazzo Ciano, *Diary 1937–1938*, translated by Andreas Mayor (London: Methuen, 1952), p. 166.

parrots, women, or such things. He was interested in the maps of Czecho-slovakia and Western fortifications. He had to liquidate Czechoslovakia he explained, because it tied down forty German divisions. "Besides the time will come when we shall have to fight side by side against France and England. All the better that it should happen while the Duce and I are the head of our countries, and still young and full of vigor."[58]

Nobody paid any attention to the Czechs. Jan Masaryk, the Czechoslo-vak minister, attended Chamberlain's speech in parliament. He was devastated. He called at the foreign office where he was told that Hitler had consented to the conference only on the condition that Czechoslovakia and Russia be excluded. "If you have sacrificed my nation to preserve the peace of the world," he exclaimed struggling for self-control, "I will be the first to applaud you. But if not, gentlemen, God help your souls."[59]

The Munich Conference was an anticlimax. Hitler got everything he demanded. After the agreement was signed (September 30 at 2:30 A.M.) and the Germans and Italians departed, the Czech representatives were summoned. The terms were explained. Daladier was silent, Chamberlain was reportedly yawning frequently. At the end the Czechs asked whether a response regarding the terms was expected from their government. "No," M. Leger, the French State Secretary for Foreign Affairs, said very quietly.

Soon Chamberlain returned home. Germans lined the streets five and six deep cheering him enthusiastically. In London he was met by a jubilant crowd. He had brought peace and "he was a jolly good fellow." Daladier too was flying back. He was worried. In the air he was told that a very large crowd was assembling at Le Bourget airfield. He feared he might be lynched. The pilot sought an alternate place to land, but all other fields in the area were closed by fog. So it had to be Le Bourget. The plane landed, the crowd surged forward, anxiously Daladier stepped out, and he heard they were cheering![60]

The travails of Czechoslovakia continued, but the story can end here. It has already been long enough to illustrate the perils of a weaker country becoming entirely dependent on a major power. This is not to say that countries heavily dependent on the United States for their security, let us say South Korea or Israel, when facing a crisis in the future can expect a fate similar to Czechoslovakia. Times change, systems change, and the

---

[58] Ibid.

[59] Wheeler-Bennett, *Munich, Prologue to Tragedy*, p. 171.

[60] In the United States *Time* magazine named as its "Man of the Year" Adolf Hitler.

differences in the personality and character of heads of government are not insignificant. Even so, neither the United States nor our friends and allies can wisely disregard the possibility altogether.

In a broader sense, recounting the details of the Munich crisis does focus on the vulnerability of democracies with their openness, freedom of press, and inclusionary, participatory method of decision-making when facing a systematic campaign by the controlled media of a highly structured authoritarian power.

8

Across the North Atlantic

The civilization of Western Europe and by extension that of Northern and Southern Europe formed the foundation of our own. Their people provided a large share of immigrants who settled and developed this country. Their values are very much like ours; their commitment to human rights and the democratic form of government is no less profound. We have been friends for a long time and comrades-at-arms with most in two great wars. Economically Western Europe offers important markets for our industry and commerce. Militarily it denies valuable jumping-off points for aggression against us.

These are weighty arguments for our friendly cooperation, but since World War II we seemed to be moving toward a consensus for a much deeper relationship: a North Atlantic Community. Initially we made some progress in that direction, but we never actually reached the point where our relationship could accurately be so characterized. And lately we are witnessing progressive deterioration. Possibly it is a case of good intentions going awry. Possibly the process was tragically handicapped by disparities exacerbated by extraordinary conditions.

Extraordinary conditions marked the very beginning. The takeoff in the development toward the North Atlantic Community occurred in the wake of World War II, and World War II was a very, very different experience for the countries and the peoples on the two sides of the Atlantic.

For Western Europeans the war was a dreadful experience. Without exception they were victims of a total war that brought uninterrupted horrors to all, combatants and civilians alike. When it was over, Germany was on its knees, but the cost to Britain, France, Belgium, and Holland was monstrous. Towns everywhere were in shambles; their inhabitants were hungry, cold, and often homeless. (The Dutch had to eat their prized storks to survive.) Their ties to their families and friends were shattered; their confidence in government was at best severely strained. The economies had collapsed. People everywhere were disoriented. Everything had a price; nothing was holy any more. In Germany American cigarettes and chocolate bars could and did buy anything and almost everyone. Indeed Western Europeans, victors and vanquished, were very much in the same boat, and a very leaky boat at that.

In sharp contrast, for Americans the war in Europe and its aftermath were rather exhilarating experiences. Our homeland was never in danger, and our casualties were modest. To the people stunned by the Great Depression, the war restored self-confidence. It demonstrated the heroism and self-reliance of our young men and women, our immense industrial capacity, our irresistible military power, and our decency and generosity. The greatness of our people and our country, we had no doubt, was there for all to see. We knew what was right; we knew what to do.

Right away the United States did a number of things to help. It gave a large loan to Britain, accepted hundreds of thousands of displaced persons, and then financed a massive and comprehensive European Recovery Program (Marshall Plan). Between 1948 and 1952 the United States gave away over $12 billion of goods, a fabulous sum in times when even a single million was highly respected. By 1952 Western European production had increased to 200 percent of prewar levels. Obviously the United States knew what to do and was prepared to do it.

Prompt, short-run rehabilitation was not all. The United States had very special ideas for long-range solutions as well. First, economic integration. The Economic Cooperation Act of 1948 made it clear that Americans were "mindful of the advantage which the United States has enjoyed through the existence of a large-scale domestic market with no internal trade barriers and [believed] that similar advantages can accrue to the countries of Europe."[1] Second, political unification. Many in government hoped that political integration would be a natural and necessary consequence of economic integration. But in any case, political unity would be compelled by common sense. Surely Western Europeans had learned the lessons of war. Had it not been for intense national divisions and rivalries, all the misery could have been avoided. Just look at the example of the United

---

[1] John Spanier, *American Foreign Policy since World War II*, 9th ed. (New York: Holt, Rinehart and Winston, 1983), p. 38.

States. Thirteen rather insignificant sovereign states united; together they spread across a whole continent and grew into a world power. *E pluribus unum*. Europe, especially Western Europe, could surely follow the example: the United States of Europe.

The Europeans were pleased with their recovery and were willing to credit the heavy inflow of American goods. They were not sanguine about the long-range solutions "Made in the USA." They went along with economic integration. When it came to a political union, however, the *pièce de résistance* of the American design was getting nowhere fast. As the economies recovered, notwithstanding American threats of "agonizing reappraisal," the momentum turned away from regional integration. Traditional solidarities reasserted themselves. Consultations and cooperation would continue, even improve in cordiality. Alliances would remain desirable, but their fundamental and increasingly explicit assumption was the sovereignty of the nation state: the right of each independently from each other and independently from the United States to determine its own national interest. General Charles de Gaulle, since 1958 once again president of France, spelled out the position: "I have already said, and I repeat, that at the present time there cannot be any other Europe than a Europe of States, apart, of course, from myths, stories, and parades."[2]

Facing so clear a challenge, the Americans would not back down; they would not abandon their design for the United States of Europe. President Kennedy reiterated the point. "It is only a fully cohesive Europe," he declared, "that can protect us all against fragmentation of the alliance. Only such a Europe will permit full reciprocity of treatment across the ocean, in facing the Atlantic agenda. With only such a Europe can we have a full give-and-take between equals, an equal sharing of responsibilities, and an equal level of sacrifice."[3]

Behind the debate over the political organization of Western Europe, however, lurked a much more fundamental issue: the role of the United States in the Atlantic community. Times have changed. Such descriptions as patron:client or doctor:patient relationships may have been fairly realistic in the 1940s though not much appreciated by Europeans. By the sixties these descriptions were inappropriate and deeply resented by them.

---

[2] Press conference, May 15, 1962. *Major Addresses, Statements and Press Conferences of General Charles de Gaulle*, May 19, 1958–January 31, 1964 (New York: French Embassy, Press and Information Division, 1964), p. 176.

[3] John F. Kennedy, Address at Frankfurt, Germany, June 25, 1963. *Department of State Bulletin*, 49, no. 1256 (July 22, 1963), p. 122.

SECURITY DOMINATES ALL

The problem was that while gross disparities were ameliorated on a wide front, they remained paramount, indeed were exacerbated, by strategic realities. Western European countries remained profoundly vulnerable. Soviet forces stationed in Eastern European countries were nearby; the Soviet Union itself was not far away. Western European countries, each by itself or even all together, were no match for Soviet military might. To be reasonably secure from predatory initiatives, for their very survival they desperately needed American support. The Soviet Union was visibly gobbling up country after country along its borders. It seemed they would never stop unless the United States drew a line and posted no trespassing signs. And that was exactly what happened, but when it did, it obscured the fundamental problem of the disparity of perspective. For the survival of Western European states in the face of Soviet aggression, their essentially regional rationale, conveniently coincided with the containment of Soviet power, the essentially global rationale of American foreign policy. It worked while it lasted, and it lasted throughout the Cold War.

In April 1949 Western Europe and North America formed the North Atlantic Treaty Organization (NATO). Initially it was an organization with no money, no forces, and no command. During the solemn signing ceremony, the Marine Corps band played, at the suggestion of the secretary of state (with a wry sense of humor) two songs from *Porgy and Bess*: "It Ain't Necessarily So" and "I've Got Plenty of Nothing." But the signatories had high hopes. They proposed to establish an integrated military command structure and called for the assignment of forces to NATO by each of the member states. Perhaps most important, they made a security commitment in Article 5 of the treaty: "The Parties agree that an armed attack against one or more of them in Europe or North America shall be considered an attack against them all."[4] As unambiguously as its constitutional provisions permitted, the United States let it be known that any military superiority which the Soviet Union might have against any Western European country (or all Western European countries together) would be more than offset by adding American strategic resources to the Western European side of the balance. In consequence, any Soviet attack

---

[4] United States, *Treaties and Other International Agreements of the United States of America 1776–1949*, Department of State Publication no. 8521 (Washington, DC, U.S. Government Printing Office, 1970), vol. 4, p. 829. NATO was later joined by Greece and Turkey (1952), West Germany (1955), and Spain (1982).

would suffer defeat, or at least the Soviet homeland would suffer enormous, unacceptable devastation.

It was a relatively simple matter during the first decade of the treaty. The United States had nuclear monopoly or at least was safe from nuclear attack. Credibly without much cost it could "extend" its own strategic deterrence by a written commitment. Our allies could feel safe under an American nuclear umbrella. Had it remained a simple matter, it would have provided an opportunity to build solidarity.

As the Soviet Union deployed its own nuclear weapons and long-range delivery systems, however, the situation changed radically. In Western Europe it triggered a haunting *déjà vu*. Many saw a balance of strategic forces of a democratic and a totalitarian government with the latter enjoying an advantage in conventional forces plus a massive propaganda apparatus reinforced by a controlled press. They wondered if this would be a prelude to a new "Munich." Had the Americans learned an essentially European lesson, would they act differently from Britain and France, the great democracies, two decades ago? In fact, would they risk a nuclear attack on their country to defend Western Europe from a conventional attack? Once the doubts that the United States would risk America to save Western Europe were shared by the Soviet leadership, the credibility of "extended deterrence" was very much in peril. Faced with the fundamentally changed strategic circumstances, three alternatives seemed indicated. First, it was still possible to believe that the United States would risk America for Western Europe. The strange combination of idealism and pragmatism that is so characteristic of Americans and has marked their foreign policy is rather unpredictable.

A second possible approach was for the major European powers to build their own independent strategic nuclear capabilities. Britain already had such a force. President de Gaulle was determined that France too should get one. The Soviet Union must be left with no illusions. Any attack on France would cost them quite a lot, way out of proportion of any possible gain. Even if the Americans were to let her down, France would still have the strategic force of its own to punish the Soviet homeland.

Then there was the third, very different, approach. Instead of relying on assured strategic punishment, a conventional attack on Western Europe could conceivably be deterred by the prospect of defeat in the field by conventional NATO forces. In 1955 West Germany was admitted to the alliance. Its forces, when added to those of France and Britain reinforced by American units, would present a formidable combination. Surely, so the argument ran, the Soviet Army is not invincible. It has problems of leadership and morale; some of its equipment is flawed, and its maintenance is spotty; and of course the supply lines of an attack on Western Europe would have to run through "satellite" countries whose people would not be wholly supportive. The Soviet Army could be defeated.

In the event, all three options were combined. Britain maintained and France built their own strategic (nuclear) forces. Meanwhile NATO collectively was building up its conventional forces. Plus the American commitment to Article 5 of NATO was constantly reiterated; public assurance never wavered. The United States would not accept the communist conquest of Europe. The Soviet Union should entertain no doubts. If everything else failed, the United States would use its full strategic retaliatory capacity to punish the aggressor. It all added up to a system of "flexible response," that is, deterrence at each level of aggression by symmetric capabilities. All in all, it was not an altogether satisfactory approach. To begin with, doubts persisted about the U.S. nuclear umbrella. President Charles de Gaulle would not believe in it at all. "Despite its power," he confided shortly after his retirement, "I don't believe the United States has a long-term policy. Its desire, and it will satisfy it one day, is to desert Europe. You will see."[5]

Then again the notion of French and British strategic nuclear forces deterring Soviet aggression was seriously flawed. Even the largest of the European powers was in modern global terms relatively small in territory. All of France could easily fit into Nevada and New Mexico; Britain could fit into either with room to spare. How could strategic weapons become survivable in such limited space? How could a relatively small strategic nuclear force deter a very much larger one?

Perhaps most important, the third component, deterrence by the prospect of defeat in the field, suffered from very serious difficulties. They were exacerbated when President de Gaulle withdrew French forces from the unified NATO command and forced the NATO Headquarters to leave his country and relocate in Brussels, Belgium. The Supreme Allied Commander for Europe for one did not mince any words: NATO's "conventional capabilities today," he said, "are clearly inadequate to meet the growing Warsaw Pact conventional threat."[6]

For a while it appeared that we could solve the problem by deploying tactical nuclear weapons. In the late 1970s we were actually ready to

---

[5] André Malraux, *Felled Oaks: Conversations with de Gaulle* (New York: Holt, Rinehart and Winston, 1971), p. 30.

[6] General Bernard W. Rogers, "The Atlantic Alliance: Prescription for a Difficult Decade." *Foreign Affairs*, 60, no. 5 (Summer 1982), p. 1152.

develop a new, enhanced radiation warhead. President Carter, however, in what was described as a very personal decision and overruling all his advisers, decided against the production of such weapons.[7]

The Soviet Union, however, was not similarly constrained. It already had fighters and short-range bombers that could deliver small nuclear bombs. It also had nuclear-capable artillery and kept building better ones and more of them. Indeed "the number of their nuclear capable artillery tubes had gone from less than 800 to over 7,700 in about ten years."[8] The time was passing when NATO disadvantages in case of aggression by conventional forces could be overcome *and deterred* by escalation to tactical nuclear weapons.

CRISIS IN DETERRENCE

Still not satisfied, the Soviet Union went one step further. It deployed a new offensive weapon: the SS-20, an intermediate-range missile.[9] It was a secure weapon. Mobile and deployed far to the East in the Soviet Union, it was beyond any NATO capability to take it out. MIRVed with three warheads the SS-20 had a range of 2,700 miles. Once fired, the SS-20 would take only a few minutes to reach NATO forces and facilities so heavily congested in West Germany. By radically improving the prospects of a Soviet surprise preemptive strike, it presented a formidable challenge to deterrence.

The SS-20 forced Europeans to think of the unthinkable: the breakdown of deterrence. That contingency always placed them in a frightful dilemma. Understandably they wished fervently that deterrence be successful and

---

[7] Cyrus Vance, *Hard Choices* (New York: Simon & Schuster, 1983), pp. 68–69; and Zbigniew Brzezinski, *Power and Principle: Memoirs of a National Security Advisor 1977–1981* (New York: Straus & Giroux, 1983), pp. 302–06. In the view of former Secretary of Defense James Schlesinger, it was a "capital blunder from which he never wholly recovered." James Schlesinger, "The Eagle and the Bear, Ruminations on Forty Years of Superpower Relations" *Foreign Affairs*, 63 (Summer 1985), p. 955.

[8] United States, House of Representatives, Subcommittee of the Committee on Appropriations, *Soviet Military Power*, 1985, pp. 39, 68. Their short-range nuclear missiles were estimated at 700 in 1983.

[9] By 1979, 120 were deployed; by 1985, 400, two-thirds opposite NATO. Collins, *U.S.-Soviet Military Balance*, p. 461; United States, House of Representatives, Subcommittee of the Committee on Appropriations, *Soviet Military Power*, 1985, p. 36.

they be spared Soviet attack. To have any chance of credible deterrence they needed and wanted the Americans: their military forces and their nuclear power. No less understandably they wanted very much, in case deterrence failed, to be spared from becoming a nuclear battlefield and ultimately ending up as a radioactive ash heap.[10] To put it simply, if deterrence failed and the Soviet Union actually did invade Western Europe, most Europeans would have found it in their vital interest to surrender. But they were not sure about the Americans, They might be quite willing to fight it out—on European soil. Contemplating that contingency, Europeans did not want the Americans: not their military forces and especially not their nuclear power.

All things considered, it was an unsatisfactory situation. Something had to be done. The Western Europeans knew it; the Americans knew it. To upgrade the credibility of NATO deterrence, American military capabilities in Europe needed to be reinforced but without overwhelmingly aggravating European public anxieties, which could be expected to be stirred by Soviet propaganda. The negotiations had their ups and downs, but by December 1979 an agreement was hammered out. It called for a dual-track approach. First, a diplomatic initiative. To appease European public opinion President Carter agreed to enter into arms control negotiations in order to try to persuade the Soviet Union to eliminate its SS-20s or at least to stop deploying them. Second, a military countermove. The plan called for the deployment of 464 new ground launched cruise missiles and most important 108 new Pershing II missiles.[11]

---

[10] In June 1955 NATO held an exercise to find out what casualties might result from tactical nuclear warfare. It was found that in less than three days 1.5 to 1.7 million people would be killed and 3.5 million wounded if only 268 bombs fell on German soil. The rate of German casualties would be five times that suffered in World War II as a whole. In 1960 NATO maneuvers in Schleswig-Holstein showed that between 300,000 and 400,000 civilian deaths could be expected within forty-eight hours of the initiation of tactical nuclear warfare. These figures did not take into account the effects of radiation and ensuing diseases. Theodore Draper, "Nuclear Temptations: Doctrinal Issues in the Nuclear Debate," in Charles W. Kegley, Jr., and Eugene Wittkopf. eds., *The Nuclear Reader: Strategy, Weapons, War* (New York: St. Martin's Press, 1985), p. 28. It does not take much imagination to conclude that by the 1980s potential casualties have multiplied many times over.

[11] To reassure public opinion that NATO was not expanding its reliance on nuclear missiles, however, 1,000 nuclear warheads already in Western Europe were

(continued...)

The Pershing II was of crucial importance. With its 1,000-plus-miles range it could reach in less than ten minutes' flight time well into the Soviet Union itself. With some alterations, invisible on the outside, its range could be extended beyond Moscow to the command centers of the Soviet armed forces. Moreover, its alleged accuracy (within sixty to120 feet of the designated target) gave it some hard-target capability. In short, while it could be used as a tactical weapon affecting the outcome of a battle, *it could also serve as a strategic weapon.*

From the point of view of deterrence, therefore, the Pershing II made a decisive difference. By reinforcing it with an additional capability, it would enormously improve credibility. The prospect that the devastations of aggression could be limited to Western European battlefields was practically eliminated. An attack on Western Europe would trigger a strategic nuclear strike from Western Europe. It risked Mother Russia.[12]

Following the "dual-track" approach, President Reagan was willing to negotiate with the Soviet Union about the reduction of "intermediate-range nuclear forces" (INF). He proposed the zero-zero option in intermediate-range ballistic missiles. "The United States is prepared," the president declared, "to cancel its deployment of the Pershing II and ground-launched missiles if the Soviets dismantle their SS-20, SS-4 and SS-5 missiles."[13]

To be sure, the zero:zero option was essentially a politically motivated compromise. We were sure they would never accept it. As President Nixon explained: "When the United States proposed in November 1981, the zero option . . . it did so not because policy makers thought that such a solution served Western interests but because it expected the Russians to reject the idea and suffer politically for doing so. It was assumed that the proposal would score political points in Europe and enable the United States to station intermediate-range nuclear forces in NATO countries."[14]

---

[11](...continued)
to be withdrawn. Brzezinski, *Power and Principle*, p. 309.

[12] In 1981 President Reagan explained our response to the SS-20. "Now the only answer to these systems," he said, "is a comparable threat to Soviet threats, to Soviet targets. In other words, a deterrent preventing the use of these Soviet weapons by a counterthreat of a like response against their own country." *The New York Times*, November 19, 1981, p. A17. Gorbachev understood the special value of the Pershing II quite well. He later declared: By signing the INF treaty we had literally removed a pistol held to our head. Gorbachev, *Memoirs*, p. 444.

[13] *The New York Times*, November 19, 1985, p. A17.

[14] *The New York Times Magazine*, March 13, 1988, p. 79.

The Soviet leadership liked one-half of the president's proposal: the American zero. Especially the Pershing II zero. But on the Soviet zero they balked. For almost two years they made all kinds of counterproposals. None of them permitted the deployment of any Pershing IIs and none dropped the permitted SS-20 level below 140. None of them could be acceptable to the United States. In November 1983 the deployment of Cruise missiles in Britain and Pershing IIs in Germany commenced, and the Soviet Union walked out of the negotiations.

THE PASSING OF PERIL

They did come back. Negotiating sessions were scheduled, delegations met and discussed a wide range of technical details, but the initiative had passed to the highest political levels. And on the highest political level fundamental changes were in progress. The Soviet Union had a new, very different leader. Mikhael Gorbachev wasted no time. Shortly after the Reykjavik Summit he stunned the world and accepted the zero:zero option.

We really had little choice but to agree. After all, it was our proposal in the first place. Moreover, the INF treaty eliminated an entire class of nuclear armed missiles, and it may have been the first successful move to start a momentum for reductions in strategic missiles. On December 8, 1987, at the Washington Summit the treaty was formally signed.[15] In it each party pledged (1) that it would eliminate all its intermediate-range missiles and launchers and their support structure and support equipment within three years;[16] (2) that it would eliminate all shorter-range missiles and launchers and their support structures and support equipment;[17] and (3) that it would not in the future produce or flight-test any intermediate- or shorter-range missiles or produce any stages or launchers of such missiles.

European leaders publicly endorsed the treaty, but privately they were utterly dismayed. They objected to the manner in which it had been arrived at: negotiations principally by the United States and the Soviet Union on a subject of vital interest to Western Europe. Some objected to its substance. The very component, which after two decades of intensive search restored a high measure of credibility to NATO deterrence with its regional

---

[15] *The New York Times*, December 9, 1987, pp. A24–25.

[16] For the United States this meant its Pershing II and its ground-launched Cruise missiles. For the Soviet Union this meant the SS-20, SS-4, and SS-5.

[17] For the United States this meant the Pershing 1A, and for the Soviet Union it meant the SS-12 and SS-23.

rationale, was sacrificed by the Americans for some global superpower purpose. We can see now by hindsight that the treaty marked a turning point. It set in motion, almost imperceptibly at first but at a rapidly accelerating rate, a fundamental reappraisal of Western European attitudes to NATO.

The United States sought to reassure its allies. Deterrence would remain in full force. President Reagan solemnly pledged that an attack on Munich was the same as an attack on Chicago.[18] In addition, America would continue to maintain massive ground forces in Europe to make any Soviet attack by conventional forces a very hazardous undertaking. Congressional leaders demanded a continued unilateral asymmetric reduction in Soviet conventional forces. The administration in turn spoke of the need for the modernization of NATO forces.[19]

American reassurance did not altogether allay Western European worries about the credibility of NATO deterrence. Worse still, American calls for "modernization" produced new anxieties. Just exactly what did they mean by it? Did the Americans have in mind the modernization of NATO tactical nuclear forces, and more specifically the short-range Lance missile? In economic terms this would not be too costly. But the INF treaty had radically reduced the range of permissible missiles, and as anyone could see: "the shorter the range the more dead Germans." In case of war short-range NATO nuclear missiles would massacre East Germans while Soviet nuclear missiles would massacre West Germans. This was not an attractive prospect to Germans but not necessarily a distressing contingency for the Soviet Union. In any case, as an increment in deterrence one could not heavily count on it.[20]

Alternatively did the Americans urge the qualitative improvement of conventional forces (troops and weapons)? It would require enormous expenditures. Given the substantial reductions in the U.S. defense budget, by the second half of the 1980s many Europeans wondered: was this the overture to a campaign of "burden sharing," that is, a demand for more European contributions?

---

[18] A few days later after the Brussels summit, the president repeated his pledge but substituted Amsterdam for Munich.

[19] *The New York Times*, March 3, 1988, p. A3.

[20] The NATO summit could agree only on an "appropriate mix of adequate and effective nuclear and conventional forces which will continue to be kept up to date." *The New York Times*, March 4, 1988, p. A6. The German translation was weaker still.

In fact, Western Europeans felt keenly that they were already bearing their share of the burden—at the very least. By their count of the standing NATO forces the Europeans provided 90 percent of the manpower, 95 percent of the divisions, 85 percent of the tanks, 95 percent of the artillery, and 80 percent of the combat aircraft. The West Germans were especially annoyed. For decades they had patiently put up with two, three, and more major military exercises per year: the damage to the roads and the fields, the infernal clanking of tanks, the deafening thunder of low flying jets (*Tiefflieger*), day and night, day and night. Too much noise, too much trouble. The cows would give no milk, the chickens laid no eggs, even the rabbits were reluctant to multiply. Then just as they were becoming sick and tired of it all, two unrelated spectacular accidents catalyzed a massive public resentment.

Late in August 1988 the American airbase of Ramstein at Kaiserslautern was host to an international airshow. It was an annual event with picnic baskets and frolicking around. Great fun. This time too the mood was festive and relaxed. The audience visited the exhibits and watched the acrobatics in the sky. Then suddenly during the performance of the Italian precision team disaster struck. Three planes collided in the air, exploded, and showered the helpless guests with flaming debris. Television covered the event. Over and over it played its own tapes and some especially dramatic footage from private videocams. Germans, their eyes riveted to their TV sets, watched in color the stark horror of human mayhem, people in panic, twisted, burning bodies, and heard in the background the plaintive cry of a distraught, searching mother: "*Anje, wo bist du?*" Annie, where are you? The casualties included some 46 dead and 500 others injured. It was one of those media spectacles that shape the mood of a people. Then before conventional wisdom could regain its equilibrium, within three and a half months (December 8, 1988) a U.S. jet fighter on a training mission plunged into a row of homes at Remscheid killing at least five people, wiping out a section of the town, and creating another set of distressing television pictures. A new tone could be heard from the commentators. They reported that this was actually the twenty-second NATO crash of the year and quoted German official complaints that the Americans had hindered rescue efforts because they were more anxious to protect the military secrets in the plane than to save human lives. The questions arose: was it possible that deterrence through preparedness was getting to be too expensive?

While these issues were still being pondered and debated in Europe and America, General Secretary, now also President Gorbachev resumed the initiative. Speaking to the United Nations on December 7, 1988, he announced the unilateral reduction of the Soviet armed forces by 500,000 men and the withdrawal of six tank divisions plus assault-landing troops from East Germany, Czechoslovakia, and Hungary.[21] This was unquestionably a very far-reaching move. For when the plan was implemented with assault crossing units relegated to the rear echelons, Soviet capability of a surprise attack would be practically eliminated or at least severely impaired. With additional reductions in total force and especially in tank units Soviet prospects of a conventional victory in the field would be substantially reduced. Apparently the Soviet Union had given up aggressive designs and was taking a "clearly defensive" stand. The momentum had shifted. The question arose: is deterrence really necessary? To all concerned any military menace against Western Europe dramatically disappeared altogether as did the significance of the strategic disparity between the Europeans and the United States. What remained, however, was the very troublesome asymmetry of perspectives. The missed opportunities of the 1960s and 1970s to build a common community had now become painfully apparent.

Most Europeans profoundly doubted that the United States had a global strategy. Indeed many were convinced that the United States was inherently incapable of formulating and implementing any strategy at all. They saw the American people as too self-centered and too impatient to persist in any larger purpose. They saw a constant turnover in political leadership. Every four years, possibly even every two years, the diplomatic corps in Washington, DC, was forced to acquaint itself and to learn to work with a group of newcomers who arrived from who knows where but who were determined to demonstrate that they had better ideas than their predecessors. In any case, Europeans felt American foreign policy was not carefully crafted according to what was reasonable and feasible in the international environment but reflected partisan advantages of the domestic environment. All too often it was shaped by the noisiest pressure group of the moment. Frankly Western Europeans were fearful to trust the fate of mankind (let alone their own fate) to the people across the Atlantic and their leaders in their capital along the Potomac. They had felt this way for quite some time, but now some in diplomatic parlance were expressing their reservations.

About the same time, having lost their accustomed position of dominance in Europe and suspecting that American public opinion was turning inward or at least had little taste for assuming global responsibilities, American decision-makers seemed to have become disoriented; their

---

[21] Ibid., December 8, 1988, p. A16.

position became wobbly. In 1991 after he had played a key role in German reunification and had just demonstrated American power and his personal skill in the Gulf War, President George Bush went to Rome for the NATO summit. There was some discussion of a "new strategic concept" and a plaintive American question: Do you want us to withdraw from Western Europe?[22] Our NATO allies obliged by a not wholly enthusiastic "no" in the final communiqué. Just as on military matters we stood down, so we made no attempts now to build on other traditional ties. As an example: President Bush missed a marvelous opportunity to celebrate together with our Western European allies the 500th anniversary of the discovery of America by a European. Instead he was intimidated by a small and noisy special interest group that caricatured Christopher Columbus as nothing but the enslaver of the native populations.

Similarly even as the crisis over the disintegration of Yugoslavia was building, President Bush did not seem to know what to do. Possibly he fervently wished it would just go away. He did not want to get involved in some European quagmire. Let the Europeans lead. We can kibitz and if our NATO allies had some requests to make, we would be ready to consider them. It was a stance that was carried on by the Clinton administration. For five years we have been in a reactive mode. With the continent in flux and the United States confused about its leadership role in the North Atlantic, Western Europeans may choose to move along a different track.

TOWARD A EUROPEAN UNION

Western Europeans may proceed collectively and press on to an integrated European community. Considerable progress has already been made toward this ideal. At first it was principally a French-German affair focusing on coal and steel. It made good sense economically. Deposits of these two important industrial raw materials were concentrated along, but separated by, national borders. For a century each country sought to gain control of these resources for its own national benefit by conquering its neighbor. Alsace-Lorraine and the Saar served as prizes in victorious wars. It was not a happy or for that matter a successful arrangement. Surely it would be far preferable for all to leave the boundaries along national lines but to remove the obstacles to the free flow of these raw materials across these lines. Moreover, the affair made excellent sense strategically. Both countries had in memory suffered through terrible horrors in two world

---

[22] Ibid., November 8, 1991, p. A1.

wars and had to endure national humiliations. France was still anxious about its security, all the more so because by the 1950s the German *Wirtschaftswunder* once again demonstrated that one cannot keep the Germans down. Not for a long time. After World War I France had hoped to protect its security by compelling German subservience. This proved to be a tragic failure. Led by two much more imaginative statesmen, Robert Schuman, foreign minister from 1948 to 1953, and Jean Monnet, his country's foremost economic planner, France now was inclined to attempt a pioneering approach of gaining peace through constructive processes of cooperation. In turn, West Germany was anxious about her self-respect and international reputation. The barbarism of her Nazi past had stamped her with a scarlet letter for aggression and atrocity. She needed to build a new record of civilized behavior, and who could better vouch for her than her traditional enemy France? And let us remember, there was one more reason for the consolidation of Western Europe, a very practical and very pressing reason at the time: the Americans liked it!

Thus, on April 19, 1951, at Paris a treaty was signed by France and Western Germany, plus—France wanted some additional voting power—Belgium, Italy, Luxembourg, and the Netherlands to establish the European Coal and Steel Community. Its goals were ambitious: to create (1) a free trade area and (2) a common market in the then-basic raw materials of any industrialized society. As economics sometimes pulls along politics, the treaty also provided a structural mechanism. There was to be a High Authority composed of nine members, including at least one from each member nation. It was stipulated that members would not be bound by their own country's interests or their own government's advice or instructions. There was to be a Council of Ministers with one delegate from each government and a Common Assembly with representatives from each country selected by national parliaments.

Actually these were rudimentary institutions. The High Authority was checked by the Council, which reflected the interest of each participating country, and required unanimity on important issues. The Common Assembly was free to debate but had only advisory powers. All the same, it was a beginning and served as a stimulus. Negotiations expanded to common communities on atomic energy and common defense. Then in 1957 at Rome through a new treaty the European Coal and Steel Community was expanded into the European Economic Community. Central to it was its Article 2: "The Community shall have as its task . . . to promote throughout the Community a harmonious development of economic activities, a continued and balanced expansion, an increase in stability, an accelerated raising of the standard of living and closer relations between the states belonging to it."[23] It was an ambitious statement, which also included social and agricultural policies, but its goals were to be accomplished by a gradual process, a very gradual process. In fact, most of the differences between national governments were untouched, left for further negotiations. The Council of Ministers and the Assembly continued as before. The High Authority was renamed European Commission with slightly less authority.

Since the members, particularly the smaller states, were leery about the prospect of centralization, the headquarters of the institutions were distributed throughout the community: the Council in Luxembourg, the Commission in Brussels, and the least important, the Assembly, in Strasbourg, France, just across the West German border. All along, notwithstanding all the treaty commitments and public declarations, members were determined to protect their own sovereignty. In 1958–1959 when the decline of energy consumption coinciding with falling oil prices created an overcapacity of coal production, the Commission (technically still the High Authority) pushed for a "community" solution. It was generally ignored. Each member sought its own uncoordinated, specific sovereign approach.

For nearly three decades no spectacular advance followed. Even so, there was some movement. The French-German cooperation was reinforced by a close relationship between President de Gaulle and Chancellor Adenauer and later with a mutual commitment to a Common Agricultural Policy.[24] Some other movement included the treaty signed in 1965 which merged the parallel institutions of the European Community and Euratom, a treaty signed in 1970 amending the budgetary procedures, and another signed in 1975 streamlining financial provisions. In 1979 the Assembly became a Parliament whose members were directly elected by the people every five years. Perhaps most important among the developments was the extension of membership. After some controversy (French veto) the United Kingdom was admitted into the Community in 1972, as were Denmark and Ireland. Greece then became a member in 1979 and Spain and Portugal in 1985. Noticeably of the six new members four were poorer countries.

---

[23] Neill Nugent, *The Government and Politics of the European Community* (Durham: Duke University Press, 1991).

[24] Free trade in the Common Market notwithstanding, the French farmers, a politically powerful group vulnerable to communist agitation, would be systematically protected. For all practical purposes the European Economic Community became a captive market for French agricultural products.

A new and major impetus for advance of the Community occurred when a Socialist, François Mitterand, was elected president of France, and Jacques Delors, another Frenchman, served as a very activist president of the EC Commission. In tandem they pushed for a firm timetable by which in 1992 a single market for the entire Community would be accomplished. During the next two years the Council approved the idea and the Commission adopted a program entitled: "The Single Act: A new frontier for Europe."

Once again the forward thrust was pulled by the French-German engine. With German power clearly on the ascendance, it became a critical necessity for Germany to exemplify the New Germany, the good European Germany, which had given up once and for all chauvinist nationalist self-aggrandizement. In turn, with the Cold War visibly waning and the cement of common security loosening rapidly, French national security became worrisome. It needed the fullest entanglement of Germany with Europe. For Mitterand, a Socialist, it meant governmental entanglement. By hindsight, moreover, we may suspect another French motive. The French have never given up their cherished nostalgia for *la gloire* and the days when it was a global power. To be sure, those days were gone and actually never quite existed. But perhaps they could return. A European Union based on what has nicely developed for a generation and a half into a pattern of policy built on German power guided by France might just be the ticket.

What was proposed and with some ambiguity agreed to by the EEC Council in December 1985 was a quantum leap. The scope of the Community was vastly extended to "establishing a common economic and social area, creating the conditions for stronger economic growth, acting decisively and in concert on matters of foreign policy, adapting the common agricultural policy to changing circumstances in the world, and ensuring that the financing of the Community is placed on a sound footing."[25]

Meanwhile the Commission under Jacques Delors assumed an increasingly activist role. Until then it had concentrated on persuading national governments to relax, even eliminate their regulations. Now with a much broader "competence" it took the offensive by setting Community-wide standards and regulations to be enforced upon the governments and peoples of its members. In December 1989 at the Strasbourg meeting of the

---

[25] European Communities Commission, *From Single Market to European Union* (Luxembourg: Office for Official Publications of the European Communities, 1992), pp. 42–43.

Council eleven heads of state adopted the Community Charter of the Fundamental Social Rights of Workers. President François Mitterand, serving as the president of the Council, declared that the necessary majority existed for the convening of an Intergovernmental Conference to draft amendments to the EEC treaty needed for the final stages of economic and monetary integration. The pace of integration had become breathtaking.

It was just too much for the British prime minister. Margaret Thatcher was never an uncritical devotee of the European Community. During her first term as prime minister she constantly carried on a campaign to reduce British contributions to the EEC budget, which she considered excessive.[26] As the French-German offensive was taking off, in her second term Margaret Thatcher's reservations became much broader and her expression of these reservations became much more determined and vehement. She did not like the operational effectiveness of what she called the French-West German axis. Behind "a sappy rhetoric of Euro-idealism" the French made policy and the West Germans paid for it. Such power concentration on the Continent was tolerable when it was checked by the Soviet threat from the outside and restrained by U.S. power on the inside. Now with the Soviet Union out of the picture and Russian power withdrawn far to the east past East Germany, past Poland, and past the Ukraine, the French-German axis was too formidable for British comfort. Especially so when the United States was visibly reducing its role in Europe.

It also bothered Margaret Thatcher that she saw an essentially reactionary socialist direction of the Community. At the time when the Soviet model was seen to have been discredited throughout the world, the Community and its Eurocrats were apparently accepting its main premises. They were steering toward a society controlled by a centralized state with an economy managed by bureaucrats. She could more or less understand French President Mitterand, whom she liked, a Socialist in a polity with a tradition of *dirigisme*. She felt puzzled and exasperated by Chancellor Kohl, whom she did not like, who was a Christian Democrat and who should have learned from his country's recent past.

Mostly though, the British prime minister was alarmed by what she intensely felt was a mistaken concept of the Community. It resembled very much the American blueprint which in the 1960s under the leadership of General de Gaulle was rejected by Europe. By the summer of 1988 another Frenchman (Jacques Delors) predicted that within ten years the Community

---

[26] After a struggle she won a commitment for a rebate, which, however, remained a festering problem.

would be the source of "80 percent of our economic legislation and perhaps even of our fiscal and social legislation as well."[27] In a major speech before the College of Europe in Bruges on September 20, 1988, the British prime minister fired back. She was no less clear and no less emphatic than President de Gaulle had been some 25 years earlier.

Willing and active cooperation between independent sovereign states is the best way to build a successful European Community. . . . Europe will be stronger precisely because it has France as France, Spain as Spain, Britain as Britain, each with its own customs, traditions and identity. It would be folly to try to fit them into some sort of identikit European personality.[28]

Nevertheless Margaret Thatcher's was an uphill battle. She could enlist the support of only a few other members of the Community: Denmark and occasionally Holland and Spain. The rest consistently followed the French-German lead. *Savoir faire* plus Deutschmarks make a powerful persuader. Mrs. Thatcher fought hard, but in the end she had to give in on the intermediate step of ERM (Exchange Rate Mechanism), which set fixed exchange rates among the currencies of the various members of the community. Even so, she mitigated defeat by negotiating a wide band of ± 6 percent flexibility of the British pound sterling. Undaunted she was determined to oppose EMU (Economic and Monetary Union), that is, a single currency and a single central bank, and she would never accept any political union that meant the subordination of national sovereignty to some federal arrangement.

Her firm, uncompromising stance cost her heavily within the European Community. At home a plurality of people (43 percent:38 percent) were with her in opposing the EMU.[29] Still her personal style antagonized members of her party and even her cabinet. Time was running out for Margaret Thatcher. On November 1, 1990, Geoffrey Howe, her foreign secretary, resigned and her days were numbered. She herself resigned four weeks later and was succeeded by her protegé, John Major.

Meanwhile the French-German locomotive was about to have a burst of speed on what now appeared a clear track. In July a full liberalization of capital movements came into effect in eight countries. Exceptions applied to four poor countries. An Intergovernmental Conference on the Economic

---

[27] Thatcher, *The Downing Street Years*, p. 72.

[28] Ibid., p. 745.

[29] Eurobarometer No. 34, December 1990.

and Monetary Union was formally scheduled to take place in Rome on December 13 and one on Political Union on December 14, 1990. They were to complete their work by December 1991 for the Maastricht Meeting of the European Council.

Idealists saw Maastricht as a further leap into the future, the foundation of total economic integration with a tight Monetary Union. It would also be a step toward a federal government. As the European Community became the European Union, any thoughts about national sovereignty were put on the defensive. Limitations on the power of the European Parliament were derogated as a "democratic deficit."

Indeed Maastricht went according to plan—well, more or less. The "Treaty on European Union" was signed by the foreign and finance ministers of all twelve members,[30] but there were exceptions and exemptions. Britain, for example, insisted on an "opt out clause." If she did not want to join the common currency, she could do so without affecting her status in the European Union. For most others the implementation of a common currency was formally set for 1997. If then in the judgment of the Council a majority of the members had met five specific criteria, a common currency would be used by them.[31] If not, the decision would be postponed to 1999, when in any case the common currency would be applied to those, even a minority of members, who met the criteria.

Questions about the four poorer nations, quite possibly Italy as well, remained. Would they really have a chance of ever meeting the criteria? National borders as barriers to the free flow of people and goods were eliminated (more or less), but on this too there were exceptions. A political union was vigorously debated. The concept of a federal system was not adopted, although not rejected outright.[32] Significantly while the European Parliament, whose members represented the citizens, gained some power, the center of gravity of the Union remained the Council of Ministers, whose members represented their respective governments and where unanimity on most important issues was required.

---

[30] Council of the European Communities, Commission of the European Communities, *Treaty on European Union*, Luxembourg. Office for Publications of the European Communities, 1992, pp. 4–6.

[31] The five conditions listed were (1) low inflation, (2) low long-term interest rates, (3) a budget deficit under 3 percent of national GDP, (4) a public debt ratio of less than 60 percent of GDP, and (5) two years of currency stability within the ERM.

[32] Ibid., pp. 8, 9.

As a matter of fact, negotiations at Maastricht even in the absence of Mrs. Thatcher, their favorite *bête noire*, were difficult and at times acrimonious. Some of the practical difficulties were coming to the fore. Then during the process of ratification they became fully visible. First rattle out of the box the Danish people by a referendum rejected the treaty. Since unanimity was required for ratification, this could have been a fatal blow. The treaty was saved by several rounds of renegotiations with Denmark, each entailing concessions of additional exemptions. Finally the Danes approved. Most of the weaker members had their own renegotiations. A crucial test was France. President Mitterand decided not to use the National Assembly dominated by his party as a means of ratification. Instead he submitted the treaty to a referendum. After a massive government campaign which, imagine this: enlisted even Chancellor Kohl's public appeal, the French people by a margin of less than 1 percent did approve the treaty. Germany was relatively easy. Britain required further concessions (exemptions).

After Maastricht four new countries were admitted into the Union. Three, Sweden (by a narrow margin), Finland, and Austria, decided to join. Norway declined. The rising momentum of 1985 through 1990 has been visibly slowing down. Traditional interests with a national focus were reasserting themselves. To begin with, new opportunities and combinations with the former Soviet satellites, with newly independent states of the former components of the USSR, and with Russia itself present daunting challenges. Next, the Socialist rule of France has ended. The National Assembly of 1984 produced an unprecedentedly large majority (80 percent) of Gaullists and their "rightist" allies. In 1995 Jacques Chirac, a Gaullist, was elected president. And not least important, in Germany attitudes may be changing. "United Germany is . . . number one in Europe. We have about 80m people. We are the country with the strongest economy. We are particularly well organized, which is very important in modern industrial society. . . . We have our plusses and minuses. But taking everything together, we will [not get into trouble] if we take our place in the [European] house. Naturally the others accept that we will need the biggest flat," declared Chancellor Kohl on television in 1995.[33]

As the Intergovernmental Conference convened in Turin, Italy, (March 29, 1996) to reexamine the treaty, Germans had another chance to look at "clarification at first hand" in conferences, seminars, and lectures by delegates from the commission and in focus groups held throughout the

---

[33] *Economist*, November 9–15, 1996, p. 20.

country. Revisions were widely discussed.[34] In most member states doubts were resurfacing.[35] Clearly a federal system was beyond the horizon. Meanwhile the activist stance of the commission, so pronounced during M. Delors' term, was replaced by the motto of his successor Jacques Santer: Do less, but better. Even so, the commission was not idle, indeed turned to issues of foreign policy. For example, it took diplomatic initiatives in the Bosnian conflict and insisted on being the only representative of EU countries at international economic conferences. Moreover, it was busy trying to undermine the powers of the Council. It kept pushing for revisions that would reduce the unanimity requirements on the most important issues to a "qualified majority," a ratio that would effectively eliminate the veto of each national government. Such voting changes would be applied to a common foreign policy and even to such domestic issues as employment and social policy. This aroused the British government and more specifically the conservative party in power. Prime Minister John Major now moved to the offensive. He made it clear that he would veto any extension of the qualified majority formula.

Meanwhile other complications have also arisen with the European Union. For one thing, the issue of the expansion of membership is now raised regularly. Poland, the Czech Republic, Hungary, Slovakia, and Turkey as well have high hopes. Their admission would exacerbate the still-unsettled "common agricultural policy" so dear to the French. Add to this the extracurricular activities of President Chirac. The Maastricht Treaty, we may recall, stated that "the common foreign and security policy ... shall include all questions related to the security of the Union, including the eventual framing of a common defence [*sic*] policy, which might in time lead to a common defence." Just what the word "common" means and how it is to be arrived at, or what "eventual" means remains for diplomats with their expertise in semantic obfuscation to explain. As far as the French president is concerned national defense and foreign policy were part of national sovereignty. Without consultation, let alone union approval, France broke the nuclear test moratorium. A few months later it intruded into the peace process of the Middle East. Other major developments had a mixed effect. On August 12, 1996, the Supreme Court of Denmark ordered a district court to hear the challenge of eleven citizens on the constitutionality of the Rome and the Maastricht treaties. The appeals process is expected to be prolonged. Mark down a minus. On May 2, 1997,

---

[34] Bonn, *Bonner Rundschau*, May 3, 1996, p. 4.
[35] *Economist*, March 23–29, 1996, p. 52.

Britain had a change in government. Within three days the new Labour Minister for Europe flew to Brussels and promised a "fresh start." Mark down a plus. At the end of same month President Chirac's coalition found its overwhelming majority in the National Assembly melt away in national elections. And with it went much of the president's political clout. Mark down a big minus. Further progress toward a European Union appears to be considerably slowed.

All along in the background the EMU caused difficulties. The Exchange Rate Mechanism has for all practical purposes collapsed. After 1993 the "fixed exchange rate" had an accepted band of ±15 percent. Moreover, while officials gave it a name (euro), no one expected a common currency to be in place in 1997, the Maastricht target date, and even the 1999 alternative deadline had become controversial. In the middle of May 1996 the European Commission released a series of relevant statistics. Only Denmark, Luxembourg, and Ireland were expected to run budget deficits within the 3 percent of GDP Maastricht requirement. Germany's deficit was approaching 4 percent, France's 4.2 percent.[36] Chancellor Kohl met the problem head-on. His 1997 budget included heavy cuts that intruded into the government-guaranteed "entitlements," seen by many as the keystone of German democracy. By the summer of 1996 the EMU was getting quite unpopular among Germans. They did not like to see their pride and joy, the Deutschmark, being replaced by the euro. They liked it less when the French demanded (*mais naturellement*) that a Frenchman head the new central bank. Poll results varied between 84 percent and 52 percent in opposition.[37] Prominent leaders were beginning to express doubts publicly, and they included Hans Tietmeyer, the president of the *Bundesbank*, Germany's central bank.[38] The French government also made some budget cuts, but it resorted heavily to creative accounting; for example, one-time revenues from the France Telecom pension fund and wildly optimistic spending and revenue estimates.[39]

Considering the matter realistically (not to mention honestly) the French budget deficit in 1997 will be about 4 percent, well above the Maastricht requirement, which presents a dilemma and hence a search for a political solution. Unfortunately the options are few, if any. First, the

---

[36] *Economist*, May 18–24, 1996, p. 51.

[37] Cited in Richard Medley, "Keeping Monetary Union on Track," *Foreign Affairs,* November/December 1996, p. 22.

[38] *Economist*, October 26–November 1, 1996, p. 62.

[39] Medley, "Keeping Monetary Union on Track," p. 24–25.

Maastricht requirements could be strictly applied. As a result, very few of the EU members would qualify, not even France. One big problem would be the relationship within the Union between the ins and the outs of EMU. A colossal problem would be the exclusion of France. Such an option is clearly a nonstarter. Second, the requirements could be generously interpreted. That would bring in practically all members but seriously compromise the hard currencies of some, Germany's for example. That too is a nonstarter. So is there a middle ground? Perhaps to close eyes and hold noses and accept the French government's budget figures—BUT apply the Maastricht requirements firmly to all other members. Frankly not much of a starter for the final decisive negotiations toward EMU. All the same, throughout 1996 most members devoted herculean efforts to meet the requirements, and there stand Chancellor Kohl and President Chirac, very determined. Any delay, they are convinced, would seriously impair the prospects of a common currency. They probably will prevail with some face-saving formula. The foundations for this were laid when on April 23 the Commission issued its forecasts for the budget deficits in 1997. It declared "the majority of the members ready to join the euro on January 1, 1999." Britain, Sweden, and Denmark would probably stay out by their own choice; Greece and Italy could be kept out by not meeting the criteria.[40] But the road toward EMU is uphill all the way, and if and when it is put in place the road will become steeper still.

THE GERMAN PROBLEM

From time to time some voices in America are raised expressing anxiety about our friends across the Atlantic becoming too strong as a regional bloc, presenting too much of an independent voice in international affairs, and too much of an economic competition. Nevertheless ever since President Kennedy (if not earlier still) the United States government has consistently encouraged the economic *and* political consolidation of Western Europe. Indeed advance toward a European Union deserves our admiration as a historic phenomenon. Political consolidation has in the past been either coerced by a rising power in search of hegemony or achieved through cooperation by political units anxious about a common threat. Exceptions are practically nonexistent. Perhaps the United States was one; the European Union may become another, achieving unification without

---

[40] The Italian government is determined to get in. The prime minister promised to resign in case of failure. *Economist*, April 26–May 2, 1997, p. 47.

subjugation or a shared fear. If so, the process is extremely instructive for a peaceful advance of human development.

Much has changed in the last forty years in Western Europe. A reactionary return to the unbridled chauvinism of the nineteenth century is a possibility, of course, but not at all a probability. Relations among Western European states suffer from ups and downs but have improved visibly. There are still tensions, and some may periodically become aggravated. Nevertheless the feeling of Western European solidarity has grown deep roots. Which does not mean, however, that national sovereignty has lost its appeal. If therefore the European Union is to mean more than a common free-trade zone but less than a political federation, a *system* of the States of Europe may emerge. The idea of General de Gaulle and Margaret Thatcher is one whose time now may have come. Not a Europe of states with all their deep traditional cleavages, their special parochial interests constantly clashing, and their perpetual anxiety about their security. Instead a *system* of the States of Europe recognizing their common interest but managed through a decentralized political structure that fully accommodates the persistence of national identities. The example of Switzerland or some model along those lines comes to mind. Very much will depend on the major European powers, more specifically on the position of Germany in the future.[41] Will it find its proper role? Will it regain its dignity?

The Haunting Past

National dignity relies heavily on the past. People must be able to recall with pride the glories of their ancestors and the collective achievements of their community, but the recent past is very troublesome for Germans. During World War II there were heroic Germans worthy of admiration. Some were civilians, others soldiers, and some even members of the *Waffen-SS*. But how could Germans celebrate heroes of a war that was clearly a war of German aggression, a war, moreover, Germany had lost?

Thinking about the past also quickly brings back memories of the Nazi period. Germans pride themselves on correct behavior. They are really a

---

[41] Located in the center of Europe, Germany has only 11 percent of the European Union land area, well below France's 17.6 percent. But in other indicators it easily outstrips its partners. In population 22 percent (82m) to France's and Britain's 16 percent. Its share in the GDP of EU is over 28 percent versus France's 18 percent and Britain's and Italy's 13 percent. Its share in world export is 10 percent, twice that of the nearest EU competitor.

very decent, if not always lovable, people. There is no facet of human development to which they did not heavily contribute. And yet the Nazi regime in Germany was among the most barbaric in human history. Not just because many (though far from most) of its citizens were monstrous brutes, and that they were, but because it systematically abused and subverted all the fine human qualities with which man is endowed and which have been developed over past millennia. It systematically catered to his primitive animal urges. One cannot help wondering how a civilized people could be ruled by such evil savages and remain loyal to them to the bitter end.

It is a question Germans wanting self-respect and a German nation seeking to resume its proper position in our civilization must face. They owe an honest answer if not to the world, at least to themselves and to their children. Ah, but there is the rub. Seeking an honest answer, Germans come face to face with a horrendous truth. Almost to the end most of them actually enjoyed the Nazi period.

Part of the explanation may be found in World War I and its aftermath. We have been taught that the war was a clear case of German aggression. It really was not.[42] Moreover, the German people did not believe that it was. Young men enthusiastically marched off to defend their country. To help with the war effort women traded in their golden wedding bands for rings of a strange gray alloy. It was, they truly believed, an act of patriotism, a sacrifice for a just cause. Hence it was a tragedy that the war was lost; it was a travesty that they were internationally stigmatized as primitive predators (the Huns) and compelled to pay enormous sums of reparations to the Allies, mostly to France. The social order was in shambles. In 1923 the economy collapsed under a runaway mega-inflation. In January one kilogram of potatoes cost twenty-three Marks; by October it cost 90 billion. In August a street car ticket cost 100,000 Marks; by November, 150 million. Workers would get paid twice a day to give them a chance to rush to the bank to deposit their salary before it lost more of its value. In just a few months all the savings—lifetime, careful savings—were wiped out. Radical devaluation restored the value of money, but the savings were gone. Then in six years in the Great Depression, which hit Germany especially hard, most of the jobs were gone as well. By 1931 one half of all German families were directly affected by unemployment. The political system was helpless; then it too collapsed. The misery was oppressive, in fact, so oppressive that people could not stand it. They had to have some

---

[42] Sidney Bradshaw Fay, *The Origins of the World War*, 2nd ed. (New York: Macmillan, 1930).

relief, if nothing else, a convenient scapegoat. To hell with the price. It was the season for demagogues. And so average Germans welcomed the Nazis.

In fact, the price was horrendous. It devastated the Jewish population in Europe, and it cast a dark shadow on future German generations. Yet at the time few noticed it; fewer still cared. It felt good to have a job again, to be able to buy decent food and clothing, to go on a vacation. It felt good to watch grand parades with colorful flags and fanfares, indeed to march together in a solid overwhelming phalanx. It felt good that Germany was no longer a pathetic pariah but could dominate, conquer, and rule foreign countries. It felt good not to feel ashamed of being German but to be proud of it. It felt very good.

But what about the holocaust? One explanation making the rounds in 1996 was that Germans as Germans with their "eliminationist mind-set" are guilty of a uniquely vile anti-Semitism. This is rubbish, in fact dangerous rubbish. For an argument that imposes upon an ethnic group immutable special traits reflects a regression in human development and a return to the dominance of ethnocentrism. Indeed if we look closely enough, we can easily see that it has the same roots and is fertilized by the same manure as Nazi doctrine. At our level of civilization it is more appropriate to assume the unity of *human* nature and search for explanations in special personal or temporary situational conditions.

As a matter of fact, Jews had been living in Germany for centuries. The relationship had its ups and downs, but for most of the time it was good to tolerable. Some Jews were successful in industry, some married into the officers' corps, some were knighted by Emperor William II. Most Germans had Jewish friends and dealt with some Jewish tradesmen. They were all right; they were *German* Jews, more accurately Jewish Germans.

As it happened, the end of World War I brought a massive influx of immigration from the East, Poland and Russia, many of whom were Jewish; quite a few were Hasidic Jews. Easy targets of scapegoating, they were people different in culture and style. They wore different clothes; they wore beards and peculiar sideburns. On top of it all, they apparently parlayed their special ethnic solidarity into an advantage in the German economy. A mass of immigrants distinguishable and quite noticeable appeared to manage quite well when everyone else in the country was miserable because they were impoverished and because they were German. The immigrants from the East became the easy targets of frustration, and since frustration and fanaticism do not differentiate, so were Germans committed to their *Vaterland* who confessed the Jewish faith. When economic conditions were improving, the Nazis claimed credit. All along, they spread their venom. They kept pointing their finger at the Jews, the Jews, the Jews as the source of all Germany's troubles. Spellbound, honest, decent people watched when Stormtroopers abused their innocent neighbors, seized their property, and brutally herded them into concentration camps. They shrugged their shoulders and thought: this does not concern me; I am not a Jew.

There is no excuse, not the miserable post-World War I conditions in Germany, not the mass immigration of *Ostjuden,* and not the coincidence of the two. But there are explanations; more to the point there are lessons to be learned. Fascism is not a special German affliction; it is a human disease of retrogression or, as some put it, negative development. A virulent form infected Germans for two decades. It has infected others as well. No nation is immune. That which feels good is not necessarily good; it may be evil. We have our reason to tell us the difference. But civilization is still a thin veneer. There is evil in men and there are still evil men. Modern mass society, one that caters to emotion and promotes the subjectivity of values, may be especially vulnerable. All the more so since the technology of communication, including propaganda, record-keeping, and government surveillance, has improved enormously. Though fascism is utterly repugnant to Americans, we are not immune. Our free press, however troublesome it may appear at times, is an invaluable asset. We must never forget the warning of Jefferson: the price of our democracy is eternal vigilance.

Germans haunted by their past, however, were hardly suited to offer this explanation. To be sure, there were some shrill voices that dismissed the holocaust as propaganda or described it as no different from the behavior of other peoples and governments, but in West Germany these were drowned out by the vast mass of silent gloom.[43]

Rising Out of Catastrophe

After twenty years a new generation was growing up. Ignorant of the tabooed subject, its members felt guilty nevertheless. Introverted, they stayed at home. At first they had little money to travel abroad; later they were too anxious to do so. But changes were already underway. The "economic miracle" was a source of pride, not merely for its phenomenal

---

[43] Just before reunification German historians engaged in a vigorous and extremely bitter debate on the issue of the Nazi period. "The New Nationalism and the Old History: Perspectives on the West German Historikerstreit," *Journal of Modern History,* 59 (December 1987), pp. 761–97.

accomplishment, but also because of its innovative participatory approach: *Mitbestimmungsrecht*. Economic policies (as well as most others) were formed by a broad consensus of all participants, e.g., employers, employees, government, and political parties. It was a harmony to be enjoyed.

By the early 1960s the German phoenix was beginning to rise out of ignominy. President de Gaulle came to visit Munich and spoke in German to the elated masses. President Kennedy declared in Berlin: "Ich bin ein Berliner." During this nascent recovery of self-confidence the 1968 student movement in France splashed across the border. Almost overnight cells of 68ers sprang up in Germany. Young men and women began to live again. They discussed issues: literature, philosophy, and politics: democracy, human rights, equality. They began to travel abroad. With caution and diffidence their parents, beneficiaries of long vacations made available by rapid economic advance, followed them. Still haunted by their past they reached out for a new identity through Europe and a dignity by being a good European.

It made a big difference. Still it was not altogether a success. Some in the excitement of the 68ers were carried into extremes, for example, the Baader-Meinhoff gang, which moved quickly to violence and terror, warning all that playing politics could still be a dangerous game in Germany. In fact, democracy was taking root; public reaction was massive and vigorous. Extremism of any kind under any pretense was not welcome in the *Bundesrepublic*.

Unquestionably, the European identity gained appeal, but it was handicapped by an absence of parallel movement in other European states. The French still preferred to be French, the Belgians preferred to be Belgians, the Italians preferred to be Italians. If anything, the popular momentum was in the other direction: fragmentation through ethnic solidarity. So Germans delighted in an exceptionally high standard of living, in physical comfort, in electronic gadgets, in entertainment, not to mention in the "freedom" of racing up and down the Autobahn at 120 miles per hour. They also enjoyed the collective rewards of belonging to social organizations and professional associations. Some thought hopefully that this would be enough. The West Germans uniquely would not need the intangible rewards of patriotism. If they needed a demonstration of solidarity, they could have parades in old-fashioned local costumes replete with lederhosen and dirndl accompanied by a brass band's um-pah-pahs.

Then came the surprising developments in Moscow and the realization by governments and people that Soviet forces would no longer be available to impose communist rule on Eastern European satellites. There was now a chance to gain freedom. At the same time, the East German economy was visibly on the verge of collapse. It was a good time to escape the storm and return to the warm, comfortable hearth. Liberty or prosperity, it is not quite clear which, probably both in combination, drew masses of East Germans to the West. In 1989 a human tide moved into Czechoslovakia and Hungary in an attempt to bypass the fortified shoot-on-sight strip of no-man's-land along their border. By the summer East German "vacationers" were crowded along the Austro-Hungarian border. Hundreds of East German border guards and secret policemen were clandestinely dispatched by their government "to talk some sense" into their errant fellow citizens.

Caught in the middle the Hungarian government vacillated. Should they abide by their Warsaw Pact obligations and forcibly repatriate the DDR Germans, or should they follow the United Nations Convention on Refugees and let them proceed as they wished? As it happened on August 19 the Paneuropa Union, an international organization with headquarters in Switzerland, planned a "picnic" in the vicinity of Sopron, a Hungarian border town. The program of the festivities included a ceremonial opening of a border gate for a short time. The news spread like wild fire, and when the time came a veritable avalanche of Germans singing "We Shall Overcome" rushed through the temporary opening. It was reported as the most spectacular mass escape from East to West in history. It also gave an idea to many, many more citizens of communist East Germany.

For a few days indications about Hungarian intentions were contradictory. The gate to Austria was once again firmly closed. Indeed on August 24 border guards launched an assault on the refugees. They shot at them (mostly above their heads) with automatic weapons and chased them with rubber truncheons, injuring men, women, and children. But the next day at a supersecret meeting at Gymnich requested by Hungarian prime minister Miklos Németh, the latter assured Chancellor Kohl that DDR citizens even without proper documents would be permitted to leave his country unmolested toward their chosen destination. Hearing this, tears came to Kohl's eyes.[44] Repeated inquiry by the chancellor whether Hungary wished for some favors in return were met by the proud pronouncement: "Hungary does not sell human beings." Kohl was very much impressed. He was grateful when on September 10 Budapest officially informed him that as of 00.00 A.M. on September 11, 1989, the Hungarian borders would be open.[45] Next month Prague followed suit. Soon hundreds of thousands of East

---

[44] Helmut Kohl, *Ich Wollte Deutschlands Einheit*, ed. Kai Diekmann and Ralf Georg Reuth (Berlin: Ullstein Buchverlage GmbH, 1996), pp. 73–75.

[45] Incidentally later Hungary benefitted from DM500 million German credit.

Germans streamed to the West; the momentum for German reunification was gaining fast.

On October 7 East Germany celebrated its fortieth anniversary. Gorbachev, who attended the festivities, warned the government, "Life punishes those who arrive too late." Two days later mass demonstrations started in Leipzig and spread to other cities. On November 7 the East German government resigned. The East German people massed in Berlin at the crossovers in the Wall demanding free access to the West. The new government desperately tried to hold the line. It did not or could not order its police to fire into the throngs. On November 9 the border was broken by a wave of surging humanity. Masses of Germans flooded to the West, some as refugees, some as visitors. Young people in blue-jeans danced on the Wall. They started chipping away, hacking at it, and then reducing it to rubble. Miles and miles of cars crept through border points. It became a colossal media event. Excitement swept through the Western world. American networks sent their top reporters and anchormen to Berlin. They ran the story over and over. The past did not matter. For the first time in many decades the American people were elated by and almost universally applauded a German achievement. Suddenly once again it felt good to be German.

Chancellor Kohl seized the historic opportunity. The time had come, he was firmly convinced, for Germany to regain her full sovereignty. No foreign troops on her territory without her consent. No four-power military occupation of Berlin. Germany had paid for Nazi aggression and atrocities; she had proven that she was a responsible country entitled to sovereign equality with all states, including the major powers. Moreover, the chancellor decided the time had come for reunification of Germany. He moved swiftly and confidently. Some of the highlights are worth recalling. With American help[46] Kohl designed a two-step process. First the two German states would have to come to an agreement; then the three victorious powers of World War II and one Germany would have to agree. As it later became known, it was the two-plus-four approach.

The outcome was far from certain. Many Germans, even some of the prominent members of Kohl's party (for example, his foreign and defense ministers), were worried about the risks and wished to proceed at a slower,

---

[46] James A. Baker III, *The Politics of Diplomacy, 1989–1992* (New York: G. P. Putnam's Sons, 1995), pp. 195–216. For a more detailed account from the German perspective see: Horst Teltschik, *329 Tage, Innenaussichten der Einigung* (Berlin: Stadler, 1991).

more careful pace. They were impressed by the difficulties at home and in their international environment. Indeed there were problems in Germany. The chancellor happened to be in Warsaw when the wall was broken. He quickly interrupted his visit. He flew to Berlin. Such were the limitations on German sovereignty four decades after World War II that he could not do so in a German plane. He had to appeal to the Americans for transport. He arrived in Berlin late in the afternoon (November 10), and then things began to go wrong. The arrangements for his visit were in chaos. He was driven to the wrong place at the wrong time. At the square of Rathaus Schöneberg he was greeted by a leftist crowd with earsplitting catcalls and whistles. Then he had to sit idly by while other subordinate officials were delivering turgid orations. It was a poor beginning—in *West* Berlin at that. Incidentally, while he was waiting, another crisis loomed. He received an urgent message from Gorbachev insisting that the chancellor calm the people. The latter was puzzled. Documents now available provide the explanation. The East German secret police (STASI) through the KGB deliberately misinformed Gorbachev that masses of Germans were about to attack Soviet army facilities. Apparently they hoped that the Soviet leader would be forced to intervene and order the tanks to roll.

The reaction of the East German people was unpredictable. Many hundreds of thousands were streaming to the West, but in an East German election the emigrés would not count. And there was still in place the communist government party organization (SED) not to mention the secret police (STASI) with its batteries of informers estimated at roughly one third of the population. So elections were scheduled for May 1990 with the government expecting an electoral victory, perhaps not much of a majority, but just enough.

Chancellor Kohl had his own calculations and quickly launched his campaign. The CDU formed a coalition with some minor East German groups and committed itself unambiguously to reunification. On December 29 Kohl visited Dresden. There were no leftist hecklers in sight; there was no shrill concert of whistles. After a ten-kilometer-long triumphal procession of cheering masses, he found several thousand people assembled in front of his hotel cheering, "Helmut, Helmut." It was a tune to his liking. Deeply touched the chancellor turned to his aide and remarked, "It's happened."[47] There followed many more trips; the crowds and the enthusiasm were visibly building. He constantly emphasized the unity of

---

[47] Karl Hugo Pruys, *Kohl, Genius of the Present* (Chicago: edition q, inc., 1996), p. 269.

the German people. He spoke of "we", of "us", and of "ours." He named his coalition "Alliance for Germany."

Kohl did more than make campaign speeches. He moved to unify the two currencies. The issue arose what the conversion rate should be between the strong Deutschmark and the worthless East German Mark. The chancellor did the unprecedented. He overruled most of his advisers and the head of the *Bundesbank*. For a substantial basic amount, 1:1 would be the ratio; for much larger amounts, 2:1.

The East German government began to worry. In order to deprive the CDU of time to organize, it moved the election date forward to March. It did not really matter. Kohl had become the focus of the campaign, and he was indefatiguable in his passionate appeal. By March 9, 1990, when he visited Rostock he found over two hundred thousand East Germans wildly cheering "their" chancellor. In Leipzig he spoke to vast masses of people who interrupted him frequently, practically after every sentence, with endless ovations. The chancellor closed his campaign with the words: "We wish that the people here be happy . . . that no one should leave his homeland because of his doubts about the future. Everyone must know: we have a good future together . . . We are proud of our homeland . . . our German fatherland and of a common European future. Let us support each other, help me along this road. God bless our fatherland."[48] In the only free elections of the DDR the chancellor's supporters won. The first part of the unification strategy, the "two" in the "two-plus-four,'" was accomplished. Kohl's party in the Federal Republic of Germany would negotiate with Kohl's party in the German Democratic Republic about the future of Germany.

There remained some steep international hurdles in the "plus four" to be overcome. The Americans, especially President Bush, were warmly supportive. At the summit meeeting with Gorbachev at Malta (December 2, 1989) and at the NATO Council meeting (December 4, 1989) Bush defined the question of reunification as a matter of self-determination. That helped a lot. But the Polish government raised vehement objections. They wanted to become part of the process. After all, World War II started when Germans invaded their country. Israel objected. They chose shrill denunciation. The Germans sought reunification, charged Prime Minister Yitzhak Shamir, so they could resume the outrages of the Nazis against the Jews.[49] The Dutch also objected. Britain did not like it either. It sought to entice

---

[48] Kohl, *Ich Wollte Deutschlands Einheit*, p. 528.

[49] Ibid., p. 241.

French support. Then there was the Soviet Union. Practically everyone believed that its opposition would remain rock solid.

Kohl sought to reassure the Dutch. The Americans tried to placate the Poles. President Bush reiterated that the United States recognized the current western border of Poland,[50] but Poland was not admitted into the process. Meanwhile Kohl responded to Israel as diplomatically as possible. The Prime Minister's charge was unwarranted and strained the otherwise stress-free (*spannungslose*) relations. But the chancellor knew that the key barriers to be overcome were France and the Soviet Union.

Just after the New Year (January 4, 1990) Kohl called on President Mitterand at his modest, rustic home in Latché on the Atlantic coast south of Bordeaux. The welcome he received was noticably restrained. Indeed Kohl had never seen the French president so out of sorts.[51] Once by themselves (with the exception of close aides) Mitterand revealed his two anxieties. First, he worried about Russia. Noticeably he did not say Soviet Union. Too many concessions by Gorbachev would lead to his undoing. "The fate of Gorbachev," he warned, "was more dependent on Helmut Kohl than on his opponents in Moscow." The former's failure would probably mean a military dictatorship with its bloody consequences. Second, Mitterand was very much concerned about East Germany. He quite understood that if eighty million people were determined on a particular course, it would be foolish to oppose them, and France had no intention of doing so. Still "for the moment the map of Europe could not stand the sharp revisions." Therefore it was necessary to proceed jointly and with caution.

Kohl was optimistic. The new decade, he said, would in his opinion prove to be a good decade for German-French relations and for Europe. He informed Mitterand that he would soon meet with Gorbachev and would assure the Soviet leader that he would do nothing to add to the difficulties of his position. In turn, he wanted to reassure Mitterand that Germany was fully committed to European integration. With France, together they would provide the engine for it. German reunification was not inimical to the process—in fact it was intimately imbedded (*eingebettet*) in it.

Although not raised at the meeting, Kohl suspected that Mitterand had another anxiety as well. A singleminded German drive toward reunification might mean a neutral Germany. Then some linkage to Moscow would be inevitable. As a consequence the Soviet sphere of influence would extend to the city limits of Strasbourg— for the French a terrifying prospect. But,

---

[50] Baker, *The Politics of Diplomacy*, p. 233.
[51] Kohl, *Ich Wollte Deutschlands Einheit*, p. 232–38.

in fact, the Germans had no intention of sacrificing NATO membership for reunification.

In conclusion Kohl made a passionate little speech. It is very important, he said, that the people of our countries feel that the German-French friendship persisted. The close Kohl-Mitterand cooperation and their common European program were quite secure. But the Germans would have to see that they had friends. The public should also know that in the Elysée Palace there sits a man who follows the development in Germany sympathetically. It was time for Mitterand to be reassuring. "I shall hold firm," he declared.

All that remained was the Soviet Union, and soon there were clues that she too would be amenable. On January 8, 1990, the Soviet ambassador requested an urgent meeting with the chancellor. On instructions from the foreign minister he inquired whether Kohl's offer of help during Gorbachev's visit to Bonn the previous June was still valid. If so, the Soviet Union urgently needed food shipments, principally meat, shortening, and cheese. "The Chancellor," recorded his foreign policy adviser in his diary, "recognizes the inquiry of Shevardnadze as a chance to improve the climate in the relationship with the Soviet Union." Within eight weeks West Germany delivered 52,000 tons of canned beef, 50,000 tons of pork, 20,000 tons of butter, 15,000 tons of powered milk, and 5,000 tons of cheese. These goods were sold at highly subsidized prices that cost the West German government DM220 million ($160 million).[52]

A month after his tête-à-tête with Mitterand (February 10, 1990) Kohl flew to Moscow. The Soviet foreign minister met him at the airport. The Germans considered this a friendly gesture and a good omen. At the summit the formal exchanges were cautious, each man trying to gauge the other's position. Gorbachev started with questions. Just how long a reunification process did the chancellor have in mind? In December (1989) it was considered to take years. Since then people voted with their feet: the East German exodus to the West. But if the process would be very much speeded up, it would surely lead to chaos. Other questions followed: the Western borders of Poland, the military status of united Germany, and the relationship between German reunification and European integration. There followed quick exchanges that gradually became visibly more friendly. Once again Kohl was firm on substance but very reassuring in style. Indeed toward the end they were discussing a visit by Gorbachev to Kohl's home in the Palatinate.

---

[52] Teltschik, *329 Tage*, pp. 100–101, 124.

No firm commitments were undertaken, but no insoluble problems had arisen. No impossible demands were made by the Soviets, no threats either. Twice Gorbachev declared: The Germans in East and West have already proven that they have learned the lessons of history and that from their soil no war will emanate. Hence in terms of unification, "the Germans must make their own choice."[53] It was, the chancellor's entourage concluded, a green light from Moscow.[54] Just five months later (July 15) at Stavropol the details were worked out. Reunited Germany would have full sovereignty and remain in NATO, but military assurances, such as a limitation on the size of the German armed forces, were given. Similarly Germany assumed the cost of the repatriation of Soviet forces and committed itself to extending massive financial aid.[55]

On October 3, 1990, reunification was proclaimed. Two months later parliamentary elections for the whole country were held. The chancellor and his party together with a coalition ally (FDP) gained a comfortable majority (359 out of 656) in the new *Bundestag*.

Struggling for the Future

Flags were waving, the celebrations were frequent, and the speeches of politicians were jubilant. Still underneath problems were festering. Forty-five years of compulsory separation heavily reinforced what had even before been a cultural and political fault line. The Rhineland and Bavaria tended to be oriented toward the West, especially France, while Prussia, in spite of Voltaire in the court of Frederick the Great or Queen Victoria's children with William II, was heavily engaged in the East.[56]

After World War II with a capital in Bonn on the Rhine West Germans once again were closing ranks to the West. Democracy began to penetrate public and private life. Increasingly people learned to relate horizontally as equals. In contrast in the East the old method of vertically defined relations continued and perhaps was even reinforced. Order meant treating people

---

[53] Ibid., p. 272.

[54] Ibid., pp. 337–43

[55] German contribution to the costs of the withdrawal of Soviet forces from East Germany were DM14.55 billion ($10 billion). Germany also assumed all the East German obligations to the Soviet Union. For starters it granted a DM5 billion credit.

[56] An exception was Saxony, which had its eyes on Vienna—and circuitously on the West.

according to their status: that is, those in higher positions differently from others below them. Authoritarian rule, indeed the cult of personality (*Führerprinzip*), was taken for granted.

The cleavage was especially profound in the two armed forces. The West German *Bundeswehr* was shaped by democratic attitudes and especially the unique value of the individual human being regardless of rank. Thus, for example, it went to great lengths to provide acceptable physical conditions for the troops. The quality of food and clothing was quite good, comparable to the high standards of the U.S. armed forces. The barracks were sturdily built, well heated, and equipped with sufficient number of showers, toilet facilities, and always hot- and cold-running water. Leaves were generous; during the weekend forces were reduced to minimum (85 percent) readiness. Moreover, through a well-enforced doctrine of *Innere Führung* the *Bundeswehr* carefully monitored relations among ranks to protect the human dignity of each soldier.

Members of the West German armed forces were expected to be democratic in orientation. They were to respect civilian political control, but were not linked to any political party. They saw people across the "internal" border to the East as fellow Germans buffeted by unfortunate historic events and forces. Their attitude and military posture toward them was entirely one of self-defense. There were many discussions especially among officers in the West about the psychological problems of civil war.

In the East German *Nationale Volksarmee* (NVA) the situation was radically different. It built its rules and procedures on the ideals of the Prussian army. Service was a patriotic duty of each young man; his individuality had to be subordinated to strict obedience in a hierarchy of rank. "*Maul halten und weiter dienen*" (Keep your trap shut and serve on) was the dominant dictum. The troops always had to be on full readiness; leaves were very few and far between. Indeed when not in training they had to spend most of their time in the barracks, a dreary existence. General Jörge Schönbohm, the commander of the new *Bundeswehr* Command East who had the task of transitional management of the NVA after reunification, noted in his diary:

A . . . visit to the [NVA] barracks reveals the sight that will later be repeated again and again . . . The furniture in the other ranks' rooms—occupied by eight to ten men—consists for each man, of a bed, a narrow locker and a stool. There is only one table for all the occupants . . . The walls are bare—there are no personal effects. In another ranks' common room chairs are grouped around a television—dark distemper is flaking the walls. Depressing grey everywhere. There is no room where one could feel comfortable and enjoy oneself. . . . In the washrooms there was, as a rule, only cold water and there were no showers or they did not work. In the more modern barracks shower blocks were built in the 1970s—for 2,500 servicemen one shower room with fifty to seventy showers. If showers were taken, each unit had to report beforehand, so there was enough warm water. If it was a cold winter and boilers were overburdened, there was often no warm water for the mass showers.[57]

The sharp contrast was not limited to physical conditions. The NVA was systematically built up as the communist party's (SED) instrument. Ninety-five percent of the officers and 50 percent of NCOs were long-standing party members heavily indoctrinated with political and ideological beliefs. Hatred was carefully nurtured. As late as 1988 the *Armeerundschau*, the official organ of the NVA, stated: "We can hate from the bottom of our hearts all that and all those who stand in the way of realizing . . . [our] longings . . . Our hate is inflamed by the crimes of imperialism . . . by attitudes such as those of the Defense Minister of the FRG [West Germany] Wörner." In a book given to servicemen when they took their oath they could read: "Your enemies are the mercenaries of imperialism . . . Whatever language they speak . . . whatever uniform they wear, that of the Bundeswehr or another imperialist army . . . whoever bears arms for imperialism and acts on its behalf is our enemy."[58] The young NVA conscript's oath began with: "I swear to serve the German Democratic Republic, my fatherland." West Germany was just like any other country, the *Bundeswehr* just like any other enemy. In a conversation with General Schönbohm where the latter revealed that the *Bundeswehr* was only at 85 percent readiness during weekends, a young former NVA officer spontaneously burst out: "General, then with a brief attack at the weekend we could have advanced to the Rhine and occupied everything. I ask myself today, why didn't we actually do it?"[59] Questions of aggression, let alone civil war, just did not occur to him.

Then there was the glaring economic disparity. The West Germans with the aid of the Marshall Plan produced their economic miracle (*Wirtschaftswunder*). In the East their Soviet masters had very little interest in

---

[57] Jörge Schönbohm, *Two Armies and One Fatherland* (Providence: Berghahn Books, 1996), pp. 59–61.

[58] Ibid., p. 27. See also: Peter M. Schmitz, "The German Democratic Republic," in Douglas J. Murray and Peter P. Viotti (eds.) *The Defense Policies of Nations: A Comparative Study* (Baltimore: Johns Hopkins University Press, 1989), pp. 191–93.

[59] Schönbohm, *Two Armies and One Fatherland*, p. 134.

regenerating a German industry. After the war they promptly dismantled anything they could put their hands on. They transferred the East German raw-material base to Poland. All the same, the East Germans were and still are inordinately proud that among Soviet satellites in the economy they were the best. Curiously, many abroad shared their belief.[60] But in fact the DDR turned out to be in worse shape than almost anyone had suspected. While West Germany built Volkswagens and BMWs, East Germany produced the Trabant, a freak: something like a motorcycle engine (some called it a lawnmower) surrounded by a particle board frame.[61] A comedian remarked we push it up a hill and then it can roll down. (*Man schiebt's hinauf und rollt hinunter.*) Worse than that, while the work ethic roused West Germans, their eastern compatriots developed a different view: they pretend to pay us, we pretend to work. As far as farmers were concerned, forget the weather, nine to five will do quite nicely.

As a result, in 1983 the DDR needed a DM10 billion "loan" from West Germany. A secret paper commissioned by the DDR government shortly before its end noted: the external deficit has become so vast that just to stop it from rising any further the 1990 standard of living would have to be cut by 25–30 percent making the country "ungovernable."[62] The magistrate of East Berlin pleaded with the Senate of West Berlin to take over all community services, including hospitals, traffic, even police.[63] In fact, East Germany had become insolvent.

Blatant disparities notwithstanding, after reunification equality was the dominant theme. They did not have to earn it by work; the East was entitled to the standard of living of the West. Up went the chants of grievances. Wages in the East were only 60 percent of those in the West. Unemploy-

---

[60] For example, in the Foreword to General Schönbohm's book General John M. Shalikashvili, chairman of the U.S. Joint Chiefs of Staff, wrote: "The East Germans had somehow succeeded in making Communism work—even more productively than the Soviets . . ." Schönbohm, *Two Armies and One Fatherland*, p. VI.

[61] In 1976 the car of a senior U.S. diplomat in East Berlin was accidentally hit by a Trabant and a larger Wartburg. All that his Volvo suffered were modest body damages; both East German cars were totaled. There followed an interesting sequel. By 1996 the Stasi files were opened and our diplomat got hold of his own. They revealed that after the accident the drivers of the two German cars were interviewed by a Stasi general who accused them of planning the accident so they could pass secret information to the Americans!

[62] *Economist*, November 9–15, 1996, Survey Germany p. 5.

[63] Kohl, *Ich Wollte Deutschlands Einheit*, p. 249.

ment was three times higher. Never mind that productivity was less than 30 percent in the East. The West had accepted a parity of currencies. Now they would have to pay for economic disparities. And they had better do it soon.

It was all getting on the nerves of the West Germans. Their compatriots in the East were becoming a gigantic pain in the anatomy. The government, however, was busily stoking the fires of optimism. To be sure, "*die neuen Bundesländer*" were economically underdeveloped; that was the communist system's fault. The people were Germans after all. Within a democratic polity opened up to private enterprise they would pull off a second German economic miracle. Massive private investment and the newest technology would naturally stream there. Just wait and see.

West Germans waited but did not see. New investment, new technology was not streaming to the East. The East German state-controlled industries to be sold to private owners and estimated to bring in DM600 billion ended up as a negative equity of around DM200 billion. One reason was titles of ownership. The Nazis had expropriated, the Soviets had expropriated, the East Germans had expropriated. The victims of such arbitrary government action had to be given a chance to recover. But who were the victims? Where were they? Many had fled to the West. Many had been murdered by the Nazis and the communists. Their heirs, if any were left, might be somewhere, anywhere, possibly in Israel or America. They might have only vague ideas about the details of the property: just what was the number of the house, indeed what was the name of the street back then? Many might discover their rights only later and then should have a right to exercise them. It is all a matter of justice. But an investor wants a clear title. No one would spend money only to discover later that the profits would have to go to someone else. That is just plain economic good sense.

By 1992 it became clear that if there was to be a stream of private investment to the East, it would take more time. Politically too much time. The government therefore decided to transfer from public funds a minimum of $100 billion per year for at least five, quite possibly ten years. A colossal sum, about three times the defense budget. How to pay for it? By deficit finance and by taxes. On March 13, 1993, to income taxes was added a "solidarity tax" of 7.5 percent across the board, hitting the West Germans and especially the middle classes, the bulwark of German democracy.

As though this was not bad enough, there came further complications—constitutional complications: Germans have a right to live in Germany. Since 1945 Germany had already integrated an enormous number of people into an area that in 1939 was populated by 41 million. At the end and during the immediate aftermath of the war came 9 million refugees and expellees from formerly German and German-occupied territories. Then before the Berlin Wall prevented further movement, 4.2 million East Germans crossed over. The rapid industrial recovery caused the recruitment of foreign "guest workers." Their number rose past 5 million (plus family members) before recruitment for workers outside of the European economic community was halted (*Anwerbestop*) in 1973.[64] In addition, there also came a trickle of ethnic Germans, an annual average of 20,000, and some asylum seekers, less than 10,000 in the 1950s,'60s, and '70s. With the collapse of the Soviet Union the members in these two last categories rose dramatically. The number of ethnic Germans entering the Bundesrepublic in 1988 jumped to 203,000. In the next six years (1989–94) 1.7 million entered Germany. The constitution recognized them as Germans (Article 116). There was no alternative but to resettle them.

The constitution with the Nazi record clearly in mind, moreover, was also very generous about political asylum (Article 16). Anyone entering Germany with a claim of being a political refugee would be admitted. His claim would be thoroughly investigated, a process that could take several years. In the meantime asylum seekers were *entitled* to food, clothing, housing, and about $800 per person, per month, regardless whether they worked at all. After examination about 4 percent were found to be legitimate political refugees. But what about the other 96 percent? It was just too difficult for the young democracy to expel them *en masse*. Their prospects of remaining were excellent. The door was wide open.

The steady trickle of asylum seekers became a flood. In 1992 their numbers reached 438,000, of which about 250,000 came from Yugoslavia. United Germany became a magnet. Entire villages from East Europe and Asia appeared on the doorsteps claiming the *rights* of asylum. West Germans, already deeply engaged in their venture of united Germany, now had to find a place for people with foreign languages, foreign cultures, and foreign values. And they had to pay for it! Their mood turned sullen (*düster*). Something had to be done. In 1993 through a bipartisan effort the right of asylum was defined. Those claimants who had to reach Germany through a third "secure" country were ruled ineligible.[65] Thereafter the numbers dropped. In 1995 there were 128,000 applicants of whom 18,000 were judged valid.

---

[64] Hermann Kurthen and Michael Minkenberg, "Germany in Transition: Immigration, Racism and the Extreme Right," *Nations and Nationalism*, I (2), 1995, p. 180.

[65] In 1996 the German constitutional court upheld this limitation. *Frankfurter Rundschau*, May 15, 1996, p. 2.

Anxiety about the political risks the chancellor was taking proved to be unwarranted. In the 1994 elections the CDU prevailed. Together with its ally, the FDP, Kohl could still operate with a ten-vote majority in the *Bundestag*. Two years later, in three important state elections the ruling coalition gained seats, while the extremist parties lost seats. All the sacrifices did not feel good, but the electorate was willing to put up with them. In April 1996 in order to reduce government deficits to meet the European Union requirements, the chancellor was confident in announcing (a) the postponement of the scheduled 1 percent reduction in the solidarity tax and (b) deep cuts in the 1997 budget. Many of these cuts necessarily affected the cherished social entitlement programs. Labor leaders, essential components of the consensus approach to economic policy, objected vigorously. The chancellor held firm. There were demonstrations on May 1 as expected but on a very much smaller scale than expected.

By the end of 1996, however, the pressures were mounting. Questions about a successor were widely discussed. Demands for tax reforms were heard throughout the land. The chancellor appointed a commission to study the matter, and its report should be ready toward the end of 1997. Meanwhile he undermined its efforts to reduce taxes by reducing expenditure. One obvious source of saving could be the coal miners' subsidies. In the last decades their numbers had dwindled and most people thought that subsidies well over a DM100,000 per person were far too extravagant and should be phased out altogether in the near term. Even so, in spring 1997 Kohl let it be known that he was determined to keep the subsidies intact.

Germany, of course, is still in a transitional stage. The cleavage between the eastern and western parts of the country have become more visible. New words entered the German language: the Ossis (eastern Germans) and the Wessis (western Germans) each endowed with different connotations according to the groups. In a June 1996 poll 89 percent of easterners but only 48 percent of westerners expressed the view that life in the eastern part is worse than in the west. Similarly 84 percent of the easterners and 9 percent of the westerners believe the government is doing little to create equal conditions; 32 percent of the westerners and 0 percent of the easterners believe it is doing much.[66] In 1994 General Schönbohm frankly admitted: "We have now been united for five years and we still do not know enough about one another to understand each other."[67] All the same, the German economy with the exception of double-digit unemploy-

---

[66] Quoted in *Economist*, November 9–15, 1996, Survey Germany p. 6.

[67] Schönbohm, *Two Armies and One Fatherland*, p. 204.

ment is doing well, and the people in the East are doing very much better. In fact, hardly anyone in Germany regrets unification.

Democratic political culture has not yet permeated the entire society. Many of the recent immigrants and East Germans still need to learn about the attitude of moderation, the process of compromise, and perhaps the value of human rights. There are in Germany, as anywhere else, peculiar people. The neo-Nazis are such a fringe group. Germany, at least the dominant western part, is perhaps more than any other country inoculated against fascism. Still government officials are extraordinarily sensitive about their tarnished reputation abroad. After an interview with the Bonn correspondent of the French newspaper *Le Monde* during which the latter without evidence charged that the Germans in their push for reunification had willfully sacrificed advance toward European unity, the chancellor's foreign policy adviser noted in his diary: the distrust against us Germans runs deep.[68]

Intellectuals are still distressed when anyone raises the issue in whatever form. Thus, when a Harvard assistant professor wrote a book in which "the judgment that all Germans were guilty [of the mass murder of Jews] is constantly—and irresponsibly—implied,"[69] alarm bells rang all over the country. At the same time, the generation that is now growing up and increasing in number in the *Bundestag* will not wear the scarlet letter. Nor will they hang their heads in shame when they are pilloried by the foreign (American) press because some of their fringe groups, neo-Nazis, skinheads, whatever, produce outrageous media events. Cautiously but determinedly they are now trying to learn about and cope with the Nazi past. The first German chancellor of the post-war generation (Kohl) was ready to address the issue of the holocaust.

We have . . . a duty to ask ourselves how it could have happened that a culture collapsed to which German Jews in particular had made such an outstanding contribution. . . . We shall not permit anything to be falsified and ameliorated. It is exactly the knowledge of this guilty entanglement, of this lack of conscience, also cowardice and failure that puts us in a position to recognize the first symptoms of destruction and to resist them, since totalitarianism, which was able to take root in Germany after January 30, 1933, is not an unrepeatable aberration, not an accident of history.[70]

---

[68] Teltschik, *329 Tage*, p. 61.

[69] *Economist*, April 27–May 3, p. 52.

[70] *Union in Deutschland*, April 25, 1985.

After about fifty years democratic institutions are now well established in Germany. The party system, however, is still vulnerable. In the eastern part of the country reactionary communism retains some voter appeal. More troublesome, a populist tendency may be on the rise. In the western part the two major parties are still dominant, but as in most democracies they are battered by the media. For some time now there has been a third party, the Free Democrats (FDP), which by shifting support could (and did) decide which of the major parties (in coalition) would hold parliamentary majority and control the government. In 1983 another "third party" entered the *Bundestag*: the Greens. They arrived as a motley crew, flaunted their image as "pacifist tree-huggers," and thrashed about like some *enfants terribles* with anti-NATO banners, clutching pine branches allegedly damaged by acid rain. They harangued about the abolition of the German army and the protection of the environment. On the latter they offered such droll approaches for the relief of pollution as a prohibition of lawn mowers and their replacement with hungry geese. Recently the party has matured and moved toward the middle. One of its leaders, Joschka Fischer, explained: "I think Bosnia was the turning point. . . . Our party was born in the peace movement, but the scenes of genocide in the Balkans changed the views of even the most hardened pacifist."[71] Indeed most Greens now support German participation in NATO and the expansion of the organization. They see no alternative to a strong U.S. presence on the continent. Their views on the ecology are still very emphatic but have been significantly moderated, focusing on the development of new technologies to protect the environment. With a new moderation, they gained support among the growing number of voters who prefer an alternative to the two major parties. In some state elections they have become *the* third party, entering in coalition to form a governing majority. Their performance further bolstered their support. By 1997 some estimates project them winning 15 percent of the votes in the 1998 parliamentary elections. If so, the question arises, will the Greens *replace* the FDP as the makers of a winning coalition, or will an entirely new (from the academic perspective, fascinating) situation arise of two major parties plus two minor parties?

Then there is the personal element. The need for strong leadership is often expressed. In fact, Helmut Kohl is a historic figure. He towers over all other party leaders. He overshadows political institutions. During the last election he pledged that he would not run for reelection. But many Germans hoped he would lead the country into the twenty-first century. In

---

[71] *Washington Post*, August 2, 1997, p. A13.

April 1997 he announced that he had changed his mind and would run again in 1998. This was hardly a surprise and will not be a disaster. After all, German democratic institutions have survived Konrad Adenauer quite well. Still it is not a healthy habit to develop in a democracy.

The most important transition for Germany is in the international environment. For fifty years Germany did not initiate any great political ventures. Even in its own region of Europe it carefully integrated its position into a collective stand, following faithfully and uncritically the American or the French lead. West Germany was painfully conscious of the legacy of Nazi aggression. However fervently they wish to put an end to this legacy, it will continue to haunt them for some time to come. There are still too many countries throughout the world who have dreadful memories of German military occupation, and there are still too many countries that are envious and believe they can make use of it for their own purposes. Undoubtedly it will try the patience of the German people and its leaders. It might produce a new Right comprising journalists, novelists, professors, and young businesspeople who would wish to strike out on their own.[72]

We cannot expect united Germany with its power and geopolitical location to play the role of "an economic giant and a political dwarf." Indeed it should not do so. It can make major contributions to peace. It would be helpful if it would choose not to play a lone hand and German policy not become too assertive. Fairly or unfairly Lawrence Eagleburger, at the time (1991) deputy secretary of state, thought German unilateral recognition of Slovenia and Croatia to be unwise. He predicted an inevitable radical Serb reaction followed by chaos and bloodshed.

There is also a question of the geographic scope of German foreign policy. Will Germany choose the regional or the global stage? Those concerned about German aggression in the past wish to contain it to the smallest possible sphere. Indeed most Germans themselves prefer to limit their involvement in international affairs to a minimum. But doing so may be a mistake. The narrower its sphere, the greater the disparity in Germany's favor. In central Europe whether it chooses to exercise it or not, German power is overwhelming. On the entire continent there is no effective counterweight except perhaps Russia. But Russia has its neighbor China with a billion plus people, many of them very smart people, to worry about. Germany, a colossus in the middle of Europe focusing on the affairs of Europe, may once again frighten its neighbors. Instead a Germany soft-

---

[72] Jacob Heilbrunn, "Germany's New Right," *Foreign Affairs*, November-December 1996, pp. 80–98.

spoken but fully engaged in global issues and responsibilities would be the most salutary prospect. In 1994 the constitution court reinterpreted the *Grundgesetz* to permit under some conditions a global projection of force. Since then Germany, following the "policy of small steps," has participated in collective peacekeeping and /or humanitarian initiatives in Somalia and Cambodia as well as in Bosnia. In March 1997 German military units carried out a very successful evacuation of foreign (including German) civilians from Tirana, Albania.

The United States of Europe, or a System of the States of Europe, or reversion to the traditional chauvinisms and power struggles. Which will it be? Germany emerging from its profane adventure with the twisted cross and probably much wiser for it will make a major difference. But a whale of a difference will be made by the United States. Will it resume a strong and creative leadership position? Possibly. Here again we have to face a new reality, for American eyes have been turning to Asia. In our daily lives we have become accustomed to rely on imports from the Pacific Rim. Since 1978 the majority of our trade has shifted to that region. Hyundai has replaced Volkswagen. Japan, Korea, and Taiwan are now principal ($100 billion) surplus countries. And Americans' eyes may be turning south to Latin America with its intense and ambivalent attitudes toward the United States, its population explosion, its chronic economic problems, its fascist perils, and perhaps its new democratic opportunities.

9

South of the Border

Much of Latin America is farther from us than is Europe (or Africa for that matter), but we have always by passive consensus taken our special relationship for granted. Physical contiguity may have contributed to this attitude, but the foundation of our common bond was intangible: the heritage of a shared venture.

When Columbus landed on the island of San Salvador, he took the first steps toward a historic enterprise: the New World. It offered much more than an opportunity to explore vast, previously (to Europeans) unknown territories. It offered to the people of the Old World an inspiring vision: the promise of a new beginning. The dichotomy was enunciated in the Monroe Doctrine. In 1823 the president foreswore any U.S. interest in Europe but committed us to hemispheric solidarity. "We should consider any attempt on their [European] part to extend their system to any portion of this hemisphere as dangerous to our peace and security" he warned in his State of the Union message.[1] As far as we were concerned the Old World and the New World were clearly separated and should remain an ocean apart.

We should not miss the fact, however, that our positive attitude to Latin America was something of an on-and-off affair. The Monroe Doctrine was not yet two years old when the United States was invited to a conference at Panama arranged by Simon Bolivar. This continental

---

[1] Thomas A. Bailey, *A Diplomatic History of the American Peple,* 3rd ed. (New York: Appleton-Century-Crofts, 1946), p. 185.

conference, to be held just after the battle of Ayacucho which finally terminated Spanish presence in South America, was convened to consolidate republican institutions in the New World. President John Quincy Adams promptly accepted and was ready to send two delegates. When he sought Senate approval for his appointees and a congressional appropriation for their expenses, however, he found little support and less interest. Although in the end the legislators reluctantly gave their consent, no U.S. delegates ever reached Panama. One delegate, poor fellow, died en route; the other started too late. He soon concluded that he could not reach his destination in time and gave up trying. Later in that century (1881) the United States itself set out to organize an Inter-American Conference. Secretary of State Blaine sent out the invitations but three weeks later, for domestic partisan reasons, decided to leave office. Latin American leaders were preparing to attend. Never mind, Blaine's successor peremptorily canceled the meeting.

And we ought not forget that quite a number of times North American special interest did not have happy consequences for Latin American countries. In the middle of the nineteenth century the United States became quite interested in Mexico. This led to a war more or less instigated by the American government, which ended by our closest neighbor's being compelled to cede to us about half of her territory.[2] Later in the century (1892) our attention was focused on the other end of the hemisphere. After an incident in which unarmed American sailors on shore leave were attacked, Chile was compelled to apologize publicly, show public respect for the Stars and Stripes, and pay $75,000 in reparations. We may have been right,[3] but the Chileans felt humiliated. Eating humble pie did not improve their appetite for a special relationship with the United States.

Soon our special interest shifted to Cuba. We were offended by the continued practice of slavery on the island. That was one reason. Another: ever since the Civil War American investment in the island had been steadily increasing. And another: as Caribbean commerce expanded, we

---

[2] The Mexican title to the land was based on the principles of "discovery" and "occupation" (less than a dozen missions in California) accepted at the time but already obsolescent. On the U.S. side a part of victory in war was the emerging principle of self-determination.

[3] Two sailors were killed, seventeen were injured, and the rest were beaten and imprisoned. The local police reportedly joined in the mob attack. A month passed without any visible Chilean regret, then another, and yet another before an American ultimatum had its effect.

were concerned about control of the inner sea. At an opportune moment (1898) we went to war with Spain to gain Cuban independence. After the colonial power was forced to withdraw, the American government compelled (the Platt Amendment) the newly independent state to lease part of its territory to us for naval and coaling stations and to include in its constitution a provision granting us the right to intervene militarily. In 1902 American forces that liberated Cuba withdrew; in 1906 they returned "to restore order." Our special interest then moved to Central America. The United States was determined to build a canal linking the Atlantic and Pacific oceans. Colombia therefore was forced to stand by while one of its provinces (Panama) was severed.

Indeed throughout the twentieth century our relationship with Latin America was punctuated by difficulties, economic difficulties, for example. The countries to our south complained about the arrogance of major American companies. United Fruit was charged with taking land out of production thereby limiting employment opportunities. American electric power companies were accused of charging too high prices and failing to serve rural areas. Some countries complained about the size of our sugar quota; others that they were not given a quota. Peru and Ecuador complained about problems in selling rice in the United States. Argentina complained that the United States depressed the world price of wheat by dumping practices. They became outright hostile when we continued to exclude Argentine beef well after the hoof-and-mouth disease had been eliminated from their cattle. There were political difficulties as well. Latin Americans resented constant U.S. pressure to follow uncritically the line of our diplomacy. Mostly though, Latin Americans resented U.S. military interventions: in the Dominican Republic, Haiti, Cuba, Grenada, Nicaragua, Honduras, Guatemala, and Mexico. There may have been explanations, even good reasons, for American actions. Private companies did bring many employment opportunities to rural areas. To provide a very lucrative sugar quota to all countries wishing for it would have either lowered the domestic price or reduced the quota amounts available to the Philippines and Hawaii. U.S. reasons for overt and covert military intervention included helping to collect customs duties for the benefit of international (particularly European) creditors, restoring internal order, and/or blocking communism. It may have been a logical and necessary consequence of the assumption by the United States of assuming global responsibilities, but Latin Americans were unsympathetic to this kind of geopolitical rationale.

This attitude of feeling aggrieved was somewhat softened when the Organization of American States was formally established after World War II (1947). It contained the solemn declaration: "No State or group of States has a right to intervene, directly or indirectly, for any reason whatever, in the internal or external affairs of any other State." More than that its governing council was composed of one representative from each member, that is twenty from Latin America and one from the United States—a very favorable voting ratio requiring constant attention and tender loving care by Washington.

More recently, however, this has changed significantly. New Caribbean countries, including former British colonies, had to be admitted into the Organization, which had carefully excluded Canada, four, five, six, ten, eleven with Surinam, now fourteen. Not only are they not Latin countries, they have shown a predisposition to vote with the United States. Washington still has to be careful to avoid an adverse majority vote, but it can now with relative ease block a two-thirds vote necessary on important issues. The OAS has changed too much, Latin American leaders now keep complaining; it is no longer very useful. Perhaps as a consequence they have begun to organize, with few concrete working results, their own regional combinations.

It all adds up to this: When we consider the utility of special relations, we have to recognize that Latin American attitudes toward us are loaded with heavy emotional baggage accumulated in the past. Needless to say, unless Latin Americans climb down from their mountain of grievances, it will be difficult to maintain a mutually satisfactory hemisphere solidarity. Meanwhile unless North Americans rise out of their usual mode of indifference and reappraise their long-term interest in their partners in the New World, no new consensus can emerge.

NEW STRATEGIC REALITIES

A major reason for United States indifference may be that as a rule Latin America was of little strategic significance to us. In 1836 there was the lamentable unpleasantness at the Alamo, but within five weeks the Texans handled it quite satisfactorily at San Jacinto. Eighty years later Francisco (Pancho) Villa tried his luck with extracurricular incursions into New Mexico, but General Pershing soon discouraged the Mexican's misguided fervor. These, however, were minor matters. In fact, the United States has never been seriously threatened by a Latin American country. What we did face occasionally were indirect challenges by European powers attempting to establish bases in Latin America in order to reach us and do us harm. In the 1820s President Monroe, or more specifically Secretary of State John Quincy Adams, was concerned about Spain's reconquering its former colonies. In the 1860s we were disturbed about

France's, or more specifically Napoleon III's, placing a puppet ruler on the Mexican "throne." During World War I Americans were aroused by a secret German note advising that in case of a U.S. declaration of war against Germany a military alliance with Mexico should be sought offering as an inducement the recovery of New Mexico, Texas, and Arizona.[4] During World War II we were annoyed that the German navy and German intelligence were receiving aid from South American governments.[5]

The situation became serious needing close American attention and determined response only during the Cold War. The Soviet Union began to invest heavily in the extension of communism to the New World. It subsidized revolutionary movements throughout the hemisphere, some with nationalist, others with social reform directions. It came perilously close to success in Guatemala, Venezuela, Peru, Chile, the Dominican Republic, and Nicaragua. It did succeed in Cuba. Then in October 1962 we discovered that the Soviet Union was installing strategic missiles on the island. Even after we forced them to withdraw their missiles, they continued to station a brigade of combat troops on Cuban soil and built a naval base. Meanwhile in Grenada and Nicaragua they helped construct airfields with runways capable of handling strategic bombers.

Fortunately this bothersome interlude was of short duration. By the final decade of the century, we were back roughly in the pre-World War I position. We could expect some periodic unpleasantness in Central America, possibly targeting the Panama Canal, but all potential indirect military threats could be easily managed. And no Latin American country could possibly pose a direct strategic threat to us.

ECONOMIC RELATIONS

The economic case for interdependence is more robust. For some time the region's share in our international trade has been significant. It accounted for 13.6 percent of our exports in 1965, well behind Europe (32.2 percent), Canada (20.3 percent), and Asia (16.5 percent). In 1975 it

---

[4] The note was intercepted by British intelligence. Because their means was top secret, the idea that it may have been a forgery was making considerable headway when the German foreign secretary frankly (naïvely) admitted its genuineness.

[5] Much of it was clandestine. When it came to public confrontation, they regularly yielded to U.S. diplomatic persuasion. Thus, for example, when the German pocket battleship *Admiral Graf Spee* sought time for repairs in Montevideo, the government of Uruguay ordered it to leave in seventy-two hours.

rose to 14.6 percent, dropped to 12.8 percent in 1986, then rose to 18.1 percent in 1994 always behind Europe, Canada, and Asia.[6] Concurrently Latin America's share in imports moved downward steadily: 17.8 percent in 1965, 12.2 percent in 1975, and 10.7 percent in 1986, but then rebounded in 1994 to 13.3 percent. Even so, we are now importing about three times (36 percent) the value of goods from East Asia.[7]

Meanwhile the composition of our trade has changed. Traditionally we have gained because the Caribbean area offered us easy and cheap access to its agricultural products (e.g., tropical fruit, sugar, coffee, and rum) and industrial raw materials (e.g., oil, bauxite, copper, and iron ore). We have gained because the rest of the continent, with the possible exception of Argentina, provided us with easy access to uncompetitive markets for our manufactured goods. Such convenient, mercantile trade patterns, however, have become obsolete.

Growing industrialization has changed the Latin American market. It has become much broader, providing new opportunities for export of U.S. capital goods (heavy machinery and farm equipment) and new opportunities for the export of agricultural products. That is the good news. At the same time Latin American countries have begun to build some manufacturing capacity of their own which may expand their intraregional trade and may link them into the world economy. U.S. exports in Latin America now face competition, indigenous and international. In addition, Latin American governments have imposed greater control over U.S. imports. They established government monopolies. They regulated and restricted trade. Mexico, for example, has limited its oil exports to its northern neighbor to 50 percent of its production and offers the rest to distant places anywhere throughout the world.

Add to this a new and very troubling phenomenon: narcotics. More than a dozen of our southern neighbors are involved in the chain of this illicit activity, which floods the United States with drugs. "Cocaine earnings in Bolivia are estimated to be three times the value of all the country's other exports. Repatriated drug profits are said to account for about 20 percent of Peru's export earnings. A similar share of Colombia's foreign exchange is earned from the drug trade, and drug income has also become a major source of dollars in Mexico. During the 1980s, when debt

---

[6] By 1986 Asia had risen to the number one spot.

[7] U.S. Department of Commerce, Bureau of Census, *Statistical Abstract of the United States, 1967* (88th edition) (Washington, DC: Government Printing Office, 1967), pp. 838–39; and op.cit. 1988, (108th Edition) p. 770.

service obligations have been rising and the prices of Latin America's legal exports have been falling, drugs have been the only significant regional export increasing in value."[8]

Apart from trade, we are involved in Latin America through private sector investment. Its range has expanded from natural resource extraction and utilities and now includes substantial investment in manufacturing and services. Its dimensions are still significant but have been declining from 38 percent of our total foreign investment in 1950 to 13 percent in 1985. To borrow some apt comparisons: "United States firms now have almost twice as much invested in Canada than in all of Latin America and the Caribbean; they have as much invested in the United Kingdom and Ireland as in all of South America; and more invested in Denmark than in all of Central America."[9]

This, however, is only part of the story, the less important part. For while U.S. investment in the Latin American private sector was declining, suddenly U.S. private credit to Latin American governments (and government corporations) rose sharply. Indeed in the mid-1970s American banks, facing recession at home and flooded with petrodollars, were prepared to lend money for almost any project and typically for *no* project at all! In 1975 Latin America and the Caribbean owed to private creditors, about two-thirds of them U.S. creditors, $34.8 billion in long-term loans. Five years later this figure more than tripled ($111 billion), in 1985 hit $222.7 billion, and was still rising! If one added the long-term loans owed to "official creditors" and the short-term loans, the total exceeded the psychedelic figure of $387 billion.[10] Specifically this meant in the case of Brazil, for example, that its external debt, which stood at 17 percent of the gross national product in 1975, jumped to 46 percent in 1984. Panama's debt exceeded 75 percent and Costa Rica's 140 percent of the gross domestic product.[11]

---

[8] Abraham F. Lowenthal, *Partners in Conflict, the United States and Latin America* (Baltimore: Johns Hopkins University Press, 1987), p. 190.

[9] Ibid., p. 54.

[10] The World Bank, *World Debt Tables 1987–1988*, First Supplement (Washington, DC: The World Bank, 1988), p. 18.

[11] Celso L. Martone, *Macroeconomic Policies, Debt Accumulation, and Adjustment in Brazil, 1965–84* (World Bank Discussion Papers) (Washington, DC: The World Bank, 1986), p. 10; and United States, *Report of the National Bipartisan Commission on Central America* (Washington, DC: National Bipartisan Commission, January 1984), p. 44.

In theory this could not go on. By the mid-1980s the hemisphere was in a debt crisis. Hundreds of U.S. banks were involved. By 1982 the nine largest of them had considerably more than 100 percent of their stockholders' equity exposed in Latin America.[12] To be sure, default is a technical term made even more elusive by various practical applications and in any case a designation devoutly to be avoided. Still whatever they would call it, very soon Latin American debtors, including Costa Rica, Peru, Mexico, and Brazil, found it impossible to pay on the principal and were even forced to suspend interest payments. Argentina required two new "bridge" loans; Bolivia was permitted to pay off its debt at eight cents on the dollar. By 1984 foreign investment was drying up, and American banks were desperately seeking formulas to avoid admitting colossal losses.

Toward the end of the decade a new feature was added to economic relations. President Bush decided to tie Mexico's economy to that of Canada and the United States. Just why he decided to do so and why he pushed the idea so single-mindedly are not entirely clear. The general umbrella argument that it is good for free trade evades the question: why Mexico? Could we not find a more suitable partner than an authoritarian and corrupt political system with a bankrupt economy heavily engaged in drug trafficking?[13] Skeptics wonder: was it because our large banks needed some assurances about the vast loans they had extended to the country? Was it because our large corporations sought opportunities for reducing the prices of their own products in order to make them more competitive? Was it an attempt to counteract regional combinations in Europe (Common Market) and Asia (ASEAN)? On closer examination none of these special interest concerns can be readily converted into American national interest especially because other special interests are vigorously opposed and have to endure harm at the very least in the short term. Or is the principal rationale for NAFTA, as so many people slyly whisper, an effort to stem the waves of illegal aliens across the Rio Grande? There are objections to that approach as well. First, it concedes that the United States is unable to protect its borders. Second, it plays on ethnic fears and antagonisms. Finally, it is empirically fundamentally flawed. Admittedly there is

---

[12] Lowenthal, *Partners in Conflict,* p. 57.

[13] It has become something of a pattern. First the admission that in the past there were serious problems with corruption and drug trafficking. Then the claim that with the new president all that is in the past, just wait and see. And finally revelations that indeed nothing has changed and the repetition that it will be much better next time.

evidence that close economic ties improve demographic mobility. In case of countries with roughly the same standard of living it promotes tourism, a flow in both directions. But, and this is a big but, in case of a significant disparity between the standards of living, close economic relations facilitate a flood of migration *one way*, from the poorer to the richer country. This distinction when applied to NAFTA makes it obviously dysfunctional. In any case, on December 17, 1992, about a month after his electoral defeat, the president signed the treaty. President Clinton, who during the campaign opposed it, changed his mind after he took office. Then followed a well-orchestrated mass mobilization effort by almost every segment of the American Establishment (business, media, academia, but not labor) as well as by Mexican public officials. After massive exertions by the president and bipartisan congressional leadership, a noticeably reluctant Congress gave its approval. According to schedule the North American Free Trade Association (NAFTA) entered into force in January 1994.

Simply put—and the treaty is far from simple[14]—it provided for a phased-in (over ten to fifteen years) elimination of tariff and nontariff barriers on regional trade. Specifically (a) the historically contentious restrictions on agricultural products, textiles, and apparel were to be liberalized, (b) U.S. investment opportunities in petrochemicals and financial services were to be opened up, and (c) cumbersome Mexican trade laws and opaque administrative practices were promised to be revised. One also hears it said, however, that the most important feature of NAFTA is that it gave hope and confidence to Mexicans.

It is too early to judge just how NAFTA will work out. Will it significantly increase trade? What will be its effect on employment in the United States? Will Mexico fully live up to its bargain?[15] How will NAFTA

---

[14] For a detailed discussion pro and con see: Gary Clyde Hufbauer and Jeffrey J. Schott, *NAFTA: An Assessment* (Washington, DC: Institute for International Economics, 1993).

[15] Possibly, for it is such a good deal for them. All the same, it is worth noting that the World Bank's experience (always expressed in tactful, diplomatic terms) with Mexico's carrying out policies to which it was committed was not always reassuring. An internal, confidential report noted for example: "The final period (1982 to 1992) showed a marked improvement in environmental policy and results. . . . Since most of these projects have not been completed and almost no environmental evaluations are available, it is not totally clear if implementation and monitoring has improved proportionately with better environmental assessment and design. However, it appears that implementation has lagged behind assessment."

(continued...)

affect trade with other Latin American countries? How will it affect illegal immigration to the United States? And not least important: just how much will it cost us? The initial investment was estimated at $40 billion.[16]

Early events did not augur well. In 1994 trade between Mexico and the United States was in balance with a slight ($1 billion) surplus in U.S. exports. In 1996 trade had indeed increased—mostly one way—producing a $12 billion U.S. trade deficit! Worse still the number of illegal immigrants who were not apprehended rose from 1 million in 1994 to 1.6 million in 1996.[17] President Carlos Salinas de Gortari of Mexico, who was lionized by leading American public opinion groups, is now forced to live in exile to avoid criminal charges.[18] Corruption is still rampant in public life. His successor, Ernesto Zedillo, is another great favorite. Nevertheless on December 20, 1994, a few days after the Summit of the Americas, Mexico suddenly devalued its currency "triggering a major crisis that threatened to engulf the Latin America and Caribbean region."[19] Undeterred by past experience, the United States was ready to organize a massive international bailout. In 1996 Mexico still owed $100 billion from the 1982 debt crisis. Add the $40 billion of NAFTA. Add the $50 billion for the bailout. Comforted international banks returned to their optimistic mood. Meanwhile Mexico has replaced Colombia as the chief source of drugs in the United States. In February 1997 General Jesus Gutierez Rebollo, the country's top antidrug fighter who was enthusiastically endorsed by President Zedillo, was charged with being on the payroll (for seven years!)

---

[15](...continued)
The World Bank, *Memorandum to the Executive Directors and the President, Subject: OED Study of Bank/Mexico Relations, 1948–1992* (Washington, DC: World Bank, Office of the Director General, 1994), p. 43.

[16] Loss of tariff revenues: $2–3 billion; retraining of American workers: $1.68 billion over five years; extra border bridges, highways, and sewage treatment: $15–20 billion over the next decade; extra customs inspectors: ?; extra spending on agricultural programs: ?. Estimated total: up to $40 billion. *The New York Times*, July 11993, p. D2.

[17] *Economist*, March 1–7, 1997, p. 43, and July 5–11, 1997, p. 23.

[18] Paul Craig Roberts and Karen LaFollette Araujo, *The Capitalist Revolution in Latin America* (New York: Oxford University Press, 1997), pp. 20–28.

[19] Burki and Edwards, *Latin America after Mexico*, p. 1. The International Monetary Fund in a report concluded the crisis was triggered by Mexican investors. For example, Mexican residents' net sales of domestic stocks and loans totaled $4.7 billion in December 1994, which is more than two-thirds of Mexican foreign exchange reserves. *Washington Post*, August 21, 1995, p. A1.

of Amado Carillo Fuentes, head of the Juarez mob and the country's top gangster. Other reports (which were denied) also implicated two governors (of the states of Sonora and Moreles).[20]

Meanwhile Marco Ruiz Massieu, a deputy attorney general (1993–94), was facing a civil trial in Houston, Texas. The U.S. government charged that the $9,041,598 deposited in an American bank were the proceeds of illegal drug trafficking. Moreover, it was a contention of the government lawyers that the case showed a pattern of corruption reaching so high in the Mexican government that it has frequently foiled U.S. efforts to halt narcotics trafficking.[21] In the end the Houston jury agreed to the U.S. seizure of the deposits. Shortly thereafter Oberto Garcia Abrego, a top drug launderer, escaped from detention. Senior American officials apparently knew about it but cooperated in keeping the news secret until a few days later when President Clinton recertified Mexico as a cooperative partner in our antidrug efforts. General Barry McCaffrey (Ret.), Director, National Drug Control Policy, "explained" that the level of violence in Mexico was "enormous." Last year there were twenty-five major assassinations and some 200 policemen were murdered. The institutions of democracy were creaking. "We have ten years of trouble ahead of us . . . but we are stuck with them culturally, politically, and economically."[22] And so we move along—as usual.

EXPERIMENTS IN DEVELOPMENT

By far the most important feature of Latin America is its position as a gigantic laboratory where important and difficult issues of our times are being addressed. For we live in an age where many countries, big and small, are struggling with a transition from authoritarian political systems with planned economies to democracies with a free market. Unfortunately there are no suitable precedents. In the past experiments by scholars and decision-makers often were seriously handicapped by the fallacy of the single factor. They focused on one dimension, for example, the economic or less often the political, and held all other factors constant, as though in the real world this would be possible. Latin American experiments are invaluable because they try to move simultaneously on both the economic and political planes.

---

[20] *The New York Times*, International, February 26, 1997, p. A1, 6.

[21] *Washington Post*, March 19, 1997, p. 1.

[22] ABC News, *This Week*, March 2, 1997.

By the early 1980s the economies of most Latin American countries were in chaos. Inflation was out of control. In 1985 consumer prices increased by 60 percent in Mexico, by 163 percent in Peru, by 227 percent in Brazil, by 672 percent in Argentina, and by 11,750 percent in Boliva! Their strategies of economic development, insofar as they actually had strategies, were failures for all to see. The public sector did not or could not perform. It produced no self-sustained economic development. Worse still, it impeded growth. But there were massive benefits for the privileged bureaucracies. Meanwhile external investment (public and private) was drying up fast. In February 1982 Mexico devalued its currency by 40 percent. Then seven months later it defaulted on its external debt.

What completed the catastrophe was their authoritarian government's losing control. Poverty remained crushingly persistent while public officials proved to be blatantly rapacious. Corruption, they seemed to hold, was a prerequisite of office. Mexican elites, for example, built mansions and felt few qualms about enriching themselves from public coffers.

Ex-Mexican president José López Portillo (1976–1982) reportedly grabbed a fortune estimated at $1 to $3 billion during his tenure. . . . He built a luxurious, thirty-two-acre estate overlooking Mexico City. . . . While many of his countrymen lived in adobe or corrugated metal shacks, López Portillo and his family have bathrooms of marble and gold. Some floors are jade, and one is transparent, with a detailed model of the Acropolis visible through it. While president, López Portillo got the public works agency, *Banobras*, to spend $33 million on the access road, sewage, and water lines for his estate.[23]

Jorge Diaz Serrano, director of Pemex (the nationalized oil company), was accused of diverting more than $4 billion in revenues in 1979 alone and was unable to account for more than 300 million barrels of oil between 1976 and 1982. In fact, López Portillo was not much worse than his predecessors; Mexico, however, was somewhat worse than the Latin American average. As the venal appetites of high and highest public officials grew, there was less to go around for their subordinates and nothing for the people. The masses were distracted by outbursts of national *machismo*, scapegoating foreigners, most often Americans. This road in April 1982 led to Argentina's invasion of the Falkland Islands (Malvinas), a grand fiasco resulting in the complete loss of confidence in President Leopoldo Galtieri and his military junta.

---

[23] Roberts and LaFollette Araujo, *The Capitalist Revolution in Latin America*, p. 75.

To be sure, there was a lot of public resentment, dissent, even some formal opposition, but when discovered these were forcibly repressed. At the universities government-paid thugs posing as students attended classes to make sure that professors followed the official party line. Any who slipped (and this was widely known) had their classes disrupted, were assaulted, or sometimes detained. Death squads roamed the streets. People were arbitrarily arrested, "taken for a ride," and never heard from again. As a matter of course official corruption and coercion inspired private banditry. Explained Alberto Dahik, vice presidential candidate in Ecuador: "If the minister himself steals, the undersecretaries will commit assaults and the department directors will engage in theft, extortion, robbery, and murder."[24]

Somewhere along the line the people of the South American subcontinent had had enough. And when the Soviet Union collapsed and the communist menace could no longer justify fascist methods, they were ready for a fresh start. To be sure, since independence there were periods of democratic exercises; here and there they were more or less genuine, but they were ephemeral in the extreme. Even as recently as two decades ago we had to deal with mostly authoritarian governments: dictators, presidents for life, or military *juntas*. Some were friendly, others persuadable. Since the 1980s, however, we have been witnessing the *resurgence of democracy* in Latin America (Castro's Cuba remains the lone holdout), and this time it seems genuine enough.

At last the New World may have a common political denominator, but it will need much help. The fact is that the political values of Latin Americans are very different from those of the Founding Fathers in Philadelphia. Latin Americans feel quite comfortable in a *corporate state* where politics means dividing up the spoils and decision-making is based on a system of special interest groups: the Church, the landed gentry (*latafundistas*), labor unions, business organizations, professional associations, etc. Similarly while we believe that government should be limited in scope, that we should look to it for remedy only as a last resort, Latin Americans are accustomed to a more comprehensive, *paternalistic* arrangement, or as some others call it: the nanny-state. People just take it for granted that the state should and would take care of their problems. In the past such predispositions supported authoritarian regimes. Just what kind of democratic institutions, if any, can comfortably rest upon them remains to be seen.

---

[24] Quoted: Ibid., p. 81.

In any case, establishing democratic systems is a prolonged and arduous process. After several centuries in the United States we still have some work to do. The task is not as simple as selecting a suitable leader, not that discovering such a leader through the electoral process is all that simple. It is a common fallacy to consider "free" elections of a chief executive as definite evidence of a democratic system. Such elections can be arranged and conducted in a very short time, thus providing an easy claim for a "democratic reputation." Actually much, much more is needed, and those things require much time.

It takes much time to build a civil community based on the common man, not just on special people distinguished by wealth, beauty, physical strength, or talent. It takes much time to turn traditions upside down and recognize the salience of rights and the principle that it is not government that bestows rights on citizens but citizens who delegate conditional authority to government. It takes time to learn to abide by rules, not in fear of punishment but from *enlightened* self-interest. It takes much effort to learn that elections are political contests among fellow citizens, not occasions of combat with the opposition as the enemy. It takes much time to learn to cherish the minority with its vital function in the system. For the legitimacy of the government is not bestowed by the majority (let alone a plurality) of voters but by the minorities that after the votes are counted publicly concede: "You won fair and square." It takes a democratic commitment to recognize that the methods of resolving disputes are negotiation, bargaining, and above all *compromise*, a compromise when one may gain but also when one must give.

Actually a stable democracy requires even more. Democratic governments, as we are proud to proclaim, are not governments by men and women but by law and institutions. To establish institutions takes enormous effort, statesmanship, and time. Nevertheless institutions have to be developed and carefully nurtured to prevent demagogues, as they did so often in the past, from capturing the system. For institutions by a judicious distribution of power forestall its concentration in one or a few hands. It takes time to develop political parties which by defining the issues shape public opinion and help manage the electoral process. It takes time to establish a legislature that is politically sensitive and can make sound rules, especially new rules required by a constantly changing environment. It takes time to establish an independent judiciary that can serve as the guardians of the continuity of the constitution, an institution that integrates into the democratic system a respect for the past and the interests of the future, and perhaps most important is the special guardian of the minorities, the weak, and the unfortunate.

Is it enough time for people and their leaders to internalize democratic norms? Can there be enough time without a breakthrough to self-sustained economic development, in fact, a breakthrough from zero-sum relations where any gain by one means a loss by another to positive sum relations where all benefit and the only question to be solved is just how much?

We are witnessing now an avowed conversion of Latin American countries to capitalism. For quite some time their political leaders have been told by foreign economists that they cannot expect miracles, nor can they simply rely on some commodity exports for economic development. They needed industrialization. It is doubtful that most Latin American governments, not to mention people, were convinced.[25] Still given the external pressures and the lure of external credits, by the late 1980s they had seriously embarked on this course.

This is in itself a gigantic undertaking. To build a vigorous and profitable private industrial sector managed by the "invisible hand" of the market has always been a difficult challenge. Until the last couple of hundred years no society could accomplish it. Even since then relatively few could do so. But as time goes on it is not getting easier. There are no premiums for the late-comer. Industrialization can no longer proceed incrementally from the relatively small scale through many decades of expansion to the global scale. By now most industrial economies have already reached the global scale with all kinds of efficiencies reaped by their vast investments in advertising, sales, and distribution. In their deep shadow reinforced by frequent invocations of the creed of free trade, infant industries have a difficult time to survive let alone mature unless they become absorbed and controlled by generally foreign-based multinationals. Moreover, we now know some of the heavy costs of capitalism: the bruising competition, the harshness of the "creative destruction" of inefficient and/or obsolescent production units together with all the jobs they provided. Plus, at least in the initial takeoff stage, the inevitability of growing disparity in incomes. Sustained growth through industrialization may be possible, but it takes time and requires enormous capacities of stable political institutions.

To summarize: (1) it is very hard to build a capitalist system, but it might be done in a favorable environment of political stability; (2) it is very difficult to establish democratic institutions, but it might be done in a

---

[25] Tom E. Davis, "The 'End' of the State in Economic Development," in Alvaro A. Zini, Jr., *The Market and the State in Economic Development in the 1990s* (Amsterdam, The Netherlands: North Holland Press, 1992), pp. 51–58.

favorable environment of economic growth; (3) how to do both at the same time is a conundrum; and (4) that is exactly the historic experiment in which the Latin American countries are now engaged. It is instructive to observe their efforts to build democratic systems; it is fascinating to watch them do so while at the same time they are using these frail and tenuous democratic processes to convert their economies to capitalism.

Actually the new democratically elected leaders are profoundly uncomfortable with the idea of building *political* institutions. They much prefer, at least during a transitional period, to rely on the conventional wisdom of a succession of great leaders. They are selected by more or less managed popular elections. So democracies in Latin America are essentially guided democracies, guided by strong presidents: Cardozo of Brazil, Menem of Argentina, Samper of Colombia, Frei of Chile, and Fujomori of Peru, to name the most notable ones. But as far as one can tell, none are engaged in building institutions or socializing democratic attitudes.

Meanwhile democratically elected Latin American leaders are also dissatisfied with the fashionable foreign advice of jumping into a free market economy with one leap.[26] They have profound reservations about the "shock treatment" of rapid radical *privatization*. They are worried about the morality of the harsh costs of sudden government withdrawal. Some people, especially those in the former bloated public sector, will inevitably get hurt, and there are quite a large number of human beings—and voting citizens.

Mexico may have topped the list of the largest number of state companies, but in 1992 Brazil had over 500 state companies and Peru at least 270. In March 1992, Peruvian finance minister Carlos Boloña estimated that there were almost 1.2 million public employees in Peru, and that one out of every six workers labored for the state. . . . In Argentina, in 1988, there were almost two million bureaucrats out of a working population of 11.5 million.[27]

Predictably public-sector employees will suffer. Some people, the entrepreneurs, the private engines of development, will reap huge profits. In

---

[26] In a memorable conversation Sir Winston Churchill advised Nikita Khrushchev, very much concerned about the Soviet economy: "A precipice can't be crossed in two leaps." Sergei Khrushchev, *Khrushchev on Khrushchev, an Inside Account of the Man and His Era* (Boston: Little, Brown and Company, 1990), p. 4.

[27] Roberts and LaFollette Araujo, *The Capitalist Revolution in Latin America*, p. 87.

consequence those who are hurt will feel aggrieved, and those with huge profits will grow arrogant. Since those aggrieved are sure to be many and those benefitting will be few, political leaders are likely to keep in mind their own chances of reelection before making massive cuts of public subsidies and massive layoffs of public employees who have no skills to operate and compete in the free market.

Argentina and Mexico moved toward capitalism with moderate determination. They began by privatizing public services: telephone, electricity, port facilities, railways. In Argentina: also petroleum; in Mexico: also banks, steel, and now the petrochemical industry. Peru proceeded more rapidly and even included privatizing some of its always profitable mines. But it was a somewhat different case because the main thrust of privatization came under President Fujomori, who shortly after taking office dissolved democratic institutions. And the most massive privatization occurred in Chile after the Allende government was over-thrown by the military (1973). General Pinochet was determined to reverse all the nationalizations by the former Popular Front (Socialist/Communist) government. Vigorous efforts of rapid privatization have recently been initiated by the government of El Salvador, which had lately emerged from a bloody civil war. Peru, Chile, and El Salvador are, of course, special cases.

Most other Latin American governments, finding themselves between a rock and a hard place, try to wiggle. They give lip service to the idea but then find ways of temporizing. Brazil, the largest of the Latin American states, chose to proceed cautiously. It introduced a new currency, part of an economic program that has cut inflation from 2,541 percent in 1993 to 35 percent in 1995.[28] It also amended the 1988 constitution to end monopolies in telecoms, oil, and mining, but most of the changes have still to be put in effect. Necessary enabling bills languish in congressional committees; other changes are still not "published" as bureaucrats manage to delay them. Noticeably there is no progress on three other constitutional amendments: reform of the civil service, tax system, and social security. A dramatic symbol of privatization, the sale of controlling shares in CYRD, the state-owned mining and transport company, promised by the government as its commitment to capitalism, was postponed by judicial action on April 29, 1997—just one example of so many complex hurdles to mount for a new Latin American democracy with a "capitalist" economy. The pattern is very similar in Uruguay. Conditions are confused and confusing in Paraguay

---

[28] Burki and Edwards, *Latin America after Mexico*, p. 26.

where the president proved unable to eliminate General Lino Oviedo from his control of the armed forces. In Ecuador Abdala Bucaram (El Loco) was elected president in July 1996. During the campaign he cursed and gestured wildly, telling people he would attack banks and monopolies if he were elected. He promptly launched a harsh economic stabilization plan. In six months after two days of massive demonstrations and a general strike he was deposed by the legislature and replaced by Speaker Fabian Alarcon.

All of these experiments are worth observing. They ought to teach scholars and decision-makers much. Perhaps the most instructive experience, however, is that of Venezuela.

THE CASE OF VENEZUELA

First a little background.[29] The country had a new democratic beginning in 1958 when the dictator, Marcos Pérez Jiménez, was forced to flee the country by a broad popular movement. Three years later a new constitution was approved, and Venezuela was on its way to a constitutional republic.

That armed guerillas were active in much of the country did not help. As it turned out, Venezuela's large oil deposits also caused much trouble. But it helped enormously that two great patriots, Rómulo Bétancourt of Accion Democratica (Social Democrats) and Rafael Caldera of COPEI (Christian Democrats), were guiding progress toward an effective two-party system with a responsible majority and a loyal opposition. They set out to build something new in Latin America: a political system based not principally on a constitution of parochial solidarities or one based on class privileges but one based on political parties mobilizing individuals with common political interests toward a winning coalition. In the first two elections the AD won. Then in 1968 Caldera and COPEI gained a small plurality. AD, the party in power and especially Bétancourt, loyally supported the transition—very much like Alexander Hamilton supported Thomas Jefferson in the transition after our 1800 election. Indeed in a quarter of a century power shifted four times from one party to the other and did so in an orderly, peaceful manner.[30] The political system seemed to be maturing.

---

[29] For a detailed discussion of the first twenty-five years of democratic development see: Mauricio Baez, *From Praetorianism to Civil Order: the Case of Venezuela* (Philadelphia: University of Pennsylvania, Ph.D. dissertation, 1981).

[30] 1968: AD to COPEI; 1973: COPEI to AD; 1978: AD to COPEI; 1983: COPEI to AD

Then world affairs took a hand. The Middle East war in October 1973, or more accurately the firm American stand in support of Israel, brought an Arab boycott of oil exports to Israel's friends. When President Caldera left office, the average price of crude oil was less than $3 a barrel; when his successor took office it had quadrupled ($13).[31] Public sector revenue jumped to 50 percent of GDP.[32] Foreign bankers rushed in to offer credit. Money was streaming into Venezuela.

A mania gripped the country. There was no effective leadership to counsel responsibility or impose prudent restraint. Caldera was out of office,[33] and Bétancourt was abroad and ill. The new president, Carlos Andrés Pérez, solemnly promised "to manage abundance with a mentality of scarcity," but soon forgot his promise.[34] The national budget tripled. The government plunged into public enterprise. Through semipublic corporations it invested heavily in electricity, aluminum, and steel. The president also accelerated a massive housing and a substantial highway program. Caracas, which was essentially a small, somewhat rural center, grew almost overnight into a modern metropolis. Suddenly masses of the lower middle classes found their quarters radically upgraded. Public sector employees, their number multiplying by the month, had their wages raised, raised, and raised again. All kinds of benefits—health, welfare, retirement funds—were piled on. In consequence, the private sector, not very sturdy in the first place, was badly hurt. It became noncompetitive and unable to break even. It could not be counted on to drive economic development. The public sector was to become the economic engine![35] Meanwhile some of the wealth also trickled down to the poor. They gained better and cheaper access to employment opportunities in the cities. Public transportation was heavily subsidized as were basic food items. Cleaner water became available, and through more regular garbage collection health risks were

---

[31] In current dollars or in constant (1980) dollars from nine to twenty-six. The World Bank, *Venezuela CEM: Living with Oil*, Report No. 12849-VE, July 21, 1995, vol. I, 3. See also Julio Sosa-Rodriguez, "Oil and Economic Perspective of Venezuela," paper presented at Symposium on Venezuela, University of Connecticut, October 31, 1984, p. 7.

[32] Moisés Naim, *Paper Tigers and Minotaurs, the Politics of Venezuela's Economic Reforms* (Washington, DC: Carnegie Endowment for International Peace, 1993), p. 76.

[33] Under the constitution the president could not succeed himself for ten years.

[34] The World Bank, *Venezuela CEM: Living with Oil*, vol. I, 7.

[35] H. Cardosa, currently the president of Brazil, referred to the comparable phenomenon in Brazil as "state capitalism."

reduced as well. All classes went on a buying spree. Venezuelans flooded Miami and bought anything they saw or heard of, some by the truckload. Refrigerators, transistor radios, cordless telephones, cosmetics, alcohol, clothes, cameras. They had plenty of money left to entertain lavishly back home. The nightlife was brisk; new, excellent, expensive restaurants opened up all over Caracas and other cities.

Life was just great, all the goodies and thrills and no need for hard work. The oil just kept bubbling forth—day and night. Those in power enjoyed the popularity that sudden prosperity brought. They, including the president, were caught up in the mood. They saw no reason why they should not get their share of the wealth, indeed a whole big chunk of it. Corruption and scandal riddled the regime and besmirched the reputation of the young democracy. By the end of 1978 statistics were clearly troublesome. Non-oil GDP growth averaged 7.9 percent, but the fiscal deficit was approaching 5 percent. Inflation reached 10.5 percent by 1975; the current account deficit reached about 14.5 percent of GDP by 1978.[36]

Meanwhile the international situation was changing again. Oil prices stabilized, then began to decline steadily. Oil revenue dropped sharply. It could not keep pace with the growing government spending, including the enormous waste and graft. To keep up the facade of prosperity the government borrowed heavily from the private foreign banks pushing the country farther and farther into debt and destabilizing the economy. To the surprise of the government and pollsters the people did notice what was going on, and in national elections the government party lost.

The new president was Louis Herrera Campins, a member of Caldera's party (Caldera was still ineligible). A comparatively honest man, he disapproved of the rampant corruption. Indeed in his inaugural address he publicly chastised his predecessor for it. He was literally "a man of the people," fairly intelligent, not especially articulate, without the charisma of Caldera, Bétancourt, or even Carlos Andrés Pérez. He promised to do his best to reduce spending, including consumer subsidies; to increase interest rates in order to encourage savings; and to eliminate price controls in order to foster private economic activity. But he never understood the complexities of a modernizing political economy. Nor did he have the stamina to bear the political costs for such an austere fiscal policy.[37] Within a year the government abandoned it before it could yield any results. In 1980 when

---

[36] The World Bank, *Venezuela CEM*, vol. I, 7.

[37] The World Bank, *Economic Memorandum on Venezuela*, Report No. 5016-VE, 1985, p. 5.

war broke out between Iran and Iraq, oil prices suddenly tripled and for a short time reached up to $40 a barrel.[38] So perhaps it was all right to keep dreaming. Alas oil prices remained at that level for just six months. As world oil demand contracted and OPEC lost control of the market, oil prices started their steady decline. By 1993 they were at $13.34 a barrel.[39] Debt financing became an increasingly acute problem. The public sector, which had become the engine of industrial development, did not live up to expectations. The private sector, crippled by President Pérez's policies, had lost confidence in the government especially after Herrera failed to shift the emphasis back to it. So GDP growth dropped from an annual average of 6 percent (1974–1978) to *minus* 1.2 percent (1979–1983). It caused an acceleration of capital flight.

The binge was over but not quite the dream. The dramatic advance had stopped, but all classes of people were still much better off than just a few years earlier. The momentum, albeit a rapidly slowing momentum, carried them along. It really felt so good, surely it must be good. Indeed it must be right. These were temporary reverses that good political leadership could correct. If they were not corrected, if the bonanza would not be resumed soon, the political leadership was at fault. During his last year in office President Herrera became a scapegoat, a much hated man. Nostalgia became the dominant mood. Nostalgia for the good old times—nostalgia for Carlos Andrés Pérez.

He was not eligible to run, but he had a stand-in, a rather innocuous local pediatrician with modest political experience, Jaime Lusinchi. Caldera, now eligible once again, opposed him as the COPEI candidate. He could not promise to restore the dream; he could not outright disown Herrera. It was an impossible quest. As is so often the case, close associates kept giving him overoptimistic reports.[40] Some, and this is my personal conclusion, gave him only superficial support, positioning themselves for the next election. So Caldera, by popular consensus the most respected Venezuelan statesman, went down in a (2:1) humiliating defeat.

---

[38] Fundación John Boulton, ed., *Politica y Economia en Venezuela, 1810–1991* (Caracas, Venezuela: Litografia Melvin, 1992), Gráfico #2 (Precio promedio de realización y valor de exportación), p. 366.

[39] Source: Banco Central de Venezuela/Memoria de Hacienda, 1995.

[40] Five days before the election a polling group within his organization assured him that he had "crossed the line" and was now ahead of his opponent. When I got hold of the raw data, it became apparent that it was based on a sample of 43 (!) taken in South Caracas.

In all fairness, President Lusinchi never had a chance. His own skills were limited; his public support was tenuous; his political patron was kibitzing; and Venezuela's financial problems had reached crisis proportions. Helpless, carried along by the socialist orthodoxy of public sector primacy, he "increased public sector spending, from 21 percent of GDP in 1983 to 26.5 percent in 1988, despite continued reduction of oil revenues, and . . . increased import protection as well as producer and consumer subsidies."[41] It was altogether counter-productive. Venezuela was sinking deeper and deeper into a financial morass. The World Bank's conclusion:

In 1988 foreign reserves have fallen to 2.5 months of imports (the lowest since 1973), annual inflation was 60 percent and increasing, the consolidated public sector deficit was 9.4 percent of GDP, and Venezuela could not service its external obligations. There were shortages of many goods and living standards had plunged. Between 1980 and 1989, real GDP per capita had fallen every year despite comparatively high oil prices until 1985, and the percentage of the population living in absolute poverty increased, according to one study from 4 percent in 1980 to 13 percent in 1989.[42]

Worse still, all the progress made toward institutionalizing democracy was now in peril. The widespread reputation for corruption among politicians now enveloped President Lusinchi.[43] It exacerbated public cynicism about the whole democratic process. Meanwhile the two-party system was breaking down. In COPEI, party officials challenged Caldera and manipulated his defeat at the 1988 convention. They nominated the secretary-general of the party, essentially an administrator, who then went down in utter defeat. Tragically Caldera, the party builder, now stood only on his own reputation, his charisma. At the same time in *Accion Democratica* Carlos Andrés Pérez detached himself from the traditional party power-brokers. He was elected president in 1988 very much on his own. His margin was the largest in 25 years. In sharp contrast his party lost its majorities in both houses of Congress leaving it in disarray.

Having come to power the second time, Carlos Andrés Pérez made a complete turnaround. With his cabinet of young technocrats he abandoned the public sector as the engine of economic development, the engine he himself built during his first term. By 1988 free market economy had

---

[41] The World Bank, *Venezuela CEM: Living with Oil*, vol. I, p. 8.

[42] Ibid.

[43] He and his wife (former private secretary) were indicted and now live abroad.

become the fashion of the times. Privatization was the theme. The only question was should it be done gradually or radically "with one leap." Carlos Andrés Pérez chose the latter, the economists' orthodoxy: "the shock treatment." It would provide the greatest economic benefit he thought, and by doing it with one stroke shortly after his great electoral victory he would have a good chance of surviving it politically.

Specifically the government adopted a program that included reforms in both fiscal and monetary policy as well as the foreign exchange regime.[44] It signed a "Debt and Debt Service Reduction Agreement" with commercial banks. It deregulated prices, privatized publicly owned industries, freed interest rates, and increased rates of electricity, water, telephone, gasoline, and transportation. The bolivar was devalued 170 percent, and interest rates soared from 13 to 40 percent. "The intention was to move from a state-led, inward-oriented strategy to one led by export growth."[45]

In terms of economic statistics the shock treatment seemed to pay off. Inflation and unemployment dropped, and the Venezuelan economy experienced one of the highest growth rates in the world. International lenders and investors regained their confidence in Venezuela; credit rating services ranked the country at the top of their world lists.

The problem was that Carlos Andrés Pérez and his technocrats were victims of the fallacy of the single factor. They neglected, if not ignored, the political dimension. On Monday, February 27, 1989, just three weeks after the inauguration before an unprecedented number of foreign dignitaries, many people in Caracas and three other major cities went on a rampage of riots and looting. They had experienced the first sample of the shock treatment: workers living in the outskirts of Caracas woke up to find a substantial increase in bus fares. The government had approved the increases, but private operators—after all it was free enterprise—topped them with an additional margin to cover their cost increases. The riots erupted spontaneously. Three days of turmoil left 300 persons dead and a country very distressed. Order was restored, but social and political unrest prevailed. Strikes and demonstrations became endemic; crime became rampant. The government was blamed "for real or perceived threats that the new policies posed for their living standards."[46] Then conditions moved from bad to worse. Halfway through his presidential term at 1:00 A.M.,

---

[44] See in detail: The World Bank, *Venezuela: Structural and Economic Reforms—the New Regime*, Report No. 10404-VE, 1993.

[45] Naim, *Paper Tigers and Minotaurs*, p. 76.

[46] Ibid., p. 61.

February 4, 1992, heavily armed forces launched an attack on the presidential palace, the presidential residence, and the nearby air force headquarters. President Pérez escaped with his life by sneaking out a back door and hiding under a coat in the back seat of an unmarked car. He reached a private television station and addressed the nation, recounting the attempted coup and pleading for military and public support.

He got it, but the key player was Caldera. In the afternoon Congress met in an emergency session. The senior statesman, without any taint of corruption, rose to speak. It was a speech televised throughout the country, a bravura performance. In clear terms he condemned the coup. Any direct threat to a constitutional system must be resisted and crushed. He then rejected the indirect threat of declaring an emergency and suspending constitutional guarantees requested by Pérez. Finally he raised serious questions about the shock treatment. A radical shift to capitalism had too many innocent victims. Clearly here was a democrat with a heart. His popularity soared to an 80-percent-plus public approval rating. The strategy of shock treatment was practically over. Other free market reforms were visibly slowed down. In any case, it was the end of Carlos Andrés Pérez. Calls for his resignation intensified, but he refused to leave office. On November 27, 1992, another coup attempt followed. It failed as well, but by now the president's days were numbered. Since he had made himself aloof from his party, his party showed no signs of wanting to defend him. He was charged with corruption.[47] Congress suspended him from office and appointed a caretaker (Velasquez) government. All the turbulence mostly canceled whatever economic benefits the shock treatment had produced. It also advanced the deinstitutionalization of the political system. Nine days after the second failed coup, state and local elections were held. Voter turnout was heavy; the results suggested a further decline in the hold of political parties over the electorate.

President Caldera returned to power in 1993. It was a personal achievement. COPEI, defying polls reporting his overwhelming popularity, nevertheless nominated another, much less qualified candidate. Caldera announced his candidacy although he was in practical terms expelled from the party he had founded. He then put together a loose coalition of political fragments. No one doubted that it was his show. With the Pérez fiasco Rómulo Bétancourt's party was disoriented. The democratic institution of a two-party system was in peril.

---

[47] Considering the real situation, the charges were no big deal. He diverted secret funds to other national security expenses.

Caldera's victory was far from robust, a little over 30 percent of the vote, but well above all the other candidates. It was a personal victory, but significantly the electorate perceived it as an emergency measure. The established party organizations (AD and COPEI) fared well in the congressional elections. They were regaining their political salience. The more or less leaderless AD elected 16 senators out of 50 and 55 deputies out of 203. Meanwhile COPEI came in second with 14 senators and 52 deputies. Caldera's conglomerate could score only five senators and twenty-four deputies. Indeed he had to rely on the support of Bétancourt's party and an ally, MAS (Movimiento al Socialismo).

In the economy Caldera inherited a mess. Indeed he had no idea how bad it was. He knew, of course, of the falling per capita GDP (-2.6 percent), of the high inflation (45.9 percent), of government deficits (-3.6 percent). These were monumental challenges in themselves, but just a few days before he took office, due to mismanagement and some criminal activity, the second largest bank (Banco Latino) collapsed. Then more, at least eight, midsize banks collapsed as well. What choice did Caldera have? As a traditionalist, paternal authority he had to protect the individual depositors; as a democratically elected president he had to protect the masses of depositors. Whatever its cost, the government deposit insurance agency (FOGADE) would have to carry the burden. Thus while some of the bankers decamped for Miami, Florida, and a comfortable life, the government had to come up with $6.1 billion, which blew the consolidated public sector deficit sky-high (17 percent of the GDP).

President Caldera had deep misgivings about the "shock treatment" approach of his predecessor. During his campaign he argued for "gradualism," a government restraint on the harsh effects on some (often poor) people of the free market. If he could not reverse it, at least he would slow the rapid advance of reform. And that was what he appeared to be doing in 1994–1995. Some tax increases were to take effect in August 1994, but they were focused on "luxury goods." In any case, their implementation kept being delayed. The IMF was willing to help, but Caldera would not accept their conditions—the World Bank and the international financial community were standing by. On September 12, 1994, a new economic plan was announced. A year later it had still not been implemented. Public services continued to be subsidized. Gasoline prices—twelve cents a gallon—would not be raised. Inflation became rampant. In spite of strict exchange control the value of the bolivar dropped to 500:1 dollar.

Whatever was Caldera doing? The electorate which had faith in him—polls still reported an 80 percent approval rating—was beginning to worry and wonder. Did he rely on wrong advisers? Was the nice man getting too old? Had the great leader lost his confidence and become all too indecisive?

It is just possible, however, that President Caldera was following an optimal politicoeconomic strategy. He would first have to create a favorable political environment for any shocks. It required careful timing. He would regularly speak of the necessity of the sacrifices needed and the hardships to be endured. The people saw the problem, but the government showed reluctance to impose any prescription. Things went from bad to worse; people wanted governmental remedies. More and more compulsively they yearned for a cure.

By the spring of 1996 Caldera's approval rating had plummeted below 30 percent. People were willing to accept any medicine, however bitter. Moreover, there were very hopeful signs. Oil prices soared (by $1.61 per barrel, i.e., 12 percent in 1995), and foreign investors showed considerable interest in the exploration of new fields. New, close economic relations with Brazil have been crafted. Oil exports to Brazil rose sharply and kept rising. In April Caldera acted. First he addressed Congress, then he spoke on television to the people. Decisively he announced a new blueprint for reform. It was the medicine of the orthodox free market, including a steep rise in sales taxes (from 12.5 percent to 16.5 percent) and a five-fold increase in gasoline prices. "To vacillate is to lose ourselves," he declared solemnly. Observed the *Economist*: "The nation that had begun to feel that something, anything must be done, knew he was right."[48] Significantly this time there were no riots, no coup attempts.

The sacrifices the Venezuelan people now have to make are enormous. The poor are not making much progress, but generally the inherently insecure middle class[49] is bearing the brunt. For nearly ten years white-collar incomes were frozen while inflation was eating away their purchasing power. Savings are mostly gone; some have lost their jobs. But, so far at least, the rich are not getting richer. Rumors about government corruption are spotty, and Caldera is still considered squeaky clean. The economy appears to be stabilizing, and the public mood seems to have improved. There are even signs of hope. The new minister for economic planning, Teodoro Petkoff, has captured the imagination of the people.[50] In 1996 with

---

[48] *Economist*, April 20–26, 1996, p. 34.

[49] See: von Vorys, *American National Interest*, pp. 145–46.

[50] Petkoff was a communist guerilla in the 1960s. During his first term President Caldera granted an amnesty to all Venezuelan insurgents. Since then

(continued...)

a windfall of oil revenues bringing in an extra $3 billion, GDP rose by 2.2 percent, inflation leveled off, the trade balance increased by $4.6 billion, and foreign currency reserves almost doubled ($11.8 billion from $6.3 billion).[51]

As he approached the final year of his presidency, Caldera continued his balancing act. Champions of the single factor urged that he use the increase in oil revenues to help service the $26 billion foreign public debt. He followed this line—up to a point. Venezuela did not draw further on its IMF credit, and its budget was balanced, perhaps even with a small surplus. The stability of the banking system was restored, with the two largest banks now in private hands. But Caldera used some of the money to nearly double public-sector salaries. Committed to slimming down the bloated (1.4 million) bureaucracy, 17 percent of the country's workers, he was not prepared to abandon them altogether. At the same time, he enlisted the full support of the unions to fundamentally revise (liberalize) labor laws.

In terms of political development, nothing was done about the constitutional reforms he proposed as a candidate. Most pressing are reforms of the judiciary and the largely ineffective system of law enforcement. The process of selecting judges is thoroughly politicized. Corruption is deeply pervasive. Some initial steps have been taken. In 1995 the government negotiated the first "Stand Alone Judicial Sector Program of the World Bank" (No. 3514) toward that purpose. Then on October 29, 1996, disaster struck. A fire broke out in La Planta prison killing some thirty inmates. Television covered the tragedy: the blaze, the charred remains of bodies, some prisoners desperately but unsuccessfully trying to escape, *and* reports that the fire had been intentionally started by National Guardsmen. The pictures stunned President Caldera and the people.[52] The tragedy, however, did not trigger a massive effort for radical reform.

The most crucial problem facing Caldera, however, is succession. Neither the economic nor the political reforms could possibly be completed by 1998, so he could plausibly ask for more time to complete the task. Like his colleagues in Argentina (Menem) and Peru (Fujimori) he could try to change the constitution to allow himself a successive term. Conceivably he

---

[50](...continued)

Petkoff became a leader of a small party, Movimiento al Socialismo (MAS), a vigorous and articulate advocate of free trade, and most recently a supporter of Caldera.

[51] *Economist*, February 15–21, 1997, p. 100.

[52] *Economist*, October 26–November 1, 1996, pp. 52, 54.

could try to start a new party on his own or designate an independent candidate as his personal stand-in successor. It is doubtful that he could succeed. But those who know Caldera best firmly believe that he would not become involved in any such machinations. Moreover, millions of his supporters believe that Caldera is a true patriot, that the constitutional republic to which he devoted his life is indescribably more important to him than any personal ambition. Possibly he may be satisfied in having reversed the trends of political and economic destabilization. He may be quite content with the 1998 elections run strictly along party lines—well perhaps with a little bit of advice from the country's elder statesman. Still there is another possibility. Speculating optimistically—and in all fairness to give a reasonable chance to the politicoeconomic approach to development—it may well be that Caldera understands political processes better than his critics do. It is generally assumed that presidential power declines rapidly toward the end of the term.[53] This may well be true, except in this case. At this point in time Caldera is still a formidable political force in Venezuela. The political party organization of COPEI is still intact and that of AD is still very effective.

In the 1995 elections for provincial governors the AD came out as a clear winner.[54] It controls Congress. If AD could nominate a candidate who would be endorsed by Caldera, he would have an enormous advantage in the 1998 presidential election. Indeed that is probably all he would need. Alternatively Caldera plus COPEI would be troublesome, and a campaign with protégés of Caldera and the reemerging Carlos Andrés Pérez added would be chaotic. Thus, during the last year before the campaign Caldera will be in a more powerful position than ever before. With its control of the legislature AD may be prepared to pay the price of supporting President Caldera's judicial reforms. Working together they could depoliticize the appointment of judges. If so, the beleaguered political institutions would benefit greatly. Such a combination with this joint achievement would restore public confidence, demonstrating that democracy is not fundamentally flawed because all politicians are *not* self-serving crooks. And the economic system could benefit because it may gain precious, crucial time for development. Above all, the people of Venezuela would gain much in the improved conditions of law and order. As the result, the advantages of the optimal politicoeconomic strategy would be demonstrated.

---

[53] Especially when the constitution bars the president from succeeding himself.

[54] It won elections for eleven governors and the mayor of Caracas. COPEI won three governorships and MAS, five.

It may not be easy to engage the interest of the American people in such crucial experiments. It does not help that through his entire first term President Clinton never set foot on Latin American soil. Still the president's position may be changing. His second administration may produce some improvement. Of course, much of Latin America is close to us, and the Latino element among our people is steadily growing. Furthermore North American banks and businesses are deeply involved in investments south of the border.

So now at last we have come to the most daunting challenge to our foreign policy, where the pressures of the international environment and those of the domestic environment are most sharply clashing. For in the twilight of the twentieth century, the American people are utterly determined not to become the policemen of the world. No less clearly, however, as we enter the twenty-first century, the unity of the human race, its implications, and the consequences will dominate our international environment. The question is: will we find an optimal balance?

10

Global Order

Ever since the Founding Fathers of the Republic the unity of the human race has been a basic value of our democracy. As a practical matter, however, most Americans did not know much about people in distant places and generally were quite content in their ignorance. In any case, isolationism in foreign policy isolationism suited us very well. It took some 150 years and the lessons of two world wars for Americans to appreciate the utility of friendly foreign countries. By 1947 a consensus was finally built for a selective commitment to alliances for purposes of security and other special reasons, but we still had perfunctory interest in countries and people who were of no particular use to us.

It was through a long and tortuous struggle marked by quantum leaps and perilous reverses that human development reached the scale of global interaction.[1] In 1757 in Bengal, India, (Plassey) forces more or less loyal to Britain defeated forces more or less loyal to France. Two years later on the other side of the globe at Quebec, Canada, (in our French and Indian War) once again forces more or less loyal to Britain (American colonial forces) were victorious. The Treaty of Paris (1763) crossed the traditional regional barriers; for the first time it was a peace settlement that was global in scope. The problem arose how to manage it, how to keep peace and order on so vastly expanded a dimension.

---

[1] For a somewhat more detailed discussion see: Karl von Vorys, *American National Interest, Virtue and Power in Foreign Policy* (New York: Praeger, 1990), pp. 152–70.

For a while in the early 1760s it seemed that the traditional method of regional consolidation could be extended to the largest human scale. Noticeably all consolidations in the past were accomplished through conquest by force and integration by a common belief system. This common belief system was based on ethnic solidarity, on law, or on a great religion. Simply put, it was the method of hegemony. Now the British Empire with its power projected to all the continents appeared to be headed in the same direction. Democracy with its potential for universal appeal could provide the common belief system. In less than a generation, however, it became apparent that the impact of democracy in international relations was rather ambivalent. Its basic axiom of human equality could be a force for unity, but its tenet of self-determination when applied to groups could drive and legitimize political separatism.

In less than a generation it became apparent that all the military power of the British Empire was still not sufficient for hegemony. The first clue came from North America. Settlers mostly from Britain established their own communities, insisted upon their democratic right to govern themselves, and when it became necessary, by force of arms won their independence from Britain (1783). More followed. The French monarchy, the foremost continental power in Europe and a recently defeated competitor in global aspirations, was overthrown (1789) and the Republic was proclaimed. Soon it became apparent, however, that its commitment to popular sovereignty did not restrain the French Republic from jeopardizing British vital interests. At the earliest opportunity it occupied Belgium and opened the Scheldt estuary. The first placed powerful French forces just across the Channel, posing a grave military threat to Britain; the second offered the port of Antwerp with its vast continental Hinterland as an alternative to London, presenting a bold challenge to the commercial structure of the Empire. Nor did the common commitment to popular sovereignty mitigate Britain's response. With bulldog determination it moved to eliminate these threats at all cost—even at the cost of an alliance with the absolute (divine right) rulers of Austria, Russia, and Prussia.

It took twenty years of more or less continuous warfare to defeat the French (the Republic, then Napoleon's Empire). When at the end of hostilities (1814–1815) the statesmen gathered in Vienna to negotiate the peace treaty, there was little room for doubt (1) that international relations had reached the global scale—the war was certainly fought on the global scale; (2) that no single power had established or could be expected to establish global hegemony—clearly the British could not do so; and (3) that no belief system, ideology, or religion could serve as a common orthodoxy—democracy was still only the theory of some intellectuals and the practice of only the important but peculiar British and the much less important and possibly more peculiar Americans. Thus the question remained: how to manage the global scale through some new, reasonably stable processes.

ORDER BY POWER POLITICS (1815)

It was a brilliant affair. Emperors, kings, princes, all with large and splendid retinues, were present. It was a fascinating affair: a summit meeting on the grandest scale. For months on end the rulers of Europe met in Vienna. They negotiated, bargained, and compromised; they struggled with the challenge of international order. In the end their answer was global order by the major powers of Europe acting in concert. They had the right and responsibility to serve as international arbiters They would define the legitimate *status quo*, and if in the future disputes would arise anywhere in the world, these powers would have the duty to meet in a congress (in our jargon: hold a summit) and would have the right to collectively determine and impose the proper settlement.

A formula based on the concert of the most powerful countries on earth was a significant advance over the conventional pattern of the hegemony of a single power in the region. It could have a chance of providing a stable arrangement, however, only if political leaders recognized and respected certain basic rules! By hindsight we can identify the most important ones.[2]

First, all major powers must be part of the system. Any power excluded would naturally form a counterpole and by constantly enticing inside members would gradually tear the system apart. Second, the major powers should be roughly equal in power. One that is much smaller or significantly declining in power would soon lose its independent position; one that is much greater or disproportionately rising in power would soon seek to dominate. Among equal and independent powers according to the theory a flexible balance[3] would emerge providing security and stability. Third, although ideologically diverse the major powers should share in a minimal consensus. At the very least all the major powers should agree that the concert system is worth preserving even at the cost of some sacrifices in national aspirations. No major power should perceive it as oppressive and

---

[2] cf: Henry A. Kissinger, *A World Restored* (New York: Grosset & Dunlap, 1964), pp. 1–3.

[3] This requirement is often used in naming the system: the balance of power system.

hence be tempted to overthrow it. In any case no major power should threaten the vital interests of its partners in the concert. Each must remain confident that all the conflicts among the partners would be held at the levels of lesser interests and hence be negotiable. Fourth, all major powers should have confidence in the commitments of their partners. Once a major power had given a pledge, others must be able to depend upon it. Changing conditions may warrant renegotiations, but obligations could be revised only by mutual consent, not by arbitrary unilateral terminations, and certainly not by deception and double dealing.

Important as they were, these rules would not be sufficient. One more precondition, indeed the most fundamental precondition of any global order, would still have to be created: a consensus on the symmetry of norms. In a quantum leap asymmetric norms would have to be replaced. The value of actions must not be determined by the actor. For example, if *he* does it to me, it is flagrant aggression, but if *I* do it to him, it is righteous self defense. Instead, the value of an act must be specific to the act itself and be independent of the actor. If *I* do it to you it must have the same value as when *you* do it to me.

The notion itself was not new at all. For millennia at least some of the human race was acquainted with the golden rule: "Do unto others as you would have others do unto you." In practical application, however, it proved to be extraordinarily difficult. People and collectives generally persisted in the tradition of radical (ascriptive) cleavages within the human race and much preferred the perversion of the dictum: "Do unto others before they will do it to you." Nevertheless with the global scale of human interaction, the time had come for the recognition of the unity of the human race, and the advance to the symmetry of norms had become a human imperative.

For about a century the Concert of Europe moved along. To be sure, there were conflicts and some wars. But the wars were not global in scope; they were localized and not too costly in life and treasure, and the conflicts were often settled through agreements by the major powers worked out at congresses.[4]

All the same, the arrangement was precarious. The close working relationship among the British, Austrian, and Russian leaders so carefully nurtured during the wars against Napoleon and the Congress of Vienna was soon terminated by events. An unsuccessful assassination plot against Czar Alexander turned this already moody monarch, bent on religious causes and

---

[4] At Troppau (1820), Laibach (1821), Verona (1822).

horrified by the prospect of revolution, into an arch-conservative zealot for the remaining few years of life (1825). And soon (1822) tragically Castlereagh died by his own hand. He was succeeded by George Canning, who had little understanding of and less interest in global affairs. Of the Big Three only Metternich, the Austrian chancellor, remained. His diplomatic skills were formidable, his personality towering, but with his country's power visibly on the decline he could do no more than a brilliant holding operation.

Not just personalities changed. With Napoleon gone and peace restored, foreign policy returned to secondary importance. The demands of the domestic environment resumed their dominance of public interest and government priorities. The Russian monarchy, heavily resting on the church and the army, was under constant pressure for causes and conquest. Austria, which dominated Germany, had become an ethnic goulash trying desperately to keep its various nationalities under control. Prussia was confused and vacillating. The army so effectively built by the Great Elector and so well employed by Frederick the Great performed pathetically against Napoleon and had become very unsure of its sovereign. The nobility and the emergent middle classes were beginning to mix with uncertain results. In France the revolution was over but the country was badly divided. The monarchists dreamed about the past and intrigued about royal succession. The bourgeoisie now in power feared the masses but could not quite decide whether they preferred the pomp and glitter of an empire or the popular participation of the republic. They knew though that they wanted *la gloire*. Great Britain was in the midst of the Industrial Revolution with all its phenomenal economic accomplishments and distressing social strains. It was still struggling with the question just what elements of its population should be qualified to vote in parliamentary elections. As far as foreign policy was concerned, Britain was interested in the peace of Europe but primarily to keep its back secure. Mostly it looked beyond the seas to the colonies and principally to India. In short, the glimmer of international order through the concert of European major powers was fading fast. Absorbed as they were in their own particular domestic concerns, their foreign policies reflected their national focus of orientation. Diplomatic activity in the chancellories of the great powers remained brisk, but there were no more summits (Congresses) for quite a while.

That was not all. Circumstances were never too favorable for an international order enforced by the European major powers in America. The United States would have none of it, and after 1823 the Monroe Doctrine declared the entire Western Hemisphere off-limits to Europe. Moreover, conditions were turning unfavorable in Asia and Africa as well.

The nineteenth century saw the European powers penetrate deeper and deeper into these continents. All the same, their imperial control was never very sturdy. They never had enough to govern the people in their colonies directly. The best thing they could manage was indirect rule. Through manipulation of succession, bribes, and coercion traditional rulers were controlled by European administrators and advisers.[5] But the former remained in control of the people. Moreover, the further colonial powers expanded their government, the thinner they had to spread their exportable surplus of control. Worse still, the further they penetrated Asia and Africa, the prospect steadily increased that colonizers from different "mother countries" would rub against each other. Thus European attention to Asia and Africa, which could in theory serve as a safety valve to reduce major power rivalries within Europe, did, in fact, boomerang. When serious conflicts arose in Asia and Africa, and they soon did, they were reflected back and further exacerbated European major power rivalries.

The growing dissonance between the Vienna arrangement and the international environment was bad enough, but what really doomed the Concert System was that as they passed the midpoint of the nineteenth century the major powers no longer followed the rules. The struggle in the heartland of the Continent reverted to a free-for-all.

Prussia was on the move. Its Iron Chancellor, Otto von Bismarck, was determined to unite all the fragmented German principalities into a new Second Reich. It meant some skillful diplomacy, some deception, and several wars. Denmark was defeated (1864), then Austria (1866), and finally France (1870–1871). When peace was restored, summit meetings were resumed, but the system had fundamentally changed. Goals were no longer limited and incremental, and they justified any means. Bismarck saw the war with France not just as a final step in German unification, but also as the first step in the struggle for German hegemony on the European continent. After French armies were defeated in the field but the population still resisted, the Iron Chancellor insisted on the bombardment of Paris. As he recalled later:

I was tormented during sleepless nights by the apprehension that our political interests, after such great successes, might be severely injured through the hesitation and delay . . . [due] to personal and predominantly female influences with no

---

[5] Britain had begun building a civil service structure in India (ICS) down into the local subdivisions, but at the turn of the century it was still in a rudimentary form.

historical justification, influences which owed their efficacy, not to political considerations but to feelings which the terms humanity and civilization, imported to us from England, still rouse in German natives.[6]

In the end with the support of the crown prince, Bismarck prevailed, and Paris was bombarded by heavy artillery. The French surrendered and were forced to sign a harsh peace treaty. They were deprived of some territory (Alsace-Lorraine). They had to pay a billion-dollar indemnity, an enormous sum at the time. Worst of all they had to endure humiliation. The country would remain occupied until the indemnity was paid in full. Prussian troops paraded through Paris, down Champs Elysées. That was not all. France was to be diplomatically isolated. The French hated it all, especially they hated the Germans, and they were thirsting for revenge. Soon the French demonstrated the cost of excluding a major power from an international order based on power.

At first France could do little, but not for long. Bismarck's system was not five years old when (1875) Czar Alexander II indicated sympathy and support for France, as did Queen Victoria.[7] For the time being French diplomacy remained low key, but France left no doubt that it had economic power that it would use for its political purposes. Patriotism was sweeping the country. Social cleavages between the nobility and the bourgeoisie notwithstanding, all Frenchmen wanted the imposed war indemnity to be paid and the Germans out. They accomplished this in an astonishingly short time. The first government loan for this purpose (1871) was hardly announced when it was doubly oversubscribed. A similar loan next year was quickly oversubscribed twelvefold![8] In a country where parsimony was legendary, money poured into the banks.[9] Then under the guidance of

---

[6] Prince Otto von Bismarck, *Reflections and Reminiscences*, edited by Theodore S. Hamerow (New York: Harper & Row, 1968), pp. 144, 200, 203–4. The Crown Princess, the wife of the Chief of the General Staff (von Moltke), the wife of the Army chief of staff (von Blumenthal), and the wife of the staff officer next in influence (von Gottberg), lamented Bismarck, were all Englishwomen.

[7] Sidney Bradshaw Fay, *The Origins of the World War*, 2nd ed. (New York: Macmillan, 1930), vol. 1, pp. 96–97.

[8] For a detailed account see: Leon Say, *Les Finances de la France sous la Troisième Republic* (Paris: Levy, 1898), vol. I, pp. 363–422.

[9] By 1874 the metallic balance of the Bank of France had risen to 1.13 billion francs; five years later it nearly doubled to 2.12 billion francs. Bernhard Mehrens, *Entstehung und Entwicklung der grossen französischen Kreditinstitute* (Stuttgart:

(continued...)

the government, private investment was directed abroad.[10] Much of it went to Russia. The first of these loans for 500 million francs was listed on the Paris Bourse in December 1888 and proved a large success. Next year two more loans to Russia, one for 700 million francs and another for 1.2 billion francs, were equally successful.[11] The loans were financially very risky, but politically the profits were enormous.

Bismarck saw the danger. He tried to discourage and discredit French economic penetration of Russia. He tried to exhibit good will toward France. French diplomats were treated with special courtesy and favor; French imperial designs in the Mediterranean and Africa were regularly and roundly encouraged. But since Bismarck could not erase bitter memories and could not return Alsace-Lorraine, the spirit of *revanche* and the urge to break up the existing international order remained the dominant mood. A nation suffering dismemberment, wrote the French ambassador in Berlin, "ought to never pardon anything, never forget anything."[12] Besides, the internally frail French Republic could always benefit from the solidarity produced by nationalism, especially an angry, aggrieved nationalism.

All along, Bismarck was very careful to keep his dominant coalition in good repair. With Austria-Hungary and Russia there were formal treaties, with their foreign ministers regular conferences, and with their rulers regular summit meetings. Bismark was especially careful not to offend Great Britain. This was something of a magic act (*ein Kunststück*), as Austrian and Russian interests clashed in the Balkans and British and Russian interests clashed in much of Asia. But Bismarck, the master-juggler, managed it; just barely he kept all three balls in the air.

In 1888 Emperor William II ascended the German throne. He yearned to conduct his own foreign policy, and soon balls were rolling all over the floor. No more consideration, no more encouragement for imperial expansions by France. Indeed Germany would by ultimatum force the resignation of the French foreign minister (Delcassé) and would challenge France in North Africa. There would also be no more strenuous efforts to maintain close relations with Russia. The treaty with her was unceremoniously left

---

[9](...continued)
J.G. Cotta'sche Buchhandlung Nachf., 1911), p. 164.

[10] In 1881–1885 French private foreign investment was practically nil. Fifteen years later (1897–1902) it had skyrocketed to 1.16–1.26 billion francs. *Bulletin de l'Institut International de Statistique* (1913), vol. XX, part II, p. 1406.

[11] Fay, *The Origins of the World War*, vol. I, p. 10.

[12] Quoted in: Ibid., vol. I, p. 100.

to lapse. Gone too was any deference to Britain. Germany would challenge her by building a High Seas fleet to rival the Royal Navy and by building a Berlin-Baghdad railroad to bring German presence to the Middle East. While Britain was engaged in a struggle with the Boers in South Africa, the Kaiser sent a gratuitous personal telegram congratulating the Boer leader for a British defeat. When the British colonial secretary (Joseph Chamberlain) offered an alliance with Germany, William II ordered a dilatory response, told the Czar that he was importuned by the British, then put it to him straight: "Now I ask you, as my old and trusted friend, to tell me what you can offer me, and what you will do for me if I refuse the British offers."[13] Evidently the German Emperor had neither tact nor finesse.

All of these acts tore the dominant Bismarck coalition apart and replaced it with a Europe of contending and increasingly hostile camps. France got through to Russia and signed an alliance in 1894. Ten years later it got through to Great Britain.[14] A British-Russian understanding in 1907 completed the triangle. France was no longer isolated but at the apex of a powerful coalition (Triple Entente). Germany was no longer secure. The possibility of encirclement was no longer just a bad dream but a very disturbing reality. It still had Austria-Hungary (plagued by nationality problems) and Italy (a very uncertain ally), but its position had become precarious. It was on the defensive and all the more arrogant. Two alliance systems were set on a collision course. As mankind entered the twentieth century, it was no longer the time when in pursuit of international order European major powers in concert could export their resources of control over the different parts of the globe. On the contrary, it was the time when some of them were becoming increasingly dependent for their prosperity upon the economic resources of their colonies and for their security upon troops recruited in Asia and Africa. The flow of power was reversing itself. Major powers still asserted their special right to define international law and settle international disputes, but matters were getting out of hand. In East Africa, in the Near East, in India, resentment and resistance to the European design was on the rise. In China the Boxer Rebellion (1900) against foreign domination had to be repressed by force, a force that now included participation by non-European powers: Japan and America. The

---

[13] Quoted in: Ibid., vol. I, p. 131.

[14] While Germany was challenging Britain's global position, French ambitions in North Africa ran into British interests in the Sudan. At Fashoda (1898) the French yielded and hauled down their flag. A humiliation in a distant land, it was a cheap price for an understanding with Britain.

crisis over Morocco was settled at Algeciras at a convention called by and influenced by Theodore Roosevelt, president of the United States.

Actually the Vienna arrangements never had a chance. Even if the rules had been adhered to more conscientiously the plan was doomed. For while the map of the world had been practically completed and most physical barriers separating people had been overcome, the world in general and Europeans in particular were not ready for the unity of the human race as a practical operational concept. Solidarity to their own usually ascriptive (ethnically) defined group invariably superceded any attachment they might have felt for the human race. The crash was inevitable. It came when after a decade of crises involving the Ottoman Empire mostly in the Balkans the heir to the Austro-Hungarian thrones, Archduke Francis Ferdinand, and his wife were assassinated on June 28, 1914. Intense diplomatic efforts backed by a genuine wish of practically all major leaders to avert war proved to be in vain. In just over a month, in the words of the British foreign secretary, "the lights went out all over Europe" and mankind was plunged into its first world war.

IF AT FIRST YOU DON'T SUCCEED (1919)

Four years later when all the horrible killing finally stopped, the war had clearly reconfirmed the global scale of human interrelationship. It left international order, however, in a shambles. Any prospect of mankind's being managed by a concert of European major powers was scuttled by chauvinism and washed away by streams of European blood. As the victors gathered at the Palace of Versailles outside of Paris to settle the terms of peace, they had no doubt that international order was the prerogative of the major powers, but they paid scant attention to the lessons of the century-long record of the Concert of Europe.

One problem was the attitude of the delegates. In a mood of vengeance each pursued his own national purpose with single-minded determination; each sought absolute security. Some were satisfied with massive territorial gains; others insisted on reducing their enemies to abject impotence. Even though this was not surprising, it was tragic all the same. Henry Kissinger's observations on the Congress of Vienna are directly to the point on Versailles.

An impotent enemy is a fact; a reconciled enemy is a conjecture. A territorial accretion represents the surety of possession; to integrate an opponent into the community of nations through self-restraint is an expression of faith. It is no accident that the advocates of "absolute security" always have popular support on their side. Theirs is the sanction of the present, but statesmanship must deal with the future.[15]

Only David Lloyd George, the British prime minister, was vaguely interested in a scheme of international order and only Woodrow Wilson, president of the United States, was devoted to it.[16] The latter's preoccupation with a long- term arrangement to safeguard peace did produce novel ideas: First, the task of settling international disputes was not left to possible, future, *ad hoc* arrangements but was assigned to a permanent institution with regular annual meetings. Problems to peaceful relations need not fester until they reached sufficiently dire crisis proportions for a congress to be convened; they could be addressed earlier by the League of Nations before they became intractable. Second, The president was insistent on ideological orthodoxy. Bubbling forth from a profound American belief that aggression was the peculiar habit of authoritarian governments was his insistence that only democratic countries could be peace-loving and that the only legitimate basis for international boundaries was the self-determination of peoples. Democracy could provide the common bond to hold the League together. *With one proviso: the peace loving (democratic) nations had a consensus backed up by preeminent power.* Quite possibly Wilson was on the right track. But, of course, the president while inspiring was not the dominant force at Versailles. It was Georges Clemenceau, the French prime minister, assisted more or less enthusiastically by his British colleague. They opted for the old ways, ways that were becoming obsolescent.

Times were changing fast. Gone (or at least going) were the days when the human race could be structured into imperial systems. The colonial powers, which dominated at Versailles and whose dominance the League enshrined, possessed coercive capacity barely sufficient to assure their control in the nineteenth century. In the twentieth century when traditional leaders were losing their legitimacy among the indigenous masses, the colonial powers needed much more and just did not have it.

---

[15] Kissinger, *A World Restored*, p. 180. At the request of the British Foreign Office Sir Charles Webster prepared a study on the lessons of the Congress of Vienna for Versailles. In Kissinger's view: "Webster's conclusion that it was one of the errors of Vienna to permit France to negotiate and the acceptance of his advice not to repeat this mistake with respect to Germany turned out to be one of the banes of the Treaty of Versailles." Ibid., p. 342.

[16] William E. Rappard, *The Quest for Peace since the World War* (Cambridge: Harvard University Press, 1940), pp. 99–102.

Nor could they rely heavily on the capacity to persuade. Back in the nineteenth century indigenous leaders were attracted to the imperial system; indeed they wanted very much to be part of it. As a young man Mahatma Gandhi "dreamt continually of going to England." When he had the chance, he took it even though he knew it was against the rule of his caste. The order went out promptly: "This boy shall be treated as an outcaste from today. Whoever helps him or goes to see him off at the dock shall be punishable with a fine of one rupee four annas."[17] While in England Gandhi meticulously "played the English gentleman," wore English clothes, and after his studies was "called to the Bar." To his intense distress he was nevertheless treated as a "coolie barrister."[18] By the twentieth century it became all too painfully clear that however much they wished to assimilate, however loyal they would be, the people of the colonies could not become full members of the Empire. The color of their skin would bar them forever. Versailles added insult to injury when it trumpeted the principle of self-determination all over central Europe but would not dream of applying it to India or Algeria. Just about the time (April 1919) when the Covenant of the League of Nations was adopted in Paris, serious riots broke out in India. At Amritsar troops firing into the demonstrators killed 376 and wounded 1,200 people. It was also the time when Gandhi led his first *hartal* (mass boycott). The movement toward independence was already underway.

What made the failure of Versailles inevitable, however, was the stubbornness with which its European architects refused to learn from the lessons of the past, from the mistakes of Bismarck, or even from the gross blunders of William II. The terms imposed on Germany were nothing short of brutal. She had to assume the burden of colossal reparations while losing all her colonies and much territory along her eastern and western borders; she was reduced to military impotence, and perhaps worst of all, had to accept the moral stigma of war-guilt. The peace of Versailles ignored the basic requirement of power politics and followed blatantly exclusionary practices. Thus the League chose to manage without Germany, but although

---

[17] M. K. Gandhi, *The Story of My Experiments with Truth,* translated by Mahadev Desai (Washington, DC: Public Affairs Press, 1960), pp. 57, 58.

[18] Ibid., pp. 136–38, 140–44, 161–64, 181–84. In 1962 the Chief Justice of Pakistan, Mohammad Shahabuddin, recounted to me an early experience in Madras where he served as District Magistrate. By tradition, arriving at a new post the wives of junior officers would call upon the wives of senior officers. There were instances when the wives of English junior officers excluded from this courtesy the wives of the native senior officers of the Indian Civil Service. His resentment for such racial affronts still rankled many, many years later.

humiliated and almost disarmed, Germany remained a place where enormous economic and human resources were concentrated. It was also a place where not unlike France of the 1870s anger and righteous indignation united the people in ferocious determination. Their single-minded purpose: to overthrow the Treaty of Versailles, and if in the process the League would be washed away, so be it.

Russia too was excluded. Its new Bolshevik rulers, guilty of regicide, guilty of betraying the Allies in a separate peace with Germany, and guilty of fomenting world revolution, could hardly be permitted to participate in regulating international relations. Still as almost anyone could see, the Russian state, renamed the Union of Soviet Socialist Republics, had formidable resources, potentially great power, a disdain for capitalist countries, and a deep resentment for being ostracized internationally. It should have been no surprise that Germany and the USSR, the two outcast states, would approach each other.[19] Their combination, excluded from the League of course, accounted for most of the Eurasian continent—no negligible loss.

There were other losses as well. Swept along by his foreign policy quest, President Wilson neglected the demands of his domestic environment. Rudely ignored in negotiations across the Atlantic, the American electorate, and more specifically the Senate, made it clear that they were not ready to participate in global ventures. Ours being a constitutional democracy, that settled the issue. The League of Nations would have to manage without its principal pillar, the United States. Add to this that Italy was disgruntled with the Versailles settlement and Japan rapidly became disenchanted with the League. In practically no time all that was actually left of the coalition of great powers was France and Great Britain—a very unenthusiastic Great Britain.

By the late 1920s Germany and the Soviet Union were admitted to the League of Nations, but that did not help much, for the League remained bound to Versailles. France and its associates in central Europe would not have it otherwise. Unless the territorial settlement of Versailles remained wholly intact, thundered the French foreign minister in Geneva, it will mean war. Unless the territorial settlement of Versailles was radically revised, the German foreign minister shouted back, it will mean war. Thus concluded Professor Quincy Wright of the University of Chicago, the American observer, we shall have war.

---

[19] As early as 1922 at Rapallo, Germany and the Soviet Union signed a treaty ostensibly on economic cooperation but with wide-ranging military ramifications.

With Adolf Hitler coming to power (1933) the German assault took shape. It was, of course, substantially assisted by French intransigence and British discomfort about the terms of Versailles. With its empire increasingly on the defensive in the face of nationalist demands in India, by 1935 Great Britain was ready to give the collective rule of great powers another chance—preferably with all the great powers present and participating: Great Britain, France, and also Germany and Italy. (The Soviet Union fell somewhere between the cracks.) The League of Nations was hopeless, but if through the policy of appeasement German grievances could be allayed, she and her Italian ally could be enlisted for a common effort. Even without ideological orthodoxy, political stability on the global scale could perhaps be restored by joint power. The risk seemed worth taking.

It was a policy that stood by idly while Hitler overthrew the Treaty of Versailles, rearmed, and then intimidated and invaded Germany's neighbors. It was a policy that led to Munich—where the British prime minister believed he had bought "peace in our time." Czechoslovakia had to pay for it with much of the territory. It was alas a policy of wishful thinking. In less than six months British illusions were shattered. On March 15, 1939, Dr. Emil Hacha, a decent and frail old president of the helpless remnant of Czechoslovakia, traveled to Berlin. In the evening he called on the German Führer to offer his fullest cooperation. To his utter astonishment and consternation he was informed that Hitler had decided to invade his country at 6:00 A.M. next morning. Any resistance would be mercilessly broken ("*mit Brachialgewalt gebrochen*"). If necessary German heavy artillery and the *Luftwaffe* would devastate Czech cities. Hacha asked for time to consider. It was denied to him. He had a heart attack. Revived he accepted the inevitable. Hitler had his way: Czechoslovakia was now smashed (*zerschlagen*).[20] In Rome Count Ciano, the Italian foreign minister, knew what it all meant. He confided in his diary:

The thing is serious, especially since Hitler had assured everyone that he did not want to annex one single Czech. This German action does not destroy, at any rate, the Czechoslovakia of Versailles, but one that was constructed at Munich. . . . What weight can be given in the future to those declarations and promises which concern us more directly?[21]

---

[20] Erwin Wickert, *Dramatische Tage In Hitlers Reich* (Stuttgart: Steingruben Verlag, 1952), pp. 226–32.

[21] Count Galeazzo Ciano, *The Ciano Diaries 1939–1943*, edited by Hugh Gibson (Garden City, NY: Doubleday, 1946), p. 42.

Ciano's boss, Mussolini, was distressed. He finally found solace in invading Albania.

Indeed it was a very serious matter. "If Chamberlain failed to understand Hitler," observed Winston Churchill, "Hitler completely underrated the nature of the British Prime Minister. He mistook his civilian aspect and passionate drive for peace for a complete explanation of his personality, and thought that his umbrella was his symbol. He did not realize that Neville Chamberlain had a very hard core, and that he did not like being cheated."[22] One might add a general fact: Nobody likes to be bullied.

The destruction of Czechoslovakia taught a valuable lesson. Cooperation with dictators is always a risky business. They tend to be impatient with the incremental approach and insensitive about anyone else's vital interests. Fanatics committed to revolutionary change will not be restrained by considerations for international order. There could be security for no one: there would be no peace on earth as long as Hitler ruled a powerful Germany. Humanity was on the threshold of the World War II.

---

[22] Sir Winston Churchill, *The Second World War: The Gathering Storm* (Boston: Houghton Mifflin, 1948), p. 344.

11

Decentralized World Order

It was much worse than the last time. The second world war lasted longer (1939–1945), it directly involved more countries, and the carnage and devastation far surpassed anything even a sick mind could conjure up. The Americans were slow getting involved in the conflict. The war had been raging in Europe for almost two years; still most Americans wanted to stay out of it. Many in the army were chalking up the motto O.H.I.O. ("over the hill in October"), the Neutrality Act of 1939 was still in force, and the extension of the draft law was passed by a single vote in the House of Representatives. The sneak attack by Japan on Pearl Harbor changed all that.

President Roosevelt took victory for granted. He was deeply interested in what seemed to him an essential, much more difficult task: to set the foundation for an orderly international environment on a global scale where peace would become the norm. At the Tehran summit (November 1943) Churchill and Stalin were interested only in discussing a strategy of winning the war. President Roosevelt, on the other hand, raised the issue of postwar order. His plan was not at all original. It was typed on a single sheet with the title in all caps: "The Four Policemen." Once again the maintenance of peace would be the prerogative of the major powers.[1]

Under constant American pressure negotiations on the postwar political order moved along. The Soviets, like the French twenty-five years earlier,

---

[1] Robert E. Sherwood, *Roosevelt and Hopkins: An Intimate History* (New York: Harper, 1948), p. 785.

insisted on absolute international security through territorial aggrandizement, and the Americans, like the Americans twenty-five years earlier,
insisted on peace through international institutions. The Soviets got everything they wanted, all of Eastern Europe and part of Southeastern and
Central Europe. After negotiations and compromises at Dumbarton Oaks,
Yalta, and San Francisco (June 1945) the United States got the Charter of
the United Nations.

The similarity with the Covenant of the League was striking. If there
were differences, they were mostly in reinforcing the great power
domination of the organization. References to international law and justice
were rarer. The smaller states could debate all they liked in the General
Assembly as long as it did not involve disputes under consideration by the
Security Council. Only the Security Council could act in matters of
international peace and security, and on it the great powers had permanent
seats and the power of the veto. Only the great powers could act, but they
could act only in concert. In concert they could impose their will any time,
any place in the world. But they were not in concert, not for long at any
rate. Quite the contrary.

Barely ten months after San Francisco (February 9, 1946) Stalin made
a campaign speech. It was marked by the usual communist rhetoric,
assertions about Soviet preparedness at the time of the German invasion,
gloating about victory, and at the end a humble bit: the expression of
gratitude for being nominated to the Supreme Soviet and the promise "to
try to justify this confidence." As the State Department read it, "He also
stated with brutal clarity the Soviet Union's postwar policy. Finding the
causes of the late war in the necessities of capitalist-imperialist monopoly
and the same forces still in control abroad, he concluded that no peaceful
international order was possible."[2] Promptly a call went out to the
American Embassy in Moscow for the "elucidation of this startling
speech."[3]

Just what the State Department expected is not quite clear. What it got
was "the long telegram" of some 8,000 words by George F. Kennan.[4] The
Chargé d'Affaires, in bed with a "cold, fever, sinus, tooth trouble, and
finally the aftereffects of the sulpha drugs administered for the relief of

---

[2] *The New York Times*, February 10, 1946, p. 30.

[3] Kennan remembered the cause of his letter differently: as an inquiry about
Soviet reluctance to join the World Bank and the International Monetary Fund.
George F. Kennan, *Memoirs 1925–1950* (Boston: Little, Brown, 1967), p. 292.

[4] Ibid., pp. 549–51.

these other miseries," saw his chance. Within a comprehensive pedagogical exercise he made his point: we cannot expect anything remotely resembling reason from the Soviet Union!

Please note that premises on which this party line is based are for most part simply not true. . . . Nevertheless, all these theses, however baseless and disproven, are being boldly put forward again today. What does this indicate? It indicates that the Soviet party line is not based on any objective analysis of the situation beyond Russia's border; that it has indeed little to do with conditions outside of Russia; that it arises mainly from basic inner-Russian necessities which existed before recent war and exist today.

In other words, however hard we may try to gain their confidence, "their neurotic view of world affairs" will abort any endeavor requiring Soviet cooperation. It was really a foolish waste of time to try at all.

The message was leaked and became an instant success. James Forrestal, secretary of the navy (and soon to become the first secretary of defense), liked it very much. The State Department was more cautious, but Dean Acheson, who in the meantime had become undersecretary of state and a man President Truman trusted, agreed that "his [Kennan's] predictions and warnings could not have been better."[5] Since the president himself was also developing profound doubts about the Russians, a consensus was forming in the government that in spite of all American hopes and efforts a concert with the Soviet Union, at least for some time to come, would only produce cacophony.

A NEW BEGINNING

Events that followed are well known. What these events meant, however, is open to various interpretations. The orthodox version holds that U.S. foreign policy was captured by national security policy. We set out to dam the communist tide and became fully absorbed in building alliance systems along the *communist* periphery. We designed and single-mindedly pursued a Cold War and called it the strategy of containment.[6] An alternative interpretation, one which I think more closely reflects the truth, is that (1) *the American government did not abandon its deeply felt commit-*

---

[5] Acheson, *Present at the Creation*, p. 151.

[6] See for example: Stanley Hoffmann, *Primacy or World Order: American Foreign Policy since the Cold War* (New York: McGraw-Hill, 1978); and John L. Gaddis, *Strategies of Containment* (New York: Oxford University Press, 1982).

ment to international order, (2) *it gave up the orthodox approach of international order through the concert of great powers and tried something new: a decentralized world order,* and (3) the government of the United States and more specifically Dean Acheson knew that the American people and the Congress so recently committed to isolation would not readily understand and support our *general interest* in international order. Since they did want popular support and needed congressional approval they thought it necessary to *resort to a ploy, to reformulate such general goals and publicly present them in terms of our special interests in helping our friends and allies and better still in terms of our vital interests to thwart a communist threat to America.*

A case in point. At the first briefing of congressional leaders at the White House on Greek and Turkish aid the secretary of state sought to place the program in the context of our general national interest and "most unusually and unhappily, flubbed his opening statement." Dean Acheson, sitting next to General Marshall, in desperation asked permission from the president and the secretary to speak.

In the past eighteen months, I said, Soviet pressure on the Straits, on Iran, and on northern Greece had brought the Balkans to the point where a highly possible Soviet breakthrough might open three continents to Soviet penetration. Like apples in a barrel infected by one rotten one, the corruption of Greece would infect Iran and all to the east. It would also carry infection to Africa through Asia Minor and Egypt, and to Europe through Italy and France, already threatened by the strongest domestic communist parties in Western Europe. The Soviet Union was playing one of the greatest gambles in history at minimal costs. . . . We and we alone were in a position to break up the play. . . . A long silence followed. Then Arthur Vandenberg[7] said solemnly, "Mr. President, if you will say that to Congress and the country, I will support you and I believe that most members will do the same."[8]

Because it seemed to work, the strategy would be repeated with "the rotten apples" eventually replaced by "falling dominoes."

A year later (1947) the secretary of state at the Harvard commencement announced the Marshall Plan and once again justified it in terms of general international cooperation. His undersecretary later recorded:

If General Marshall believed, which I am sure he did not, that the American people would be moved to so great an effort as he contemplated by as Platonic a purpose

---

[7] Ranking Republican on the Senate Foreign Relations Committee.
[8] Acheson, *Present at the Creation*, p. 219.

as combating "hunger, poverty, desperation, and chaos," he was mistaken. *But he was wholly right in stating this as the American governmental purpose.*[9]

While American aid to Europe was getting underway, historic events in other parts of the globe were moving along at an inexorable pace. In August 1947 India and Pakistan became independent, and that was just the beginning. New states based on the principle of self-determination were emerging all over the globe. The old colonial order was gone forever. The United States with all its awesome power had no interest whatever in gaining world hegemony but had not the slightest inclination to permit the Soviet Union to do so. In his inaugural address (1949) Harry S Truman, elected president in his own right, warned of the "false philosophy" of communism but went far beyond that. He pledged American leadership for a cooperative enterprise in which all nations work together . . . a world-wide effort for the achievement of peace, plenty and freedom." Afterwards he explained to reporters in the Oval Office: "I spend most of my time going to that globe back there, trying to figure out ways to make peace in the world."[10]

One further point, NSC 68 was a national policy statement recommended by the secretaries of state and defense on April 7, 1950. It has often been quoted as evidence that containment of the Soviet Union was the overriding objective of American foreign policy for more than four decades afterwards. The document was even castigated as a principal culprit of the Cold War. Actually the impact of this document was more complex. For one thing, there were other national policy statements as well, for example, NSC 20/4 and NSC 162/2 where the purpose of "containment" was not as emphatic. Indeed even NSC 68 was not as single-minded as it was often fashionably portrayed. In the section on the "U.S. Intentions and Capabilities" we can read:

Our overall policy at the present time may be described as one designed to foster a world environment in which the American system can survive and flourish. It therefore rejects the concept of isolation and affirms the necessity of our positive participation in the world community.

This broad intention embraces two subsidiary policies. One is a policy which we would probably pursue even if there were no Soviet threat. It is a policy of attempting to develop a healthy international community. The other is the policy of "containing" the Soviet system. These two policies are closely interrelated and

---

[9] Ibid., p. 233. [Italics added.]

[10] Truman, *Memoirs*, vol. II, pp. 226–27, 233.

interact on one another. Nevertheless, the distinction between them is basically valid and contributes to a clearer understanding of what we are trying to do.[11]

Thus it serves accuracy best to recognize a steadfast moral commitment of American foreign policy to international order even during the Cold War. Confronted with the obvious failure of the previous three attempts to manage a global order through a concert of major powers, President Truman and Secretary of State Acheson did not just give up and withdraw into a Fortress America reinforced by a system of military alliances. They persisted and tried something new. My colleague, Walter McDougall, highlights the conclusion: "For forty years Americans did sacrifice, and not for their own comfort and [s]elf, but that other nations might be reborn. That is why NSC 68 was, for better or worse, a sublime expression of the Judeo-Christian culture it purposed to defend."[12]

Decentralized world order was indeed a radical departure from conventional wisdom. Power was not the organizing principle. It was based on the novel proposition that international order was not the privilege of the major powers but the right and responsibility of *all* states collectively. If any state were to be given greater weight in settlements, this would not be because of the product of its military power but because of its geographic proximity. Smaller states nearby would be entitled to greater weight than large powers in the distance.

This, of course, did not mean that major powers would stop imposing their solutions upon the disputes of others let alone stop meddling in the business of smaller states. It did mean that they could not do so *as a matter of course*. They would have to have an excuse and would have to go to great lengths to justify themselves to a skeptical world.

Decentralized world order, however, was still only a concept, at best a design. Formidable obstacles would have to be overcome before it could become a reality. Some were quantitative. The system of great powers had four or five, at any rate few decisive components. It was difficult to get agreement, let alone a consensus, but it could be done. But decentralized world order with the "sovereign equality" of all the various states vastly inflated the decision-making number: 50, 100, and 150. Agreement among so large a number, not to mention a consensus, was a very different, quite possibly unmanageable task.

---

[11] Ernest R. May (ed.), *American Cold War Strategy: Interpreting NSC 68* (Boston: Bedford Books of St. Martin's Press, 1993), pp. 40–41.

[12] Ibid., p. 171.

Worse still were qualitative obstacles. There was the contradiction that while all members of a decentralized world order were by definition equal in sovereignty, in fact they were very much unequal in their power. Since the effectiveness of decision-making depends on the ability to implement decisions, the majority rule becomes untenable. In the real world a major power simply cannot be compelled to accept any decision against its will, not even by a majority vote. This has been the reality all through history; this was the reality that the founders of the United Nations recognized when they insisted on a veto for the major powers in the Security Council; and this remains the reality in our time.

No less troubling was another contradiction. While all countries would be entitled to participate in the management of world order, many of them were actually unable to manage satisfactorily their own domestic affairs. Most of the newly independent, postcolonial countries of Africa and Asia, not to mention other smaller states of Latin America and Europe, actually lacked the minimal capacities of a modern state: they were not only economically underdeveloped, but also politically unstable.

If decentralized world order was to have a chance at all, a special temporary transitional effort was needed by the United States. We would have to help build the political stability of the newly independent states of Asia and Africa. President Truman accepted the responsibility. As they emerged, American initiatives had a dual thrust: (1) to generate economic development thus reducing the *demands* on government and (2) to improve administrative skills and internal security forces thus increasing the *resources* of government.

The strategy had serious theoretical flaws,[13] but its most serious practical deficiency was its neglect of the possibility of external predatory initiatives. States with unstable political systems are not only vulnerable to internal revolution, they are also magnets of external aggression. And, of course, the Soviet Union was not sitting idly by. It used its propaganda to discredit world order made in the United States, and its power and influence to challenge it. Sunday morning, June 25, 1950, the regular forces of communist North Korea invaded the Republic of South Korea.

As a case of unprovoked aggression the North Korean attack was an affront to international order. It was also a communist challenge, a Soviet challenge by proxy, to the United States. Dean Acheson, now the secretary

---

[13] For example: (a) technical administrative expertise plus police force do not add up to political legitimacy; and (b) economic growth does not necessarily produce political stability.

of state, explained: "To back away from this challenge, in view of our capacity for meeting it would be highly destructive of the power and prestige of the United States."[14] Accordingly the American response was swift and massive. U.S. air, naval, and ground forces were committed to repel the aggressor. Since at the time the Soviet Union was boycotting the Security Council, this could be done under United Nations auspices. All the same, it was a very troubling matter. It was one thing to provide aid—economic or even military supplies and training—in order to build political stability in distant lands for the purpose of international order; to shed American blood for this purpose was something else again. For so great a sacrifice at least in the past we needed a more direct and a more clearly perceived threat. Just three days after the invasion the secretary of state warned that the administration "could not count on the continuance of enthusiastic support that our staunch attitude in Korea had worked in the country and in the world. Firm leadership would be less popular if it should involve casualties and taxes."[15]

Casualties were rising soon enough, but popular support remained enthusiastic. We were winning. Our troops destroyed the North Korean forces, captured their capital, and seemed ready to liberate practically all their country. Then communist China intervened, and suddenly we came face to face with the full costs of a decentralized world order. We could, of course, withdraw and abandon our cherished international design, but Americans do not easily accept defeat. Or we could escalate and "shoot the works." General MacArthur, the supreme allied commander in the Far East, was ready to do the latter, and the American public—while the option remained academic—was wildly in favor of this. But the risks were enormous: the risk of a full-scale war with China, perhaps the Soviet Union, the risk of Soviet initiatives anywhere else on the globe (perhaps Western Europe), and the risk of scaring our allies (for example, British Prime Minister Attlee) out of their wits. All these risks might be warranted in case of a threat to our vital interests but were surely not justified by a challenge to our general interest in international order. What we actually needed was a limited response to a limited purpose. We needed firm leadership steering a moderate course, a president with careful judgment, a moderate temperament, and a feel for a delicate balance. We also needed an American electorate patient and understanding with a war in support of an Asian government perhaps friendly to us but with not the slightest inclination to

---

[14] Acheson, *Present at the Creation*, p. 405.

[15] Ibid., p. 411.

democratic values. We needed an American electorate patient and understanding with a war without glory, endlessly devouring American lives, money, and prestige. Possibly we had the necessary executive leadership; certainly we did not have the public patience and understanding. President Truman managed a stalemate in South Korea—at colossal political cost.

Dwight D. Eisenhower, his successor, had known for quite some time that international order had become an integral part of America's national interest. As Supreme Allied Commander in Europe he faithfully supported the contemporary view of an international order built on a coalition of great powers and went to great lengths to build the confidence and enlist the cooperation of the Soviet Union. As president he was no less determined to try to make decentralized world order work. He recognized the weakness that the stalemate in Korea exposed, but given a "New Look" he believed a corrective could be developed. The problem, as everyone (including our enemies) could see, was that the American people had concluded that under existing conditions the price for the protection of vulnerable foreign states by American arms was prohibitive. But did it have to be? Quite possibly, as his secretary of state suggested, the flaw in the Truman-Acheson approach was their commitment to a "symmetric response." It granted the aggressor the choice of place and weapons, a generosity even old-fashioned gentlemen duelers would not indulge in. Certainly John Foster Dulles would not. He did not mince words. "The way to deter aggression," he said, "is for the free community to be willing and able to respond vigorously at places and with means of its own choosing." To make it perfectly clear he wrote: "A would-be aggressor will hesitate to commit aggression if he knows in advance that he thereby not only exposes those particular forces which he chooses to use for his aggression, but also deprives his other assets of 'sanctuary' status." The Truman administration's self-restraint was counterproductive.

Early in his administration Eisenhower passed a message through the Indian government to Beijing. The United States was determined to end the war in Korea. Cease-fire negotiations had been going on for over a year at Panmunjon with no results. All they did was offer the communist delegates an opportunity to verbally abuse the United States. We had listened patiently, but now our patience was at an end. Unless within a very short time an agreement would be signed, the United States, using means of its own choice on targets of its own choice, would put an end to the impasse. Just in case this message was not fully understood, the United States shipped atomic bombs to forward areas in the Pacific. The move was secret but intentionally not so secret that it would escape the attention of Soviet and Chinese intelligence agents.[16] The communist filibuster at Panmunjon ended; a cease-fire agreement was signed; the concept of decentralized world order was still intact.

With Eisenhower in charge North Korea, China, the Soviet Union, and everyone else was on "public notice that if the communists were to violate the armistice and renew the aggression the response of the United Nations Command would not necessarily be confined to Korea."[17] Let them heed the warning: a country invading its neighbor will be punished by "instantaneous, massive retaliation." Then sensing a new danger, John Foster Dulles specifically warned China of "grave consequences which might not be confined to Indo-China" in case it were to turn its aggression to the south. Through the "imaginative use of the deterrent capabilities of these [nuclear] new weapons," he explained, the United States would get more bang for the buck, actually the biggest gosh-darn bang anyone could imagine. Altogether it was the most economical way to deter and punish aggressors anywhere in the world.

The secretary was closer to the traditional power politics school. Even so, he was part of the continued American preoccupation with international order. "It is a fact, unfortunate though it be," he echoed Acheson, "that in promoting our programs in Congress we have to make evident the international communist menace. Otherwise such programs . . . would be decimated."[18] President Eisenhower himself regularly and dramatically demonstrated his own commitment to a new decentralized order. He had no faith in an international system linked to European colonial rule. He respected our special interest which tied us to our NATO allies—as a matter of *regional* security. On the global scale, however, he thought our general interest to be on the side of the emerging newly independent Asian and African states. Preferably noncommunist, of course. In 1954 when France desperately needed American military support in Indochina (Dien Bien Phu), he overruled his secretary of state and other senior advisers and

---

[16] No written record of the shipment of atom bombs is available; perhaps it does not exist. In the private meeting with President Johnson (February 17, 1965) discussing strategy in Vietnam, President Eisenhower recounted his successful solution of the Korean War.

[17] Speech to the Council of Foreign Relations, January 12, 1954, Department of the State *Bulletin*, vol. XXX (January 25, 1954), p. 108 and "Policy for Security and Peace," *Foreign Affairs*, vol. 32, no. 3 (April 1954), p. 359.

[18] Speech to the Associated Press, New York, April 23, 1956, Department of the State *Bulletin*, vol. XXXIV (April 30, 1954), p. 708.

refused to become involved in a scheme to restore the rule of a colonial power over subject peoples. Two years later during the Suez Crisis he supported the sovereign integrity of an unfriendly, even hostile Egypt against the military action of Britain and France (not to mention Israel), our close World War II allies but former imperial powers.

Thus, with the Eisenhower-Dulles corrective of "massive retaliation," decentralized world order was given a new lease on life. Alas not for long. "Massive retaliation," or "asymmetric response" as the jargon went, rested on the pinpoint of American nuclear invulnerability. Though it was wildly unlikely, it was imaginable for some that America would bomb a country back into the Stone Age as an imposed penalty while she remained completely safe. But after October 1957 with *Sputnik* in the skies revealing a vigorously pursued and rapidly advancing Soviet space program, America could be completely safe not much longer. That it should use its nuclear power against a communist aggressor far beyond the seas, thereby risking a nuclear response from the Soviet Union remained wildly unlikely but had become imaginable for almost anyone.

Still the American concept of decentralized world order was a very inspiring one, and to give up at all, let alone to give up easily, is not an American trait. It certainly was not part of the character of John Fitzgerald Kennedy. Understanding quite well all the new international realities he proclaimed at his inauguration: "Let every nation know, whether it wishes us well or ill, that we shall pay any price, bear any burden, meet any hardship, support any friend, oppose any foe to assure the survival and success of liberty."[19] It was a bold challenge. Just two weeks before, Nikita S. Khrushchev, the First Secretary of the Communist Party of the Soviet Union, had announced active Soviet support for "wars of liberation." Such wars, he said, "will continue to exist as long as imperialism exists, as long as colonialism exists. These are revolutionary wars. Such wars are not only admissible but inevitable."[20] Confronting the Dulles warning he used as his principal example of wars of liberation "the armed struggle of the Vietnamese people." We were on a collision course, a course that led us to Vietnam and, as it turned out, to a historic test of decentralized world order.

---

[19] *The New York Times*, January 21, 1961, p. 8.

[20] Nikita S. Khrushchev, Speech to the Higher Party School of the Institute of Marxism-Leninism of the Central Committee of the CPSU, January 6, 1961, quoted in Alvin Z. Rubinstein, *The Foreign Policy of the Soviet Union*, 3rd ed. (New York: Random House, 1972), p. 268.

CONFRONTATION IN VIETNAM

As a matter of fact, 1954–1959 was a relatively peaceful time after the French defeat in Indochina during which the newly established government of South Vietnam under President Ngo Dinh Diem could have consolidated its position.[21] The communists were busy in the North consolidating their position. In the South, American aid was generous. U.S. officials[22] in Saigon thought Diem could be successful. They watched with dismay several of the wrong turns. First, they had hoped that some kind of land reform would be undertaken which through the opportunity of private ownership would tie the interests of the rural masses to the anticommunist government. President Diem took no action. Land ownership continued to be concentrated in the hands of the often-absent few. Thus the masses of rural people had nothing to lose to the communists, and perhaps they felt that they had something to gain by getting even with the landlords. Second, US AID officials hoped that given the reality that some 90 percent of the South Vietnamese people did not share the religious beliefs of the president, his government would proceed along generally secular lines and strive to be inclusionary toward all Vietnamese elements. On this, too, they were disappointed. President Diem, a devout Catholic, carried his faith into his politics. He surrounded himself with Catholics. His government visibly favored the Roman Catholic minority. Many of these, in fact, were recently arrived refugees from the north and actually strangers to the community. In the highest civil service academy, for example, Catholics were noticeably preferred and Catholic doctrine was regularly taught. Missions from the Vatican were occasions of government-sponsored public celebrations with special banners, nightly illuminations, and fireworks. Cardinal Spellman of New York regularly visited the country. Pictures of his meetings with President Diem were widely published and distributed conveying a legitimacy flowing from the Church and America. Finally it was hoped that in contrast to the previous rulers in Indochina President Diem would be honest and would vigorously root out corruption. In fact, by all reports he was honest; but unfortunately he did not insist that others around him

---

[21] For a brief review of some of the preceding events see: von Vorys, *American National Interest*, pp. 196–202.

[22] For example, Dr. Milton J. Esman, the Program Officer of US AID in Saigon. Earlier Dr. Esman was one of General McArthur's advisers on the Japanese constitution and later a senior adviser to the Malaysian government. More recently he held the John Knight chair of international relations at Cornell University.

follow his example. The traditional habits of corruption continued into his administration, indeed infected his closest coterie. In sum, the net result was that he missed the opportunity to build popular support and loyalty. The rural population remained largely indifferent, the majority of religious elements were apprehensive, and the small nascent group of intellectuals was cynical about his system.

After 1959 the situation turned to bad and then to worse. Communist forces infiltrated South Vietnam from the north. Local Vietcong cadres were activated. A systematic assassination of rural leaders commenced; worse still, hit-and-run attacks on military establishments and supply routes were becoming frequent. Occasionally communist guerillas seized a district or provincial capital, held it for a while, meted out revolutionary justice (i.e., massacred some people), and then as government forces were approaching slowly and carefully—very slowly and very carefully—withdrew. The American ambassador, though not the senior military representatives, became very nervous.

Vietnam Becomes Our General Interest

In Washington members of a new administration were just beginning to know each other in the spring of 1961. President Kennedy's principal advisers were Robert McNamara, secretary of defense lured away from the presidency of Ford Motor Company; General Maxwell Taylor, Kennedy's most trusted military adviser; Allen Dulles, head of the CIA who was a holdover from the Eisenhower administration; Dean Rusk, secretary of state and former head of the Rockefeller Foundation; plus a familiar face, McGeorge Bundy, national security adviser and former dean of Harvard College. Always on call was Robert F. Kennedy (young Bobby), the attorney general, who at the time was rather absorbed in the problems of the Justice Department (e.g., civil rights and J. Edgar Hoover, director of the FBI).

In May 1961 in response to distressing reports from South Vietnam Vice President Johnson, carefully chaperoned by a presidential sister and brother-in-law, visited Saigon. During a discussion with Diem he offered American aid. Diem was very much impressed "particularly because we have not become accustomed to being asked for our own views on our needs" and took him up on it. He asked for equipment to nearly double his army from 150,000 to 270,000 men and "a considerable expansion of the United States Military Advisory Group." Then, in five months, (October 1) the South Vietnamese president surprised the American ambassador by asking for a U.S.–South Vietnam defense treaty. Disturbed, President

Kennedy sent General Taylor and Walt Rostow from the National Security Council on another fact-finding mission to Saigon.

The idea of South Vietnam as a test case for decentralized world order did not appeal to President Kennedy. The Geneva Agreement (1954), which set up South Vietnam, intended it only as a transitional arrangement. The combination of internal insurgency and external incursion added further complexity. Furthermore the prospects of a viable political system emerging in this fragment of former Indochina were far too uncertain. Personally he was willing to give it his sympathy, but as a policy he much preferred benign neglect.

All the same, President Kennedy was in a difficult position. He was steadily being *pulled* into the conflict. By hindsight it seems most unlikely that the communist powers would have let him experiment with a variety of minimal to moderate means. Ho Chi Minh, the ruler of communist North Vietnam, was in fact prepared to pay any price, bear any burden for the success of his cause. China and the Soviet Union relished the prospect of haranguing throughout the world about our impotence and their successes. Meanwhile the president was *pushed* into the conflict. The pressure of the political Right was formidable. The outrages of the McCarthy era had become bad memories. Even so, the suspicion that the "Democrats were soft on communism" lingered on. It did not help that his first eighteen months in office were marked by a series of setbacks in foreign policy. The bungling into and at the Bay of Pigs. An indifferent performance at the Vienna Summit with Khrushchev. Indecision on Berlin and impotence at the Wall. Persistent trouble in Laos. Voices were raised: does he know anything, can he do anything right? Pressure was building for "bold leadership." Another "loss to the communists" could prove politically fatal.

Remarkably the president was also pushed from the political Left. John F. Kennedy liked the company of young intellectuals, many of them academics, attractive men who had accumulated vast knowledge in their respective areas of specialization. Much like Franklin Roosevelt he brought a large number into his administration in middle-level policy positions. As it happened some became major actors in the Vietnam decisions. They included, for example, Roger Hilsman, assistant secretary of state for Far Eastern affairs, and Michael Forrestal, son of the first secretary of defense and a member of the NSC staff.

General Taylor, having returned from his mission to Saigon, had no doubt that U.S. military involvement was necessary to save South Vietnam. Still he was cautious in his report. All he recommended was a very modest, primarily logistical support, a task force of "6–8000 troops . . . for the purpose of participating in flood relief." He was especially cautious about

American meddling in the political processes of the country. He did not shrink from a candid estimate of the moral deficiencies of the government or the political peculiarities of its president, but General Taylor rejected "his removal in favor of a military dictatorship . . . would be dangerous under present tense circumstances, since it is by no means certain that we could control its consequences and potentialities or communist exploitation." Our intervention was to assure "Diem of our readiness to join him in a military showdown with the Viet Cong or Viet Minh."[23]

On November 11, 1961, in a joint recommendation the secretary of state, the secretary of defense, and the Joint Chiefs of Staff urged that we "commit ourselves to the objective of preventing the fall of South Vietnam to communism." John F. Kennedy could not stop the momentum, only slow it down. He approved the aid, but any reference to a commitment "of preventing the fall of South Vietnam to communism" was omitted from the formal decision paper (NSAM 111). Shortly before Christmas 1961 two U.S. helicopter companies arrived in South Vietnam,[24] and South Vietnam became part of our general interest. This was not an unreasonable position, but soon the Kennedy administration involved us very much deeper still.

Escalation to Special Interest: Loss of Contact with International Reality

In two years the number of U.S. advisers rose from 900 to 16,000, South Vietnamese military strength was approaching 225,000 men, and their cost to us exceeded a quarter billion dollars. At first it seemed to be worth it. In 1962 insurgency seemed to decline steadily. All through the year Secretary of Defense McNamara was issuing—in retrospect, he admitted—overoptimistic reports. For example, on October 9, 1962, at Andrews Air Force Base he told the press: "I think it is too early to say that the tide has turned or to predict the final outcome, but a tremendous amount of progress has been made during the past year."[25] On May 6, 1963, Secretary of Defense McNamara explained at a briefing in Honolulu that

---

[23] United States, House of Representatives, Committee on Armed Services, *United States–Vietnam Relations 1945–1967*, vol. 2, pp. B1, 125–33. Much of the data and analyses of our Vietnam involvement are based on the above source, popularly known as the *Pentagon Papers*. Therefore unless otherwise indicated, all citations come from this elaborate study.

[24] *The New York Times*, December 11, 1961, p. 21.

[25] Robert McNamara, *In Retrospect* (New York: Times Books, 1995), p. 47.

in his view the South Vietnamese government will have gained control of the insurgency by 1965 and that U.S. aid could be reduced. Accordingly, he announced, he decided to withdraw about 1,000 U.S. military personnel by December 1963.

Two days later the troubles really began. At the celebration of Buddha's 2,525 birthday Thich Tri Quang, a Buddhist leader from the North, denounced the Diem government as anti-Buddhist and then led an aroused mass of people to the radio station where they demanded that the tape of his speech be broadcast. When troops arrived a riot broke out. There were explosions, set by the Viet Cong the government insisted, but not believed by the American correspondents.[26] A month later (June 11) an aged Buddhist monk got out of a car in Saigon, assumed the lotus position, two associates poured gasoline over him, he lit a match and was engulfed in flames. Given advance warning, the Associated Press correspondent and his photographer were there. Next morning all of America heard about it and saw the pictures. Madame Nhu, President Diem's sister-in-law and officially South Vietnam's First Lady, explained the spectacular event on NBC News: "[The Buddhist leaders] have done nothing but barbecue a monk, and, at that, not even with self-sufficient means, since they had to import gasoline." The American people were not amused.

The administration was shocked. The policy settled in 1961 became an issue suddenly just when it seemed to be working so well, and the news was getting worse. Guerilla attacks intensified. Buddhist mass demonstrations became more frequent and more widespread. Other monks chose to immolate themselves. President Diem was slow in responding to American diplomatic pressure. His brother, Ngo Dinh Nhu, head of the security forces, however, was altogether too forceful for American tastes. In a carefully planned operation after telephone lines to the U.S. Embassy and to the private homes of all senior U.S. personnel had been cut, Buddhist pagodas were invaded, and about 1400 Buddhist monks were arrested.[27] The news disoriented the foreign policy decision-making in Washington, leading through most bizarre practices to an American-sponsored *coup d'état* in Saigon.

The enemies of the Diem regime in Washington saw their chance. Their position, moreover, was reinforced by two appointments who proved to be

---

[26] Russ Braley, *Bad News, the Foreign Policy of The New York Times* (Chicago: Regnery Gateway, 1984), p. 192.

[27] Not their leader; Thich Tri Quang escaped and was given sanctuary in the American Embassy.

quick converts. First, Averell Harriman, a man with extraordinary diplomatic experience during the Roosevelt and Truman administrations, was promoted to undersecretary of state, Roger Hilsman's immediate superior. Second, at the insistence of Secretary of State Rusk a new ambassador was sent to Saigon: Henry Cabot Lodge, a scion of an old New England family, recently a U.S. Senator from Massachusetts. Dean Rusk knew him quite well, and just before Lodge left for Saigon Rusk "told him that he was deeply distressed over the Buddhist crisis and wanted him to take a strong lead to bring about a greater degree of peace and security in the country."[28]

August 24, 1963, was a Saturday. The secretary of state was in New York; the secretary of defense and the director of the C.I.A. were away on vacation. President Kennedy was relaxing at Hyannis Port. Roger Hilsman was drafting instructions to Ambassador Lodge. It included the following unambiguous and far-reaching paragraphs.[29]

U.S. Government cannot tolerate situation in which power lies in Nhu's hands. Diem must be given chance to rid himself of Nhu and his coterie and replace them with best military and political personalities available.
If, in spite of all your efforts, Diem remains obdurate and refuses, then we must face the possibility that Diem himself cannot be preserved.

Clearly these were instructions to prepare a coup. When the president read them, he agreed provided the senior cabinet officers endorsed it. By a sly maneuver their assent was gained after they were informed that the president had seen the message (true) and had already signed off on it (not quite true). So the message was sent. In Saigon Ambassador Lodge was eager to proceed. He was ready to contact the Vietnamese generals. In the event the American military mission would oppose such machinations (a shrewd guess), Lodge decided to use the CIA as the instrument of his dealings.

Upon his return to Washington, President Kennedy learned that General Taylor, Chairman of the Joint Chiefs, had not been consulted and was utterly opposed.[30] He was annoyed and insisted on polling the table

---

[28] Thomas J. Schoenbaum, *Waging Peace and War, Dean Rusk in the Truman, Kennedy and Johnson Years* (New York: Simon & Schuster, 1988), p. 395.

[29] McNamara, *In Retrospect*, pp. 52–53.

[30] In retrospect McNamara had his own deep misgivings: "It shocks and saddens me today [1995] to realize that action which eventually led to the overthrow and murder of Diem began while U.S. officials in both Washington and
(continued...)

asking each of his advisers for his position on the cable. "Do you want to cancel it, Mr. McNamara? . . . Do you want to cancel it, General Taylor? Yes or no? . . . " Each man said "no."[31] Shortly thereafter the CIA sent out a cable to Saigon station: "Headquarters instruct . . . to discuss the coup with the generals based on the August 24 cable."[32]

Contact was soon established. On August 29 Lodge cabled "We are launched on a course from which there is no respectable turning back: the overthrow of the Diem Government. There is no turning back in part because U.S. prestige is already publicly committed to this end in large measure and will become more so as facts leak out."

Alas it was not as simple as that. A week after the August 24 cable General Tran Thien Khiem, speaking for General Duong Van Minh, leader of the plot, called the head of the U.S. military mission (not the CIA!). There would be no coup, not now anyway. Lodge passed on the message to Washington. "There is neither the will nor the organization among the generals to accomplish anything."[33] It did not discourage the American ambassador. He kept pushing on. Just two weeks later (September 11) he recommended: "Renewed efforts should be made to activate by whatever positive inducements we can offer the man who would take over the government." In the guise of improving his position to *negotiate* with Diem he asked for authority to announce all U.S. aid would depend on his own discretion. When he received this authority, he used it in his efforts to *overthrow* Diem.

While the plotting proceeded in Saigon behind the back of the American Military Advisory Group (not to mention Diem), in Washington there were meetings after meetings without any clear conclusion.[34] Robert Kennedy was taking an increasingly active role. He would keep asking sensible questions. For example, on September 10: "We have been trying to overthrow Diem, but we have no alternatives I am aware of. Therefore

---

[30](...continued)
Saigon remained deeply divided over the wisdom of his removal; no careful examination and evaluation of alternatives to Diem had been made by me or others."

[31] Richard Reeves, *President Kennedy, Profile of Power* (New York: Simon & Schuster, 1993), pp. 567–68.

[32] Ibid., p. 568.

[33] Ibid., p. 576.

[34] August 27, August 28 (2 meetings), September 3, September 6, September 10, September 17, September 23, 1963.

we are making it impossible to continue working with Diem on the one hand and, on the other, we are not developing an alternative solution. We should go back to what we were doing three weeks ago."[35] Finally on September 17 the president decided to send two trusted senior advisers, Secretary McNamara and General Taylor, plus Deputy Undersecretary of State U. Alexis Johnson to Saigon for a closer look. The middle-level officials in Washington opposed the idea violently as did Ambassador Lodge. All the same, the president insisted. On September 23 his instructions to his special envoys were conciliatory: extensive consultations with Lodge, but "in executing this mission you should take as much time as is necessary for a thorough examination both in Saigon and in the field."[36] While the president's envoys were flying to Saigon, Hilsman sent his own message to Lodge.[37]

Dear Cabot: I am taking advantage of Mike Forrestal's safe hands [*sic*] to deliver this message. . . . I have the feeling that more and more of the town is coming around to our view [i.e., that Diem must be removed by a coup] and that if you in Saigon and we in the Department stick to our guns the rest will also come around. As Mike will tell you, a determined group here will back you all the . . . way.

Secretary McNamara and his colleagues did conduct some extensive examinations. They interviewed government officials, private businessmen, labor leaders, indeed practically anyone they could think of. Their advice was mixed. Most views were pessimistic about the Diem regime but no viable alternative could be suggested. The papal delegate admitted that South Vietnam had become a police state but complained that American officials were sending vague and contradictory messages. At the end of the visit the presidential envoys accompanied by Ambassador Lodge called on President Diem, who with his interminable monologue and inflexible views made a poor impression. On October 2 upon return their report generally urged a firm hand with Diem, but it "particularly emphasized that we did not believe action to organize a coup should be taken at that time."[38]

---

[35] McNamara, *In Retrospect*, p. 64.

[36] Memorandum from the president to the secretary of defense, September 21, 1963, and Memorandum of the Record of a Meeting, September 23, 1963 (U.S. Department of State, Foreign Relations of the United States 1961–1963, Washington, DC, U.S. Government Printing Office, 1988) vol. 4, pp. 278–82.

[37] McNamara, *In Retrospect*, p. 70.

[38] Ibid., pp. 77–79.

Although the president endorsed the recommendations, the plotting under American auspices continued in Saigon.

Lodge somewhat dramatically threatened dire consequences in case Diem was assassinated, which he characterized a rather remote contingency. This at the time the Vietnamese generals were confiding to American contacts their plans for the assassination of Diem's two brothers. Indeed Lodge himself was informed, "The generals are planning the complete removal of the Ngo family."[39] To assist the cause information was passed back to Washington that Diem and especially Nhu were negotiating with the communists. They might ask the United States to withdraw. Interestingly by then we were determined to stay regardless.

In Washington the inconclusive debate continued. Robert Kennedy could see no sense in instigating a coup. It meant "putting the future of South Vietnam—indeed the future of all Southeast Asia—in the hands of someone whose identity and intentions remained unknown to us." The director of the CIA remarked: "If I was manager of a baseball team, and I had one pitcher, I'd keep him in the box whether he was a good pitcher or not."[40]

Still Lodge persisted. On October 25 he cabled that the plotting among South Vietnamese generals was so far-advanced that "we should not thwart a coup." Secretary of State Rusk was in Germany at the time when the State Department "green light" cable for the coup was sent to Lodge on October 27.[41] The next day General Don, a major plotter, asked his CIA contact for money to pass out to the other generals in case the coup would fail. The agent rushed to the embassy and collected all the money he could put his hands on: $42,000.[42]

Finally on November 1 the generals acted. At 4:30 P.M. President Diem called the American ambassador on the phone. "Some units have made a rebellion and I want to know what is the attitude of the U.S.?" The ambassador feigned ignorance: "I do not feel well enough informed to be able to tell you. I have heard the shooting, but am not acquainted with all the facts. Also it is 4:40 A.M. in Washington and the U.S. Government cannot possibly have a view." All Lodge would do was to express concern for Diem's physical safety. The coup proceeded. Diem and Nhu fled the palace. Next morning they called the generals and on the assurance of safe

---

[39] Reeves, *President Kennedy*, p. 640.

[40] McNamara, *In Retrospect*, p. 81.

[41] Schoenbaum, *Waging Peace and War*, p. 400.

[42] Reeves, *President Kennedy*, p. 640.

conduct agreed to surrender and revealed their location. They expected to be taken to an American airbase and evacuated to the United States. A military convoy came for them; they climbed into an armored personnel carrier; the convoy roared off to South Vietnamese military headquarters. When it arrived there, "both bodies were already stretched out on the ground. . . . Diem had been shot in the back of the head, Nhu had been stabbed in the chest and numerous times in the back of the head and in the back. The hands of both victims were tied behind their backs."[43]

It was a case of "accidental suicides," our new protégés declared. President Kennedy did not believe a word of it. The news brought tears to his eyes. He was deeply distressed by the sordid end of this not very inspiring and not particularly sensible episode of his administration. Still no official expression of sorrow or regret was forthcoming—only a pretense that it was all a Vietnamese idea. Of course, the government knew better. The judgment of the *Pentagon Papers* was not too harsh and its conclusion directly on target. "For the military coup d'état against Ngo Dinh Diem, the U.S. must accept its full share of responsibility. . . . Thus, as the nine-year rule of Diem came to a bloody end, our complicity in his overthrow *heightened our responsibilities and our commitment in an essentially leaderless Vietnam.*"[44] Indeed by the time of the tragedy we were already deeply involved. Some 16,657 American troops had been sent there. Sixty-nine of them had been killed. After the coup we were trapped. Other countries, whether they wished us well or ill, knew just what had happened. We had made Vietnam our special interest, a test of our determination and by implication a test of the viability of decentralized world order.

Escalation to Vital Interest: Loss of Contact with Domestic Reality

We had a tragedy at home as well—one that brought tears to most American eyes. By the time Ambassador Lodge returned home, we had a new president. Lyndon Johnson went along when his advisers wanted him to reiterate (NSAM 273) that "it remains the central objective of the United States in Vietnam to assist the people and governments of that country to win their contest against the externally directed and supported communist conspiracy." "I was not going to be the president who saw Southeast Asia

---

[43] Marguerite Higgins, *Our Vietnam Nightmare* (New York: Harper & Row, 1965), pp. 218–19.

[44] *Pentagon Papers*, vol. 3, p. IVB–5.3. [Italics added.]

go the way China went," he explained.[45] But he had profound doubts about the events and the methods of the recent past. "I believed the assassination of President Diem had created more problems for the Vietnamese than it solved. I saw very little evidence that men of experience and ability were available in Vietnam, ready to help lead their country. I was deeply concerned that more political turmoil might lie ahead in Saigon."[46] Senior officials quickly followed Johnson's lead. The activist middle-level group started leaving the government within a month. Soon they resumed their activism with renewed vigor, this time from the outside and this time against any involvement in Vietnam.

In fact, South Vietnam was not better off without Diem. It was a mess. The coup leaders lasted for less than three months. There followed another coup, then another, and another with distressing regularity. Progress in the struggle for the minds and hearts of the people, primarily statistical in the past, became largely illusory. Time and again the president raised the option "to pack up and go home," only to be convinced without much difficulty by his advisers that

The American investment is very large, and American responsibility is a fact of life which is palpable in the atmosphere of Asia, and even elsewhere. The international prestige of the United States, and a substantial part of our influence are directly at risk in Vietnam. There is no way of unloading the burden on the Vietnamese themselves and there is no way of negotiating ourselves out of Vietnam which offers any serious promise at present.[47]

Whenever President Johnson hesitated or tried to insulate himself from events in Vietnam, the communists escalated. Confrontation, getting America deeper and deeper involved, was evidently what they wanted. Just before the Democratic National Convention reports reached Washington that North Vietnamese torpedo boats twice attacked American destroyers in the Gulf of Tonkin. Subsequent investigations raised some doubts

---

[45] David Halberstam, *The Best and the Brightest* (New York: Random House, 1969), p. 298.

[46] Lyndon Baines Johnson, *The Vantage Point, Perspectives of the Presidency 1963–1969* (New York: Holt, Rinehart and Winston, 1971), pp. 44–45. Richard Nixon held very similar views. It was, he said a week before the coup, a choice "not between President Diem and somebody better . . . [but] between Diem and somebody infinitely worse."

[47] Report by "Mac Bundy and his specialists" quoted in Johnson, *The Vantage Point,* p. 126.

whether the second incident actually occurred,[48] though not whether the Navy personnel on the spot believed that they were under attack. There are no doubts that two days before the presidential election communist forces hit our airbase at Bien Hoa. Six planes were destroyed, 5 Americans were killed and 76 wounded. On Christmas Eve they bombed the U.S. officers billets. In February 1965 while the president deliberated on our future course, they attacked American installations in Pleiku, destroying aircraft, killing 7 and wounding 109. They then assaulted the barracks in Qui Nhon, killing 23 and wounding 21 American soldiers.

Faced with such strategically timed dramatic challenges President Johnson was left no choice but to respond, but foreign policy was a weak link in his broad range of political experience. He needed help. President Eisenhower, visiting the White House on February 17, 1965, urged a clear decision one way or another. If we would decide to deny Southeast Asia to the communists, he cautioned, we would have to share this purpose with other nations of the Western world, "and they should be brought to acknowledge and support this effort." We would have to engage in a massive information campaign in Vietnam and throughout the world. More than that President Eisenhower, "stressed strongly that the U.S. Government must tell our own people just what we are doing in the area, i.e., what our policy is, and what course of action we are following." In any case we must be firm. We cannot negotiate from weakness. We have learned that Munichs win nothing. Indeed "the greatest danger in his judgement in the present situation is that the Chinese get the idea that we will go just so far and no further in terms of the level of war we would conduct. That would be the beginning of the end, since they would know all they had to do was go further than we do."[49]

President Johnson's official advisers counseled restraint and moderation. He himself did not feel sufficiently confident for clear-cut action. He could not get himself to give up in battle, but he was never comfortable with the use of military force. He could never appreciate the basic rule of deadly quarrels: if you must use force, use overwhelming force! In consequence what emerged was a colossal blunder, the policy of gradual, incremental escalation, the very thing Eisenhower warned against. We should try to persuade Ho Chi Minh, President Johnson thought, to stop underwriting the insurrection. He waved the stick. In the South we would

---

[48] McNamara, *In Retrospect*, pp. 131–34.

[49] "Memorandum of Meeting with the President, 17 February 1965" by Lt. General A. J. Goodpaster. Eisenhower Library, Abilene, Kansas.

use forces in the field to demonstrate that a communist victory was impossible. In the North we would use air power to make the point that an aggressor can enjoy no sanctuary. But it would not be a very big stick, just large enough to hold our own in the South and not large enough to cause crippling damage in the North. And he forever dangled a very large carrot. We would negotiate without preconditions, we would be satisfied with an independent and neutral South Vietnam, and we would be willing to contribute to the economic development of the area and have North Vietnam share in a billion-dollar program.[50]

That Ho Chi Minh was a devout believer in his cause was one of our main problems. He was neither intimidated nor visibly tempted. Another problem was the cost of holding our own in the South. It had been rising steadily and sharply. At first our troops were there for training purposes, then their mission was expanded to include guarding our facilities, and further expanded to permit active and aggressive patrolling. By June 1965 permission was granted to assist Vietnamese forces under attack when no other reserves were available. Toward the end of the month permission was granted to commit U.S. combat forces independently *to search and destroy*. As late as mid-April 1965 there were only 33,000 American troops in South Vietnam. In July the president decided to "give our commanders in the field the men and supplies they say they need."[51] In this way the massive buildup commenced. By October 1967 480,000 men, 40 percent of our combat-ready divisions, half of our tactical airpower, and at least a third of our naval strength were waging a counterinsurgency effort in a far distant country about which the American people knew nothing. Our casualties were running at 1,000 dead and 5,500 wounded per month. Meanwhile the annual dollar cost passed twenty-five billion.

Faced with such figures and a steady reporting in word and pictures from the field, the American people became interested. They wanted an explanation; they wanted assurance. It was too much for President Johnson (and perhaps for any president) to explain the sacrifices he asked for in terms of the actual value of South Vietnam to us, that is in terms of our

---

[50] President Johnson's speech at Johns Hopkins University on April 7, 1965. *The New York Times*, April 8, 1965, p. 1.

[51] Johnson, *The Vantage Point*, p. 149. A year later the president wanted to be sure that troop reinforcements were sufficiently accelerated "so that General Westmoreland can feel assured that he has all the men he needs as soon as possible." The secretary of defense checked with the Joint Chiefs who (in their own jargon) reported that they were getting all they needed.

general interest in international order. It was even too much in terms of the level of special interest, a definition bequeathed to him by the Kennedy administration. He inflated the stakes further.

He justified the enormous American effort as a far-sighted, long-term strategy to protect our *vital interest*. The domino theory once again became the rationale of our strategy. "Let me say as solemnly as I can," warned the secretary of state, "that those who would place in question the credibility of the pledged word of the United States under our mutual security treaties would *subject this nation to mortal danger*. If any who would be our adversary should suppose that our treaties are a bluff, or will be abandoned if the going gets tough, the result could be catastrophe for all mankind."[52] Meanwhile the administration through announcements and pronouncements offered reassurance. We were making continued military progress, declared the secretary of defense in June 1966. The first quarter's operations "exceeded our expectations."[53] In July the president himself reported that our troops were giving excellent account of themselves. As a result the enemy was losing ten men for every one of ours. Between 15 and 20 percent of their troops now were 12- to 16-year-old boys.[54] In August General Westmoreland, the American military commander in South Vietnam, declared: "A Communist military take-over of South Vietnam is no longer improbable. As long as the United States and our brave allies are in the field it is impossible."[55] By November General Wheeler, chairman of the Joint Chiefs of Staff, publicly reported a series of successful operations to the president. "The war," he concluded, "continues in a very favorable fashion. General Westmoreland retains the initiative and in every operation to date he has managed to defeat the enemy."[56] Thus the barrage of good news continued. A year later things were better still. "I have never been more encouraged in my four years in Vietnam,"[57] announced General Westmoreland.

Behind the scenes, however, the administration was rent by doubts and incessant debates. There was, in truth, little confidence that progress was being made. Enemy losses were high, but their resupply seemed endless. Our losses were getting high, but few thought the patience of the American

---

[52] *The New York Times*, October 13, 1967, p. 14. [Italics added.]
[53] Ibid., June 12, 1966, p. 1
[54] Ibid., July 21, 1966, p. A12
[55] Ibid., August 15, 1966, p. 1.
[56] Ibid., November 11, 1966, p. 18.
[57] Ibid., November 16, 1967, p. 1.

people was endless. In the judgment of Alain Enthoven, the Pentagon's chief systems analyst, enemy (Viet Cong/North Vietnam Army) losses remained below their replacement capabilities. *"On the most optimistic basis,"* he warned the secretary of defense (May 1, 1967), "200,000 more Americans would raise their weekly losses to about 3,700, or about 400 a week more than they could stand, *In theory, we'd then wipe them out in 10 years.*"[58]

Most Americans really wanted to believe their government, but their common sense was getting strained. They were unclear about why we were in Vietnam. They never understood the application of the domino theory; it seemed that an unbelievably long row of distant countries would have to fall to communism before it would come to one which they could identify. They could not imagine how events in Vietnam could become a mortal danger to the United States. Americans were also dubious about just how we were doing. They were not reassured when official reports of progress were regularly accompanied by requests for additional numbers of young Americans being sent over there.

Actually much progress was being made on the battlefield. The insurgents and the North Vietnamese infiltrators were suffering heavy casualties. North Vietnam had to do something, something that might ignite American public opinion. On January 31, 1968, during the Chinese New Year (Tet) celebrations the communists broke the announced cease-fire and launched a dramatic, broad-scale offensive. Some of the targets were military: they attacked American bases. Most were political: they penetrated urban centers and captured some. They infiltrated Saigon, even invaded the American Embassy compound. When government forces were withdrawn from the rural areas to help out in the cities, communist cadres quickly moved into the hamlets.

The American military response was quick and fierce. Cities and towns were vigorously defended; within a month those that had fallen to the enemy were recaptured. Khe Sanh (a Marine Corps base projected by propaganda as the American Dien Bien Phu) held and was relieved. The American forces suffered heavy casualties—about 1,100 killed and 5,500 wounded. The cities suffered more. While the communists held Hue, they summarily executed 300 local officials and prominent citizens and dumped their bodies into a mass grave. When the Americans fought their way back, their firepower devastated much of the ancient capital. It was the communist insurgents, however, who suffered most. Estimates range from 33,000

---

[58] *Pentagon Papers*, vol. V, pp. IV, C, 6, 122. [Italics added.]

up to 45,000 killed. In any case, after the Tet offensive the Viet Cong ceased to play a significant military role. The fighting was carried on primarily by North Vietnamese troops.[59]

Scholars may debate whether the Tet offensive was a military surprise to our government, and a good case can be made that for our armed forces the outcome was a military victory. What is perfectly clear, however, is that for most Americans, the communist attack was a wholly unexpected shock and for the administration it was a major political explosion. Its fallout produced a fundamental reorientation in policy.

In Congress and in classrooms old doubts were recounted with a heightened moral tone and with more resonance. Then Walter Cronkite, anchorman of CBS Evening News, supplied the refrain. Without any expertise in the subject after a short visit in the area he solemnly pronounced his verdict on the air. "It is increasingly clear to this reporter that the only way out then will be to negotiate, not as victors, but as honorable people who lived up to their pledge to defend democracy, and did the best they could."[60]

The events in Vietnam and its consequences on the home front distressed the president. Even so he was willing to hold the line. Just three days after it had begun he pronounced the Tet offensive "a military failure for the enemy." He offered reassurance. When at a press conference he was asked about the possibility of additional deployment, he answered with confidence: "There is not *anything* in *any* of the developments that would justify the press in leaving the impression that any great new overall moves are going to be made that would involve substantial movements in that direction."[61] But then something incredible happened.

With the American people still in shock and the noise of opposition rising to crescendo, General Earle Wheeler, Chairman of the Joint Chiefs of Staff, a man who persistently filled the record with optimistic evaluations, just home from a post-Tet inspection trip endorsed General Westmoreland's request for reinforcement: about 205,000 more American

---

[59] Ibid., p. 382; Harry G. Summers, *On Strategy, a Critical Analysis of the Vietnam War* (Novato, CA: Presidio Press, 1982), p. 138: Townsend Hoopes, *The Limits of Intervention* (New York: David McKay Co., 1969), p. 142.

[60] Some years later David Halberstam wrote with some satisfaction: "It was the first time in American history that a war had been declared over by a commentator." Gary Paul Gates, *Air Time: The Inside Story of CBS News* (New York: Harper & Row, 1978), p. 211.

[61] Johnson, *The Vantage Point*, p. 383.

men and who knows how many more American dollars! It was the straw that broke the camel's back. The president, beleaguered and distraught, was nobody's fool. He prepared for a major policy speech on Vietnam at the end of the month and in preparation for it ordered a general review of existing policies with a "new pair of eyes and a fresh outlook."[62]   And that is exactly what he got.

The chairman of the task force was the new secretary of defense, Clark Clifford, a counsel to President Truman and the personal attorney of John F. Kennedy, a very savvy political operator with vast experience in domestic affairs. Little did the president know that even before the first meeting of the task force he appointed to study the Joint Chief's recommendation Clifford "was already unalterably opposed to the request for more troops"[63]

The other key member of the group was Secretary of State Dean Rusk. His position on Vietnam was eclectic, but he usually vigorously opposed any policy that might cause a loss of American/presidential prestige. He knew from the first that the troop increase "had almost no chance of approval," and he "began his own private process of reexamining the premises of the war, which would transform him into a force for modera-tion."[64]

The early (March 2, 3, and 4) meetings of the task force tended to be dominated by the "hawks." Further escalation was proposed, even the invasion of North Vietnam. Clifford had his hands full trying to restrain some very aggressive options, especially since he suspected that those were exactly what the president wished to hear. It was Dean Rusk who slowed down the momentum by suggesting a conciliatory gesture of a bombing halt. It would not make much difference as during the monsoon period bombing was in any case not very effective, but it could be a symbolic act. It may have seemed to be a modest move but its impact was profound: it shifted the focus of discussion from "war" to "peace." Clark Clifford claims credit for managing it, and his critics blame him fully for it. In any case a policy turnaround was about to take place.

On March 12, 1968, New Hampshire held the nation's first presidential primary. On the Democratic side, a relatively unknown senator from Minnesota, Eugene McCarthy, received 42 percent of the vote. The

---

[62] Clark Clifford, *Counsel to the President* (New York: Random House, 1991), p. 486.

[63] Ibid., p. 493.

[64] Schoenbaum, *Waging Peace and War*, p. 469.

president, who did not campaign, received a write-in vote of 49 percent, but the difference was too close for comfort. For the first time President Johnson felt the pent-up domestic pressures on his foreign policy. Then Robert Kennedy got in the act. On March 16 against the advice of his closest political confidant, Ted Sorensen, he announced his candidacy for the Democratic presidential nomination. It was no longer a relatively unknown senator from Minnesota, but the heir of Camelot, who challenged his president on the Vietnam policy.

The draft for the prospective speech on March 31 was still in the war mode, as was the president. To the convention of the National Farmers' Union in Minneapolis he declared: "Your president has come to ask you people, and all the other people of the nation, to join us in a *total national effort* to win the war. . . . We will—make no mistake about it—win. . . . We are not doing enough to win it the way we are doing it now."[65]

The task force, however, kept moving along the peace mode step by step. The problem became less and less to gain a significant majority (if not a consensus) in the group, but to sway the president. Clifford, having "realized the degree to which Dean Acheson had become disillusioned with the war," urged an A-to-Z review by a broader advisory group, the "Wise Men," which would include the prestigious former secretary of state, who was "present at the creation" of decentralized world order. The president was reluctant but then was persuaded by Dean Rusk.[66] While Robert Kennedy tried to isolate President Johnson in his party, Clark Clifford was busy separating him from his closest advisers. On March 25 and 26 the "Wise Men" met for a briefing. The presentations were provocative. Secretary Rusk said they were unbalanced and overly pessimistic. "President Johnson, [National Security Adviser Walter] Rostow and [Chairman of the Joint Chiefs of Staff General Maxwell] Taylor and the military all felt that they had been betrayed by the briefings, if not the briefers."[67] But the battle was over. On the second day the president knew it too.

The speech was fundamentally rewritten. It shifted from war to peace. On Sunday, March 31, 1968, President Johnson addressed the nation on television. He had made his decision. No increase in American forces in Vietnam. We would abandon the effort to gain military victory in the South and would no longer attempt to intimidate through bombing in the North.

---

[65] Clifford, *Counsel to the President*, p. 507.

[66] Ibid., p. 507.

[67] Ibid., p. 512.

We would rely entirely on negotiation. Finally he himself would forgo any further personal political ambition. "Accordingly, I shall not seek, and will not accept, the nomination of my Party for another term as your president."

Surely one of the most dramatic speeches on American television; it meant the tragic end to the political career of a great American, *a leader with a vision of the "Great Society"* and the effective champion of social justice. It also meant the end of our quest for a system of decentralized world order. For in effect it let every nation know, whether it wished us well or ill, that we shall *not* pay any price, we shall *not* bear any burden, we shall *not* meet any hardship, we shall *not* support any friend, we shall *not* oppose any foe to assure the survival and success of liberty.

12

Power Politics Once Again

It was very sad. The most innovative and inspiring American design for global order was a spectacular failure. Our idealism had carried us away in the international environment far beyond the limits set by the exigencies of the domestic environment. The echos of Walter Cronkite's palliative were heard throughout the land. We had indeed lived up to our pledge to defend democracy. We had tried our very best; we had done more than any country before us. Nostalgia about earlier and happier times gripped the country. Our traditions were sound: do not get entangled with the often bizarre affairs of the Old World. Concentrate on the unfinished business at home.

DÉTENTE

As it happened, perhaps the mark of American destiny, national elections brought a new president. Richard Nixon had extraordinary talent, experience, and intense interest in international affairs. He had served under President Eisenhower and observed him more or less closely in action. His mentor, however, was John Foster Dulles. There was no question now of decentralized world order. Ideals were useful, but the real world with real peace and real war, Nixon was convinced, rested on power. He had no intention of standing idly by while his country withdrew behind its ocean fronts, whatever the popular mood. Such a course was not worthy of America; besides America could not afford it. First, he selected Henry Kissinger, a brilliant academic with a keen appreciation of the practical and a marvelous sense of humor, as his chief foreign policy adviser. Kissinger, whose Ph.D. dissertation was a masterly analysis of the Congress of

Vienna, was (and apparently still is) convinced that there are *only two alternatives* for international order: hegemony or the balance of power. President Nixon then set out to restore America's position in the world and to construct "a framework of peace."[1]

By 1969 it had become perfectly clear once again that hegemony was no option. The United States had not the slightest intention of imposing any preferred pattern of global political arrangement, but quite probably it was powerful enough to prevent other powers from doing so. Still what about a system of balance of power? It had proved impossible in 1946, but had conditions changed? The differences between the values of Soviet communism and American democracy were still profound and the tensions were severe, but not necessarily more so than were the differences and tensions between Czarist Russia and parliamentary Britain at Vienna some 150 years earlier. By 1969 the rise of their military power might have alleviated Soviet anxieties that others could push them around. The Soviet system might have matured sufficiently to recognize its vested interest in peace. In any case, given the existing distressing disarray they might have thought it useful to try relaxing tensions between the superpowers and thus bring about some cooperation on matters of international order (détente). A summit meeting to cover all the major issues dividing the superpowers was arranged for May 1972. For the sake of lasting peace, President Nixon was prepared to travel to Moscow.

In order for balance of power politics to be built into a system, however, two major conditions must be met. First, the balance, while dynamic, must be stable. A brief diversion into theory may be helpful on this. A bipolar system, that is, a pattern with two groups of major powers (as in the nineteenth century) or two superpowers (as in the second half of the twentieth) facing each other, is inherently unstable. Predictably each side will be striving vigorously and perhaps covertly to gain a decisive edge. There is no systemic restraint.

The system, however, may be stabilized by an independent major power, one which is significant but not quite in the same category with the two superpowers and one whose vital interest requires that neither of the superpowers should gain hegemony. If either side appears to be gaining an advantage, this "holder of the balance" will shift and join the other side,

---

[1] Whether "international" order was a main motivating force or just a byproduct is for me somewhat of a puzzle, however. His public statements from the Guam Doctrine on indicated concern, but when I once complimented him on his achievements in this field, he gave me a most peculiar, quizzical look.

and together they would overwhelm the excessively ambitious power. Since this prospect is both predictable and undesirable, it could serve as a restraint and keep the system in rough equilibrium.

Thus the question became acute: Was there a suitable "holder of the balance," and as a corollary could we integrate it into the system? India was independent, but hardly a major power. Britain, which had played this role in the nineteenth century, was now an American ally, and its power was visibly declining. The Russians feared the Germans, but with Germany divided and each part closely attached to one of the superpowers that would not work either. There was one power though that would be well suited: China had become independent of the Soviet Union, and the Russians were very much worried about it. The problem was that relations between China and the United States were almost nonexistent, and what little there was, was bad.

President Nixon set out to solve the problem. He had some assets: considerable talent in his National Security Council, his own skills reinforced by the tendency of others (especially his enemies) to underestimate him, and his reputation as an implacable anticommunist. Meanwhile the Chinese had become concerned about their military vulnerability. They needed some modern weapons; they needed a diplomatic counterweight to their northern, now "not altogether fraternal" neighbor. Moreover, their prime minister, Chou En-lai, was by all reports a very astute global strategist. It took some doing, false starts through Warsaw and Bucharest, but by 1971 with the help of Pakistan, the great diplomatic coup of our time was already in motion. President Nixon was invited to China. He visited it in February 1972, was courteously, even cordially received, and after extensive discussions opened up a constructive dialogue between their government and ours. China would fill the key role of the holder of the balance.

CONFRONTATION IN VIETNAM REVISITED

There remained, however, a second condition for world order based on a balance between the superpowers: the credibility of their power. No one doubted the enormous power of the Soviet Union and that it was prepared to use it. No one doubted the enormous power of the United States, but many wondered whether we would use it. The doubts were persistent. How could a superpower have become bogged down in a distant, highly complex, but essentially third-rate local conflict in Vietnam? How could the Soviet Union respect us and the Chinese rely on us for counterbalance when we were being visibly pushed around by a third-class state like North

Vietnam? For the United States to play its proper role in the balance of power politics, it would have to first regain its credibility and emerge from Vietnam with honor. This was a challenge that surpassed that of the "opening to China" and one that President Nixon also set out to meet.

It was an awesome task. The domestic environment was in an uproar. After a momentary lull from every part of the country, from every element of society, people were screaming imprecations and expletives demanding every kind of action from him regarding Vietnam. Through all the noise he had to keep a steady course. It is a wonder that he could do so. Fortunately, here too President Nixon had significant assets: foreign assets. Our allies in Western Europe respected him. More important though was the change in the perspectives of the Soviet Union and China. While in the past they had seen the American model of decentralized world order as inimical to their national interests, the idea now advanced by the Americans (Nixon-Kissinger) of managing global affairs through a partnership (albeit a competitive partnership) of superpowers was decidedly to their liking. So much so that it was worth it to them that the United States should restore its credibility in Vietnam.

Soon fundamental international changes were in progress with profound repercussions throughout the globe. This was especially so in Vietnam, for within a framework of a decentralized world order North Vietnam and South Vietnam mattered. They had value of their own, indeed in the rhetoric were equal in their sovereignty with the major powers. Not any more. They were reduced to means, no more than pawns in power politics. Military policy options consistently rejected by President Johnson as inappropriate now became available. The president was free to press the war aggressively: to bomb North Vietnam, to search and destroy in the South, and even to invade Cambodia and Laos.

Neither Congress nor the American people had any idea what was actually taking place. President Nixon chose not to enlighten them. North Vietnam was the first to recognize its brutally altered circumstances. In the face of President Nixon's evident determination, Hanoi decided to force the hand of her increasingly uncertain allies. Late in March 1972 it launched a massive invasion across the Demilitarized Zone; within a month it expanded its offensive to the Central Highlands.[2] Then in a "brutal" secret negotiating session with Henry Kissinger, after a harangue of quotes from American domestic sources and after reciting repeatedly his "epic poem of

---

[2] By May 2 they had made visible progress. They had taken Quang Tri, surrounded An Loc, and imperiled Pleiku.

American treachery and Vietnamese heroism," the chief North Vietnamese negotiator "laid down terms." As a practical matter South Vietnam would have to surrender. President Thieu would have to resign immediately; the remaining Saigon administration would have to dismantle its military and police forces promptly.[3] If the Nixon administration would accept these terms, that was fine. Possibly American domestic opposition might compel it to do so. But if the United States chose to resist and fight back, surely the Chinese and the Soviets would have no alternative but to dramatically demonstrate their fraternal (communist) solidarity and come to the aid of North Vietnam.

Nixon, however, was made of sterner stuff. On May 8 he announced his decision. He ordered the total military isolation of North Vietnam by U.S. forces. All entrances of its ports would be mined; all internal waterways would be interdicted, all rail and other communications would be cut off. The president then made it perfectly clear to "other nations especially those which are allied with North Vietnam: The actions I have announced tonight are not directed against you." He closed his television address to the American people by asking for their support. "The world," he said, "will be watching."[4]

The congressional (Democratic) leadership, television commentators, newspaper editors, columnists, and academic experts joined in a chorus of disapproval. The North Vietnamese could not have expected better. They were to be sadly disappointed, however, by their allies. Surely China should feel betrayed by such a massive American military action so soon after Nixon's historic visit. Surely the Soviet Union would angrily cancel the summit meeting scheduled for later that month. But the Chinese now saw the geopolitical advantages of balance-of-power politics in which the United States played a vigorous role. They saw no benefit in an American paper tiger. They protested but only in the mildest terms and did not challenge the American blockade. The Soviet Union also saw the geo-

---

[3] "When I asked him to explain why a Vietnamese government could abandon a policy of Vietnamization, he reverted again to Hanoi's unchanging demand for a tripartite coalition government in which the anticommunist government, decapitated and deprived of its police and army, was supposed to join a coalition with 'neutralists' (approved by Hanoi) and the fully armed communists backed by the North Vietnamese army, which coalition would then negotiate with the fully armed Viet Cong, backed by Hanoi's entire field army. That is what Xuan Thuy called the 'real situation' in South Vietnam." Kissinger, *White House Years*, pp. 1160–73.

[4] *The New York Times*, May 9, 1972, p. 19.

political advantages in a détente with the United States.[5] Official Soviet news reports were restrained. TASS even called special attention to the president's assurance that American military operations were not directed at any other country. On May 10 just two days after the announcement the Soviet ambassador called on the president's national security adviser.

Dobrynin was a good chess player. At the end of the meeting, out of the blue, he asked whether the president had as yet decided on receiving Trade Minister Patolichev (who at the time was visiting Washington). I was a little startled by the request; it could only mean that the Soviet leaders had decided to fall in with our approach of business as usual. Trying to match the Ambassador's studied casualness, I allowed that I probably would be able to arrange a meeting in the Oval Office. Playing a little chess myself, I mentioned that it was customary on these occasions to invite press photographers. Dobrynin thought this highly appropriate.[6]

The meeting was arranged, and pictures of a senior Soviet delegation chatting amicably with the president who had just closed off North Vietnam from all its military supplies were there for all to see. Evidently ". . . all the major powers—the United States, China and the Soviet Union—were painting on a canvas larger than Indochina."[7] The summit took place as scheduled. Treaties between the United States and the Soviet Union were signed. President Nixon was proud and pleased; Chairman Brezhnev was beaming, even playful. The Cold War was over; the era of détente was about to begin. With it returned the international order of power politics.

There still remained the matter of Vietnam, now a manageable nuisance. The North Vietnamese had read the signs, and just to make sure after the conclusion of the summit Podgorny, the president of the Soviet Union, flew to Hanoi to explain the developments. His exposition was received with "an attentive attitude, Brezhnev reported to Nixon."[8] When Henry Kissinger met the North Vietnamese negotiators on July 19, the

---

[5] During his secret visit to Moscow on April 22 Kissinger became convinced that "Brezhnev wants a summit at almost any cost," but after the mining expected its cancellation. Kissinger, *White House Years*, p. 1159–1200. Nixon, in turn, believed that without a strong military response in Vietnam he would have too weak a position and could not afford to go to Moscow. At one time *he* was seriously considering canceling the Summit. Indeed he ordered the May 8th measures so he *could* go to Moscow!

[6] Ibid., p. 1193.

[7] Ibid., p. 1105.

[8] Ibid., p. 1303.

whole atmosphere had changed. Gone were the ideological harangues, the studied discourtesies, the arrogant setting of terms. Le Duc Tho was polite, subtly deferential, eager to conciliate.

Serious negotiations were finally underway. At the next meeting (August 1) signs of a sense of urgency on Hanoi's side became discernible. Significant movement toward a settlement entirely by the communists was taking place. September 15 brought further advance and their request for longer sessions. Next time (September 26–27) the meetings lasted two days and brought further concessions, followed by (October 8–10) three days of meetings and a basic agreement.

It was an extraordinary achievement. The terms were far better than congressional leaders, media commentators, and academic experts expected, and far, far better than the terms for which they would have settled. The South Vietnamese government was not dismantled, indeed its military and police forces remained intact. "We thought with reason," observed Henry Kissinger, "that Saigon, generously armed and supported by the United States, would be able to deal with moderate violations of the agreements; that the United States would stand by to enforce the agreement and punish major violations."[9] There were, however, concessions. Some, involving the designation of a few joint commissions, were symbolic; one was substantial. Communist forces, including North Vietnamese units, were conceded areas of control within South Vietnam. In fact, they had been holding these areas for some time. We could not dislodge them. All the same, their recognition was a visible violation of South Vietnamese sovereignty. Looking at it from the perspective of a United States engaged in global power politics, it was no big deal. From the perspective of the president and his national security advisor who were convinced that come next spring Congress would cut off appropriations for the war,[10] it was indeed a pretty good deal. But the president of South Vietnam, General Nguyen Van Thieu, did not notice or would not recognize the changed American and international realities. His perspective was that of decentralized world order and of the sovereign equality of states. In those terms the American concessions were intolerable.

When Kissinger arrived in Saigon to brief the South Vietnamese on the negotiations, he was prepared to apply enormous pressure to gain compli-

---

[9] Ibid., p. 1359.

[10] Early in January 1973 the Democratic Caucus in the House voted 154 to 75 to cut off all funds for Indochina military operations. The Senate Democratic Caucus more than matched it with a 36 to 12 ratio. Nixon, *RN*, p. 742.

ance. All the same, the president of the small country and a government which since Ngo Dinh Diem had become totally dependent on us refused to act the pawn in a great power game. General Thieu rejected an agreement made by the United States, a superpower and ally, and supported by the Soviet Union, another superpower, and China, the preeminent regional power.[11] He insisted that any settlement must contain absolute guarantees of the Demilitarized Zone and the complete withdrawal of North Vietnamese forces.[12] After all, was not the building and protecting of an independent South Vietnam the purpose of American military intervention in the first place? Kissinger, utterly frustrated, returned to Washington.

A few days before our national elections it was a fair-sized crisis. What made it worse was that most Americans had no idea just what was holding up the settlement, and those who knew did not worry that South Vietnam was being sacrificed as a pawn in a gambit for strategic advantage. Americans had had it with South Vietnam. The communists could have it. With our compliments.

All along, the Soviets and the Chinese were watching closely. Each for its own special reasons remained curious: just how far would America go in using military power to support its foreign policy? What they witnessed was a calculated, at times raw, exercise of American power against friend and foe alike. North Vietnam would be forced dramatically to make further concessions. Our demands were mostly cosmetic, but the point was that they were *our* demands. Hanoi balked and had to face our military might. The president ordered the reseeding of the mines in Haiphong Harbor, the resumption of aerial reconnaissance, and most dramatic of all: massive B-52 strikes on the Hanoi-Haiphong area.[13] Within days the enemy had had enough and were ready to settle.

---

[11] Some similarities with the pre-Munich negotiations are indeed striking.

[12] Nixon, *RN*, p. 702.

[13] The North Vietnamese, the Soviets, and the Chinese knew what this was all about, but just in case some Americans, particularly some of our military leaders, might be slow in understanding, the president made it clear. "The day after the bombing began I think I shook Admiral Moore (Chairman of the Joint Chiefs of Staff) when I called him and said, `I don't want any more of this crap about the fact that we couldn't hit this target or that one. This is your chance to use military power effectively to win this war, and if you don't, I'll consider you responsible!' I stressed that we must hit and hit hard or there was no point in doing it at all. If the enemy detected any reticence in our actions, they would discount the whole exercise." Nixon, *RN*, p. 734.

South Vietnam too would be forced dramatically. Kissinger's deputy, General Haig, flew to Saigon with the new, somewhat improved draft, but one which still permitted organized communist forces to control some areas of the country. On January 16 he saw President Thieu and presented him with a letter from the president of the United States. In it Nixon made it clear that he had decided to initial the agreement on January 23 and sign it on January 27. "I will do so," he wrote, "if necessary, alone." He continued: In that case I shall have to explain publicly that your government obstructs peace. The result will be an inevitable and immediate termination of U.S. economic and military assistance which cannot be forestalled by a change of personnel in your government.[14] It was an ultimatum, simple and brutal, with a fixed, very short time limit. No diplomatic fuss, no muss. You must do what we tell you or ELSE. President Thieu, reluctant and resisting to the very last minute, looked across his desk at the American special envoy. "I have done my best," he said woefully. "I have done all that I can do for my country." Then he accepted the agreement. In a world where the superpowers at least tacitly cooperated in the settling of disputes, he had no more of a choice than had his North Vietnamese counterpart.

The agreement was duly signed. U.S. forces were withdrawn from Indochina "with honor," and our foreign policy could turn to other, global matters. The United Nations was meeting regularly in New York, but what really mattered were regular high-level exchanges among the United States, the Soviet Union, and China and annual summit meetings between the United States and the Soviet Union.

THE UNRAVELING OF DÉTENTE

An understanding between the superpowers of a shared vested interest in world peace was surely a plus, but balance-of-power politics, though perhaps better than international anarchy, did present serious problems to American foreign policy. To begin with, it was hard on our alliances. Our friends, some until recently very powerful countries themselves, were accustomed to participate in shaping international events. With détente when all the great issues would be discussed and possibly settled by Nixon and Brezhnev (with some assistance from China), the position of our allies in decision-making would be reduced to a subsidiary role. Our allies moreover had their own interests, which to them were of special, often vital

---

[14] Ibid., p. 746.

significance. Now in superpower politics their interests would be reduced to secondary importance. That is how it was, and under this scheme that is how it must be. All the same, our allies did not like it. Across the Pacific the Japanese were grumbling about "Nixon shocks." Across the Atlantic people were not amused when the president announced his intention to make 1973 "The Year of Europe," nor when he ordered a global military alert in October 1973 but did not consult them and (with the exception of Britain) did not even inform them until two hours after the fact. To the South Latin Americans saw new evidence of *Yanqui* arrogance and neglect. Governments and people everywhere wondered what America was doing, what the United States and the Soviet Union with the help of China would decide about their fate.

Détente and balance-of-power politics were also hard on the nonaligned states of Asia and Africa. They had enjoyed much profit from the conflict of major powers. Indeed their security they firmly believed rested largely on it. They had even more at stake. Until recently most were colonies, part of an imperial system. As such they did enjoy some benefits but paid a very high tribute in human dignity. They had struggled for and attained independence. Now at last they would hear no more nonsense about the inferiority of the "colored races," or the "dependency" of certain peoples. In the United Nations General Assembly—the Security Council was dead-locked by the Cold War—they were equal for all to see with their former colonial rulers. Regardless of race or color: one state, one vote. As human beings in world affairs they had a *right* to be treated as equals. It felt good. It felt good to be able to address the General Assembly or other interna-tional forums and harangue about imperialist exploitation while delegates from Western Europe sat in respectful silence.

It felt good to assume a superior moral tone against the United States. During Prime Minister Nehru's visit President Kennedy tried to develop a dialogue, but "question after question [the Indian prime minister] answered with monosyllables or a sentence or two at most." The president found it very discouraging but he kept his good humor and kept on trying.[15] Afterwards somewhat anxiously he asked his ambassador to India how he thought things had gone. India was important. Nehru was satisfied. His daughter, Prime Minister Indira Gandhi, used her toast at a state dinner in Washington to instruct Lyndon B. Johnson on morality and the Vietnam War. He was furious; she was pleased.

---

[15] John Kenneth Galbraith, *Ambassador's Journal* (Boston: Houghton Mifflin, 1969), p. 248.

All this was changing now. Henry Kissinger, visiting New Delhi on his secret trip to China, was subjected to a similar treatment. He did not bother to debate. Her country, alas, was not important, and it didn't matter that she was not pleased or satisfied. Another example of the new reality. In 1973 while war raged in the Middle East, the United Nations Security Council stood by helplessly until Henry Kissinger flew to Moscow and negotiated an agreement. Suddenly the two superpowers introduced a joint resolution for cease-fire, and China let it be known that while it disapproved, it would not vote against it. In less than four hours the Security Council by unanimous vote (with one abstention) approved the resolution. This was remarkable in itself, but otherwise the debate was made noteworthy by a lament of the Indian ambassador that the smaller powers had become irrelevant. In a world order where power dominated and a concert of superpowers decided, the rhetoric on sovereign equality sounded hollow. Vast masses of mankind could hardly help wonder whether their change from a dependent colony to a third-class independent state was really an advance. Certainly in terms of human dignity after the experiment in decentralized world order, it represented a keenly felt retrogression.

The most unsatisfactory consequence of balance-of-power politics, however, is that it focuses single-mindedly on the realities of the international environment and in general ignores the exigencies of the domestic environment. This is a no-win strategy. As our Vietnam experience should teach us, in any straight confrontation the domestic environment is bound to win. In our democratic system with elected officials the mood and will of domestic constituencies will trump any strategy that rests principally on the logic of external conditions. These conditions influence our elections indirectly, but they rarely decide their outcome.

VIETNAM ONCE AGAIN—THE END GAME

Whether a successful system of balance-of-power politics—something along the lines of the nineteenth century—could have emerged in the late twentieth century may be moot. With the Watergate scandal engulfing the Nixon administration, such an endeavor became a hopeless quest. By the Second Supplemental Appropriations Act for Fiscal Year 1973 Congress tied the president's hand in Indochina. It prohibited any American military action in the area.

President Nixon resigned in August 1974. Kissinger stayed on. His reputation helped, but American credibility began to slide down a slippery slope under President Ford. In early March 1975 communist forces felt secure enough to assume the offensive in Cambodia and from their enclaves in South Vietnam. Neither the Cambodian nor the South Vietnamese army performed with distinction. What about the United States of America? How did we do? On March 17 at a news conference President Ford allowed that events in Southeast Asia tended to validate the "domino theory" and insisted that the existence of a noncommunist government in Cambodia was vital to our interests. This, five days after the House of Representatives by a resounding margin refused to vote any more money for the region. By the end of the month defenses were crumbling all over Indochina. "Neither friend nor adversaries," intoned the president of the United States (April 3, 1975), "should interpret South Vietnamese losses as a sign that U.S. commitments will not be honored world wide." And the losses were about to become total. Panic gripped the land. Riots by South Vietnamese seeking to escape were becoming commonplace. Before the end of the month the State Department was considering the evacuation of civilian refugees. Congress had no intention to help and was busy making sure that the president should have no chance to do so either. Corralled, all President Ford could think of was the evacuation by air of Vietnamese orphans. This was at most a faint symbolic gesture, and even that went wrong when early in April a U.S. transport plane crashed and burned killing at least 100 children. It was, of course, far too late, but on April 10 the president requested $722 million emergency aid. Congress refused to consider any support for the South Vietnamese armed forces. To be sure, the Senate was willing to consider granting some funds, provided they were used only for humanitarian aid, and the House was willing to permit the use of American forces to protect evacuation from Saigon. It was all a charade. By April 23, that is in six weeks, the president tossed in the towel. "The war in Indochina is finished as far as America is concerned," he announced. A week later Cambodia had fallen; South Vietnam surrendered.[16]

All in all this was not a very impressive performance by America—not at all worthy of a superpower. There followed a ludicrous sequel. Two weeks later (May 12) a U.S. merchant vessel, the *Mayaguez*, was seized off the shores of Cambodia by a communist band. Cambodia had no navy and whatever government it had was busy murdering or forcing its own people out of the cities. At last here was a challenge we could handle. The U.S. Navy was ordered into action. The U.S. Marines stormed an island. The *Mayaguez* was released. The "rescue" should demonstrate to the world, proclaimed Secretary of State Kissinger, that "there are limits beyond

---

[16] *The New York Times*, March 13, 18, 29, April 4, 5, 11, 23, 24 and 30. All front-page stories.

which the U.S. cannot be pushed."[17] Two days later the president complimented our military men for "the skill and courage" of those engaged in the
rescue. It made only page twenty-one of *The New York Times*. Page four
reported an interview with the captain of the *Mayaguez*. Apparently the
marines had stormed the wrong island after the ship had already been
released!

MUDDLING THROUGH

And so it went. Before the year was out there was trouble in Africa.
Portugal withdrew from its colony of Angola. The Popular Movement for
the Liberation of Angola was supported by the Soviet Union. Its surrogate,
Cuba, had sent regular forces to the country. They were opposed by another
group which the U.S. government preferred. Well, perhaps not the U.S.
government, just the Executive Branch. On December 16 Congress voted
to prohibit American military intervention in the area. Three days later the
Senate felt it necessary to vote (54:22) to cut off funds even for covert
operations in the area. Unintimidated by such firmness, President Castro
announced that Cuban military forces would stay in Angola to keep peace.[18]
When global initiatives from the Western Hemisphere came from Cuba and
not the United States, international order was clearly in shambles again.

It did not help that the public had not yet recovered from the Watergate
scandal and still lacked confidence in presidential leadership. It did not help
that congressmen and senators, senior and junior, each and all thought they
knew just what to do in foreign affairs. And it did not help that the man
who moved into the White House on January 20, 1977, had practically no
experience in world politics.

President Jimmy Carter had ideals and definite views on American
foreign policy, but if he had a broad concept, a global framework of his
own, it escaped discovery. During the campaign he showed disdain for
détente, but once in office he and his secretary of state took pride in
"steering a balanced course." Specifically in the case of the Soviet Union
he thought that "balancing competition with cooperation" described the
proper course, a description that simply explained in English what détente
really meant.[19] During the campaign Jimmy Carter also rejected what he
called the "Lone Ranger" approach to foreign policy, but all along his

---

[17] Ibid., May 17, p. 1.

[18] Ibid., December 17, p. 1; December 20, p. 8; December 23, p. 5.

[19] Vance, *Hard Choices*, pp. 84, 120 ff.

national security adviser saw international relations as a grand power play starring the Soviet Union and the United States with China and possibly Western Europe in supporting roles. Lesser assignments would be granted to "the newly emerging regional 'influentials'" specified at one point as Venezuela, Nigeria, Saudi Arabia, Iran, India, and Indonesia.[20] The rest were extras—just filling the stage. It is worth noting that when Zbigniew Brzezinski published his memoirs he chose the title *Power and Principle*. Power came first. No less revealing is that the large section under the heading "On the Same Earth" (124 pages) in the president's own memoirs was devoted mostly (two-thirds) to relations with the Nixon partners, the Soviet Union and China.

Early in the administration some thought to find a clue to the president's global (macro) vision in his determination to negotiate, sign, and manage ratification of the Panama Canal treaty, which gave up our control of the Canal Zone and promised to turn over management of the Canal itself to Panama by the end of the century. Strategically it was a hazardous, and in terms of domestic politics, a controversial move. The question arose: did the president take the security risks, was he willing to pay the enormous political price at home as an investment in hemisphere solidarity, the rock upon which he hoped to build an American global design? It was certainly an interesting idea, but a closer examination revealed all kinds of contradictions. Just a few months into his administration (March 11, 1977) Brazil, the largest South American power, felt compelled to cancel the military assistance treaty that had been mutually satisfactory for twenty-five years. By the fall of the next year (November 1978) tensions with Mexico, our closest Latin neighbor, had risen to such alarming levels that a set of new policies (Presidential Review Memo #41) was proposed. Then there were the *faux pas*. Venezuela held democratic elections, the opposition won, power was transferred in a peaceful, orderly manner. Quite a significant achievement. To the inauguration of the new president the democratic countries of the hemisphere sent their heads of state. The United States was represented by the wife of the vice president. Another case: President Carter's visit to Mexico where during his toast at the state *dinner* he unaccountably dragged in a reference to "Montezuma's revenge." If indeed there had ever been an intention to build hemispheric solidarity, it was lost in implementation.

The Carter administration, of course, had other initiatives as well. American diplomacy mounted an offensive against white minority

---

[20] Brzezinski, *Power and Principle*, pp. 53–54.

governments in Africa; we would set an example by being more "humane and moral" in our foreign relations. The president himself guided "the peace process" in the Middle East leading to the Camp David accords and their partial implementation. These, however, were moves of primarily regional significance and reflected (if not motivated by) domestic political pressures. We were not engaged in building international order. Meanwhile our credibility as a superpower continued to erode. In Nicaragua we helped to overthrow the pro-American Somoza dictatorship but did little when its successors established a hostile communist tyranny. In Ethiopia with Soviet and *Cuban* help a brutal communist dictatorship was murdering its own people. The Soviet Union invaded and occupied its neighbor Afghanistan. Iran callously violated the most rudimentary international law by invading the American embassy and by holding our diplomats hostage.

During much of his first administration President Reagan was absorbed in domestic issues. Even so he quickly moved to restore American power and improve American credibility. Noticeably his initiatives were military. He significantly accelerated the military modernization and buildup that had begun under his predecessor. Then in Lebanon, Grenada, and Libya he demonstrated that the United States was once again able and willing to project force overseas but without getting trapped into escalation by it. Meanwhile the peace process in the Middle East was not pressed; the Caribbean Basin development never really got off the ground; the quiet diplomacy in Southern Africa was practically inaudible. Noticeably U.S. foreign policy was *ad hoc* and reactive. Others set our agenda for action. Unlike in the days of Truman, Eisenhower, Kennedy, and Nixon we did not project a vision of the future. Our policy was an aggregate of fragments. Insofar as the administration had a concept of the international environment, it lacked subtlety. It was a world of stark contrasts (of communist red and true blue), where all issues were reduced to a common denominator: the mortal struggle between the forces of peace and disorder. The world was a stage with only two stars and many more or less inconsequential extras.

In the fall of 1985 the president had a particularly suitable opportunity to air his view of the world. He was addressing the fortieth anniversary session of the United Nations General Assembly and was offering "a new commitment, a fresh start." It would be based on the plain and simple fact that "the differences between America and the Soviet Union are deep and abiding." Management of these differences, he explained to an audience composed mostly of the representatives of the "Third World" countries, was the principal task. Conflict in Afghanistan, Cambodia, Ethiopia, Angola, and Nicaragua all "share the common characteristic: they are the consequence of an ideology imposed from without, dividing nations and creating regimes that are, almost from the day they take power, at war with their own people."[21] The approach, the president suggested, was a three-tier process. First, bring together the communist and democratic elements of the country (or region) for purposes of negotiation. Second, provide Soviet and U.S. help toward achieving agreement. Third, welcome each country back into the world economy (presumably with some economic assistance). It was not much of a design for international order. It was not an approach that was new or particularly relevant to most in the audience. They applauded politely.

The position did not change under his successor. President Bush was suspicious, at times disdainful of "that vision thing." He did have a brief shining moment during the Gulf Crisis, and he did take a controversial initiative on the North American Free Trade Area, but for the rest of the time, e.g., in Somalia, his foreign policy was reluctantly reactive. President Clinton was more or less dragged into the Middle East peace process. After the Israelis and the PLO, then the Israelis and Jordan, made their historic breakthroughs, he presided over the ceremonies handsomely. After much vacillation, the United States took the initiative of orchestrating the signing of a peace treaty on Bosnia and organizing an implementation force.

We seem to be once again in a muddle-through mode.

---

[21] *The New York Times*, October 25, 1985, p. A11.

Conclusion

Toward Leadership Abroad

We may be tempted to indulge in an essentially reactive posture of muddling through in foreign policy. The world is full of surprises. Indeed surprises are more the rule than the exception. Regularly we have to respond on very short notice to unanticipated events. Saddam Hussein's invasion of Kuwait, the collapse of the Soviet Union, and the unification of Germany are only a few recent examples. We may carefully design stacks of option papers covering all kinds of contingencies, but when confronted by actual challenges, it is best to discard them and to start anew. Else we may become misled by preconceived patterns that, although sagacious when formulated, often miss a key element and might misguide us. A fresh look when the unpredictable actually happens has definite advantages.

Then there is the temptation of subordinating foreign policy to domestic and/or partisan rationales. Arguably President Clinton had this in mind when he insisted that "we must break down the walls in our minds between foreign and domestic policy."[1] In a way it is a matter of priorities. We can easily understand that even under normal circumstances there are not enough hours in a day for the president of the United States to cope with all the problems that need his decision. He has to delegate some, and inevitably he has to neglect some. Even problems to which he gives his

---

[1] White House Press Release, *Remarks by the President on American Security in a Changing World*, Washington, DC: George Washington University, August 3, 1996.

personal attention are necessarily ranked in importance. In our time foreign policy has become a very time-consuming subject. It is not just that there are many more countries now with which we have diplomatic relations than there were a generation ago. It is not even that international relations have become a much more complex, many more faceted, affair. The greatest burden comes from our contemporary reality that to be successful foreign policy needs not only to be effective abroad but also popular at home. Educating the American people about the main ingredients, never mind the subtleties of all the international issues, is in itself more than a full-time task. Quite probably President Carter made a sincere effort, but by his second year in office, certainly after the Camp David negotiations, he realized that he could not accomplish this. Since we no longer live in national peril and our domestic agenda is long and pressing, the opportunity costs are especially high. In presidential campaigns foreign policy rarely plays an important role. Thus, it is not too surprising that foreign issues are likely to be relegated to a low priority. The president will be inclined to address international matters when they are dramatically brought to his attention by domestic policy.

For many reasons these temptations are worth resisting. The political power ratios among the special interest groups within the American polity are not at all congruent with either the power ratios on the global scale or with the relative salience of our strategic goals. Thus, a foreign policy driven by the pressures of special interest groups is likely to be distorted. If we choose to look at the world through a telescope—which by itself may not be a bad idea—we must be certain that we do not look through the wrong end. Tyrannical governments are obnoxious to us wherever they may be. In Haiti, Liberia, Nigeria, Burma, North Korea, Cuba, and many other countries. But it is not statesmanship *nor is it in our national interest* to tolerate all of them except one (Haiti), where we forcibly intervened because a special interest activist in Washington announced a hunger strike. Similarly foreign policy guided by the sensations of media headlines are likely to be arbitrarily selective. Tragically there are starving, emaciated children in many parts of the world. In Bangladesh, Cambodia, Sri Lanka, Paraguay to name only a few. To help them is in the best American tradition. But it is not statesmanship *nor is it in our national interest* to single out Somalia for our intervention because of high national media coverage and *ignore* such conditions elsewhere, including the much greater misery in nearby Sudan. Special interest groups pursuing their own at-times-questionable political or economic purposes due to their excessive influence may push American foreign policy to oppose and thwart the needs of those states whose policies are more in the right and whose interests may well coincide with ours. Or to put it plainly: *powerful special interest groups through their clout in Washington may well line us up on the wrong side of a conflict.*

A reactive foreign policy flitting from crisis to crisis, moreover, has other severe handicaps affecting the quality of decisions. First, by the time a conflict has reached crisis proportions and hence attracted our public attention, its solution has become extremely urgent. There is little time for careful deliberation, and often the multiplier effects on broader geographic areas or long-term consequences are ignored. The conflict may have become intractable. Our choices then are reduced to massive military intervention or accepting the *fait accompli* of the aggressor. Domestic politics would generally favor the latter, which would *appear to be cheaper* in American lives and treasure. We may easily become victims of the well-known syndrome. At first we rationalize that it is too early to know the merits of the situation, that we must give the matter a careful look. Soon we slip into the second rationalization: ah, well, it is really too bad, but by now it is too late. Sorry, there is nothing we can now do about it anyway.

Perhaps the worst aspect of *ad hoc* foreign policy, however, is this: it is unworthy of America. Indeed from the very beginning of the Republic Americans were sensitive to their obligations to the human race. Jefferson called his country the world's best hope, and Lincoln called it the last best hope of earth. Later Americans would quote: "Humanity with all its fear, with all the hopes of future years, is hanging breathless on thy fate."[2] As we entered the twentieth century and our power grew with rapidly rising prominence, our vision of international order was kept alive by Presidents Wilson, Roosevelt, and Truman. President Kennedy, speaking at American University (June 12, 1963), was perhaps most eloquent in defining our international aspirations:

What kind of peace do I mean? Not the peace of the grave or the security of the slave. I am talking about genuine peace, the kind of peace that makes life on earth worth living, the kind that enables men and nations to grow and to hope and build a better life for their children—not merely peace for Americans but peace for all men and women—not merely peace in our time but peace for all time.

Most recently, President Clinton called the United States the only indispensable country.

---

[2] Henry Steele Commager, *The American Mind* (New Haven: Yale University Press, 1952), p. 11.

Considering it fairly, it is undeniable that American leadership has helped advance human development in the last centuries. Admittedly so far we have not accomplished a breakthrough to international order, but that is no reason for us to give up. Most other countries look to us for leadership. Especially because we are now in a unique position. The United States, in fact, is the only superpower. Ours is the largest economy. Perhaps more important we are at the leading edge of the information revolution. We have enormous leverage on the global scale. And this is not all. Not least important is the moral dimension. We must keep reminding ourselves: the world is now in a very fragile transitional stage. The danger of regression into the preeminence of ethnicity and other radically divisive ascriptive solidarities is increasingly menacing. A reactive foreign policy is not likely to prevent it. At the same time, we do have a *unique opportunity* for a new quantum leap toward global order. A reactive foreign policy will surely blow it.

Saying all this, to speak of peace and the imperative of American leadership abroad, to provide arguments in support, however, is the easy part. It might discredit *ad hoc* reactive foreign policy, but what is needed is to build a positive national consensus, in fact, a proactive public conviction that international order has become an integral part of our national interest. And that is much more difficult in the absence of a clear and present danger to our national security. What makes it especially difficult is that we do not have a model to follow. It presents the daunting challenge of historic innovation. But the question is: if not we, then who?

Let us keep in mind: it would be a tragic mistake if we would simply replicate past efforts and thus repeat past mistakes. Conventional wisdom we have inherited from the Europeans holds, and past history supports the notion, that international relations is a struggle for power, and hence order depended on power. Our choices were hegemony, the traditional method of regional empires, or a "system" of balance of power. In the event the United States, its people, and its government have no interest whatever in hegemony but will not permit any other country to impose its own, so the question does not arise. But from time to time we have been enticed by the formula of a balance of power. During the Cold War, it is said, we followed a bipolar power pattern. Now statesmen and scholars look for stability in a multipolar system, reminiscent of the formula posited by the Congress of Vienna (1815). That seems to be the compass of their vision.

There are just three things wrong with the balance-of-power approach. First, it does not seem to work. Even in theory a bipolar system is inherently unstable. There is never a satisfactory balance because neither major power or coalition is content with equivalence. The uncertainty factor was discussed previously.[3] Neither side can afford to relax. Both keep worrying that the other will surreptitiously gain a decisive advantage. The theoretical solution of a "balancer" was clearly imaginative but did not help much in the past. For example, Britain, the balancer in the late nineteenth century, did not restrain a contentious arms race and growing national antagonisms on the continent. Indeed she joined one side and then launched a massive ship-building program.[4] More recently in 1972 Nixon's détente was in place with China as the balancer. It did not restrain the Soviet Union's desperate gamble in the 1970s to achieve first-strike capability. And in the 1980s it did not restrain the United States from responding with its own massive buildup. All along, China was busy developing its own nuclear weapons arsenal.

Second, as a practical matter the multipolar model has no relevance now. A precondition of the Congress of Vienna system that the major powers be roughly equal in power simply does not apply. The United States is just too powerful. What kind of combination could offer some balancing equivalence? Why would the Europeans want to take an adversary position to us? Indeed what would be the basis of the adversary position of any other bloc? Ideology: democracy versus fascism? Political conflicts built on a chauvinist pursuit of power? Ah yes, the economic competition of the free market: a world of regional economic blocs. Just how it would work in reality is unclear. Just how it would work when the gross disparities in military capabilities and communications resources are added is anybody's guess.

Third and perhaps most important, the American people have never been comfortable with the notion of peace through balance of tension among states in juxtaposition. In case of a national security imperative they would use military force in self-defense and use it with gusto. In support of international order they have at times resorted to military and economic power reluctantly, usually with indifferent results. Frankly Americans do not have much confidence that power politics would bring peace.

That does not mean that in the past the American approach to peace and order discounted power in international relations, but *it placed its faith primarily on institutions.* They, we hoped, would prove to be more reliable in the long run. They would be more just and stable because they could transcend the fashions and passions of national moods as well as the

---

[3] See Chapter 12, p. 298.

[4] Robert K. Massie, *Dreadnaught: Britain, Germany, and the Coming of the Great War* (New York: Random House, 1991).

vicissitudes of personal successions. Above all, institutionalized processes of settling disputes through compromise were likely to be more peaceful and generally more agreeable. American statesmen felt confident that their approach was validated by empirical evidence on a smaller scale. Delegates at Philadelphia met in 1787. They wrote the American constitution, and it worked. For more than 200 years we did have (mostly) peace and order at home. Surely it is a sound precedent for the international environment.

Which is all true enough but not altogether correct. There is a caveat about the effectiveness of institutions. It requires a *minimum solidarity of a community*. Perhaps we did not notice this because our eyes casually slid over the realities of 1789. It was a time too precious to American heritage. After a victorious common struggle for independence the thirteen new states qualified at least rudimentarily as a community. Actually they were culturally and ideologically homogeneous. The Indians were excluded as foreigners, the Negroes were disqualified as less than human, and the Loyalists were chased into Canada. Moreover, after the constitution was signed, it was ratified by all the political components of the new Union. So the institutions designed in 1787 had a chance—and even then it took a civil war before the concept of the United States as singular had become generally accepted. Until then the title was in plural: These United States.

We may be moving toward an international community. The idea of the unity of the human race is more or less universally proclaimed. But in reality we did not have an international community at Versailles, we did not have one at San Francisco, and we do not have one now. Radical discontinuities within humanity, racism, ethnicity, and tribalism, we need to emphasize again and again, are still alive if not altogether well. Most recently we had dramatic demonstrations in Somalia, Rwanda, Sri Lanka, Canada, France, Belgium, not to mention the United States. Bosnia is so deeply divided that people dig up their dead to prevent them from having to rest in land controlled by their "fellow citizens" belonging to a different ethnic group. We need to emphasize over and over again: in the absence of a community and a commitment to the collective good, centrifugal forces subvert norms and soon tear apart or at the minimum trivialize institutions. With radical discontinuities among many "sovereign" states, rhetoric notwithstanding, each would apply norms according to its subjective perspective, and institutions would be used (abused) as instruments to gain parochial advantages.

The point is: this may be an auspicious time for building an international community. For one thing powerful forces that traditionally tended to divide humanity are at the moment muted. Just now, for example, we happen to be free of bitter zero-sum struggles accompanied by government-sponsored hate campaigns among the major powers. And, at least for the moment, a secular attitude is on the ascent. The comprehensive hold of religion has been loosened practically everywhere in the world. Increasingly faith has become a private matter of conscience. The radical discontinuity between faithful and unbeliever or between the believers of one religion and the believers of another has been visibly ameliorated. Ecumenicalism, tolerance, friendly relations, intermarriage have become normal. Crusades, *jihads*, and other holy wars are out of fashion—at least for now. To be sure, religion continues to play a major role in the lives of most people, and this may not, indeed need not, change. We do have some time and unless secularism is pushed as a new orthodoxy with single-minded zeal, reactionary "fundamentalist" forces (we hope) will not regain dominance.

At the same time, positive conditions that tend to intertwine human lives all over the world are multiplying almost daily. We are witnessing the spreading appeal of democracy. Its emphasis on the human individual and life on earth accentuates the improvement of the quality of life. Its egalitarian theme appeals to all classes of people. The appetite for consumer goods seems insatiable. That they are actually very similar consumer goods replicating very similar situations will quite probably expand the common experiences shared by all people—at least for a while. Here too forces of reaction are discernible. The persistence of glaring national and/or class disparities well into the future may fuel resentment then hostility and produce volatile cleavages. For some time, though, capitalism and democracy have been in fashion throughout the world.

What makes this a uniquely opportune time, however, are recent phenomenal breakthroughs in technology, which transcend customary human barriers. The second half of our century saw extraordinary advances in transportation and communication. Jumbo jet airplanes, long-distance/direct-dial telephones, television, satellite dishes. In about a day we can travel to almost any part of the globe; in just minutes we can reach and speak to most persons; with a push of a button we can see the news and the surrounding conditions in distant lands.

Meanwhile we can now observe evidence that people all over the world would indeed welcome a chance to get to know each other, that they enjoy getting together and working toward common accomplishments. The United Nations and its specialized agencies have developed the habit of sponsoring worldwide conferences on a whole variety of subjects, as have regional groupings. In addition, nongovernmental organizations (NGOs), private venture operations (PVOs), international regimes, and all sorts of other combinations assemble regularly to exchange ideas. And, of course, there are the Olympics. The centennial games (1996) were attended by more than 200 "national" teams. President Clinton made the point:

I believe we love the Olympics because they work the way we think the world ought to work. They are possible because all different kinds of people come together in mutual respect and mutual acceptance of the rules of the game. No one wins by breaking their opponents' legs or by bad-mouthing their opponents in a public forum. Instead victory comes from doing well in a good way. And all who strive are honored as we saw when our volunteers cleared the track for the brave, injured marathon runner who was the very last finisher in the race.[5]

Just recently, exponential development in computer technology has immeasurably expanded our individual capabilities to address complex issues and manage multidimensional problems. A combination of all the new technologies produced the "third wave." Internet, at first an arrangement among some major universities to pool quickly and easily vast stores of available information, burst out of its limits providing commercial access (dot com) to practically anyone on a World Wide Web. And this is just the beginning. We are moving fast into a new information age that we cannot even imagine.

Two consequences are already clear. First, with very little effort we can establish personal relations with masses of fellow human beings; we can learn much about them and quite possibly learn to like them. Second, we may now be able to manage previously intractable challenges. True, a reaction may set in revisiting the Tower of Babel and its tragic aftermath. It is no less true that together men and women all over the world may move into a very much better world. Hence the question: if not now, then when?

If we were to choose to assume once again the leadership toward international order, it may be wise to try a somewhat different approach. In fact, a double-track approach. First, we need to recognize the possibility of human regression and be prepared to meet that contingency. Thus, we must still keep watchful eyes on the contemporary reality of power and be prepared for all the perils to our security we can foresee. Second and no less important, *we should take a chance on human advance* and invest our leadership in the long-term goal of transforming the international arena into an international community. For this an enormous effort would be required, nothing less than a fundamental reorientation of the mind-set of the opinion-leading groups.

---

[5] White House Press Release, *Remarks by the President on American Security*, August 5, 1996.

Moving along the second track, first and foremost we shall have to agree upon and then declare time and time again that our foreign policy is guided by universalist motives, specifically a commitment to the unity of the human race. It will mean reiterating words of Jefferson, Lincoln, and all the other great Americans. John Kennedy told the Irish parliament (June 28, 1963): "The supreme reality of our time . . . [is] our indivisibility as children of God and our common vulnerability on this planet." Most recently in January 1997 those who attended President Clinton's second inauguration and visited the tents on the Mall with the theme of a "celebration of American civilization," those who attended the inaugural gala, and those who listened to his inaugural address were left with no doubt: the unity of the human race is our national goal; we are on our way to global civilization.

Inspiring as such pronouncements and symbols are, we need to be more specific by putting their meaning into the context of our time. For the reaction is already out there, in our international environment, even in very sophisticated circles at home. "The principal responsibility of Western leaders," wrote Samuel P. Huntington, a very distinguished political scientist, "is . . . to preserve and renew the unique qualities of Western civilization. . . . Neither globalism nor isolationism, neither multilaterism nor unilaterism will serve American interests."[6] For many it is a very attractive argument. The golden mean. It may become a great temptation for Americans who much prefer minding their own domestic business. Indeed if progress toward a global community will fail or will not even be attempted, it may well become the national choice by default.

A close look, however, reveals its reactionary direction: "The future of the West depends in large part on the unity of the West" or such alarmist admonitions as "the peoples of the West must hang together, or they will hang separately."[7] These are exclusionary, divisive views perhaps more characteristic of culturally stagnant, nationally homogeneous Western European countries than dynamic America. Obviously they are in direct conflict with the direction of our inclusionary domestic environment so proud of its diversity.

Our ethnic composition is becoming more universal. Citizens with Western European ancestors are becoming a smaller and smaller minority. WASPs are becoming an endangered species. President Reagan in his

---

[6] Samuel P. Huntington, "The West Unique, Not Universal," *Foreign Affairs*, November/December 1996, pp. 45–46.

[7] Ibid., pp. 43, 45.

address to the United Nations General Assembly (1985) vividly made the point: "The blood of each nation courses through the American vein and feeds the spirit that compels us to involve ourselves in the fate of this good earth." And that is not just rhetoric. It is a fact. Look around. Watch our television programs, attend our popular concerts, take in a Broadway show. Observe our patterns of social interaction and you can easily see an interracial, interethnic, and intercultural mix, e.g., Tiger Woods, American. In terms of economic relations we have begun to reinforce the American market with NAFTA. Meeting in December 1994 in Miami, thirty-four of the hemisphere's leaders (all but Cuba) agreed to work toward a free-trade area of the Americas (FTAA). In his visit to Central America (May 1997) President Clinton recommitted the United States to this goal.

Meanwhile American eyes have been turning to Asia. In our daily lives we have become accustomed to relying on imports from the Pacific Rim. Since 1978 the majority of our trade has shifted to that region, and our values have become more global. Unquestionably American culture is embedded in Western civilization with its Christian, Greco-Roman, and Hebrew roots. Justifiably we may be proud of this. But at least during the last generation we have been enriched by massive contributions from the East, from the great civilizations of China, India, and Islam. Add to this the ancient cultures of Africa. Strictly speaking ours is no longer a Western civilization, not even the American phase of Western civilization. Each year our country is less and less oriented toward Europe. It may be sad, but there it is. We really need a public debate on this. Predictably any such debate would be a ding-dong affair. But at the core of the contest will be the vital question: *just what does it mean to be an American*? It is hoped the president will lead the debate, and possibly in the end we shall arrive at a national consensus.

There are, of course, invaluable elements in Western civilization that must be recognized as pillars of a global civilization. One is the unique value of the human individual. "All things have a price," wrote Immanuel Kant, "only man [*Mensch*] has dignity. It is contrary to the nature of man to be used as a means; he is an end in himself." Another valuable element of Western civilization is its proposition that "all men are created equal." No radical cleavages among human beings; ethnic and other ascriptive commitments must give way to the overriding value of the unity of the human race. Finally, we need a general commitment of settling all disputes through compromise preferably by the disputants and those in closest geographic proximity. Beyond these three tenets, however, there is room for wide latitude about social and political values and respect for the different ways of our fellow human beings. Monarchies are not inherently inferior, and the system of separation of church and state is not universally preferable, to mention only two examples.

On our way toward an international community we must make it clear that we would avoid two excesses. We must resist the panacea of world government. We have enough problems with public institutions on the national scale. Indeed national solidarity can make a constructive contribution by reinforcing a person's identity and dignity. The love of one's own country is a noble passion, but its limits are well expressed by Edith Cavell. An English nurse, she was convicted by the Germans of spying during World War I. Just before her execution her last words were: ". . . patriotism is not enough. [We] must have no hatred . . . toward anyone." Similarly we must make it clear that in our view the advancement to global civilization emphatically does not mean inculturation into Western civilization. We have learned at home that integrated diversity is much preferable to homogenized assimilation. Publicly and dramatically, privately and diplomatically, we ought to make these points.

Still in the final analysis our leadership would have to rest on our own example, what we do, not what we say. For some time now we have been engaged in a monumental effort: a United States of America where homogeneity is not the preferred standard, where diversity is not just a transitional inconvenience along the way to assimilation. It is a cherished value, and a successful integration into a community is a positive goal. No one claims that we have succeeded altogether. Obviously we have a long way to go, and there is much we need to learn. Even so, any fair evaluation will conclude that our progress has been phenomenal. Look back in history and find anything like it. Look around the world today and find a country that can match it. But we have to keep pushing and experimenting. And we have to set an example of being determined to get to know our fellow human beings beyond our political borders and being eager to help them and to learn from them.[8] Through our own example of moderation and tolerance we could try to help advance the progressive integration of the human race. Carefully, incrementally we could move together toward a community through contributions from many races, religions, and regions that would blend together the traditions and dignities of all the civilized elements of the human race.

---

[8] In the 1994–1995 school year the number of Americans studying abroad rose to 84,403, which is a 10.8 percent increase over the previous two years. Associate Press dispatch on a report by the Institute of International Education, December 1, 1996.

INDISPENSABLES

Since power is an international reality, we cannot simply ignore it and soar blithely to the ethereal heights of idealism. Indeed power is quite useful, even necessary, in setting and enforcing the parameters of civilized behavior. But when we use it, we should do so sparingly, deliberately, and prudently: not merely when leading elements of our domestic environment are annoyed or just because others act in a manner of which many of us disapprove. There has to be a major challenge to peace and international order so clearly evident that it would attract the solidarity of other countries to a common sanction. Whether we shall assume leadership toward a global community or remain content with a reactive foreign policy posture, however, we must not tolerate three kinds of international behavior. Nuclear proliferation, genocide, and terrorism are serious threats to our national interest, as well as being inimical to civilization. It would be wise to build an international consensus or at the very least a national consensus behind the use of *all necessary means* to discourage and punish, if not eliminate, these practices.

We can have no prospect for peace as long as radical or potentially radical governments can acquire *strategic nuclear weapons*. Graduate students engaged in research can now find out from publicly available sources how to build nuclear bombs. A Princeton undergraduate did just that. The necessary raw materials may now be bought or stolen in the former Soviet Union.[9] The delivery systems (long-range missiles) are still a big problem but may not be for very long.[10] Many countries are busily working on this. Testifying before a Senate committee James Woolsey,

---

[9] There are six known incidents. In September 1992 1.5 kilograms of weapons-grade HEU were diverted from the Luch Scientific Production Association in Russia by a Luch employee. In November 1993 a captain of the Russian navy stole ten pounds of HEU from a submarine fuel storage facility in Murmansk. In March 1994 three men were arrested in St. Petersberg trying to sell 3.05 kilograms of weapons-usable HEU. In May 1994 5.6 grams of nearly pure plutonium-239 were seized by German officials. In August 1994 560 grams of an oxide-uranium-plutonium mixture were seized at Munich Airport from a flight originating in Moscow. In December 1994 2.72 kilograms of weapons-grade uranium were seized by police in Prague. Graham T. Allison et al., *Avoiding Nuclear Anarchy: Containing the Threat of Loose Russian Nuclear Weapons and Fissile Material,* Cambridge, MA.: MIT Press, 1996.

[10] The National Intelligence Estimate in 1996 (though originally drafted in 1995) estimated that no new countries can acquire strategic missiles before 2010.

director of the CIA, warned (February 24, 1993): "Nonproliferation poses one of the most complex challenges the intelligence community will face the remainder of the century."

In 1968 we did sign with the United Kingdom and the Soviet Union a Treaty on the Non-Proliferation of Nuclear Weapons. In it the powers pledged not to transfer materials and technology needed for the development of nuclear weapons to other states. By the time the treaty came into force in 1970 some one hundred "non-nuclear weapon states also joined promising to forego the development of such weapons and to permit international inspection of their nuclear facilities." On May 11, 1995, more than 170 nations agreed to "extend in perpetuity" the 1968 treaty.[11]

Which is fine but not quite enough. Those countries that did not sign are, of course, not bound by it. Some that signed, moreover, were in the past violating it in secret. Will that change in the future? Or will others follow their lead? Will it get worse? What remedies are available? One is a preemptive strike. Recognizing Iraqi nuclear ambitions as a mortal threat, Israel did just that. Before the Iraqis could develop a bomb, not much before, Israeli jets swooped down and destroyed their plant at Osirak. The Soviet Union may have considered such action against China in the early 1970s. Though denied by all official sources, it is widely held that Soviet diplomats raised at least hypothetically a joint strike with the United States on Chinese facilities.

In the past the United States was wholly opposed to any such action. It is just not our way of doing things. Not in the movies. John Wayne or Gary Cooper would never draw first. Not in reality. When during the Korean War the subject of "preventive war" was raised by his secretary of the navy, President Truman quickly and sternly disciplined him. "I have always been opposed even to the thought of such a war," he explained in his memoirs. "There is nothing more foolish than to think that war can be stopped by war. You don't 'prevent' anything by war except peace."[12] A decade later during the Cuban Missile Crisis, a crisis far more perilous to our national existence, some members of the highest level Executive Committee urged a surprise air strike. They were firmly admonished. During the discussion Attorney General Robert Kennedy made it abundantly clear that "with all the memory of Pearl Harbor and all the responsibility we would have to bear in the world the United States could [not] possibly order such an

---

[11] *The New York Times*, May 12, 1995, p. A-1.

[12] Harry S. Truman, *Memoirs*, vol. 2 (Garden City, NY: Doubleday, 1956), p. 383.

operation. For 175 years we had not been such a country. . . . We were fighting for something more than survival, and a sneak attack would constitute a betrayal of our heritage and our ideals."[13] All the same, we ought to think about it. What would we do were we to learn that Iran or Libya, for example, was on the threshold of producing nuclear weapons? Even if we would not preempt, we may be unwise to publicly foreclose the option.

There may be another option—one much more in line with American tradition. Instead of using military force, use money. Buy restraint! Surely it is reasonable for any government to wish to improve the quality of life of its people. Often such programs require energy resources. Surely it is reasonable for Americans to help. We could subsidize programs based on nonnuclear energy. In extreme cases we could subsidize nuclear power programs that would be limited for peaceful economic purposes.

Actually this is a very recent, highly controversial notion. Its parent was former president Jimmy Carter who negotiated the "deal" with Kim Il Sung, the Supreme Ruler of North Korea. The "deal" was approved after the latter's death and the succession of his son in a personal pledge by President Clinton. He addressed it to His Excellency Kim Jong Il, Supreme Leader of the Democratic People's Republic of Korea.

I wish to confirm to you that I will use the full powers of my office to facilitate arrangements for the financing and construction of a light-water nuclear power reactor project within the DPRK and the funding and implementation of interim energy alterations for the Democratic People's Republic of Korea pending completion of the first reactor unit of the light-water reactor project. In addition, in the event that this reactor project is not completed for reasons beyond the control of the DPRK, I will use the full powers of my office to provide to the extent necessary, such as a project from the United States, subject to the approval of the U.S. Congress.

It is noteworthy that by this agreement the president proposed to subsidize economic development in a recalcitrant communist state that during its entire existence placed highest priority on military power and was visibly unconcerned about the material well-being, least of all the human rights, of its people. It is now a pathetically bankrupt state under the control of a man with a very unstable personality. So how would this Carter/Clinton innovation work as a general policy? Probably not at all.

---

[13] Arthur M. Schlessinger, Jr., *A Thousand Days: John F. Kennedy in the White House* (Boston: Houghton Mifflin, 1965), pp. 806–807.

Questions abound. For example: Are we paying nuclear blackmail? Are we prepared to underwrite the energy needs of other countries, more democratic countries, friendlier countries?

Meanwhile the peril persists. The clock is ticking without any consensus solutions emerging. If we were to think about it dispassionately, one approach would probably prove to have much merit: space-based strategic defense named SDI or Star Wars according to taste. Creating a system that would severely curtail the prospects of strategic offense could conceivably deter any would-be Saddam or Khadaffi. Even if they could manage a clandestine development of nuclear weapons, they could be prevented from using them. Not by *our* first strike but the interception of *their* first strike. Admittedly it would be a colossal task. It would take quite some time, a decade at least. But we still have some time. It would cost countless billions of dollars. One estimate suggests $60 billion, but such estimates are notoriously short of the actual cost. We could manage the money if we really wanted to.

Meanwhile some countries continued testing nuclear devices. In the face of almost unanimous global condemnation of their recent series of nuclear tests, China and France pledged to desist and signed a treaty to that effect. Solemnly before the United Nations with all the media coverage mobilized, President Clinton himself penned his name on it on September 24, 1996. But alas it was just one of those things. The treaty would not be binding unless all forty-four countries involved would ratify it! Actually one such country, India, refused outright even to sign it, and another, Pakistan, reportedly had its own approach. It would sign the treaty—that would keep the United States happy—and then not ratify it—that would remove the need to have to abide by it.

Another example of activity we ought not tolerate in any circumstances is *genocide*. With the holocaust fresh in human memory there should be no difficulty for Americans, indeed all civilized people, to agree on this. But again the issue of enforcing this norm causes considerable disagreement abroad as well as at home. The problem is that the guilty ones, those who perpetrate the atrocities and even more so those who introduce the venom, are usually protected by a shield of spellbound followers. It is extremely difficult to get at the criminals—it took a world war to do so with the Nazis—and it involved heavy innocent casualties. Thus, the reluctance to do anything at all is understandable. All the same, we may have to discuss this publicly and privately at home and abroad. For there are at least two reasons why it is vital to punish the criminals. First, we need to do so to discourage such practices in other countries. Second, we need to do so to begin the healing of the pent-up passions of the survivors of the victimized group. The zeal with which the survivors of the holocaust pursue those Germans and Eastern Europeans guilty of genocide is not just a matter of revenge. It is motivated to a great measure by a yearning for justice. After all the frightful miseries they witnessed and endured, they wish to feel that they live in a reasonably just world. They wish to be reassured that their fellow human beings care about the injustice done to them and are determined to punish crimes against the human race. It was not our finest hour when for years faced with evidence of genocide in Bosnia we, unmoved by the lessons of the 1930s, loudly condemned it but then sat back and explained that after all it was a European affair. Worse still, we supported an embargo of arms on the victims and could think of nothing more than to conspire with Iran so that they could smuggle in some weapons. Not until Congress through veto-proof majorities intervened, did the administration become active and brokered the Dayton agreement of uncertain merit. It did have a provision for the trial of mass murderers. Typically they are pursued pragmatically with a lamentable lack of vigor. This is just not good enough. To make the desired impression may require the use of force, massive force. It may mean American casualties, sacrifices for our self-respect and the progress of human civilization. A very tough sell indeed. It will need historic leadership!

A close relative of genocide is terrorism and especially *state-supported terrorism*. Buses are bombed in Jerusalem; the victims are Jewish civilians murdered because they are Jews. Bombs explode in London; the victims are British citizens killed simply because they are British. At times the victims are Americans. Fortunately so far the United States has been mostly spared from a major terrorist offensive. But the news is not good. Chemical and bacteriological weapons are now being developed by Iran, Libya, and quite possibly other governments as well. Their possibilities are distressingly manifold. Carried in small, light vessels they might be added, for example, to our central water supply or to the air we breathe. By the time we realized what had happened, masses of our people could have been poisoned or succumbed to an epidemic.

We must not let our imagination run wild. The danger is real but not immediate or indefensible. We can try to develop systems of protection. One approach is antidotes and vaccines. This, however, is a very difficult course because we cannot predict what poison or virus may be used. By far the best protection is a massive intelligence operation. But here again when it comes to implementation, it is difficult to find an agreement. Systematic international cooperation on sharing information on terrorist organizations is essential and at times has been forthcoming. Frequently though it is hindered by separate policy perspectives. Some of our European allies wish to maintain diplomatic and commercial relations with countries the United States has condemned as terrorist states. Moreover, each intelligence service jealously guards its "means and sources" secrets. To share information might reveal the way it was acquired. When the Korean Airline KL007 was shot down by Soviet fighters, Japanese intelligence had recorded the conversations between the Soviet pilots and their commanders. These clearly revealed that the pilots and their ground-based superiors knew it was a civilian airliner when the order to fire was given. Indeed the Japanese had also recorded the exuberant elation the pilots expressed at the destruction of the civilian plane. Still it required the direct personal appeal of President Reagan before the Japanese government most reluctantly was willing to release the tape.

President Clinton is optimistic. In August 1996 he reported:

Over the past four years, our intelligence services have been sharing more information than ever with other nations. We've opened up a law enforcement academy in Budapest which is training people from twenty-three nations, an FBI office in Moscow, . . . Congress gave us the funding for FBI offices in Cairo, Islamabad, Tel Aviv and Beijing.[14]

Noticeably although those are mostly overseas operations, the president assigned the tasks to the FBI. The CIA is a favored target of media attack. It is also a target of budget cuts. During the Clinton administration the CIA budget was cut 20 percent.[15] The reduction of agency personnel was about 30 percent. The phenomenal turnover rate of directors of the CIA is striking—seven in six years. Each of them ready to institute reforms. It usually ends up by undermining covert operations in order to shift resources from human to technical assets, which is no help at all. It does not help since only rarely can we discover a terrorist conspiracy from satellites in the sky or by communications intercepts on the ground. And in the case of state-sponsored terrorism with rare exceptions we, unlike the Israelis, are reluctant to use overt force in retaliation. Here indeed is a decisive justification for the human (especially deep cover) assets of the CIA and its capability to conduct covert operations. And here indeed is a pressing need to generate popular understanding and a consensus to undertake a massive national effort.

---

[14] White House Press Release, *Remarks by the President on American Security*, August 5, 1996, p. 4.

[15] Testimony by Anthony Lake, CIA Director designate at his Senate confirmation hearings, March 12, 1997.

UNCERTAINTIES

We must keep emphasizing this, however: Investing in American leadership toward international order will be a very difficult effort, requiring all the traditional optimism and perseverance of Americans. Obviously we cannot do it alone; we need the support of practically all countries. As a *sine qua non* we need the cooperation of China and Russia, two states in transition. They may end up as predators, but they could become our partners. We can not do much about this: it will depend on their own mostly autonomous development. There is the risk—and there is the opportunity.

We may speculate freely about the long-term secular trends in *China* and arrive at a series of "yes and then again no" possibilities. First, the obvious demographic generality. China has the largest population of any country in the world: the Chinese themselves often cite this feature. In the 1930s the story went around: if every Chinese would spit into the Pacific Ocean (or the Japanese Sea; it was never made quite clear which), Japan would sink below the ocean.

One might suppose that a state with so large a population would be tempted to go for military adventures, even to try for hegemony. As a matter of fact, that was not the record of China. In the case of its first unification (221 B.C.), a relatively small state through guile and war gained the upper hand over the much more populous parts of the country. This was also the case during the nineteenth and the first half of the twentieth century. Remote European countries with a fraction of China's population dominated, in fact, humiliated her. And, of course, in the 1930s armed forces from a relatively small island across the sea, never mind any expectoration by the masses of Chinese, moved into the mainland, conquered much of it, and would have subjugated all of China had she not been saved by massive foreign assistance. In all fairness we should add that China in the past has not been an expansive imperialist country. Since it was first united, its territory has at times been internally fragmented and then reunified, but with rare exceptions foreign conquest was not a national driving force. Military virtues were never admired; soldiers were considered very much a lower class. In the past China was more often a victim of aggression rather than its perpetrator.

One important variable may be the enormously high density of the population. Much of its western provinces are desolate. Most Chinese are concentrated in a 1,000-mile strip along the east coast. Consider this illustration: Move all Americans to the east of the Mississippi and then multiply their number by five. You then get an idea of the population density in China. Quite possibly such enormous population pressures may exacerbate the problem of internal control keeping the government too busy to experiment with external adventures. But then again the government may seek to cope with the problem by mobilization behind irredentist causes and external challenges, for example, Taiwan and its protectors.

As it happens, the current government is very much interested in limiting population growth. They have adopted draconian measures to enforce a program of one-child families. The consequences are high personal anxiety and social stress. For example, little baby girls are murdered to keep the family eligible for a male heir. But many of the senior leaders have large families (birth control cannot be made retroactive), and in much of rural China government orders are ignored or evaded. So the population keeps rising. It was hoped that it would stabilize at 1.2 billion early in the twenty-first century. In fact, it has already surpassed that number. The World Bank is now talking about 1.6 billion as a level of stabilization.

There is also the economic argument. China's current economic growth rate is phenomenal, officially about 9 percent a year. If this growth rate continues and if all that the United States can manage is a 2 percent annual increment, in 2008 China could claim to be the world's largest economy. So what does this mean? If indeed these estimates become reality, China may possibly enjoy the euphoria and move for hegemony. On the other hand, the Chinese people emerging from centuries of misery might enjoy their newly acquired material benefits and be more reluctant to risk them on military adventures.

There is, however, another worrisome prospect. Chinese economic development may suffer a decline, quite possibly a reverse. The agricultural sector is in parlous condition. President Jiang is publicly worried about the growing food, more specifically the grain, problem. Arable land is severely limited by both the quality of soil and the scarcity of rainfall. Meanwhile growing urban populations have steadily increased their demand for food and water. In 1994 China exported eight million tons of grain. In 1995 it *imported* sixteen million tons.

The industrial sector produces its own troubling statistics. It is divided into (1) the much-touted "socialist market economy," and (2) the "state-owned enterprises" (SOES). The first category involves a vibrant group of small- and medium-sized businesses that are fairly efficient and attract heavy foreign investment. They are the reluctant concessions of a pragmatic Chinese communist state. The second category is composed of heavy industries, state-owned vestiges of the past. They are the principal beneficiaries of state support, and they are also a heavy drag on the economy. They still employ the vast majority of China's labor force, but their contribution is less than a third of the country's industrial output. More than one-third of SOES have liabilities that exceed their assets. In other words, they are bankrupt. They survive on heavy loans from the state-controlled banks. Their total debt has risen from $86 billion in 1993 to $120 billion in 1996. We can now see inflation rising as are China's foreign debts.

Two examples further illustrate the fantasy of a linear projection of Chinese growth to the largest economy of the world by 2008. There are about 100 million cars in the United States and 480 million throughout the world. For China to match our current fleet it would have to acquire 600 million cars in twelve years. In 1994 it produced only a total of 350,000. Another comparison: Americans now own about 40 percent of the world's computers, 1 per 3 households. In China the comparable figure is less than 1 per 1,000. For China to reach in 2008 even the 1996 relative U.S. level would mean acquiring and installing 400 million computers in private homes. So the question arises: what will be the reaction to an economic slow down—more cooperation or more hostility?

Then there is the political variable. Chinese government officials emphatically assert that China will have political stability. Whatever questions there were about the succession to the leadership of Deng Xiaoping have now been resolved, they say. A new leader for the future has been selected. Jiang Zemin is president, party chief, and chairman of the all-powerful military committee. All of which is true but not conclusive. One may entertain doubts about the stability of the transition to the "third generation" of leadership. It may appear to have been stable principally because the second generation (Deng Xiaoping) until recently (February 27, 1997) was still around to support it. Transition from one authoritarian ruler to another (unless it is reinforced by a "mandate from heaven") is a notoriously tricky affair. Rarely does it proceed according to plan. Certainly the transition in China from the first generation (Mao) to the second (Deng) did not do so. Worse still, unlike Mao and Deng, President Jiang is not obviously head and shoulders above his senior colleagues. Few expect radical changes in leadership during the 15th Communist Party Congress to be held in October 1997. Instead the eyes are on the National People's Congress scheduled for March 1998. According to the rule, no senior government official can hold his post for more than ten years. This will mean (if it is adhered to) the replacement of several members of the current top leadership. The foremost question is what will happen to the current Prime Minister Li Peng, who has (or had) much party support? In any case, the jockeying for power must be in full swing now. Debates on the wisdom of the 1996 Taiwan Straits military exercises and, in fact, the most appropriate relationship with the United States have leaked out. Just how accurate the reports are, of course, is another matter. Thus, to bet on a period of political instability and the emergence of a new leader, whoever he may be, is not altogether unreasonable.

Difficulties may well arise in political *control*. There is trouble brewing in the vast western provinces. Tibet and Inner Mongolia with their ethnic minorities have never been pleased with Chinese domination. More recently in Xinjiang the Uighors, who make up seven million of the total of sixteen million provincial population, have resorted to violence. Bombs have been exploding on buses in the capital (Urumqi); bloody ethnic clashes have become frequent. Although the Chinese government denies this, a bomb that destroyed a bus in Beijing on March 4, 1997, killing two and injuring thirty was popularly seen as evidence of spreading ethnic unrest.

In addition, the People's Liberation Army (PLA), the coercive capacity of the state, has not always been wholly reliable. During the Cultural Revolution (1966) it conceded the streets to the radical "students," who then went on a rampage and committed all kinds of atrocities. (Deng Xiaoping's son was thrown out of a window and crippled for life.) Even the Great Helmsman Mao, who probably inspired it all, had to concede that things were out of control. It took him several years to restore order. More recently during the Tiananmen Square crisis the leadership was practically besieged in Zhongnanhai, where the quarters of senior government officials are concentrated. Some of the army units they called on proved to be less than reliable, a spotty performance to be seen on television abroad *and* in China. In any case, upon the death of Deng Xiaoping, Jiang Zemin wasted no time (March 4, 1997) in telling the armed forces: "The party's absolute leadership over the army is fundamental." Two days later a new draft law was announced that "legalises the principle of the party commanding the gun."[16]

Finally, we need to consider the uncertainties of social change. To begin with, China is still principally a rural country. About three-quarters of the population live in rural areas. That is nine hundred million people, an enormous number, hard to imagine and harder to manage. Worse still, in the second half of the twentieth century they were subjected to four major upheavals. One of the first things chairman Mao Zedong did upon the proclamation of the People's Republic of China (1950–52) was to impose

---

[16] *Economist*, March 8–14, 1997, p. 38.

land reforms. Figuratively, and in many cases literally, these wiped out the traditional land owners (rich peasants and gentry-landlords) and redistributed their property among the landless or land-short peasants. "The social result was an essentially capitalist system of individual peasant proprietorships with government-issued title deeds officially confirming the private ownership of family farms."[17]

This policy did not last long. It was soon (1953) followed by a sharp reversal. Suddenly private landownership in the villages was abolished and was forcibly replaced by the socialist method of collectivization. Shortly thereafter (1958) in another leap, "the leap to communist utopia," the new collective farms were combined into large agricultural communes. The method once again was harsh compulsion, and in the process leadership in the countryside passed into the hands of centrally controlled party bureaucrats. The economic consequences were predictable. Agricultural output dropped, then slowly crept up to the Chinese Yuan 80–100 billion level in the 1970s. More recently in another radical turn around of the Deng reforms, agriculture was decollectivized and returned to a system of individual family farming. In the 1980s agricultural output rose sharply from Chinese Yuan 135.8 (1980) to 480 (1990), stimulating the rise of a rural petty bourgeoisie.

The recently established political bureaucrats at first opposed the reforms but soon fell in line. They may have feared the retaliation of the local peasantry, they may have decided to do their bureaucratic duty, or they may have discovered special advantages from which they could profit. "It became commonplace for local officials to acquire the largest and best parcels of land for themselves."[18]

The fate of this "bureaucratic-compadore capitalism" remains to be seen. In 1996 elections for local offices were held. Some 150,000, it was said, but probably closer to a million contests. The traditional Chinese values were shedding their communist overlay. Quite possibly a different type of leadership may emerge in the vast rural areas of China. Their effectiveness and direction are part of the incalculables.

In the meantime, after all the Maoist bungles in industrialization, the Deng Xiaoping reforms produced remarkable advances in that sector as well. The disparity in the annual economic growth rate of the private

---

[17] Maurice Meisner, *The Deng Xiaoping Era: an Inquiry into the Fate of Chinese Socialism (1978–1994)* (New York: Hill and Wang, 1996), p. 28.

[18] Meisner, *The Deng Xiaoping Era*, p. 311. See supporting empirical evidence pp. 311–18.

industrialized sector (15 percent) and the public sector (5 percent) is striking. But rapid economic development driven by the private sector produces a new middle class (not to mention criminal organizations) and quite a number of plutocrats. With Hong Kong reunited with China in 1997, the middle classes may reach 200 million and the plutocrats well over a million. Their economic power will be further increased, and they may challenge the existing structure of party officials and bureaucrats. Will this lead to a desperate struggle or will a constructive coalition emerge? Possibly it will be the former, but we can hope it will be the latter. We cannot predict the outcome, but on the margins conceivably we may affect it.

If we do want to affect the outcome, we ought to keep at least three special conditions in mind. First, unlike in the rest of the world the communist party in China has not been discredited. The humiliating experiences in the eighteenth, nineteenth, and first half of the twentieth centuries have not been forgotten; their hurt still festers. The communists have restored Chinese dignity. With pride most will quote the words of Chairman Mao when he proclaimed the People's Republic of China: From today the Chinese people have stood up.

Second, the Chinese are a proud people, proud of their civilization and their historic contributions to human development. About the time Socrates, Plato, and Aristotle were pondering the meaning of truth, virtue, and justice and thus setting the foundation of Western civilization, Chinese sages were pondering the norms of their civilization. Mo-tzu identified the most important calamities:

I say that the attack on the small states by the large ones, disturbances of the small houses by the large ones, oppression of the weak by the strong, misuse of the few [minority] by the many [majority], deception of the simple by the cunning, disdain toward the humble by the honored: these are the misfortunes of the world.[19]

On the issue of unification King Hui of Liang asked: "How may the world be at peace?" Mencius the philosopher replied: "When there is unity, there will be peace."[20]

Third, the Chinese government is convinced that it is following the right course. It has concluded that economic development can occur only

---

[19] Fung Yu-lan, *A Short History of Chinese Philosophy*, edited by Derek Bodde (New York: Free Press, 1966), p. 179.

[20] Ibid., p. 180.

within a framework of political stability. Hundreds of millions of Chinese live in poverty. Their most pressing and most salient human right is sheer survival *and* a minimum quality of life that permits them to function as human beings. Once that has been accomplished, other human and political rights become relevant. Until then to support a steady advance in the standard of living, if necessary extraordinary measures which assure political stability are warranted. Indeed that is the only moral course. Government officials are very surprised and resentful about what they deeply believe is Western hypocrisy, of Westerners looking down their long noses treating them to unsolicited lectures on morality. They remember too well the Opium War (1839) when British naval forces proclaiming their doctrine of free trade invaded China and imposed all kinds of indignities on its government. What the British actually wanted was free access to the Chinese people for opium shipped from British India.

We can expect some difficult times regarding Taiwan. Sooner or later China will insist that its "province" be fully returned. Quite possibly it will use military force. The problem is that we do have some interests in the island: strategic interests in the case of power politics, human rights interests in the case of advancement toward human unity. In both cases we have an interest that the Chinese (or any other country) resist the temptation of using military force. We may send aircraft carrier task forces to the area, but it is highly unlikely that we would go to a major war over Taiwan. We should be prepared with prudent options for a variety of contingencies. Similarly if the Chinese were to invade the off-shore islands, it is most unlikely that we could do anything about it. Would it make sense to try? Does it make sense to pretend that we would?

In terms of our long-term expectations about Chinese behavior there are more important indicators. First, how will China behave in terms of established international norms? Is she going to systematically ignore international conventions on copyright? Second, how will China behave in terms of international order? Will she make nuclear weapons and/or strategic missiles available to rogue states? Third, how will she treat Hong Kong after 1997? Will she respect a measure of economic autonomy and accept some democratic institutions there?

American foreign policy in the 1990s tended to be full of harsh criticisms of China occasioned by the annual debate over the president's extension for *one more year* a most favored nations status to Chinese trade. Most recently, however, under the leadership of Secretary of State Madeleine Albright, the United States has taken a much more enlightened position. Her formula of a "multifaceted" relationship includes frequent high-level contacts. China in the near future will be treated with respect for her dignity. Our tone will be friendly; our practice, regular consultations. We might then get some clue about the long-term intentions of the Chinese government. For the moment the signals are not encouraging. Recently we have been treated to a Chinese refrain that the United States is seeking to "contain" China.

The charge sows distrust and is counterproductive because it seems so at variance with the economic, the technological, and the cultural ties that are being built between the two countries, and because it inspires Americans to question whether Beijing desires good relations or simply desires to drive a wedge between Washington and its traditional friends in East Asia. It also strengthens suspicions in the United States and other countries that the Chinese leadership now views Washington as a primary strategic enemy.[21]

Another problem is perhaps even more fundamental. During his visit to Washington, DC, where he was widely honored, including being received at the White House, General Chi Haotian, Chinese Minister of Defense, in a lecture at the National Defense University (December 10, 1996) declared "very seriously" that during the Tiananmen crisis no one was killed on the square, and outside of it "there was some shoving." He also disclaimed any religious or political persecutions or violations of human rights in China. His audience applauded his speech, but probably few, if any, Americans believed his assertions. Congressmen held public hearings where they wanted to know just how we could have constructive relations with a government whose senior officials lie so blatantly and think that we would believe them. Quite possibly the Chinese are testing us.

The situation in *Russia* is even more obscure. There is not a single fixed point from which we can project into the future with confidence. Russia suffers from the shock of the collapse of the Soviet Union and its subsequent aftershocks. People have become anxious about their identity. The old communist values have been discredited; no new ones are taking their place. People desperately seek a moral anchor. Some look abroad, some idealize the past, but most are just floating. We need to keep in mind that while the focus was emphatically on the collective, the Soviet system did provide certain personal satisfactions. The people did vicariously enjoy the dignity of Soviet military accomplishments. They were proud of their victory in the Great Patriotic War (World War II). They appreciated the

---

[21] National Committee on U.S.-China Relations, *Toward Strategic Understanding between America and China*, Policy Series No. 13, December 1996, p. 13.

many monuments erected to memorialize the heroism and glory of Soviet citizens (for example, in Leningrad) as well as those of the Red Army. Military parades were always heavily attended with veterans proudly displaying their medals in rows all across their chests. Moreover, after the war Soviet citizens (especially the Russians) quite probably derived some pride from the superpower status of their country. Possibly they noted with satisfaction that much of the world looked at it with fear, while part of the world welcomed its constraints on American power. To be sure, Soviet citizens did not have the benefits of democracy, but it is not clear just how much they missed them.

They also enjoyed other benefits. Growing up they could count on an opportunity for schooling. Practically all became literate and those with appropriate talents received a good education in science. As adults they were assured a job, and all along they had access to free health care. The problem was that their personal standard of living was low. Food was scarce; people had to stand in line for it. Clothing was uniform, drab, and often shabby. Housing was at a premium; people were crowded into small apartments with primitive appliances and not always reliable utilities. People yearned for a higher standard of living, and once they became aware that others, their neighbors in Western Europe not to mention the legendary Americans, lived very much better, they became intensely frustrated. For relief they turned more and more to vodka. "Perhaps the saddest thing was," observed Mikhail Gorbachev, "that although there was a severe shortage of consumer goods, the authorities could not think of any way to maintain monetary circulation other than by selling alcohol to make people drunk."[22] Indeed it is not too much of an overstatement that the principal preoccupation of the Soviet people when they were sober was thinking of consumer goods and when they were drunk dreaming about having some.

In 1986 Gorbachev led a movement for the "acceleration of the social and economic development of the country." Relying on "old methods," his solution was a more complete reliance on the "advantages of Socialism."[23] It was not a notable success, but the people apparently drew fresh hope when his successor, Boris Yeltsin, embraced the "free market." So far this too has been very much less than a success. In fact, all the reforms notwithstanding, the economy has been mostly going down.

There has been a high turnover in finance ministers, each with his own ideas about the proper rate and means of reform. Under Yeltsin it started

---

[22] Gorbachev, *Memoirs*, p. 220.

[23] Ibid., p. 217.

with Yegor Gaidar, who followed "a little voice" that told him to proceed rapidly with liberalization. The cost of the shock treatment was confusing to the economy and heavy on the citizens. As a result of the reforms the people lost socialist entitlements: guaranteed education, jobs, and health care. Benefits were dissipated with subsequent shifts in policy. Gaidar's successors moved toward more and more gradualist approaches. The results were no better.

The economy has become incoherent. It is no longer a socialist command system, nor a market system, nor one with any clear direction. Privatization is sporadic. A notable contradiction is cited by Sergei Khrushchev.

According to the State Property Committee, 2,621 medium and large enterprises became private on 1 June 1994 . . . thereafter 86 percent of workers were employed in the private sector. This sector now produces 62 percent of Russia's gross national product, a higher proportion than Italy's free market economy. According to another source, 90 percent of property is *still controlled by government, which kept the majority of stock in private enterprises.*[24]

During the Soviet Union, state-owned industries bought the needed raw materials and goods through what might be described as ledger transfers (*Beznalichnie*). The owner of both the buyers and the suppliers was the government. But under a market system private owners had to pay each other in real money. This they could not or would not do. By January 1992 about 35 billion rubles of such debt was unpaid. Within six months the nonpayment among enterprises rose to 3.5 trillion rubles. By September 1994 it moved to 112 trillion rubles, and in June 1995 it reached 297.9 trillion rubles.[25] Bizarre conditions were epitomized in 1995 when the electric company shut off the power supply of Russia's Northern Fleet Headquarters for nonpayment.

Russian statistics are not usually of the highest quality. Indeed the World Bank often does not include them in its tables.[26] These are some fragments from various sources: (1) The GNP has been declining at an annual rate of 41 percent between 1985 and 1994. In 1994 the GNP decline was 15 percent; in 1995 it was 4 percent. By 1996 Russian per capita GNP at purchasing power parity had dropped to less than 70 percent of the

---

[24] Sergei N. Khrushchev, "The Three Circles of Russian Market Reform," *Mediterranean Quarterly*, vol. 6, no. 4, Fall 1995, p. 25.

[25] Ibid., pp. 12, 14.

[26] The World Bank, *World Development Report 1996*, p. 186, 188 ff.

Mexican level.[27] (2) Overall the decline of manufacturing (1989–1993) was more than 50 percent. In 1994 alone it fell by 21 percent, then in 1995 dropped "only" 7 percent. (3) In 1994 the decline in the food industry was 33 percent, in light industry it was 42 to 44 percent.

Inflation was very high, in triple digits. It has subsided recently to double digits, but the danger of runaway inflation is constantly present. Unemployment is high; worse still even those who do work are paid only sporadically. According to one source, 35 million people fell below the poverty line. According to another, the figure is between 31 and 42 percent of the population.[28] The government has turned to massive domestic and foreign borrowing. By 1996, however, most corporate and household bank deposits had been sucked into treasury bills. Alarmed the IMF withheld a $330 million monthly payment on a $10.1 billion three-year loan.

Wage arrears have become an epidemic. By 1995 the government's debt for salaries had risen to 5.6 trillion rubles or more than $1.1 billion. Most alarming Russian rocket forces, which control the country's strategic nuclear weapons, had not been paid for three months in 1996.[29] Just think if this will go on how these officers and men will behave. How will they try to get some money to live on and provide for their families? How frustrated and hostile they may become.

The problem is exacerbated by the very marked income disparities. While most Russians became poorer, some are now much richer. Many people in Moscow, St. Petersburg, and in some of the regions heavily endowed with natural resources, not to mention heavy mafia activity, have visibly improved their standard of living. Consumer goods of high quality are available to them more regularly. They are eating better; they dress more fashionably. There are many more privately owned passenger cars; indeed traffic jams and gridlock have become frequent. It is estimated that residents of Moscow live ten times better than other Russians. Another relevant comparison: In Russia the top decile earns 38.7 percent of the total income; the top two deciles: 53.8 percent. In the United States the comparative figures are 25 percent and 41.9 percent.[30] The good news is that Russians, witnessing the sharp rise in the standard of living of a few, draw hope that they might do as well. The bad news is that they are becoming impatient.

---

[27] *Economist*, May 17–23, 1997, p. 38.

[28] Ibid., p. 6.

[29] Senator Sam Nunn, "Meet the Press," November 24, 1996.

[30] The World Bank, *World Development Report 1996*, p. 197.

During the presidential election campaign in 1996 Boris Yeltsin made many public spending promises and tax concessions. They may have helped his reelection. After the election, orders issued in Yeltsin's name returned to fiscal stringency. Once again the country had a new finance minister, Alexander Livshits. It was the government's intention to reduce the budget deficit to 3.85 percent of GDP for the year through budget cuts and increased taxes. Reportedly the 1997 budget plans to shrink the deficit further to 3.3 percent, which is roughly the Western European level. The IMF apparently regained its optimism. On August 21, 1996, it announced resumption of its monthly payments on its three-year loan. Surely this is economic progress of a sort. But by December 1996 strikes led by coal miners swept the country.

Shortly after the first round of the presidential elections, Yeltsin noticeably receded from public view. His enemies spread rumors (a) that he was engaged in extended and excessive alcoholic celebration and (b) that he was too ill to perform the functions of his office. In any case, the planned summit meeting with President Clinton in the United States had to be shifted to Helsinki to accommodate the Russian president. Some of the questions were answered by an open heart surgery and his resumptions of the presidency. At Helsinki (March 17–18) he seemed to be his own vigorous self according to Clinton. Indeed just a few days earlier, he ordered a radical streamlining of his government. He appointed yet another new economic team: a tandem arrangement with his chief of staff, Anatoly Chubais, promoted to first deputy prime minister as well as finance minister, and Boris Nemtsov, the young provincial governor of Nizhny Novgorod also promoted to first deputy prime minister. Yeltsin also promised to pay the salaries so long in arrears. His initiatives were treated with approval abroad, and most of the Russian people appear to be giving him another chance.[31]

Meanwhile the political system remains chaotic. Indeed the word "system" is a euphemism. There is a constitution but no serious commitment to it. All sides use it for their own purposes. The most powerful will determine its meaning. Internal security has broken down. Organized crime is unchecked; it is busily taking over businesses and building working relations with government. One source, Alexander Gurov, asserts that about 70 percent of Russian banks are controlled by the mafia. The Ministry of International Affairs estimates a smaller number: about 500 banks. In addition, according to the Ministry more than 5,000

---

[31] *Economist*, March 22–28, 1997, p. 64–65.

enterprises are controlled by the mafia.[32] None of this is reassuring. The armed forces are demoralized; effective command control is in the balance. "Free" elections for the Duma (legislature) were held in 1995 resulting in a communist-led plurality. Presidential elections were held in 1996 with Boris Yeltsin making for some a surprising comeback. Significantly even in the face of massive support for him by the government-managed media, more than 40 percent of the Russian people voted for his communist opponent. The odds that he will serve out his term are not very high; the odds against any orderly succession are considerable.

Political conditions have been further complicated by the collapse of the Soviet Union. The cohesion of the empire is gone. Centrifugal forces are on the ascendance. Some of the former Soviet Union's major components, e.g., the Ukraine, Belorus, Kazakhstan, are linked to Russia only by the flimsy ties of the Confederation of Independent States. On the periphery of what remained of Russia (principally in the Caucasus and the Eastern Balkans) movements of independence are vigorously asserting themselves. Russia is trying to deal with them with so far indifferent results. And within the heartland of Russia power is visibly devolving on regional and local government. Moscow and St. Petersburg now have powerful and determined mayors. Elsewhere the "Great Volga Association" and the "Great Ural Association" are demanding more attention and authority. And so are all the various local units (*krays* and *oblasts*) of the Russian Federation. Are we witnessing a democracy built from below? Well hardly. A survey of local leaders reveals little appeal for democratic values and procedures. Conflict resolution, political equality, and participation score negatively. Their political orientation toward the communist party scores 6.5 percent; democratic orientation scores 17.5. But independents score 33 percent, and "no answer" scores 36.8.[33] Viktor Ishayev, appointed by President Yeltsin to head the administration of Khabarovsk Kray, put it this way: "What sort of a social base do we have for our administration? The democratic stratum consists of a few people. Business is not yet developed. Where, if not from old sources, would we get the personnel?" He then reported that in a local opinion poll 90 percent

---

[32] Khrushchev, "The Three Circles of Russian Market Reform," *Mediterranean Quarterly*, p. 23, 29.

[33] Juri Avdeyev, Jane Grischenko, and Alexandra Jasinska-Kania, "The Russian National Report" in *Democracy and Local Governance, Ten Empirical Studies*, Betty M. Jacob, Krzysztof Ostrowski, and Henry Teune, eds. (Honolulu: The Matsunaga Institute for Peace, 1993), pp. 151–58.

of the respondents expressed the belief that political parties were unnecessary.[34]

With the empire gone the vicarious pleasures of national pride belong to the past. The people, no doubt, are still fond of Mother Russia and would defend it with their lives. All the same, the heady days when they were citizens of a superpower have now receded into nostalgia. When they think about their reduced circumstances, they know that they are no match for the Americans; indeed many worry about being hemmed in between an expanding NATO and a rapidly rising Chinese colossus. They very much need reassurances about the future. Mostly they need reassurances and respect from the Americans.

For the moment most Russians apparently have set their hearts on consumer goods. In the 1996 presidential election extreme nationalistic rhetoric and socialist appeals were not the winning ticket. Most who voted against Yeltsin seemed to be motivated less by opposition to the direction he promised to lead them than by a disappointment with his progress. Incidentally, a 1997 survey by the Moscow Center of International Sociological Research reported some interesting results. Seventy-three percent of the Russians would like to visit, but only 22 percent would like to live in, the United States. Sixty-five percent of Russian women would like to marry an American man, but only 22 percent of Russian men would like to marry an American women. By a 2:1 ratio (54:26) Russians favor copying the American way of life. Indeed 33 percent would approve of the Americanization of the world.[35]

Needless to say, we cannot expect the Russians to forego forever the pride of nationalism. Just possibly if the government soon (let us say within a decade) successfully addresses the economic problems and the tap of consumer goods is opened wide throughout the country, Russian nationalism may be expressed in constructive patriotism. One thing is certain, if the government fails on this score, the ensuing frustrations will go ballistic and turn into raging chauvinism.

These are the challenges the Russians themselves have to meet. But we can help some. The capitalist system and democracy are full of subtleties and complexities. We could provide some advice and technical assistance. We could, as did France at the end of the nineteenth century, encourage

---

[34] Quoted in: Rolf H. W. Theen, "Russia at the Grassroots: Reform at the Local and Regional Levels," *In Depth, Journal for Values and Public Policy*, Winter 1993, pp. 80–81.

[35] *Economist*, March 22–27, 1997, p. 62.

private investment. We could offer public financial assistance, as we do for Israel, in loans and grants.[36]

Most important, we could follow a foreign policy that might convince them that we have no intention of taking advantage of their time of troubles. We may prudently curtail any further development of offensive strategic weapons systems, indeed through reciprocal agreement cautiously reduce our current stockpile.[37] Another possible confidence-building move: In a dramatic initiative we may commit ourselves not to recruit their citizens to spy for us and become traitors to their country. All along, we may treat them as a politically most-favored nation and consult them regularly on all international issues. We could seek their cooperation in every region and exclude them from none. In the end it may not be enough. Domestic and geopolitical pressures may push the Russians into an inimical position. So we need to stay alert and follow President Reagan's dictum: trust but verify.

Simply put, we need to keep in mind that Russia's ability to sabotage any American leadership is enormous; its support as a partner is essential. The prospects are not hopeless. After an agreement was signed at the NATO-Russia summit in Paris on May 27, 1997, President Yeltsin made a surprising announcement. He would order the dismounting of all nuclear warheads from missiles targeted on his new partners. Transparently it was a grandstand. In fact, there should not be any such missiles. In Europe the INF Treaty had mandated the destruction of all intermediate-range ballistic missiles; in the United States a formal Bush-Gorbachev agreement pledged the retargeting of strategic weapons away from each other's country.

Even so, President Yeltsin's statement had enormous symbolic significance. Dramatically he made the point that he was in charge at home. More important, he clearly sent the message that in Russia there are people, even at the highest level, who want very much to be friends with America. So it is just possible that if they become convinced that we did not take advantage of them while they were weak, they may show more appreciation for our help for their economic development. Indeed their evolving societal norms may prove to be harmonious with our own. Thus, we could take a chance that Russia will turn out to be a partner not a predator.

---

[36] In March 1997 the U.S. Agency for International Development asked for Congress to approve $242 million for Russia.

[37] At the Helsinki Summit (March 27–28, 1997), President Clinton suggested a reduction to 80 percent below cold war levels. It would probably mean a reduction below the overkill level. And, if so, that would be too much.

AGONIZING REAPPRAISAL

Keeping in mind the two-track approach advocated in this book, that is (1) maintaining our national security in good repair and (2) leading the advance toward an international community, we now come to a very delicate subject. Special relations, we need to remember, are usually the products of special circumstances, and this is true especially of alliances. For our first century and a half American foreign policy was generally disposed to be friendly to foreign countries, perhaps more friendly to some than to others. But with the possible exception of Latin America, we tended to avoid any "military entanglements." This changed after the post-World War II Soviet aggression on the global scale. Our country found itself in mortal menace; countries along the Soviet border were in danger of intimidation and invasion; and practically all countries on earth were subject to communist subversion orchestrated in Moscow. New circumstances required new approaches. The United States entered into a series of defensive alliances whose common, obvious, and well-defined object was a predatory USSR.

Now that the geopolitical realities have changed once again, it stands to reason that fresh thinking is warranted. Which is awkward all the same. Our friends and allies, in fact, have been loyal to us. We cannot simply say: you have served our purpose, now good-bye, especially since we have become genuinely fond of most of them. Now let us look at the other side of the coin. For decades our friends and allies very much needed us for security and felt compelled to put up with various aspects of American leadership they were less than enthusiastic about. Now that they are not militarily dependent on us, they are showing much political and economic independence. Still they are grateful to us for past favors, and, in any case, they would rather not offend the only superpower.

It is conceivable that the Russians and/or the Chinese are secretly contemplating a surge to hegemony, but at the least in the near- and medium-term, we need not be greatly preoccupied with it. Without any help from others, we still have awesome strategic retaliatory capabilities, and with a modicum of prudence, we shall keep these intact. In any case, we should have the time necessary to discover and thwart such menacing intentions.

For the time being, we are free of a palpable global aggressor mandating military alliances. Unfortunately we are not free of "rogue states," and they do present dangers to the rest of the world in their own pathetic way. But they are being constantly watched closely for mischief and probably can be handled by *ad hoc* collective or if absolutely necessary by unilateral U.S. action. Finally, conditions are ripe for all kinds of local unpleasantness in the Third World. We may have to face sudden explosions of political, economic, or social desperation, outbursts of revenge for past grievances, or deadly flare-ups of traditional ascriptive hatreds. What makes them especially troublesome is that they are unpredictable, widely dispersed throughout the globe, and usually occur below the level of states. Prefabricated military combinations are not likely to be of much help.

Upon consideration we may conclude that our alliance systems so carefully built and nurtured during the Cold War have become obsolete. Worse still, there is the possibility that they are detrimental to our long-range purposes. For if we were to take advantage of the window of opportunity to advance human unity, our course must be essentially inclusionary. Only recalcitrants may be left out and only temporarily. But under existing conditions alliances are inherently divisive within the human race. Diplomats can exude good will all over the place, but those countries not included in military pacts will harbor dark suspicions about a hostile collusion. Their constructive cooperation with a historic effort to advance human development will predictably be impaired.

For most countries, alliances were a way of life. In contrast, for the United States they were temporary aberrations brought about by special circumstances of the recent past. So unless we have become dedicated to the proposition that a mortal threat to us will *inevitably* reemerge in the near future, we now have the opportunity to shift back to our traditional inclusionary universalist orientation. If for some reason we simply have to have alliances, *it may be wise to shift to the economic base*. The annual G-7 meeting has already become the Summit of Eight and may be expanded to the Summit of Nine, which would then include China. It may also be advisable to augment such arrangements *with open and free-access multilateral agreements of friendship and cooperation*. Through them we may open up opportunities in new, previously less congenial regions, and we could enhance our traditional friendships in many political, economic, and cultural ways without the complicating factor of the overwhelming disparity in military capacities. And, in case of aggression anywhere, we would have flexibility and be able to respond with the most appropriate coalition just as we did in the Persian Gulf War.

Actually on some major security issues we have already led with this approach. All states were invited to join in the nuclear nonproliferation treaty, the nuclear test ban treaty, and the chemical weapons ban treaty. With few exceptions all appropriate states declared their solidarity. The exceptions cannot be ignored; neither should they be permitted to sabotage our agenda. We might perhaps follow up with a global nonaggression treaty. In many ways the United Nations Charter is just that, but a renewed educational effort could not hurt. Come ye, one and all, and join us and Russia and China and anyone else in a solemn commitment not to plan and initiate war. Let us all be friends

Given the uncertainties of future Chinese and Russian behavior it is impossible to chart a fixed course for American relations in the *North Pacific Asia Rim*. South Korea, the strategic pivot between these two great powers, obviously is of major interest to the United States. To station more or less token American forces in the country, as long as the people there welcome us, will remain sound policy for some time to come. *Japan*, an economic heavyweight, is somewhat more of a problem. In case of serious trouble with Russia and/or China, it would be an essential ally. Under more optimistic conditions the Japanese could be our good friends; for the last three generations they have been so. Still, we have to be cautious. Hiroshima left a deep mark. The surrender in Tokyo Bay had shamed and confused the people. For some time under the spell of General MacArthur they mechanically followed American leadership. Then came his summary dismissal, American bungling in Vietnam, the "opening" to China, and Japan's economic surge. Adjustments to changing conditions at home are now working themselves out. Will demography complicate this process? For the Japanese population is shrinking. Some project a Japan in 2010 of only 80 million people.[38] But in terms of its external position the Japanese are still in a muddle. They have learned that their sun is not rising to a global zenith, but it will NOT sink into the night either. They soon will be searching to define their own international identity.

Southeast Asia has not been of preeminent geopolitical salience. But a number of countries there have proven to be tigers in economic development. Moreover, they are generally multiracial. They experience the tension of traditional radical discontinuities within their populations. They try to manage it. Malaysia in 1969 had for all a very distressing experience of massive race riots.[39] It apparently has learned its lesson, and under Prime Minister Dr. Mahathir bin Mohamad it has been trying to build a nation based on material affluence. So far so good, but in case of a serious economic downturn, these tigers will bare their fangs.

---

[38] I am deeply suspicious of such projections. Moreover, I think it makes a difference what the quality (admittedly a dirty word) of the population is. How will Japan with 80 million people compare to the 160 million Russians?

[39] See: Karl von Vorys, *Democracy Without Consensus, Communialism and Political Stability in Malaysia* (Princeton, NJ: Princeton University Press, 1975.)

In any case, in Southeast Asia we now may have an example of what could prove to be a most instructive development, an example of open, free-access, multilateral, inclusionary arrangement: the Asia-Pacific Economic Cooperation (APEC). Organized in 1989 after a number of security arrangements of the post-Vietnam period, it was initially an effort to coordinate regional trade. Since then, however, at the urging of Malaysia, it blossomed into a major forum of dialogue on the relationship between economic development and political stability. Two special features are worth highlighting. First, the discussions are on a high intellectual, idea-generating level without any influences of relative power positions. Second, very high officials not only from Southeast Asian countries plus Australia, Canada, Japan, New Zealand, South Korea, and the United States, but also from China, Hong Kong, *and* Taiwan have been attending regularly.[40]

Above all, solidarity with *our transatlantic allies* will continue to be of major importance—and it is where the need for reappraisal is most agonizing. Western Europeans are generally ambivalent about U.S. leadership. They like it in principle but not the kind they feel they have been getting during the past two or three decades. Some (for example, the French) wish we would be out of Europe altogether, some consider an American policy of *ad hoc* reactions ill advised, and none would be flattered by any prospect of serving as America's regional viceroys.

If we were to set as a foreign policy goal advance toward a global community, Europeans would have to play a major role. Quite possibly they would greet our leadership with mirth and assign it to American naïveté. Moreover, they could muddy the waters. Europeans, as the fountains of Western civilization, may want to change the direction of the development. Again, quite possibly, they would disregard or denigrate the advances achieved by the United States toward integrated diversity and might see as the proper goal of further advance the enculturation of all people throughout the globe into Western civilization.

These perhaps theoretical ambiguities are exacerbated by structural obsolescence. NATO is, in fact, the principal institution shared by Western Europe and North America. When it was established, its mission was unambiguous. In the face of mortal peril it served as a military alliance to defend Western Europe against Soviet aggression, preferably by deterrence. In this it was remarkably successful. For forty years NATO built a powerful

---

[40] See: William T. Tow, "Contending Security Approaches in the Asia-Pacific Region," *Security Studies 3* (London: Frank Cass), no. 1, Autumn 1993, pp. 75–116.

unified military force. In fact, there was no Soviet aggression. The unambiguous military mission, however, has become obsolete. Western Europe is safe now. Still the vested interests in the structure are carried along by their own, powerful momentums.

One option is for NATO to stand by as a framework organization with capabilities to rapidly expand as a protection against a resurgent Russia. One problem with this is that very few people worry now about a possible Russian resurgence. And another is that it might turn into a self-fulfilling prophecy. Even if the Russians were now inclined for peaceful and constructive cooperation, they may be offended by our continued expectation of their aggression and project relentless hostility to us. Certainly not something that we wish to happen.

NATO might be left to wither away. Continued radical reductions in U.S. troop commitments—we have already reduced them by two thirds—is one way of doing it. Another sure way is to politicize a professional military structure. The selection of a Spanish socialist to be its secretary-general seems to suggest the rise of political over military criteria. And so does the signing of the NATO-Russia agreement (1997) in Paris. For both Spain and France insist on remaining outside the NATO military structure. Incidentally, as one condition for their rejoining it the French demanded a rebalancing between the American and the European role, specifically that NATO-South be commanded by a French admiral. (It is curious that they felt entitled not to mention competent to order around the captains of American aircraft carriers. Is there a French word for *chutzpah*?)

Alternatively NATO's effective force structure may be redirected from a purely defensive posture to positive force projection in support of peace and global order. In which case it may make good sense for NATO to reorient itself from the east to the south. We can expect many demands for peace-keeping in Africa in the near future. Moreover, all through North Africa, West Asia, and practically all across Asia runs an axis of trouble. At its western terminus Morocco is a conventional monarchy without visible opposition, but vulnerable to both Muslim fundamentalists and secular modernizers. Far to the east are five former Soviet states of central Asia: Uzbekistan, Kazakhstan, Kyrgystan, Tajikistan, and Turkmenistan. It would be a mistake to simply lump all five countries under a common heading, but they do share some common characteristics. Mostly Muslim people, they are controlled by traditional tribal leaders. While under Soviet control such leaders were decimated, and communists, often Russian communists, were placed in charge supported by troops under Russian officers. Still, in spite of all Soviet efforts, broad-based resentment regularly bubbled forth into open resistance. Russian influence and Russian troops are now gone from all except Tajikistan, which is still under their control and where a civil war is on and off. In the other four the floodgates of Islamic revivalism burst open. So far fundamentalism is (1) retarded by Sufism, a mystical tradition that had its origins in central Asia, and (2) challenged by the rise of ethnic nationalism. Both are moderated by the replacement of Russians in prominent political and lucrative economic positions by their own people. The indigenous tribes for the moment are quite pleased by their own progress. But poverty, the absence of any firm notion about how to generate economic development, and normative confusion will predictably intensify tension and instability.

Exacerbating the potential danger, moreover, are leftover Soviet arms. Negotiations about the strategic nuclear arms in Kazakhstan are marked by solemn formal agreements and then not entirely reliable implementation. In 1992 rumors abounded that in Tajikistan enriched uranium was being sold for $100,000 a kilogram. A brisk black market trade in conventional weapons was also regularly reported.[41]

It remains an open question just which direction the newly independent Central Asian countries will choose. They are not short of wooers. Russia is working very hard to retain some influence. The Americans, government officials, and private entrepreneurs keep coming, bringing along their elaborate samples cases. Pakistan has entered into agreements, including the construction of pipelines. Many of its leaders speculate about regional combinations to the north. Taking advantage of the common language (Persian) of the people in Iran, northern Afghanistan, and Tajikistan, Iran's president Rafsanjani has his own regional bloc in mind. During May 1997 he was vigorously lobbying in Dushanbe, Tajikistan's capital. So far though the newly independent Central Asian states have been looking mostly to Turkey, a secular Muslim state and a member of NATO, for external inspiration. The problem is that lately the Turks have been annoyed by the European Community, which admitted Greece (a fellow NATO member) but consistently excluded them. They also have problems with American diplomacy. President Bush went to great length to consult regularly with the Turkish president. His successor has done much less. In 1996 the Turks had trouble with the inept manner in which the Americans handled the growing division among the Kurds in the Northern Security Zone, the

---

[41] The Soviet armed forces left behind some 4,000 tanks, 10,000 armored personnel carriers, 3,200 artillery pieces, and 220 aircraft. Ahmed Rashid, *The Resurgence of Central Asia, Islam or Nationalism* (Karachi: Oxford University Press, 1994), pp. 233–34.

subsequent intervention of Saddam Hussein, and the American response. Domestically Turkey suffers from deep economic problems, and lately its political system has been buffeted by unpredictable coalition politics. We can now also see the rise of Muslim fundamentalism in the country.

Along a more or less straight line, between Morocco and Central Asia practically all countries are either controlled by Muslim fundamentalists or by governments imperiled by fundamentalists, all hostile to the West and especially to the United States. In the May 1997 elections Iranian voters elected a moderate religious leader president. What it means for a religious leader to be a moderate in Iran remains to be seen. In the civil war of Afghanistan the Taliban seems to have the upper hand. When they at first captured Kabul, the capital, they promptly ordered all women to wear veils and all men to grow beards in six months. This is not exactly a threat to us or Europe, but if such reactionary movements across two continents become consolidated, they could cause much trouble. A militarily strong and effective NATO, able to project decisive force into this strip of trouble in support of more moderate regimes, may have a salutary effect not only in terms of regional security but also as a brake on reactionary fundamentalism.

Just now NATO is preoccupied with very much of a political matter: its "expansion of membership." It has become a done deal. The German chancellor has advanced the idea, and Secretary of State Christopher was emphatically pushing it. In an address at Stuttgart (September 6, 1996) the latter insisted that expansion will come, let nobody doubt it. Shortly after the American presidential elections he would proceed with vigorous consultations in NATO, negotiations with Russia, and the issuance of invitations to suitable eastern European (now called central European) countries. Poland, Hungary, and the Czech Republic are often mentioned and are eager to join. The new secretary of state, Madeleine Albright, is pursuing the schedule with even greater vigor.

It is now probably too late to change the outcome, but to take a closer look, to ask some questions, and to critically evaluate official answers may still be instructive. First set of questions: what kind of new security guarantees are we talking about? Would Article 5 of the NATO treaty be extended to the new members? Would the United States consider an attack on Warsaw or Budapest the same as an attack on Chicago? Would the invasion of the Czech Republic with conventional forces start the Third World War? We may not want to say it but the odds on favorite answer is "no." Second set of questions: Will NATO (and the United States) extend its conventional approach of forward deployment to the new members? Will NATO troops be stationed in Poland and the Czech Republic (some are already stationed in Hungary)? The probable answer is also "no," certainly not with strategic nuclear weapons. This would predictably provoke the Russians enormously if we would and quite probably trigger an unfriendly riposte. In fact, it would force a terrible dilemma upon us to choose between our old friends and allies, who are desirable in building an international community, and the Russians who are indispensable.[42]

Third set of questions: What effect would extension of NATO membership have on the alliance and specifically on the United States? If NATO is about to wither away, it really does not make much difference one way or another. It could provide a spectacular extended solemn ceremony of a first-class funeral. If NATO is to continue its original function in anticipation of the resurgence of a Russian military threat, the proposed extension of membership would be some help to us in moving Russian jumping-off positions farther east. It would offer some possibility of a defense in depth with the initial battlefield being on the territory of the new rather than the old members. Finally, if we were to redefine the NATO mission to a peace-keeping force, possibly focused on the North Africa-Central Asia axis, these additional members from Eastern Europe would serve little purpose for us at all. Recently Hungary did provide NATO with a staging area and transit opportunities for its intervention in Bosnia. In case of trouble in the Islamic belt, however, Pakistan and Israel would be of far greater significance.

Fourth set of questions: Who will pay for the upgrading of the Polish, Czech, and Hungarian armed forces? Will we have to do it? The sums involved will not be negligible. Fifth set of questions: Can any of the candidates be admitted after a realistic application of announced NATO standards? Are any of them "stable democracies"? In fact, their governments are riddled with communists. With the possible exception of the Czech Republic, none have any extended democratic experience. It is doubtful that the people know what democratic values are, let alone are committed to them. Do they actually have market economies? Have they

---

[42] Two statements on December 25, 1996, ought not be ignored. Said Russian Defense Minister Igor Rodionov: "The activity of the North Atlantic alliance, which has made a radical decision to expand eastward, is a serious modern challenge and a potential source of danger, which can grow into a military threat." Said Deputy Atomic Energy Minister Yevgeny Reshetnikov: "A contract might be signed as early as mid-1997 to equip a nuclear plant in China with Russian reactors." Associate Press dispatch from Moscow by Sergei Shargorodsky, December 25, 1996. General Rodionov was fired by an angry President Yeltsin on May 21, 1997.

sorted out all territorial and minority disputes amicably? How much of a fudge factor is tolerable? Is "progress" toward meeting these standards sufficient? How will such progress be judged? What happens if after admission they revert to traditional authoritarianism? Fifth set of questions: how will other applicants, unwilling members of the former Soviet empire not selected in the first draft, respond? Will the Baltic states, which were among the first to mount a heroic resistance to Soviet rule and which incidentally contributed significantly to America's demographic diversity, feel rudely slighted? Finally, there is the question once again of Russia. The persistence of NATO after Soviet threat has visibly dissolved is a difficult enough pill for them to swallow. But now NATO wants to move farther eastward. Is it because the Americans want to take advantage of Russia's temporary weakness?[43] They are paranoid enough. Do we benefit by exacerbating their anxieties? Of course, we do not.

So one more question arises: is it possible that there is a hidden agenda—worry about German aggression? Surely the Poles sitting on vast, traditionally German territories and remembering well four partitions must suffer acute anxieties. The Czechs in turn may be uneasy about the way they treated their German minorities after the World War II. They may have felt justified because the Germans mistreated them badly from 1938 to 1945. But in 1945 the Czechs paid them back in spades. They physically abused them and then peremptorily expelled them. In Bavaria, especially in Munich, there is a very influential Sudeten minority whose hostility to the Czechs does not seem to have abated.[44] And let us not forget that some of the Western Europeans may also harbor hidden anxieties. For years it has been said, informally of course, that NATO had three purposes: (1) to

---

[43] On May 14, 1997, the Russians agreed to NATO extension. Admitted a sad President Yeltsin on television: In view of "historical" and "practical realities" Russia will "have to reckon" with a broader alliance. *The Washington Post*, May 15, 1997, p. 1.

[44] Hungary is a different matter. The Hungarians have nothing to fear from Germany, however powerful it may become. In the past they had close relations, and historically Hungary had close cultural ties with Western Europe. Moreover, recently it was the Hungarian government, still in the shadow of Moscow, that had the courage to first open its borders to the West and that provided important information about intra-Warsaw Pact activities in 1989–1990. In recognition of vital Hungarian support, shortly after the Wall fell, Chancellor Kohl traveled to Budapest to accept an honorary doctorate and to acknowledge with gratitude that it was Hungary that knocked out the first stone of the Wall. "...*den ersten Stein aus der Maurer geschlagen*." Teltschik, *329 Tage*, pp. 82–83, 201.

keep the Russians out, (2) to keep the Americans in, and (3) to keep the Germans down.

One may speculate that the main driving force behind NATO expansion is another brilliant Kohl finesse. The Chancellor faced with heavy opposition throughout Europe and faint-hearted colleagues at home, with phenomenal deftness finessed the unification of Germany and the restoration of full sovereignty. He thus succeeded in eliminating the consequences of the disastrous defeat in 1945. The stigma of Nazi atrocities and above all the atonement for the holocaust may need more time. But now in addition to formal bilateral German assurances[45] through a solemn multilateral guarantee to Germany's eastern neighbors, Chancellor Kohl may seek to put a historic final line (*ein Schluβstrich*) under the past record of German aggression and lay the cornerstone of a lasting peace in Europe. If so, the Russians have nothing to fear, in fact should welcome this event.

On May 27, 1997, in Paris the heads of all NATO governments and Russian president Yeltsin signed a "partnership" dealing principally with the expansion of NATO. It was a festive and *gemütlich* occasion. The next day one of Germany's foremost newspapers started its lead editorial with the following sentences:

Who would have thought it possible? Since the prospect of joining NATO—and secondarily the European Union—is approaching in the foreseeable future for some states, a reconciliation of historic proportions is taking place in East and Southern Europe. As though led by an invisible hand, statesmen of Middle and East Europe sit down at a table and seal with their signatures "reconciliation," "understanding," "recognition of borders," and "good neighborly relations," barely after they have just started. Suddenly all difficulties seem solvable, bitter pasts can be easily overcome.[46]

THAT VISION THING

If we choose to assume leadership toward global international order and decide not to base it principally on the present reality of power that is unequally distributed throughout the world, but on the ideal of global community in the future where human equality would be the dominant feature, we shall have to address the mind-boggling problem of Sub-Sahara Africa.

---

[45] With Poland on November 14, 1990, and with the Czech Republic on February 27, 1992.

[46] *Frankfurter Allgemeine Zeitung für Deutschland*, May 28, 1997, p. 16.

Just think of a simple comparison. While the per capita income in the United States is about $25,000 per year, and the poverty line for a family of four is set by the government at about $14,000, the GNP per person is estimated at $460 in Sub-Sahara Africa. And just try to imagine this: it is $410 a year in Ghana, $280 in Nigeria, $250 in Kenya, $190 in Uganda, $140 in Tanzania, and $80 in Rwanda.[47] And these may well be somewhat optimistic (if not cooked) figures. Still they cannot begin to give us a picture of the miserable existence some 500 million of our fellow human beings concentrated in the region must daily endure.

However much Americans are sensitive to their slums, we cannot imagine what abject poverty means. It means much more than living below the national average on public welfare. It means being constantly at the mercy of the extreme forces of nature; it means being tired and hungry all the time, of listening helplessly to the plaintive cries of emaciated children. It means, to put it plainly, the existence of human beings who are alive but cannot function as rational persons. Just a simple example: for a person to function as a human being, he or she needs to consume a minimum amount of protein. Without it *kwashiorkor*, a condition of protein deficiency,[48] will set in radically reducing attention span and impairing rational deliberation. Here again statistics are scarce and not too reliable, but some United Nations Food and Agricultural Organization data indicate that the average level of protein consumption in Sub-Sahara Africa is below that of German concentration camps in 1943. According to some other World Bank selected and cited statistics, only 25 percent of the population of Ghana had access to health care, 28 percent had safe water in Kenya, 51 percent had sanitation in Uganda, 43 percent of the children under five years old suffered from serious malnutrition in Nigeria. All kinds of diseases, including AIDS, ravish the body. Life expectancy in Sub-Sahara Africa is the lowest of any region: 52 years.[49]

These dismal conditions are bad enough. What is infinitely worse, economic conditions do not seem to be improving. The growth rate from 1985 to 1994 averaged -1.2 percent. Far from catching up with the rest of

---

[47] The World Bank, *World Development Report 1996* (New York: Oxford University Press, 1996), pp. 188–89. See also: Sartaj Aziz (ed.), *Hunger, Politics, and Markets: The Real Issues in the Food Crisis* (New York: New York University Press, 1975), pp. 9–42, 65–72, 117–21, 123.

[48] Karl von Vorys, *Political Development in Pakistan* (Princeton, N.J.: Princeton University Press, 1965), p. 12.

[49] Ibid., pp. 198, 198–99.

the world, they are falling farther and farther behind. Regarding education the regional average for primary schooling: male 77 percent, female 64 percent; secondary schooling (1980) is: male 20 percent, female 10 percent; tertiary: 1 percent. Low scores in secondary and tertiary education are striking; just what, if anything, the 75 percent of the children who finish the first four grades in Rwanda actually learn is anyone's guess.

This tragic situation in education is further exacerbated by a "brain drain." Some Sub-Sahara African children, mostly sons of leaders in the "modern" political and/or economic sectors, do get a chance to study abroad. Actually they do quite well. But when the time comes to return, they prefer to stay abroad, often in the United States. One reason is that they are attracted by the American way of life. But another is that they have heard that those who did return were badly treated. They run into barriers of envy and hostility by those who did not have the opportunity to study aboard. Worse still, they run into the harsh realities of ethnic (tribal) hostilities. Perhaps an illustration that I believe is not an untypical case may help. During the Biafra War some young Nigerians were able to come to the United States. One went to Yale, received his Ph.D. in political science, and was appointed assistant professor at the University of Pennsylvania. His record at Yale was very good; at Penn he proved to be a fine teacher and a sound scholar. With or without affirmative action he could expect tenure in due time. Meanwhile his wife began to study anthropology at Penn. Her professors spoke highly of her performance, and soon she earned her Ph.D. With her ability and her education from one of the best departments in the country, there would have been no problem for an appointment at a major American university, including Penn itself. The couple with two lovely children, out of patriotism and loyalty to their homeland, decided to return to Nigeria. Alas, they were not greeted with accolades, not even with scant courtesy. That they had lived and studied abroad made their colleagues feel threatened. That they were Ibos, a minority tribe, decided their fate. The Nigerian government, which desperately needs good educators not to mention patriots, would not give them a place at any university (never mind a major university). It assigned the couple to a remote town where they were told to provide basic instruction to nearly illiterate villagers.

The horrendous fact is that Sub-Sahara African countries, perhaps more than any other countries, are helplessly caught in the vicious cycle of poverty with little chance to break out. Their chances of development, moreover, may be foreclosed by international borders that are clearly unsuitable. During the previous centuries when colonial rule was imposed on Africa, these borders were drawn by purely external criteria: the economic advantages or the administrative conveniences of distant European powers. They artificially combined different ascriptive (tribal or ethnic) groups that for centuries had been separated by hostility and bloody conflict. At the same time, they arbitrarily split groups that had been tied together by kinship and common tradition. Neither did the borders make economic sense. Often the colonies were so small and their configuration so peculiar that they could not possibly contain the resources to be self-sufficient or to generate development. Yet remarkably after the various European dependencies in a balkanized Africa finally gained their independence, they not only preserved these arcane borders but through the Organization of African Unity have repeatedly proclaimed them to be sacrosanct.

Admittedly people live in abject poverty in other parts of the world, but only in Sub-Sahara Africa is the concentration so high. It is an appalling reality screaming to high heaven. But frankly most people in the world just do not want to think about it. Americans seem content with "benign neglect." During the first Clinton administration the secretary of state visited Sub-Sahara Africa just once, shortly before the 1996 election; the president did not even do that. Regularly our state department requests and our Congress votes for foreign aid. In the case of all of Sub-Sahara Africa this has amounted to a declining $1.325 billion in 1994, $1.198 billion in 1995, and $1.069 billion in 1996, about 10 percent of our total "economic and military assistance" throughout the world.[50] There may be a variety of reasons for this: (1) the region seems to be far away, (2) no serious military threat to us is likely to emerge there, (3) physical conditions are too uncomfortable for reporters to stay and put up with, (4) the dimensions of the problem boggle the minds of scholars, (5) Africans are not eager to have Americans poking around in their countries, (6) African-Americans do not generally look to Africa with pride, and (7) rational examination of the problems is all too frequently preempted by easy and cheap recourse to imprecations of racism.

Having said all this, however, the fundamental fact remains that the dreadful realities of 10 percent of our fellow human beings will not just go away. The information revolution may be slow to penetrate Sub-Sahara Africa, but it certainly will not pass it by. There are many valuable raw materials below its soil; there is much potential and real human talent

---

[50] U.S. Agency for International Development, *Congressional Presentation, Summary Tables Fiscal Year 1996* (Washington, DC: Government Printing Office), pp. 10–11, 16–17, 22–23.

above it. But the vicious circle of poverty can only be broken by enlightened help from abroad in close cooperation with the African people and their responsible leaders. There is the rub: What enlightened help? What responsible leaders?

In America we might learn the lessons of our own history. We have paid a very heavy price for the practice of slavery during the first century of the Republic. And this is directly to the point: We are still paying an enormous price for the time after the Civil War, after the Thirteenth, Fourteenth, and Fifteenth Amendments when most Americans preferred not to see and some actually abetted the gross discrimination against African-Americans. We do not wish to remember it, but lynchings were frequent and remained unpunished in some states well into the twentieth century. Indeed some senators were elected with the solicited help of the Ku Klux Klan. Consider this: in 1936 shortly after his historic accomplishments at the Berlin Olympics Jesse Owens reportedly was snubbed by Adolf Hitler who refused to shake the champion's hand. The story was not entirely true. What was true and hurt Owens deeply was that when he came home his own president chose not to shake his hand.

Any enlightened help in so mind-boggling a problem as breaking the vicious circle of poverty will require much thought, much inspiration, much effort, and much good will. We might start by shifting the focus of our foreign aid for the Middle East to Sub-Sahara Africa. Then we could mobilize the industrialized countries (G-7) to a war on hunger, perhaps to assure that each human being can count on a daily intake of 1,800 calories and a better diet with more protein and fresh vegetables. Through special presidential attention we may reinvigorate the Peace Corps and its good work in the areas of education and health. Furthermore we may organize an international consortium of private and public agencies to help finance linkages to the Internet (World Wide Web). By assisting a country's information needs we could aid "a country in utilizing meager resources more effectively. For example, communications between agricultural researchers and extensionists will encourage dissemination of new approaches ultimately leading to better maize harvests. And fast Internet communications will improve response to emergencies: drought, locust infestation, epidemic."[51] Incidentally it would also improve personal skills enormously.

---

[51] A report by Lishan Adam, Coordinator, Electronic Communications Projects, Pan African Development Information System, *The FAO Review*, No. 158, March–April 1996.

We may sponsor the realignment of political boundaries gradually or through international conferences. These are just a few possible ideas that would still have to be developed and tested. Obviously governments and the people of Africa must be fully engaged in the process, and they must become motivated. They must have hope, and clearly they must feel that we care, that we are really trying to help, and that together we may break the chains of mass poverty. Conceivably we could make the dream of Martin Luther King, Jr. for America our vision for the human race.

We have now come full circle. We started with the proposition that our world is seriously threatened by a reversion into the acceptance of radical cleavages in the human race, cleavages, moreover, that are ascriptive, usually ethnocentric, and hence intractable. Sensitive to the sterility of stark realism, as well as the pitfalls of sweeping idealism, and keeping in mind the exasperating complexities of foreign policy decision-making, the astonishing changes in our recent past, and the lack of a consensus blueprint for international order in the future, we have now arrive at the conclusion. We live in an age that does offer phenomenal opportunities to advance incrementally but steadily toward the unity of the human race.

The United States, and only the United States, has the global reach, culturally, economically, and militarily. Thus, as we enter the twenty-first century, we may confidently concentrate on our own business, frittering away our enormous forces and resources and piling up pages in the chronicles of wasted time. Or we could seize the moment, build a national consensus to invest in the continued advance of human development, and add vibrant chapters to human history.

The opportunity is here, the result is not foreordained, the choice is ours.

Keep the faith, America. Lead, kindly Light.

Selected Bibliography

Allison, Graham T., et al. *Avoiding Nuclear Anarchy: Containing the Threat of Loose Russian Nuclear Weapons and Fissile Material*. Cambridge, MA: MIT Press, 1996.

Aziz, Sartaj, ed. *Hunger, Politics, and Markets: The Real Issues in the Food Crisis*. New York: New York University Press, 1975.

Baez, Mauricio. *From Praetorianism to Civil Order: The Case of Venezuela*. Philadelphia: University of Pennsylvania, Ph.D. dissertation, 1981.

Bailey, Thomas A. *A Diplomatic History of the American People*, 3rd ed. New York: Appleton-Century-Crofts, 1946.

Baker, James A., III. *The Politics of Diplomacy, Revolution, War and Peace (1989–1992)*. New York: G. P. Putnam's Sons, 1995.

Bethe, Hans; Richard L. Garwin; Kurt Gottfried; and Henry W. Kendall. "Space-based Ballistic Missile Defense," *Scientific American*. October 1984, vol. 251, no 4.

Bismarck, Prince Otto von. *Reflections and Reminiscences*, edited by Theodore S. Hamerow. New York: Harper & Row, 1968.

Blancké, W. Wendell. *The Foreign Service of the United States*. New York: Praeger, 1969.

Blitzer, Wolf. *Territory of Lies*. New York: Harper & Row, 1989.

Bonnet, Georges. *De Munich a là Guerre, Defense de la Paix*. Paris: Plon, 1967.

Boulton, Fundación John, ed., *Politica y Economia en Venezuela, 1810–1991*. Caracas, Venezuela: Litografia Melvin, 1992, Gráfico #2.

Braley, Russ. *Bad News, The Foreign Policy of The New York Times*. Chicago: Regnery Gateway, 1984.

Brzezinski, Zbigniew. *Power and Principle: Memoirs of a National Security Advisor 1977–1981*. New York: Straus & Giroux, 1983.

Bulletin de l'Institut International de Statistique. 1913. vol. XX, part II.

Burki, Shahid Javed, and Sebastian Edwards. *Latin America after Mexico: Quickening the Pace*. Washington, DC: The World Bank, 1995.

Caesar, Julius. *War Commentaries*. Translated by Rex Warner. New York: New American Library, 1960.

Calder, Kent E. "Asia's Empty Tank," *Foreign Affairs*, March–April 1996, vol. 75, no. 2.

Carter, Ashton B. *Directed Energy Missile Defense in Space*. Background Paper. Washington, DC: Office of Technology Assessment, April 1984.

Christopher, Warren. *The International Affairs Budget: Large Returns from a Small Investment*, Statement before the Subcommittee on Commerce, Justice, State, the Judiciary and Related Agencies of the House Appropriations Committee. Washington, DC, May 15, 1996, *U.S. Department of State Dispatch*, May 20, 1996, vol. 7, no. 21.

Ciano, Count Galeazzo. *Diary 1937–1938*. Translated by Andreas Mayor. London: Methuen, 1952.

———. *The Ciano Diaries 1939–1943*. Edited by Hugh Gibson. Garden City, NY: Doubleday & Co., 1946.

Clifford, Clark. *Counsel to the President*. New York: Random House, 1991.

Collins, John M. *U.S.-Soviet Military Balance: Concepts and Capabilities, 1960–1980*. New York: McGraw-Hill, 1980.

Colodny, Len, and Robert Gettlin. *Silent Coup, The Removal of a President*. New York: St. Martin's Press, 1991.

Commager, Henry Steele. *The American Mind*. New Haven: Yale University Press, 1952.

Davis, Tom E. "The 'End' of the State in Economic Development," in Alvaro A. Zini Jr., *The Market and the State in Economic Development in the 1990s*. Amsterdam, The Netherlands: North Holland Press, 1992.

de Gaulle, General Charles. *Major Addresses, Statements and Press Conferences*, May 19, 1958–January 31, 1964. New York: French Embassy, Press and Information Division, 1964.

Dobrynin, Anatoly. *In Confidence, Moscow's Ambassador to America's Six Cold War Presidents*. 1962–1986. New York: Times Books, 1995.

Documents on British Foreign Policy 1919–1939. London: His Majesty's Stationary Office, 1949, Third Series, vol. 1.

Documents on German Foreign Policy 1918–1945. Series D, volume II. Washington, DC: U.S. Government Printing Office, 1949.

Dulles, John Foster. "Policy for Security and Peace," *Foreign Affairs*, vol. 32, no. 3. April 1954.

———. Speech to the Council of Foreign Relations, January 12, 1954, Department of State *Bulletin* XXX. January 25, 1954.

———. Speech to the Associated Press, New York, April 23, 1956, Department of State *Bulletin* XXXIV. April 30, 1954.

Earley, Pete. *Confessions of a Spy, the Real Story of Aldrich Ames*. New York: G.P. Putnam's Sons, 1997.

Erlich, P.R., et. al. "The Long-Term Biological Consequences of Nuclear War," *Science* 222, December 23, 1983.

European Community Commission. *From Single Market to European Union.* Luxembourg: Office for Official Publications of the European Communities, 1992.

————. *Treaty on European Union*, Luxembourg. Office for Official Publications of the European Communities, 1992.

Fay, Sidney Bradshaw. *The Origins of the World War*, 2nd ed. New York: Macmillan, 1930.

Feiling, Keith. *The Life of Neville Chamberlain.* Hamden, CT: Archon Books, 1970.

François-Ponçet, André. *The Fateful Years.* Translated by Jacques LeClerq. New York: Howard Fertig, 1972.

Galbraith, John Kenneth. *Ambassador's Journal.* Boston: Houghton Mifflin, 1969.

Gallup, George H. *The Gallup Poll: Public Opinion, 1983.* Wilmington, DE: Scholarly Resources, Inc., 1984.

Gandhi, M. K. *The Story of My Experiments with Truth.* Translated by Mahadev Desai. Washington, DC: Public Affairs Press, 1960.

Gates, Gary Paul. *Air Time: The Inside Story of CBS News.* New York: Harper & Row, 1978.

George, David Lloyd. *The Truth about the Peace Treaties.* London: Victor Gollancz Ltd, 1938, vol. II.

Gorbachev, Mikhail. *Memoirs.* New York: Doubleday, 1993.

Gordon, Michael R., and Bernard E. Trainor. *The Generals' War, the Inside Story of the Conflict in the Gulf.* Boston: Little, Brown & Co., 1995.

Halberstam, David. *The Best and the Brightest.* New York: Random House, 1969.

Haldeman, H. R. *The Haldeman Diaries.* New York: G. P. Putnam's Sons, 1994.

Heilbrunn, Jacob. "Germany's New Right," *Foreign Affairs*, November/December 1996.

Higgins, Marguerite. *Our Vietnam Nightmare.* New York: Harper & Row, 1965.

Hoffmann, Stanley. *Primacy or World Order: American Foreign Policy since the Cold War.* New York: McGraw-Hill, 1978.

Holy Bible, 1 Kings 15:2, 3, 7, 8, 9, 11.

Hoopes, Townsend. *The Limits of Intervention.* New York: David McKay Co., 1969.

Hufbauer, Gary Clyde, and Jeffrey J. Schott, *NAFTA: An Assessment.* Washington, DC: Institute for International Economics, 1993.

Huntington, Samuel P. "The West Unique, Not Universal," *Foreign Affairs*, November/December 1996.

Johnson, Lyndon Baines. *The Vantage Point, Perspectives of the Presidency 1963–1969.* New York: Holt, Rinehart & Winston, 1971.

Kegley, Charles W., Jr., and Eugene Wittkopf, eds. *The Nuclear Reader: Strategy, Weapons, War.* New York: St. Martin's Press, 1985.

Kennan, George F. *Memoirs 1925–1950.* Boston: Little, Brown & Co., 1967.

Kennedy, John F. Address at Frankfurt, Germany, June 25, 1963. *Department of State Bulletin* 49, no. 1256. July 22, 1963.

Kennedy, Robert F. *Thirteen Days*. New York: W. W. Norton & Co., 1969.

Khalid bin Sultan, HRH General. *Desert Warrior, a Personal View of the Gulf War by the Joint Forces Commander*. New York: HarperCollins, 1995.

Khrushchev, Sergei. *Khrushchev on Khrushchev, An Inside Account of the Man and his Era*. Boston: Little, Brown and Company, 1990.

———. "The Three Circles of Russian Market Reform," *Mediterranean Quarterly*, vol. 6, no. 4, Fall 1995.

Kissinger, Henry A. *A World Restored*. New York: Grosset & Dunlap, 1964.

———. *White House Years*. Boston: Little, Brown & Co., 1979.

———. *Years of Upheaval*. Boston: Little, Brown & Co., 1982.

Kohl, Helmut. *Ich Wollte Deutshlands Einheit*. Berlin: Ullstein Buchverlag GmbH, 1996.

Kordt, Theo. *Nicht aus den Akten*. Stuttgart: Union Deutsche Verlagsgesellschaft, 1950.

Kral, Vaclav. *Das Abkommen von München 1938*. Praha: Nakladatelstri Ĉeskoslovenske Akademie Ved, 1968.

Kurthen, Hermann, and Michael Minkenberg. "Germany in Transition: Immigration, Racism and the Extreme Right," *Nations and Nationalism* I, 2, 1995.

Lowenthal, Abraham F. *Partners in Conflict, The United States and Latin America*. Baltimore: Johns Hopkins University Press, 1987.

Malraux, André. *Felled Oaks: Conversations with de Gaulle*. New York: Holt, Rinehart & Winston, 1971.

Martone, Celso L. *Macroeconomic Policies, Debt Accumulation, and Adjustment in Brazil, 1965–84*. World Bank Discussion Papers. Washington, DC: The World Bank, 1986.

Massie, Robert K. *Dreadnaught: Britain, Germany, and the Coming of the Great War*. New York: Random House, 1991.

May, Ernest R., ed. *American Cold War Strategy: Interpreting NSC 68*. Boston: Bedford Books of St. Martin's Press, 1993.

McFarlane, Robert C. *Special Trust*. New York: Cadell E. Davies. 1994.

McNamara, Robert. *In Retrospect*. New York: Times Books, 1995.

Medley, Richard. "Keeping Monetary Union on Track," *Foreign Affairs*, November/December 1996.

Mehrens, Bernhard. *Entstehung und Entwicklung der grossen französischen Kreditinstitute*. Stuttgart: J. G. Cotta'sche Buchhandlung Nachf., 1911.

Meisner, Maurice. *The Deng Xiaoping Era, an Inquiry into the Fate of Chinese Socialism, 1978–1994*. New York: Hill and Wang, 1996.

Menaul, Stewart. *The Illustrated Encyclopedia of the Strategy, Tactics, and Weapons of Russian Military Power*. New York: St. Martin's Press, 1980.

Moulton, Harland B. *From Superiority to Parity: The United States and the Strategic Arms Race, 1961–1971*. Westport, CT: Greenwood Press, 1973.

Naim, Moisés. *Paper Tigers and Minotaurs, The Politics of Venezuela's Economic Reforms*. Washington, DC: Carnegie Endowment for International Peace, 1993.

National Committee on U.S.-China Relations, *Toward Strategic Understanding between America and China*, Policy Series No. 13, December 1996.

"The New Nationalism and the Old History: Perspectives on the West German Historikerstreit," *Journal of Modern History*, 59, December 1987.

Nixon, Richard. *Beyond Peace*. New York: Random House, 1994.

————. *RN*. New York: Grosset & Dunlap, 1978.

North, Oliver. *Under Fire*. New York: Harper Collins, 1991.

Nugent, Neill. *The Government and Politics of the European Community*. Durham: Duke University Press, 1991.

Powell, Colin L. *My American Journey*. New York: Random House, 1995.

Price, Raymond. *With Nixon*. New York: Viking Press, 1977.

Pruys, Karl Hugo. *Kohl, Genius of the Present*. Chicago: edition q, inc., 1996.

Quayle, Dan. *Standing Firm, a Vice-Presidential Memoir*. New York: HarperCollins, 1994.

Rappard, William E. *The Quest for Peace since the World War*. Cambridge: Harvard University Press, 1940.

Reeves, Richard. *President Kennedy, Profile of Power*. New York: Simon & Schuster, 1993.

Robbins, Keith. *Munich 1938*. London: Cassell, 1968.

Rogers, Gen. Bernard W. "The Atlantic Alliance: Prescription for a Difficult Decade," *Foreign Affairs*, 60, no. 5. Summer 1982.

Rossiter, Clinton. *American Presidency*. New York: Time, Inc., 1963.

Rubinstein, Alvin Z. *The Foreign Policy of the Soviet Union*, 3rd ed. New York: Random House, 1972.

Salinger, Pierre. *P.S. A Memoir*. New York: St. Martin's Press, 1995.

Say, Leon. *Les Finances de la France sous la Troisième Republic*. Paris: Levy, 1898. vol. I.

Schapiro, Leonard. "The Great Purge," in B. H. Liddell Hart, ed. *The Red Army*. New York: Harcourt, Brace & Co., 1956.

Schell, Jonathan. *The Fate of the Earth*. New York: Alfred A. Knopf, 1982.

Schlesinger, James. "The Eagle and the Bear, Ruminations on Forty Years of Superpower Relations," *Foreign Affairs*, 63. Summer 1985.

Schlessinger Jr., Arthur M. *A Thousand Days: John F. Kennedy in the White House*. Boston: Houghton Mifflin, 1965.

Schmitz, Peter M. "The German Democratic Republic," in Douglas J. Murray and Peter P. Viotti, eds. *The Defense Policies of Nations: A Comparative Study*. Baltimore: Johns Hopkins University Press, 1989.

Schoenbaum, Thomas J. *Waging Peace and War, Dean Rusk in the Truman, Kennedy and Johnson Years*. New York: Simon & Schuster, 1988.

Schönbohm, Jörge. *Two Armies and One Fatherland*. Providence: Berghahn Books, 1996.

Schwarzkopf, H. Norman. *It Doesn't Take a Hero*. New York: Bantam Books, 1992.

Sherwood, Robert E. *Roosevelt and Hopkins: An Intimate History*. New York: Harper, 1948.

Shvets, Yuri B. *Washington Station, My Life as a KGB Spy in America*. New York: Simon & Schuster, 1994.

Sobchak, Anatoly. *For a New Russia*. New York: Free Press, 1992.

Sosa-Rodriguez, Julio. "Oil and Economic Perspective of Venezuela," paper presented at Symposium on Venezuela, University of Connecticut, October 31, 1984.

Spanier, John. *American Foreign Policy Since World War II*, 9th ed. New York: Holt, Rinehart & Winston, 1983.

Stimson, Henry L. *On Active Service in Peace and War*. New York: Harper & Brothers, 1947.

Sumaida, Hussein. *Circle of Fear, My Life as an Israeli and Iraqi Spy*. Washington, DC: Brassey's, 1994.

Summers, Harry G. *On Strategy, a Critical Analysis of the Vietnam War*. Novato, CA: Presidio Press, 1982.

Sura IV:I, *The Holy Qur'an*, text, translation, and commentary by A. Yusef Ali. Brentwood, MD: Amana Corp., 1983.

Talbott, Strobe. *End Game, The Inside Story of SALT II*. New York: Harper & Row, 1979.

————, trans. and ed. *Khrushchev Remembers*. Boston: Little, Brown & Co., 1970.

Teltschik, Horst. *329 Tage, Innenaussichten der Einigung*. Berlin: Stadler, 1991.

Thatcher, Margaret. *The Downing Street Years*. New York: HarperCollins, 1993.

Thucydides, *The History of the Peloponnesian War*. Translated by Richard Crawley. New York: Dutton, 1974.

Travertine, Gregory F. *Making American Foreign Policy*. Englewood Cliffs, NY: Prentice-Hall, 1994.

Truman, Harry S. *Memoirs*. Garden City, NY: Doubleday & Co., 1955.

United States Agency for International Development, *Congressional Presentation, Summary Tables Fiscal Year 1996*. Washington, DC: U.S. Government Printing Office.

United States Congress. *135 Congressional Record* H2312 and S618, June 6, 1989.

United States Congress, Office of Technology Assessment. *Strategic Defenses, Ballistic Missile Defense Technologies, Anti-Satellite Weapons, Countermeasures and Arms Control*. Princeton: Princeton University Press, 1986.

United States, Court of Appeals for the District of Columbia Circuit, *Final Report of the Independent Counsel for Iran/Contra Matters*, Washington, DC: August 4, 1993, vol. I.

United States, Department of Commerce, Bureau of Census, *Statistical Abstract of the United States, 1967*, 88th ed. Washington, DC: U.S. Government

Printing Office, 1967; and 108th ed., 1988.

———. *Statistical Abstract of the United States, 1986*, 106th ed. Washington, DC: U.S. Government Printing Office, 1986.

United States, Department of State, *American Foreign Policy 1950–1955, Basic Documents.* Washington, DC: U.S. Government Printing Office, 1954.

———. Foreign Relations of the United States 1961–1963, "Memorandum from the President to the Secretary of Defense, September 21, 1963," and "Memorandum of the Record of a Meeting, September 23, 1963." Washington, DC, U.S. Government Printing Office, 1988.

United States, House of Representatives, Committee on Armed Services, *United States—Vietnam Relations 1945–1967.*

———. Subcommittee on Europe and the Middle East of the Committee on Foreign Affairs, *Hearing on United States–Iraqi Relations, March 21, 1991.* Washington, DC: U.S. Government Printing Office, 1991.

United States, National Bipartisan Commission on Central America. *Report.* Washington, DC: National Bipartisan Commission, January 1984.

United States, Office of the Management and Budget. *Budget Supplement, Fiscal Year 1997.* Washington, DC: U.S. Government Printing Office, 1996.

United States. *Treaties and Other International Agreements of the United States of America 1776–1949*, Department of State Publication no. 8521. Washington, DC: U.S. Government Printing Office, 1970.

———. *Treaties and Other International Agreements.* Washington, DC: U.S. Government Printing Office, 1973.

U.S. News & World Report, *Triumph without Victory.* New York: Random House, 1992.

Vance, Cyrus. *Hard Choices: Critical Years in America's Foreign Policy.* New York: Simon & Schuster, 1983.

von Vorys, Karl. *American National Interest, Virtue and Power in Foreign Policy.* New York: Praeger, 1990.

———. *Democracy without Consensus, Communalism and Political Stability in Malaysia.* Princeton, NJ: Princeton University Press, 1975.

———. *Political Development in Pakistan,* Princeton, NJ: Princeton University Press, 1965.

Weinberger, Casper W. *Fighting for Peace, Seven Critical Years in the Pentagon.* New York: Warner Books, 1990.

Weizsäcker, Ernst von. *Memoirs of Ernst von Weizsäcker,* translated by John Andrews. Chicago: Henry Regnery Co., 1951.

Wheeler-Bennett, John W. *Munich, Prologue to Tragedy.* New York: Duell, Sloan & Pearce, 1962.

Wickert, Erwin. *Dramatische Tage In Hitlers Reich.* Stuttgart: Steingruben Verlag, 1952.

Woodward, Bob. *The Commanders.* New York: Simon & Schuster, 1991.

The World Bank, *Economic Memorandum on Venezuela,* Report No. 5016-VE, 1985.

————. *Memorandum to the Executive Directors and the President, Subject: OED Study of Bank/Mexico Relations, 1948–1992*. Washington, DC: World Bank, Office of the Director General, 1994.

————. *Venezuela CEM: Living with Oil*, Report No. 12849-VE, July 21, 1995.

————. *Venezuela: Structural and Economic Reforms-The New Regime*, Report No. 10404-VE, 1993.

————. *World Debt Tables 1987–1988*, First Supplement. Washington, DC: The World Bank, 1988.

————. *World Development Report 1996*. New York: Oxford University Press, 1996)

Wright, Peter. *Spy Catcher, the Candid Autobiography of a Senior Intelligence Officer*. New York: Viking, 1987.

Yu-lan, Fung. *A Short History of Chinese Philosphy*, edited by Derek Bodde. New York: Free Press, 1966.

Index

About the Author

KARL VON VORYS is Professor of Political Science at the University of Pennsylvania. His previous works include *American National Interest* (Praeger, 1990), *Democracy Without Consensus: The Politics of Communalism in Malaysia* (1975), and *Political Development in Pakistan* (1965).